Outclassed

Outclassed

How the Left Lost
the Working Class and
How to Win Them Back

Joan C. Williams

ST. MARTIN'S PRESS
NEW YORK

First published in the United States by St. Martin's Press, an imprint of
St. Martin's Publishing Group

OUTCLASSED. Copyright © 2025 by Joan C. Williams. All rights reserved.
Printed in the United States of America. For information, address St. Martin's
Publishing Group, 120 Broadway, New York, NY 10271.

www.stmartins.com

Design by Meryl Sussman Levavi

The Library of Congress Cataloging-in-Publication Data
is available upon request.

ISBN 978-1-250-36896-6 (hardcover)
ISBN 978-1-250-36897-3 (ebook)

Our books may be purchased in bulk for promotional, educational, or business
use. Please contact your local bookseller or the Macmillan Corporate and
Premium Sales Department at 1-800-221-7945, extension 5442, or by email
at MacmillanSpecialMarkets@macmillan.com.

First Edition: 2025

1 3 5 7 9 10 8 6 4 2

To Livia, with hopes for her future, and
Ruth: her memory is a blessing

Contents

¿No ves que yo no sé qué hacer
Con mis dos universos paralelos?
—JORGE DREXLER,
"Universos Paralelos"

Introduction

Everything was weird.

First, his factory-worker father freaked out that the wedding would not be in the Rust Belt town where my fiancé was born. Every single person my father-in-law knew was from the same town, so every single person he knew got married there. Then my mother worked herself into a frenzy cleaning my family's old farmhouse outside Woodstock, Vermont, where we planned to have the reception. No one had lived there for decades; my grandfather bought it in the 1920s, and my dad used it just to putter around in. All I could think about were the beautiful views of Killington Peak. All my mom could think about was dust. When I finally asked her why, she snapped, "The only thing those lace-curtain Irish understand is *clean*." I felt like I'd been slapped.

After the wedding came and went, my husband and I were going to Harvard Law School when his parents visited us in Cambridge. More weirdness. His parents stayed in our apartment—who even does that?—and instead of going out to dinner, we cooked at home. My mother hated to cook, and my father hadn't a clue how to, so that weirded me out, too. Slowly, slowly, it dawned on me that my family stayed in a hotel and ate in restaurants because we were, ahem, rich enough to do so.

It all came together one night during that visit when dinner was finished in our triple-decker apartment and we were all cleaning up together. "Where do you keep the butter?" asked my mother-in-law.

"Under the bed," I quipped. What did she think I was, a Martian?

Apparently so. She went into the bedroom and put the butter under the bed. Then it hit me. She thinks I'm as weird as I think she is weird. This was my introduction to the terrain where I spent my next half century. In those early days of my marriage, I learned that social class shapes everything. It shapes whether we think dust bunnies are kinda funny or a moral lapse. It shapes not just how parents visit adult children but whether they have to—or whether those children stay in their hometowns to swap house-work and childcare, eldercare, and roof repair with their families of origin. Class shapes everything from how you define a good cup of coffee to what you see as the purpose of life.

This book explains how I overcame being class blind. That's important because being class blind doesn't work any better than being "color-blind." People who think they're color-blind are actually *more* biased than those who don't, because color blindness "decreases sensitivity to racism." Class blindness is equally implausible: Americans are more likely than not to pin-point someone's social class after hearing them speak just seven words. Class is as inescapable in America as race; overcoming class blindness requires that you understand the power of class in American society and politics.[1]

Class blindness fuels the "diploma divide" between Americans who graduated from college and those who didn't. Here's the irony: sharp in-creases in inequality have been accompanied by decreasing rates of support for Democrats among both white and nonwhite noncollege voters—despite the fact that far-right policies exacerbate inequality.[2]

Democrats long prided themselves on being the party of the have-nots, depicting Republicans as the party of the haves. By 2018, the have-nots disagreed: Democrats were doing much better with voters in the top two quintiles of Americans, while Republicans were doing much better with less affluent voters.[3]

And it's not just the US. This is a transnational trend. Thomas Piketty has documented the striking parallels in the US, the UK, and France in the alliance between the working class and the Merchant Right (think: Koch brothers) against the Brahmin Left (think: Ezra Klein). Though I tap the large literature studying authoritarian populism in Europe, mostly I cite evidence from the US to keep this book to a manageable size. But the deep structure of far-right populism is the same transnationally. So this is not just a book about the US—or Donald Trump, though I will cite a lot of studies about his impact. Trump's just the symptom. The real question is why his MAGA base became so passionately attached to him. (MAGA, of course, stems from his original campaign motto to "Make America Great Again.")[4]

You don't need me to tell you what's wrong with the racist, anti-immigrant, anti-science politics of the Far Right. Instead, I want to explain how class blindness on the Left helps the Right. A glaring example is when progressives deny that authoritarian populism is about class. The dictionary definition of *populism* is a political movement driven by anger against elites. Anger against elites is class anger. Two-thirds of Americans don't believe class conflict is strong, which makes understanding its role in contemporary politics a stretch—one I hope to help you make.[5]

Another gift to the Right is to deny that economic populism is about economics. Many studies from the Left purport to prove it isn't, typically by focusing on the fact that low-income voters have not swerved right. That's true, but irrelevant: what drives populism is *precarity, not poverty.* A study of three European countries found that the voters flocking to populists are middle-status workers in routine jobs warily watching the hollowing out of the middle class. Virtually all Americans (90 percent) did better than their parents in the decades after World War II, but only half of those born in 1980 will, with particularly sharp declines in the South and industrial Midwest.[6]

No wonder people are pissed.

My message to liberals is that we will lose elections, or scrape by so narrowly we can't implement progressive changes, unless we can secure more votes from these middle-status voters in routine jobs feeling left behind. So if you care about climate change or abortion rights or defending democracy, you need to care about these lower-middle-class voters.

Taking a step back: How did we get here?

The short answer is neoliberalism—faith that unfettered markets would raise all boats—which dominated American politics by the 1990s. Neoliberalism posited that the best way to cure the (high-unemployment, high-inflation) stagflation of the 1970s was to reinvigorate the "turgid American economy" by unleashing the power of markets (to quote David Leonhardt). The neoliberal consensus embraced free trade, outsourcing, and deregulation, while decentering unions and other job protections. Liberals as well as conservatives believed that free trade would turn China into a democracy and increase GDP throughout the world by having each nation concentrate on its core competencies to produce goods most efficiently. This dream of world freedom and prosperity was so dominant in both parties that I and other liberals used to joke we belonged to "the Democratic wing of the Democratic Party." People saw the growing inequality in the American workforce, of course, but economists reassured most with their claims that the turf lost by noncollege grads was inevitable due to the onward march of technology. In fact, the growing inequality reflected neoliberal policies that undermined workers' bargaining power: "the decline of unions; a succession of trade deals with low-wage countries; and increasingly common arrangements like 'fissuring,' in which companies outsource work to lower-paying firms, and noncompete clauses in employment contracts, which make it hard for workers to leave for a competitor." The leftist Economic Policy Institute estimated that these policies produced more than three-fourths of the 43 percent differential between what workers earn today and what they would have earned if wages had kept pace with productivity.[7]

The rise of economic populism reflects that neoliberalism fueled inequality both between *individuals* and inequality between *regions*, producing a new geography of wealth that fit poorly with political systems that have winner-take-all elections in geographically defined districts. This set the stage for a revolt of the regions left behind, expressed in Brexit in the UK (fueled by votes from the deindustrialized north of England) and Trump's election in 2016 (fueled by rural areas and the deindustrialized Midwest). Far-right populism in Europe also has its greatest support in rural areas.[8]

Often this point is lost on liberals, who, instead of recognizing the anger of areas left behind, blame them for their stupidity in voting for the Far Right. This common formula was articulated most famously by Thomas Frank in *What's the Matter with Kansas?*, which depicts gullible Midwesterners voting against their self-interest. Frank had changed his tune by 2016, but this brand of condescension lives on. It ignores a central fact: by electing Donald Trump in 2016, noncollege voters got precisely what they wanted, which was to smash the neoliberal consensus. Donald Trump broke with traditional Republicans who wanted to gut Social Security and Medicare, and moved both parties away from free trade, globalism, and reflexive embrace of China. Trump "abolished" NAFTA, torpedoed the Trans-Pacific Partnership, imposed tariffs on China, and announced his intention to Make America Great Again. He also said he'd raise taxes on people like himself (he lied), breaking the celebration of the rich as untouchable job creators. MAGA ended the neoliberal consensus.[9]

Trump tapped into a narrative the Far Right had been seeding for a long time. Most progressives only know Fox News from dismissive sound bites on MSNBC or the mocking references of their favorite comedy show, but if you go back and watch Tucker Carlson during his time on Fox, you'll see his critique of neoliberal economics. In a 2018 episode titled "There Is Nothing Free About This Market," Carlson slammed Walmart and Uber for exploiting their workers and praised Bernie Sanders for pressuring Amazon CEO Jeff Bezos to raise wages. Media scholar Reece Peck told me, "Carlson consistently copies Trump's greatest rhetorical trick, which is to co-opt left-populist critiques against war, wealth concentration, and corporate power to build support for the Far Right." This is attractive to both Fox's older viewers and younger voters who are former Democrats. In 2021, Carlson gained more Democratic viewers in the twenty-five-to-fifty-four age demographic than MSNBC and CNN, a stat that "should keep Democratic strategists up at night," Peck said.[10]

At the height of neoliberalism, college-educated liberals' attention shifted onto "post-materialist" concerns like gender and environmental issues. As of the 1980s, and as late as 2000, white college grads placed about twice as much weight on culture-wars issues as those without college degrees. It was college grads, not non-elites, who started the culture wars. White college grads traditionally had voted Republican at higher rates than noncollege whites from the 1950s to the 1970s, but the new focus on cultural issues changed that. College grads' new focus on cultural issues orphaned noncollege voters, who tend to be economically progressive but culturally conservative, creating what political scientists call the "representation gap." That persisted until far-right populists from Donald Trump in the US to Giorgia Meloni in Italy to Viktor Orbán in Hungary stepped in to fill that void.[11]

The cultural piece is important. "Many liberals continue to believe that a full-throated support of 'economic populist' materialist-distributive policies is all that is needed to defeat the cultural populist identity politics of the right," notes Reece Peck. But class identity is expressed not only through economics but also through cultural differences. As the French sociologist Pierre Bourdieu pointed out in the 1970s, people from different classes have different values, different traditions of talk, and different attitudes toward tradition itself. A zillion focus groups and surveys keep rediscovering over and over again bits and pieces of what's been called the *class culture gap* between elites and non-elites—without understanding how the logic of life differs for each group. It's less gap and more like parallel universes.[12]

Culture wars began with fights over the Equal Rights Amendment and busing, but the Right has long since learned how to turn anything into a culture war, from climate change to Covid response to religion to election procedures to gun control to abortion rights to LGBTQIA+ youth. (From here on, I typically use the term "LGBTQ" for brevity.) Culture wars fueled the Moral Majority in 1968 and 1972; Reagan Democrats in the 1980s; the Angry White Men in 1994; the Tea Party in 2010; and MAGA today. Culture wars allow economic elites to deflect anger away from themselves onto cultural elites, allowing one segment of college grads (the Merchant Right) to gain power over a different segment of college grads (the Brahmin Left).[13]

The Merchant Right connects with noncollege voters through resentment; liberals need to connect with working-class voters through respect. But to do that, *we need to actually respect them.* The central message of this book is that what's needed is not to fix noncollege voters *but to fix the broken relationship between noncollege voters and the Brahmin Left.*

It's high time for liberals to stop being played, again and again, from the same playbook. If the Far Right sculpts economic anger into culture wars, we need to sculpt it back. Doing so will require building cultural competence that's often lacking, because "those above" typically know less about "those below" than vice versa.[14]

The Far Right connects culturally with noncollege grads by:

- expressing anger against elites;
- standing up for traditional institutions that anchor blue-collar self-esteem in the scrum for social honor: morality, religion, the military, and traditional gender roles;
- adopting blue-collar talk traditions;
- stressing workers' hard-work worship and their respect for small business; and
- tapping into blue-collar traditions of manliness.

The Far Right has sculpted all these into a "master identity" so strong it now overrides even evangelicals' identification with their church. The far-right narrative explains in terms that are vivid, compelling—and wrong—why non-elite Americans feel hopeless and embattled. It makes them feel strong and hopeful. The only way to peel back the power of far-right populism is to offer an equally compelling and empowering progressive alternative. This book provides the cultural competence to begin that process.[15]

How does racism enter into this? After all, high levels of racial resentment strongly predict Trump voting. But this doesn't explain why Trump won. He won in 2024 because he attracted increased percentages of people of color. He won in 2016 because he attracted a much larger group of voters with moderate racial resentment. It's important to distinguish between two types of Trump voters who hold progressive economic views. One group, totaling 20 percent of 2016 Trump voters, polled as "American preservationists": being white and Christian was central to their identity, and they had cold feelings toward people of color. Liberals cannot appeal to these voters, nor should they try to. But a second group, totaling 19 percent of Trump voters, polled as "anti-elites": they had feelings toward people of color about the same as non-Trump voters, as well as moderate views on immigration, gay marriage, and the environment. If Democrats could peel off even a moderate percentage of these anti-elites, they could win handily in both presidential and congressional elections.[16]

Progressives need to be laser-focused on anti-elites. Note I am not arguing that anti-elites, or indeed any other group of whites, is immune from racism. Racism is pervasive both among elites and non-elites. Instead, my argument is that it's possible to build a multiracial coalition that includes whites—both elite and non-elite—who are not chiefly motivated by racial dog whistles.

So much ink has been spilled about whether economic populism is about race or class that the powerful gender dynamics are often ignored. They shouldn't be. Endorsement of hegemonic masculinity (a.k.a. macho) predicts Trump voting in both men and women—and it predicts Trump fandom even more than racism. Class, race, and gender are all powerfully available categories that are tapped early and often to achieve political goals. The fancy word for this is *intersectionality*, but it's really just common sense. Everyone has a race, class, and gender. These fundamental identities interact in complicated ways. That's all intersectionality means.[17]

Which brings me back to that butter melting under the bed. In nearly fifty years of marriage, I've come to realize that not only is my mother-in-law weird, I'm weird, too. She's now 101 years old, and she's learned some things from me—but I've also learned a lot from her. One thing she taught me is that elites are hyper-individualistic, a malady not shared by non-elites. Studies have made clear the downsides of hyper-pressured helicopter parenting, which non-elites have largely avoided. Research for this book has taught me that progressive elites feel more pressure to conform than any other group does. This confirms what I have learned over the course of nearly five decades of marriage: in some important ways, non-elites have their heads screwed on straight, perhaps more so than elites. Read on: there's a lot more.[18]

Part I taps research in economics that documents the role of increasing inequality in driving economic populism, as well as the polling and political science that document the diploma divide. It also responds to the common claim that the only way to win back noncollege voters is to move to the center. Not so. That reflects the assumption that the only way to make cultural connections with working-class voters is to do so in the same way the Far Right does—by reversing liberal positions on abortion rights or climate change. In fact, the key is for liberals and progressives to build very different kinds of cultural connections with noncollege voters, which is why it's so important they develop the cultural competence to do so. Parts II and III will provide the tools.

Part I taps sociology, social psychology, political science, and media studies to explain how far-right populism connects with values of the Missing Middle. In the scrum for social honor, lower-middle-class people can't claim to have won in the white-collar "meritocracy." Instead, their claims for social honor rest on their identity as people grounded in common sense, who keep the world in moral order. This section explains how blue-collar values reflect the material conditions of lower-middle-class life.

If you're reading this, you're probably from the Brahmin Left, as am I. Part III describes the water we swim in. Blue-collar voters have a stiletto touch for pinpointing the little white lies we tell ourselves that translate privilege into "merit," "enlightenment," and "sophistication." The result is condescension that's rocket fuel for the Far Right. Remedying this requires understanding not just how blue-collar truths reflect blue-collar lives but also how white-collar truths reflect white-collar lives.

Part IV provides a game plan for bridging the diploma divide. It contains concrete guidance for mutually respectful coalition building capable of delivering real progress on specific issues, including anti-racism, redistribution, gun control, climate change, and more. Included are messaging tips for campaigns and advocates, but also some hard questions about whether college grads are willing to cede some of their power to set priorities without regard to the priorities of non-elites.

There's a flood of talk about authoritarian populism, but most is either political science replete with regressions or campaign advice from inside-the-Beltway consultants. My goal is different: to change the Manichean frame within which American politics are currently being waged. Finding a path past polarization means returning to politics as power: as the arena where people who, in good faith, have a plurality of values can work together to reach an ever-shifting set of accommodations so they can live peaceably together. No one can get everything they want—not because the other side is evil, but because the other side is different. That's the path past populism.[19]

To quote the ever-astute Ezra Klein right after Trump won the 2024 presidential election, we have to get curious about why people vote for far-right populists. This book is for the curious.

Part I

Aren't You Sick of Losing Elections or Just Scraping By?

The forces that fuel MAGA have been attracting American voters since the 1990s; many MAGA themes originated in the campaigns of Pat Buchanan and Ross Perot. Far-right populism also continues to gain strength in Europe. The far-right party longest in power is in Hungary, where Fidesz won 68 percent of parliamentary seats in 2010 and again in 2022. In Poland the far-right Law and Justice Party governed from 2015 until 2023, when it lost control of the government (though it still garnered the most votes of any party). Giorgia Meloni's Brothers of Italy, which mirrors key elements of Trump's playbook, has been in power since late 2022. The Finns Party won the second largest vote share in the 2023 Finnish elections, leading to a coalition government that pledged to halve the number of refugees. In France the National Rally won 41 percent of the vote in the 2022 presidential election and won more seats than any other party in the 2024 E.U. parliamentary elections. Geert Wilders won the largest vote share in the Dutch 2023 parliamentary elections; he did not become prime minister but the government adopted far-right positions on immigration and climate change. In Austria, the far-right Freedom Party came first in both the 2024 national and EU parliamentary elections, winning 28.8 and 25.5 percent of the vote, respectively. The Alternative for Germany has polled as the second most popular party since 2023.[1]

Far-right dominance is neither inevitable nor irreversible: Poland voted out the Far Right in 2023 and the French Left defeated the National Rally in 2024. So it's not just that, in the US, the Left has been losing or just squeaking by for years. Something's going on both in the US and Europe that's worth understanding so we can begin to work systematically to turn things around.

Is There Really a Diploma Divide?

*Too many Americans . . . feel that Washington has turned its
back on them. They know they work hard, and they believe
that anyone who works hard in America deserves to earn a
stable middle-class life at least. Whether you're a Democrat,
independent, or Republican, . . . you need to understand the
depth of the anger that is driving American politics today.*

—Mark Cuban[1]

In 2023, Representative Marcy Kaptur wowed her Democratic colleagues
with a simple chart. It showed a sea of blue on the first page, which listed
congressional districts with the highest median incomes; the second
page, which listed districts with the lowest, was a sea of red. Her fellow
Democrats were shocked. They thought of themselves as representing the
have-nots.[2]

This was true as late as 2010, when Democrats still represented more
districts with median household incomes in the bottom 40 percent. It's
not true today: Democrats now tend to win in top 40 percent districts,
increasingly losing districts in the bottom 60 percent. We see the same
pattern if we look at the standard proxy for social class: college graduation. The percentage of Democrats who are college grads almost doubled
between 1996 and 2018, with "diploma divide" particularly pronounced
among whites. Nearly 60 percent of Bill Clinton's supporters were
whites without degrees, as compared to 27 percent of Biden's in 2020. In
1996, 59 percent of noncollege whites were Democrats or Democratic
leaners; today, only about a quarter are. Defections were particularly
strong among manual workers, but also evident among clerks and service
workers. The diploma divide increased again in 2024, when Republicans

carried noncollege voters by the highest margin ever recorded, and won voters making under $50,000 for the first time ever (the latter result probably driven by inflation).[3]

Donald Trump put this dynamic into hyperdrive, with a diploma divide much larger than in prior elections. The Merchant Right voted Republican as they always do. But about two-thirds of noncollege whites voted for him, too, in 2016, 2020, and 2024. In 2016, Trump won white noncollege voters by 39 points, doubling the diploma divide just eight years earlier; in 2024, he increased his share of noncollege voters again by six points as compared with 2020. This is vitally important because white noncollege voters predominate in rural areas and in swing states, where their votes carry more weight in the Senate because of small state bias built into the Constitution: a senator in California represents thirty-nine million voters, while a senator in North Dakota represents around eight hundred thousand. The current design of the Electoral College also gives more power to votes in low-population states. The math's simple: "There simply aren't enough affluent, educated, socially liberal voters to generate strong majorities in national elections," notes Nicholas Lemann.[4]

And that's just the federal government. As post-*Dobbs* antiabortion activism shows vividly, many important matters are decided at the state level. In nearly twenty western and Southern states, Democrats are virtually shut out of statewide offices largely due to their inability to attract noncollege whites.[5]

Similar patterns emerge in Europe. Almost two-thirds of manual workers voted for Brexit compared with less than half of managers or professionals. Close to 40 percent of manual workers voted for Marine Le Pen in the first round of the 2017 French presidential elections, compared to only 14 percent of managers or professionals.[6]

In the face of all this evidence, it's downright quirky that some on the Left still deny the existence of a diploma divide. Partly this stems from confusion about which noncollege voters are swerving right. Comparative political scientist Thomas Kurer shows that it's not the poor: economic hardship actually *reduces* support for the Far Right. Instead, far-right populism attracts lower-middle-class voters holding on for dear life and worried about their future. Routine jobs account for about 25–30 percent of the labor force and at least one-fifth of the electorate. Far-right parties in the three European countries Kurer studied "find support among 'survivors' in routine work, who share a bright past but rather bleak future prospects." The radical Right attracts "those who are both threatened by automation and are still 'just about managing' economically," found another study of eleven European countries.[7]

These findings jibe with studies of Trump voters that find his support concentrated in the lower-middle class: the truck driver married to a cashier. Cashiers already are being automated out of a job; truck drivers are just waiting to be. "Trump won his largest vote shares among voters of all races with some college but no degree, in voters with annual incomes between $50,000 and $100,000—precisely the precarious middle-class," notes Daniel Markovits. In 2016, the Pew Research Center found that 81 percent of Trump voters agreed that "life for people like you today is worse than it was 50 years ago," compared to only 19 percent of Clinton voters (who were, on average, richer).[8]

Globalization both lifted millions of Chinese workers out of abject poverty and hurt the prospects of middle-status workers in advanced industrial democracies. That's why admirable progress in ending world hunger has been accompanied by the rise of authoritarian populism in both the US and Europe.[9]

The process that led to where we are now began in the 1970s. Traditionally, Democrats were the party of workers tightly focused on securing economic opportunity and stability for the white working class, but my generation of "New Left" Democrats shifted attention to "post-materialist" issues like ending the Vietnam War, environmentalism, and the race and gender equality projects to which I have dedicated my working life. This is how Bill Clinton (who grew up working class) dissected the generational conflict my crowd was so proud of, describing the 1968 Democratic convention:

> The Democrats limped out of Chicago divided and discouraged . . . The kids and their supporters saw the mayor and the cops as authoritarian, ignorant, violent bigots. The mayor and his largely blue-collar ethnic police force saw the kids as foul-mouthed, immoral, unpatriotic, soft upper-class kids who were too spoiled to respect authority, too selfish to appreciate what it takes to hold a society together, too cowardly to serve in Vietnam.[10]

Ouch.

Clinton pinpoints a rarely noted but important element of contemporary politics both in the US and Europe: what upper-middle-class kids often don't realize—I certainly didn't—is that what they see as admirable idealism and personal authenticity, lower-middle-class people often see as class privilege ("spoiled kids"). Since at least the 1970s, children of college-educated parents often declared their independence by embracing progressive causes and bohemian lifestyles, dismissing their parents' values as bourgeoise or not sufficiently radical. Their college-educated parents view all this as a rite of passage and a badge of sophistication (mixed, perhaps, with annoyance or resignation). Keep in mind, too, that generational divides affect both white communities and communities of color. Older Black activists often were less enthusiastic than younger ones about "defund the police": in 2022, over three times as many young Blacks (eighteen to twenty-nine) as older ones (over sixty-four) supported a decrease in police funding.[11]

Meanwhile, in 1970, liberals in Europe and America still held progressive pro-worker views on economic issues. Then the neoliberal consensus swept in from around 1995, when Bill Clinton promised a new era of smaller government; it was still in place in 2011, when Barack Obama promised "painful cuts" to domestic spending. "Who in power ever even mentions the widening gaps in income and opportunity that have accompanied the 1990s economic boom?" asked political scientist Theda Skocpol in 2000, protesting the neoliberal Zen that markets would take care of it. After the Great Recession of 2008, establishment politicians of both parties quickly bailed out banks with cheap loans and subsidies while leaving 10 million people to lose their homes. Democrats tolerated high unemployment and stood by as employers undercut unions, shipped jobs overseas, and slashed wages and benefits for those blue-collar workers who remained employed. "I think the largest newspaper in the country to editorialize against NAFTA was the *Toledo Blade*," said Sherrod Brown, senator from Ohio (who opposed NAFTA, as did key unions). Antitrust was dropped from the Democratic Party platform in 1992 and not restored until 2016. Greed, after all, was good.[12]

Gone was the focus in the decades after World War II on creating a middle-class life for workers. Liberals' fairness concerns shifted away from policies that promoted good jobs in favor of free market policies combined with government redistribution to the poor. Neoliberal policies helped college-educated elites: "Free trade makes the products we buy cheaper, and our jobs are unlikely to be moved to China. Open immigration makes our service staff cheaper, but new, less-educated immigrants aren't likely to put downward pressures on our wages," notes David Brooks.[13]

Republicans began to make inroads on the "Scaffle" vote: lower-middle-class people who are social conservatives (SC) but fiscal liberals (FL). The Scaffle vote explains why deep-red states like Arkansas, Florida, Missouri, and Nebraska have passed minimum wage increases and why Idaho, Missouri, Nebraska, and Utah have expanded Medicaid through Obamacare.[14]

Scaffle voters, of course, bring us back to the representation gap that was filled by far-right parties that combine progressive economics with conservative cultural values. Trump is a good example. Trump "completely moved the Republican Party away from reducing Social Security and Medicare spending," said a chagrined commentator from the conservative American Enterprise Institute, though it's unclear that's a line he can hold (or even wants to). Trump's positions on this wiggle dizzily, but that's the point: he broke the Republican "entitlements are out of control" consensus. Trump also shattered the free-trade consensus that had long dominated both parties. I'm no Trump fan, but credit where credit is due. One analysis of his speeches in the 2016 election cycle found economic concerns mentioned more than any other topic.[15]

In Europe, small employers are the key group that swings between the center Right and the radical Right. The role of small employers' votes is woefully understudied. They are particularly important in the US because they represent twice the proportion of voters as compared to Europe, but even more importantly because workers tend to identify deeply with small business. That's partly because, for men, the chief way to "make good" in the working class is to own a small business. So it should come as no surprise that nearly a third of business owners did not graduate from college.[16]

"To many American workers, self-employment—however remote a possibility—seems to offer a more realistic chance to escape from working-class subordination than does a socialist transformation," wryly note sociologists Reeve Vanneman and Lynn Weber Cannon. A machine operator put it this way: "The main thing is to be independent and give your own orders and not have to take them from anybody else." "The dream of self-employment is one expression of his class consciousness, not a denial of it," they note astutely. It's the dream of an order-taker to be an order-giver. In the US, manual workers' views on economic issues are unusually close to those of small employers as compared to other countries. The lower-middle class often votes "not as workers but as future business owners and *pre*-rich citizens." Corporate interests have been busy sculpting support for small business into support for policies that help big business since the 1970s, just when wages began to stall out. Trump promised to "massively cut tax rates for workers and small business." Democrats let them do so by failing to highlight that what's good for big business is not typically good for small businesses. After all, Walmart drove mom-and-pops out of business in the 1990s, and Amazon does so today.[17]

All this leaves a very concrete path forward. When Trump won, as noted, 19 percent of Trump voters were economically progressive anti-elites: 83 percent of whom thought the system was biased in favor of the wealthiest Americans, only 24 percent thought money and wealth are distributed fairly, and 68 percent favored raising taxes on the wealthy. Fully 40 percent of these predominantly noncollege voters had favorable views of Bernie Sanders. On climate change, 64 percent said that global warming is happening, 67 percent said it's a serious problem, and a plurality said that human activities are causing it. Many (59 percent) believed that women lose out on good jobs due to discrimination. On immigration, they were less liberal, but 45 percent supported a path to citizenship for immigrants without papers. Unlike American preservationists, anti-elites reported feelings toward people of color as warm as those of Democrats'. They were the most liberal of any group on same-sex marriage. They were the least loyal to Republicans. Democrats should be laser-focused on peeling off a chunk of anti-elites.[18]

Notice the name. Far-right populism not only taps non-elites' sense of having lost ground; it provides an explanation why: elites. In fact, far-right populism has three elements: anger against elites, an insistence on giving power back to the "common people," and defining that in-group ("common people") in reference to one or more undeserving out-groups who supposedly have been favored by elites.

One thing that blocks some progressives from understanding class dynamics is that they resist the notion that they are elites. There's a New Class Bubble Quiz to help. Let's look at some data. The cutoff for households in the top 20 percent is $130,545. If your household earns that, I'd say you're part of the elite; after all, 80 percent of US households earn less. The reason this doesn't feel elite is that elites, as Pierre Bourdieu noted in *Distinction*, tend to obsess about what fraction of the elite they're in. Elites tend to compare up, not down, and the rich make many in the elite feel distinctly middle-class. The cutoff for households in the top 10 percent is $167,639; for the top 1 percent, it's $819,324. That's one dynamic that leads elites to deny they are elites. That, and the universal tendency for the privileged to deny privilege, something the racial justice movement has sought to remedy.[19]

It's important to include incomes for clarity—of course, noncollege graduate Bill Gates is undeniably an elite—but overall education is a better proxy for class. That's because a truck driver (average wage about $50,000) married to a bank teller (nearly $40,000) can together make six figures. However, assuming neither is a college grad, they're likely to be culturally blue-collar. On the other hand, high-human-capital but low-income professions, like a librarian (around $60,000) married to a social worker ($64,000), are likely to be culturally more like more affluent college-educated families than like the truck driver–bank teller family.[20]

That's why college graduation is more often used in political polling than income. It's a very flawed proxy, given that college grads also include graduates of Bob Jones University in Greenville, South Carolina, and Oral Roberts University in Tulsa, Oklahoma, whom I suspect are highly conservative. The diploma divide is robust despite these conservative college grads—which just shows you the strength of the link between college graduation and political liberalism.

I define three politically relevant social classes in the US as:

1. The professionals: families in the top 20 percent with at least one college grad; their median family income is $244,006;
2. The poor: families in the bottom 30 percent, whose median household income is $28,430;
3. The middle: roughly the middle 50 percent, with incomes ranging from about $41,005 to $95,650 and a median household income of $75,144.[21]

The key class conflict driving far-right populism is between the professionals and the middle.

The next challenge is what to call the different groups. This is difficult because *middle class* means such different things to different groups. The voters in routine jobs would typically self-describe as "middle class" (with upper-middle-class professionals described as rich). *Lower-middle class* is clearer, so I sometimes use that. Sometimes I use *blue-collar* or *working-class*, in order not to drive the reader insane with clunky terminology. When I do use *blue-collar*, keep in mind that I'm also referring to routine white- and pink-collar work; clerical workers typically are culturally blue-collar because they come from blue-collar families. I generally avoid the term *working-class* because progressives typically use that term to refer to the poor, which erases routine workers from existence. This is the point Theda Skocpol made in calling routine workers the "Missing Middle," to highlight how often public policies focus on the poor or professionals, missing the middle. To complicate things even more, being "middle class" typically means something different in Black households than white: police officers or bus drivers would typically be considered working-class whites, but middle-class Blacks, and middle-class white couples are three to four times more likely to contain a husband in a managerial position. But enough! Just keep in mind that the Far Right thrives on the anxieties and anger of people with a precarious hold on routine blue-, pink-, and white-collar jobs.[22]

Here's the bottom line: among whites, nearly two-thirds (62 percent) of college grads but less than half of noncollege grads (46 percent) still believe the American dream. That's a key source of the nostalgia and anger that drive far-right populism.[23]

Key Takeaways:

1. In both Europe and the US, non-elites who used to vote with the Left have veered far-right.
2. Precarity, not poverty, drives far-right support. The Far Right attracts not the poor, but lower-middle-class voters in routine jobs holding on for dear life and worried about their future.
3. For decades, no party offered these voters what they wanted: a party that was economically progressive but socially conservative. Far-right populism filled this "representation gap."
4. Take the New Class Bubble Quiz at classbubblequiz.com to gain some perspective on your own class bubble!

Isn't It Just the *White* Working Class?

Democrats can win with college-educated whites plus nonwhite voters. They can't win with more defection from nonwhite voters.

—Eitan Hersh[1]

Sometimes the instinct is to dismiss the importance of the diploma divide on the grounds that it's only a divide among white people. It's true that the gap between those with and without college degrees yawns much wider among whites than among people of color: about two-thirds of whites without degrees voted for Trump in 2020. It's also true that Democrats' support among people of color is startlingly higher than among whites: 93 percent of Black voters, 60 percent of Latinos, and 68 percent of Asian American voters, but only 41 percent of whites, voted Democratic in the 2022 midterms.[2]

But here's the problem: white noncollege grads are such a large voting bloc in the country—44 percent of the 2020 electorate—that if Democrats lose them overwhelmingly, they need the overwhelming support and turn-out among people of color to win. Instead, "Democrats have lost ground among non-white voters in almost every election over the past decade," to quote Nate Cohn. Compared to the 2018 midterm elections, non-white noncollege voters shifted away from Democrats by 15 percentage points in 2022. During the same period, Black men shifted 11 points away, Black women 7 points and Latina women 14 points away from Democrats; for Latino men, the shift was a breathtaking 21 points. Clearly, Democrats can't assume consistent, sky-high levels of support from people of color. This became only too clear in 2024, when nonwhite noncollege voters shifted toward Trump by 14 points and nonwhite college grads did so by 10 points.[3]

The bottom line: Democrats can't depend on unstinting support from people of color to make up for their deficit with working-class whites. A 2024 Gallup poll concluded the Democratic Party still held advantages among people of color, "but in 2023 it was in a weaker position among these groups than at any point in the past quarter century."[4]

The largest bleed has been among Latinos. Latinos' support for Democratic presidential candidates fell from 71 percent in 2012 to 59 percent in 2020. In 2024, a majority of Latinos (54 percent) voted for Trump, shifting toward him by 33 points, while Latinas shifted toward him by 15 points as compared to 2020 (these are early exit poll numbers, which may change). Latinos also show a diploma divide. In 2020, 41 percent of noncollege Latino voters cast votes for Trump. Biden won Latino college grads by 39 points but non-grads by only 14 points. It's something about Trump that appeals: only 27 percent of noncollege Latinos voted Republican in the 2018 midterms.[5]

A Gallup poll showed that Democrats' edge among Black voters shrank nearly 20 points between 2020 and 2023. In 2024 Biden was winning Black voters by only 50 points, "a rightward swing of nearly 30 points from his 2020 margins." In the 2024 election, Harris garnered support from African Americans at about the same level as Biden (though much lower than Obama's sky-high levels). Although younger Black voters seemed to warm up to Harris, an earlier poll found that Black voters under 45 shifted 22 points toward Republicans between 2018 and 2022. Black support for Democrats had fallen 10 points in 10 years, found a poll from February 2024.[6]

Exit polls in 2020 showed Trump up by 7 points among Asian Americans as compared to 2016; in 2024 Trump support grew again, by 4 points as compared to 2020. The class effect among Asian Americans is much weaker because 51 percent of Asian Americans have college degrees, as compared with 30 percent of Blacks and 20 percent of Latinos. That helps explain why Asian Americans are more liberal as a group than Americans in general (31 percent versus 21 percent). A 2023 poll found that nearly 70 percent of college-educated Asian Americans identify as Democrats, but among noncollege grads, the percentage is in the mid-50s.[7]

The Asian American experience highlights that "people of color" is an aspirational term, not a description. (The term caught on in Black newspapers in the 1990s to stress the need for solidarity among various quite different "minorities," the then current term.) Not only is *people of color* an aspirational term; so is *Asian American*. Aggregating people of Asian descent into one (homogeneous?) community presents even more challenges than for other groups. For example, while 72 percent of Indian Americans twenty-five and older have at least a college degree, only 9 percent of Bhutanese do. These dramatic class differences are matched by dramatic cultural differences, making averages misleading.[8]

An insightful 2023 study found that the data "does not imply that Donald Trump received more votes from minority voters, only that the minority voters who turned out to vote supported Trump at a higher rate." In 2020, Democrats garnered more Black voters because their higher turnout "more than compensated for the small shifts in vote choice." On the other hand, Latinos "swung moderately towards Trump in 2020 relative to 2016." Latinos still are heavily Democratic and an increasing proportion of the population, which holds the promise of more votes for Democrats in the future. But the bottom line is that Democrats' edge among voters of color is diminishing and that the solution is for Democrats to pay more—not less—attention to communities of color.[9]

Sometimes overlooked is that in key parts of the country, voters of color express their dissatisfaction through low turnout. When Trump won in 2016, it was not only because working-class whites swerved sharply toward him but because of low turnout among people of color. Kurer and others find high levels of nonvoting among the unemployed, and the unemployment rate is much higher for Black Americans. Presumably, life becomes so overwhelming when unemployment hits, perhaps followed by eviction and bankruptcy, that voting falls by the wayside. Republicans' gains in the midterms were driven chiefly by a turnout advantage.[10]

Long gone are the days when Democrats comforted themselves that "demography is destiny": that as the US became "majority minority," an emerging Democratic majority would give sustained support for progressive policies and eliminate the need to attract white working-class voters, as Steve Phillips argued in 2016 in *Brown Is the New White*. Phillips's optimism rested on two then widely held assumptions. The first assumption was that people of color would turn out for Democrats at the same rates they did for Barack Obama. In fact, African Americans' sky-high turnout for Barack Obama has never been repeated as of August 2024. Low turn-out among Blacks in key swing states *combined* with strong Trump support among working-class whites is what cost Hillary Clinton the election in swing states.[11]

The second assumption was that people of color in general would skew as strongly Democratic as Black Americans do. They don't. Why not?

The high level of support for Democrats reflects Black Americans' strong sense of linked fate: 73 percent of African Americans say being Black is at least somewhat important to how they see themselves. They are more likely than other groups to see racial solidarity as their only reliable choice. Black adults (65 percent) also are substantially more likely to prioritize addressing issues around race than Hispanic (42 percent), Asian (32 percent), or White adults (23 percent). A key driver is the widespread experience of discrimination: 69 percent of African Americans report a lot of discrimination against Blacks, dramatically higher than any other group. The less individual Blacks believed that discrimination persists, the less they preferred their group over whites. The same held for Latinos.[12]

Digging deeper, ethnographies show that noncollege Black Americans are more like the French working class than white noncollege Americans in their insight into structural inequality. This extends beyond their own group: African Americans (74 percent) are more likely than Latinos (58 percent) to believe that it is harder to be Latino than white. Not surprisingly, voters with the weakest attachment to their Black identity have a higher likelihood of voting for Trump.[13]

The rightward shift among Latinos is much larger than among Black voters. Particularly sobering for Democrats was that Trump in 2020 made his biggest gains with Latinos among people who typically don't vote. Trump support is fueled by votes of men: in 2024, Latinos were 18 points more likely than Latinas to vote for Trump, up from 7 points in 2020.[14]

While it's important to recognize that Latino voters helped Democrats retain the White House in 2020 and the Senate in 2022, it's undeniable that Latinos are very different from African Americans. They have the lowest sense of a linked fate among people of color: only about 25 percent do. Probably related: immigration was a top issue for only 22 percent of Latinos in battleground districts and states in 2022.[15]

Latinos have a lower level of linked fate than Latinas, which may help explain their greater rightward swing. Latinos' sense of linked fate decreased between 2006 and 2016. "I'm Hispanic, but I'm an American," said one Latina when asked about Trump's insulting comments about Mexicans.[16]

Asian Americans are a much smaller segment of voters (4 percent) than African Americans (11 percent) and Latinos (10 percent). Overall, they tend to vote with Democrats, but Trump gained 7 percentage points in 2020 despite his calling Covid the "China virus," which spurred attacks on Asian Americans in San Francisco and other cities.[17]

Asian Americans are dramatically less likely to say that their race is important to their identity: 30–44 percent say it's not at all important. Another study found that 46 percent of Asian Americans had no group consciousness. Only 13 percent of Asian Americans say discrimination is a major problem for their group.[18] Said one Asian American of the counsel offered by parents:

> "The nail that sticks up gets hammered down," they said. They encouraged us to blend in, to adopt cultural camouflage, to avoid standing out in ways that might make us vulnerable to the racial targeting that they may have experienced themselves.[19]

Perhaps not surprisingly, Asian Americans (73 percent) were more likely than white Americans (63 percent) or Latinos (57 percent) to agree that "many people nowadays are too sensitive about things to do with race." A 2005 study found that 36 percent of Asians ticked the "white box," whereas 22 percent ticked the "Asian box," and the rest chose a mixed category. "When their children grow up . . . many of them may view themselves as whites," concluded sociologist Richard Alba. So perhaps it's not surprising that Asian Americans sometimes are more similar to whites than to other people of color—for example, in the low percentage of each group (38 percent) that prioritizes problems of the poor. Asian Americans are actually more likely (69 percent) than other Americans (58 percent) to say people can get ahead if they are willing to work hard. Hard work is a central value; 93 percent of Asian Americans "describe members of their country of origin group as 'very hardworking.'"[20] To quote Jennifer Lee:

> Politically conservative Asian immigrants who are calling for a retreat from race do not seek to deny opportunity for all. They believe in the American

dream and immigrated to the United States because they subscribe to the [credo that] . . . those who get ahead do so on the bases of talent, hard work, and grit. They also believe that one's racial status should be neither a penalty nor a reward, and are committed to protecting the opportunities for their U.S.-born children.[21]

MAGA offers a "multicultural politics of whiteness," to quote Cristina Beltrán. A clever social psychology study dramatizes how true this is. Mara Ostfeld and her colleague first developed a new scale for measuring skin tones from dark to light. Then they stopped every fourth passerby going to soccer games, parades, indoor markets, a county fair, used the scale to assess their skin tone, and also asked them to rate their skin tone on the same scale. They found that Latino Americans who think their skin is darker than it really is skew Democratic, whereas those who think their skin is lighter than it really is skew Republican. Another study found that Latinos who identified as "people of color" supported Biden over Trump with a gap of 61 percent; other Latinos favored Biden over Trump by just 24 percent. The Ostfeld finding that 38 percent voted for Trump among those who most overestimated their skin's lightness is consistent with a central insight of critical race theory: that race is a social construction. In a society where whiteness is valuable, people of color make different strategic decisions about whether to get ahead through racial solidarity or by assimilating into whiteness.[22]

Insight into the strategic decisions people make is offered by critical race theorist Ian Haney López. He found that only a quarter of Latino Americans share Black Americans' sense that they are "people of color" with a linked fate, while another third believe they will become part of the American mainstream just as white ethnics did. These "white ethnic" Latinos are three times as likely as "people of color" Latinos to believe that people who can't get ahead are responsible for their own situations. Another 28 percent, "bootstrappers," are the most likely to be Republican and to believe that people can get ahead through hard work. Racism plays a role: racial resentment strongly predicts Trump voting among Latinos. Here's the bottom line: the social construction of race means that "brown is the new white"— but in a way that hurts Democrats, not helps them.[23]

Key Takeaways:

1. People of color vote much more heavily Democratic than white people do.
2. Working-class whites are such a large percentage of the electorate that Democrats can't afford many defections among people of color and still win.
3. Defections among Latinos, especially those without college degrees, as well as smaller losses among Asian Americans and younger and male Black voters, threaten Democrats' coalition.
4. MAGA's multicultural politics of whiteness appeals to people of color whose survival strategy is to align with the majority.

Isn't It Bizarre When the Left Denies the Impact of Inequality on Politics?

The education gap among whites this year wasn't about education. It was about race.

—*The Washington Post* op-ed, 2016[1]

Sometimes it seems that progressives spend the first half of the day decrying the evils of inequality and the second half denying that economic populism is about economics. This makes no sense.

The economy just isn't working for a lot of people, both at home and abroad. To quote a supporter of far-right Marine Le Pen in France: "Apart from two pregnancies, I worked nonstop from age 14 to 60, and now I have a pension of 1,160 euros a month. It's pathetic, with almost half going to rent but [French President] Macron doesn't care." Far-right figures tap this anger. Said Trump in 2020, "From day one I've been fighting for the forgotten men and women of America." I didn't believe him. Many who voted for him didn't believe him either, but at least they felt *seen*.[2]

A 2017 study of Trump's speeches found constant and positive references to "workers." Most important, Trump "removed blame for their downward mobility by pointing to globalization as a structural force that negatively affected their social position." This reaffirmed workers' self-image as responsible, hardworking people who had been robbed. And he identified who robbed them: immigrants both stole their jobs and were "sponging off the system." When it comes to reassuring downwardly mobile Americans, Trump has perfect pitch. Democrats did not learn from their mistakes: only 18 percent of Democratic television ads in 2022 mentioned jobs at all, and less than 2 percent mentioned good, high-paying, living-wage or union jobs.[3]

As of 2023, noncollege voters were slightly more likely (+2 points) to believe the GOP cared more about them. Nearly 4 in 10 (37 percent) believe neither party is invested in helping the middle class. That's the heritage of neoliberalism. This is part of a larger problem. Martin Gilens's 2012 study found that low- and middle-income Americans' preferences had *no* influence on public policy. Those voters noticed.[4]

The cottage industry denying that economic populism is about economics is ironic. Leftist think tanks and a huge economics literature document the hollowing out of the American middle class. From 1979 to 2013, productivity grew eight times faster than wages. This is in sharp contrast to the decades after World War II, when wages kept pace with productivity; if that had continued, wages would be 43 percent higher than they are today. Tellingly, three-fourths of the post–World War II decline occurred between 2000 and 2016.[5]

The decline in workers' share of income has been particularly marked in the US. As incomes fell, debt rose: the ratio of household debt to gross domestic product doubled between 1983 and 2007. Today, the US ranks as the most unequal developed country in the world.[6]

Meanwhile, by 2000, the winner-take-all economy meant that the top 1 percent of households had more wealth than the bottom 95 percent, and the top 1 percent of earners (2.7 million people) earned more than the poorest 100 million. This trend continued: annual pay increases grew 138 percent for the top 1 percent but only 15 percent for the bottom 90 percent between 1979 and 2013. Average CEO pay, which rose only modestly in the decades after World War II, rose sharply after 1980 and exponentially after 1990, as the FDR-initiated era of corporate self-restraint gave way to the era of "greed is good."[7]

The US economy polarized into jobs at the bottom and jobs at the top, with workers formerly in middle-class jobs falling into low-paid dead-end service jobs: the Walmart greeter or the McDonald's cashier. About a quarter of routine white- and blue-collar jobs disappeared, while higher-level jobs increased by 34 percent and low-paid jobs increased by 11 percent between 1982 and 2017. Nearly all the net growth in employment between 2005 and 2015 was in short-term jobs and gig work. Many employers hived off major parts of their workforce into staffing companies that offered few, if any, of the benefits offered to employees—economists call this *fissuring*.[8]

The upper-middle class did well. Wages have increased by 83 percent for college graduates since 1989, but hardly at all for noncollege grads. The college wage premium *doubled* between 1980 and 2000—the 40 percent wage differential between college grads and noncollege grads rose to 80 percent.[9]

Unemployment rose sharply: it was 20 percent at the end of the Great Recession, and 14 percent long into the recovery, in 2018. Neoliberalism's deregulation of the financial industry led directly to the Great Recession, which also did a job on people's wealth. Americans in the wealthiest 95th percentile lost a lot but recovered quickly; those in the bottom 25th percentile lost about 85 percent of their net worth and many never recovered. As recently as the 1990s, wealth was evenly split between college grads and noncollege grads, but today, college grads own three-fourths of it.[10]

Neoliberalism meant not only the decline of private sector jobs but also government jobs earning between $30,000 and $50,000; cutbacks hurt noncollege grads in general and African Americans in particular. Loss of blue-collar jobs can be particularly devastating for men "whose masculine identities are often tied not only to paid labor and breadwinning, but also to work in specific "industries"—autoworker, steelworker.[11]

Identity threat is triggered even more by declining labor force participation. In 1960, class-based differences in men's workforce participation were "barely detectable," but by 2011, 90 percent of male college grads were employed—but only 76 percent of high school graduates, devastating their dignity as well as their finances. Middle-class incomes declined at a faster rate than the nation as a whole, and the "great risk shift" made Americans far more vulnerable to being wiped out by illness, old age, and unexpected job loss—risks formerly shouldered by their employers. Localities more exposed to competition from Chinese imports saw substantially larger reductions in manufacturing, resulting in more people unemployed or not in the labor force; workers without college degrees were affected most. Chinese imports accounted for between a quarter to half of the manufacturing jobs lost in the US.[12]

All this helps explain why the share of Americans who earn more than their parents has plummeted by 40 points, with the largest declines for families in the middle class and the industrial Midwest.[13]

It's not just the US either. If we compare different deciles of population between 1989 and 2008, almost 90 percent of the worst performing deciles were from mature economies; 90 percent of the best performing were in Asia. The "elephant curve" pinpoints only one group that lost ground during the recent wave of globalization: citizens with low to mid-dling incomes in rich countries.[14]

Since the 1970s, the real incomes of college grads have risen around 50 percent while those of noncollege grads have stagnated. The earnings ratio between less- and more-educated workers' salaries increased sharply. Law firm partners made five times what legal secretaries did in 1960 but forty times as much by 2020. Bank presidents made fifty times as much as bank tellers in 1960 but a thousand times as much by 2020. We live in a new Gilded Age, with a wealth gap reminiscent of the 1890s.[15]

All this fueled the rise in despair deaths from drug overdose, alcohol-ism, and suicide among noncollege grads—among whites starting around 1992 and among Blacks and Latinos after 2010. The rising mortality rate among working-class middle-aged white men was a "demographic re-versal that had never previously been observed in any group in North America or Europe except in times of war, pandemics or genocide." Life expectancy for Americans without college degrees has plummeted, and is now eight and a half years less than that for college grads. The suicide rate among working-class white men rose nearly 40 percent between 1999 and 2013; no other group of Americans was similarly affected. When a researcher asked what caused her informant's friends to turn to drugs, the answer was simple: "Lack of jobs, I think. Yeah—hard on people. It's not that easy, you know." Two economists found that depressed labor force participation was related to opioid use, with "the arrows of causation run-ning in both directions."[16]

Political scientist Justin Gest found that, in both the US and the UK, "nostalgic deprivation" predicts support for the Far Right. Other studies document this in other countries. It's nostalgia for the decades after World War II when incomes nearly doubled and non-elites could achieve the American dream: the house, the car, the washing machine, maybe a cabin by a lake. Gest found that people's sense of nostalgic deprivation played a particularly large role in the US: moving from least to most increased sup-port for Trump by 41 points.[17]

It has long been known that economic hardship tends to give rise to right-wing populist movements, and research on far-right voters had "become a minor industry" as early as 2009. One study found that labor market changes, chiefly decreases in manufacturing jobs, produced two-thirds of the total effect on voting. Many studies document that increasing imports from China (and occasionally other countries) are correlated with increases in voting for the Far Right both in Europe and the US. Following their research on the "China Shock," David Autor and coauthors found in another study that congressional districts in local labor markets affected by Chinese imports tended to veer far-right if they were majority white, and far-left if they were majority non-white.[18]

The beauty for Republicans is that both those shifts generally came at the expense of moderate Democrats. Other studies have found similar effects in France, Germany, and the UK (measured as support for Brexit). Still others document a far-right veer of voters in regions more exposed to automation in Western Europe and the US. Their fears are not irrational: automation decreases the wages of low- and medium-skilled workers and increases the wages of managers and high-skilled workers. Workers more exposed to automation prefer a larger role for government in reducing inequality—which the neoliberal consensus largely precluded.[19]

Jobs were not the only predictors of Trump voting. Counties that shifted from Obama to Trump had unusually high rates of negative home equity, which of course makes it more difficult "to start a small business, send a child to college, handle a family emergency, or move to a more advantageous location. For homeowners, this can result not only in economic harm but also in a feeling that their way of life is slipping away." *The Economist* found that public health metrics were the second-most significant factor predicting Trump's gains as compared with Mitt Romney. Other studies found that regions with lower job growth, credit scores, social mobility, and workforce participation all swung for Trump, as did counties that saw a decline or stagnation in life expectancy.[20]

When Thomas Frank argued that middle-status voters vote cluelessly against their own self-interest, none of this research existed. Nor did the research on the representation gap. "The reason voters don't vote based on economics is that they absolutely don't believe that either Democrats or Republicans will ever deliver for them," pollster David Mermin remarked to me in 2023. "Non-college swing voters in particular constantly tell us that neither party is on their side, and both parties are dominated by wealthy interests and corporate money."[21]

It's not that Democrats didn't try. Joe Biden made an effort, but it's a long road back. Famously, Biden walked the picket line with striking autoworkers in 2023. "Our Family Can Have a Future," read a *New York Times* article after the strike was resolved. It told the story of David and

Bailey Hodge, both autoworkers at a Ford Motor plant in Michigan who had been working twelve-hour shifts, seven days a week, just to cover monthly bills, car payments, and their mortgage, and to put aside a little money for retirement and college education for their children. One reason the family was so strapped was because Mr. Hodge had started as a temporary worker and had to give up his twenty-seven-dollar-an-hour wage and start again at fifteen dollars an hour when he finally landed a permanent position at the same plant five years later—the result of concessions the union had given to the car companies during the era when they were experiencing financial difficulties because of free-trade policies that had flooded the American market with foreign cars produced in countries with lower wages and/or pensions financed at a national level instead of by individual employers.[22]

"You just sleep all the time you're not at work," said Ms. Hodge, aged twenty-five. "Tag-teaming," where mom works one shift and dad works a different one, is most common among middle-status families, because they can't afford good quality childcare. Ms. Hodge worked the night shift, so she would wake up in the afternoon, get dinner for the kids, then go to work. Sometimes she would get to see her eight-year-old son off to school when she returned home in the morning. Sometimes not. Then she slept until the kids came home from school, and the cycle began again. When the workers struck, she said, "you were happy to have some time off and have dinner as a family, put the kids to bed"—simple pleasures elites take for granted.[23]

Under the new contract, Mr. Hodge makes almost thirty-nine dollars an hour, up from thirty-two dollars. Ms. Hodge will make thirty-five dollars an hour, up from twenty. "I was super happy," said Mr. Hodge. "It makes me feel like our family can have a future now." Ms. Hodge said, "It will be great just doing some overtime, not overtime all the time." "And we'll start doing things with the kids. Maybe take them to a hotel that has a swimming pool. That would be nice."[24]

One common argument writes off working-class nostalgia for family-sustaining jobs as nostalgia for white privilege. The kernel of truth is that the post–World War II "working man's paradise" was chiefly a paradise for whites: African Americans never enjoyed the kind of intergenerational mobility working-class whites did, and African Americans and Latinos remain more likely than whites to fall out of the middle class. The Great Recession increased racial wealth disparities: Latino families lost 44–50 percent and Black families lost 31–34 percent of mean wealth while white families lost only 10–13 percent. Neoliberal attacks on government employment disproportionately hurt Blacks because about one in five employed Blacks worked in government jobs, a significantly higher proportion than whites. The decline in manufacturing jobs also disproportionately hurt African Americans more than whites. From 1998 to 2000, there was a "30.4% decline in total Black manufacturing employment." The result? "A 13% increase in the racial wealth gap for men," among other increases in racial inequality. It goes without saying that it's inexcusable that people of color were systematically excluded from the workers' paradise.[25]

Whites are more pessimistic because—though they've always had more—they've also lost what they once had: primarily white mining and manufacturing communities have the highest rates of despair and deaths. "Working-class adults often make comparisons between their own and their parents' standard of living when their parents were their age," which leads to more "negative assessments among whites than minorities" because open racism has diminished but class disadvantage has increased. A recent study compared Black and white millennials born poor to same-race Gen Xers and found Blacks more likely—but whites less likely—to outearn their parents' generation. No wonder communities of color have higher rates of optimism and better health indicators—until recently when despair deaths began to rise among people of color.[26]

"I have no sympathy for them," one leftist told me, speaking of the white working class. "They were just sucking on the teat of the federal government. Now they can't, so they're whining." It's true that whites' mobility was fueled by government programs that excluded most African Americans (notably FHA loans and the GI Bill). But it seems odd for the Left to heap scorn on redistributive programs that were startlingly effective. Wouldn't it be better to bring back intergenerational mobility for Americans of all races rather than to fault whites for mourning its loss?

I've often heard progressives point out that now that white people's futures are being gutted, it's suddenly a crisis, asking why it was not a crisis when the same thing happened to people of color several decades earlier. They're right: that's an artifact of white privilege. But surely the solution, to quote Rev. Al Sharpton, is to have "rural whites and Blacks and migrants and Browns come together. [Then we] could really force real change." To quote Erica Etelson, "If the left doesn't channel populist resentment, we know who will."[27]

Key Takeaways:

1. Economic populism is about economics: today's winner-take-all economy is not working for a lot of people.
2. Many formerly middle-class Americans are unemployed or falling into unstable, low-paid service jobs or gig work—or fear they soon will.
3. MAGA attracts people who feel that neither party is serious about stopping the erosion of the American middle class.
4. MAGA is about white privilege in the sense that stable middle-class life circa 1945–1975 was offered far more to whites than people of color—but isn't the solution to create an economy that works for Americans of all races?

Why Are Rural and Rust Belts Red?

Voters here haven't known economic expansion in decades . . .
There is a strong sense in these communities, and not
unreasonably, of suffering endless condescension—the feeling
that urban America has written off the rural lifestyle as a relic or,
worse, as a joke.

—Matt Bai[1]

The story of far-right populism is typically told without reference to place. This is unwise. Trump's election in 2016 was the revolt of rural and Rust Belt counties, as was Brexit. These revolts highlight that neoliberalism fueled not just inequality between *individuals* but also inequality between *regions*. Economic opportunity has become highly stratified geographically, with a small number of cities that account for "a large and growing share of jobs, income, wealth, venture-capital and more," notes David Leonhardt. The end result: the 2,584 counties Trump won accounted for only a third of US GDP; the 472 counties Clinton won accounted for two-thirds. Trump won areas left behind by neoliberalism; Clinton won the winners.[2]

This happened in the UK and US because both have winner-take-all legislative districts defined by geography, which gives rural areas disproportionate power—unlike in democracies where winners are chosen proportionally. The Electoral College exacerbates the problem, giving king-making power to a few key Rust Belt states in presidential elections. And Congress's inability to pass virtually anything has heightened the importance of state legislatures, which in rural states are elected chiefly by rural votes.[3] The rural-urban divide drives polarization in both the US and Europe, driven by an economic system that channels wealth away from rural and Rust Belt areas into a few large cities. That economic system does not fit with a political system that gives disproportionate power to precisely those rural and Rust Belt areas.[4]

It wasn't always this way. During the first half of the twentieth century, wealth was shared more broadly not just between classes but also between regions. Pittsburgh was the king of steel; my mother-in-law's hometown of Waterbury, Connecticut, proudly proclaimed itself brass capital of the world; Rochester, New York, was headquarters of Kodak; High Point, North Carolina, was the furniture capital. Each city had its own elite that invested not only in local jobs but also in civic improvements.[5]

But starting in the second half of the twentieth century, the place-based manufacturing-heavy industrialized Old Economy shifted to a globalized human-capital-based New Economy. Between 1979 and 2019, professional and business jobs jumped from 8 percent to 14 percent of the US economy. In the same time period, manufacturing jobs decreased by 35 percent as free trade policies outsourced jobs overseas. During and since the pandemic, rural hospitals are closing, too, bought up by the same kinds of monied interests that earlier liquidated factories.[6]

The New Economy drained resources and wealth away from small and midsize cities and rural areas, concentrating wealth in a few winner-take-all cities mostly on the coasts. What urbanist Richard Florida celebrated in 2002 as the "rise of the creative class" was a triumphalist tale of this new geographical concentration of wealth, attributing it to the personal quality elites respect most: creativity. But here's the other side of the story: "In my small town, we have no local police, and our health system is woefully underfunded. Internet is expensive or nonexistent. Our main streets are a shadow of their former selves. And worst of all, Covid drove city folks to move here and turn affordable rental properties into expensive homes and Airbnbs. Now housing is unaffordable," said a Maine resident.[7]

The shift to the New Economy was justified by neoliberal consensus that celebrated globalization and free markets on the assumption that "markets were a neutral instrument for divining the public good." After the fall of the Soviet Union, the so-called end of history reflected the belief that free trade and free markets would raise GDP, lift millions out of poverty, and even lure China in the direction of democracy. It was unfashionable to worry about how that new wealth would get distributed. The neoliberal consensus was shared by Republicans and Democrats. Historian Gary Gerstle pinpoints its triumph quite precisely to Bill Clinton's administration. In 1992, Clinton campaigned on helping the industrial-ized workers who had long been the mainstay of the Democratic Party: he advocated labor law reform to level the playing field for unions, as well as industrial policy and a state-backed bank to revive manufacturing.[8]

But while Clinton campaigned for the Old Economy, he governed for the New Economy. He accelerated the decline of manufacturing by em-bracing free trade without protections against outsourcing. The end result: only in the UK was the loss of manufacturing jobs greater than in the US. The decline in manufacturing jobs as a share of total jobs exceeded the rate of loss during the Great Depression. The New Economy leached jobs into winner-take-all cities: fifty-three large metropolitan areas accounted for 96.4 percent of US growth (2014–2018) and 73 percent of employ-ment gains (2010–2016). As good jobs increasingly located in big cities, wage growth has been low or nil outside large urban centers. "People had realistic wages and benefits. . . . a local person should be able to get a good job. With benefits," one rural resident told sociologist Jennifer Sherman ruefully.[9]

Clinton also helped orchestrate the ascendance of the finance industry, with tax advantages and deregulation that fueled huge profits for bank-ers, followed by the implosion of the housing market due to the finance industry's readily abusable subprime mortgages, which led to the 2008 Great Recession. Many in the Midwest fumed as Obama bailed out Wall Street even as their own homes were foreclosed. Clinton stood by as union busting accelerated, failed to deliver on his promise to strengthen unions, instead diminishing unions' voice and influence in the Democratic Party. His embrace of NAFTA and other free trade policies "[was] widely understood as both a betrayal and an existential threat to many commu-nities in the Midwest," as was his normalization of trade with China.[10]

Studies document the impact of all this on politics. Counties with both manufacturing job losses and health care declines shifted most sharply to the GOP, accounting for 50 percent of total gains. A study of 537 small and midsize "factory town counties" in ten states mostly in the Mid-west found that the steeper the percentage of manufacturing jobs lost, the greater the vote shift to Republicans. In ten largely Midwestern states, Democrats lost 1.2 million more votes among "factory towns" than they gained in metropolitan, college, and suburban counties. Rural counties more reliant on manufacturing twenty years ago shifted hardest to the right between 2012 and 2020.[11]

What's the relationship between rural areas, Rust Belts, and college graduation? At one level, it's simple: only 21 percent of rural residents graduated from college, compared with 37 percent of urban residents. More complicated is the overlap between manufacturing and rural areas. Manufacturing counties are concentrated not only in the deindustrialized Midwest but also in Iowa and Missouri. Chicken-processing factories are chiefly located in the rural South.[12]

In rural areas, the decline in manufacturing dovetailed with changes in agriculture as it merged into a global supply chain, with profits siphoned off by large corporations. The free market neoliberal consensus meant that both political parties held fire on enforcing the antitrust laws as the power of agribusiness grew, with predictable results: farmers' share of the retail food dollar fell from roughly 50 percent (1952) to 15 percent in 2020. The meat industry consolidated under the Obama administration due to its failure to enforce the Packers and Stockyards Act and the Country of Origin acts. The transfer of power from farmers to big business accelerated after the Obama Justice Department and Federal Trade Commission allowed high-profile corporate mergers of Kraft-Heinz, JBS-Cargill, and other huge conglomerates with monopoly power. As a result, today "corporations control more and more of the agriculture business—from the seed and fertilizer farmers buy to the grain, milk and meat they sell—sucking off profits instead of giving farmers a fair price or a fair shot at the market," noted Bill Hogseth, once chair of the Dunn County Democratic Party in Wisconsin. "A farmer in the Midwest used to have five companies competing for his cattle," noted Democratic senator and 2020 presidential candidate Cory Booker of New Jersey. "Now he has one. Corporate concentration is killing his family." Robert Reich has documented how laws have been shaped to favor monopolistic companies and disfavor smaller businesses. The result is that huge chains like Walmart and Dollar General drove mom-and-pops on Main Street out of business, replacing the middle-class dignity of owning your own small business with mostly low-wage jobs.[13]

"We've been in a recession up here for 30, 40 years. We don't know any different," said a resident of a Wisconsin logging town. Half the groups Katherine Cramer spoke with for her influential *The Politics of Resentment* felt that government was dismissive of their concerns. This helps explain anti-tax sentiment: "The government must be mishandling my hard-earned dollars, because my taxes keep going up and clearly they are not coming back to benefit people like me." Nearly 70 percent of rural residents felt that rural areas didn't get their fair share, as opposed to 16 percent of suburban and 25 percent of urban residents in Wisconsin. In addition, in an era when middle-class families typically need two incomes, the lack of any semblance of a childcare system hits rural areas particularly hard: rural areas have ten infants and toddlers for every day care slot. Kids can't do homework or adults start a small business, due to widespread lack of internet access.[14]

Big Pharma targeted areas with high levels of pain to push opioids; as of 2023, 42 percent of rural residents said they or someone in their family were or had been addicted to opioids. Then Covid-related cash-flow problems closed down many rural hospitals that were one of the few remaining sources of steady work. By 2016, rural men in their prime working years are much more likely to be out of the labor force than men in metropolitan areas. The suicide rate in rural areas soared, reflecting "an inescapable feeling of failure and an overwhelming sense that there is no future here," concludes Hogseth. The rural-urban mortality gap widened across every racial group in the past twenty years; the decline in lifespan was steeper for working-age whites than people of color, and steepest for rural women. "Mortality rate increases since the early 1990s for nonmetro females have been startling." Rates rose everywhere, "but the increase was over twice as large for [rural prime-age] females" (aged twenty-five to forty-four).[15]

Tellingly, the erosion of rural support for Democrats began in 1990. But commentators who write off rural voters forget that Democrats were competitive in rural areas until quite recently: Obama won 40 percent of rural votes in 2008. Twelve years later, Joe Biden was in the 20s in some of the same counties. The chickens had come home to roost.[16]

The neoliberal consensus also meant that Clinton, and Margaret Thatcher in the UK, replaced the promise of good jobs with the promise of assets—stocks and houses—as the path to social mobility. This promise was short-lived, as many middle-class families lost money invested in stock during the tech bubble of 2000 and even more lost equity when the housing markets crashed during the Great Recession. Rural areas' recovery from the Great Recession overall has been very uneven. To add insult to injury, venture capitalists started buying from scrapyards all over Ohio around 2009, shipping everything from aluminum siding to manhole covers to street lighting to China to fuel its industrial boom fueled by outsourced jobs. The New Economy was literally selling the Old Economy for scrap.[17]

Adding fuel to the fire, "many of the same counties that hemorrhaged factory jobs also saw large increases in undocumented immigrants competing for the unskilled jobs that remained—cleaning hotel rooms, slaughtering chickens, mowing lawns. Their arrival fueled still more resentment," noted *New York Times* reporter Farah Stockman, who followed a group of steelworkers from Indiana.[18]

Progressives who scoff at people who vote against their own self-interest typically don't recognize that rural and Rust Belt areas felt abandoned by *both* parties—and the representation-gap literature shows they were. One autoworker articulated it this way: "[After NAFTA] I realized these parties were not so different. They are all there to make money on our backs." Factory town voters in 2022 saw Republicans as "in the pocket of wealthy CEOs and corporations" and Democrats as "too weak and incompetent to get anything done."[19]

If the decline of the Midwest and rural areas has been gaining speed since the 1990s, why was the rural and Rust Belt revolt not felt until 2016? The best explanation I've seen is from Michael McQuarrie. He explains that "civic associations, labor unions and political institutions unravel[ed] long after the industrialization itself." Unions were a key reason the representation gap was not felt for so long: they continued to channel members' votes to Democrats until large numbers of union members voted for Trump in 2016. In addition, massive transfers of federal funds for economic development "tied local business leaders, community leaders, and local politicians to federal program managers and Congressmen in an 'iron triangle' that was exceedingly hard for the Republican party to crack" until competitive grants replaced federal transfers to municipalities. Another crucial factor was Trump's anti-elitist rhetoric that decried the greed and ineptitude of politicians, which channeled white workers' hostility "to the political class that had silenced the Rust Belt as it was [being] dismantled."[20]

Trump also offered an economically progressive message that tapped deep roots. First and foremost, he ended the free-trade consensus embraced for decades by both parties and virtually all leading economists. In his first debate with Hillary Clinton, he mentioned "unfair" trade deals nine times, NAFTA eight times, and kept reminding viewers that Clinton's husband signed it. "By the time Donald Trump came around in 2016, many rural voters were desperate. He promised to bring back factory jobs. He promised to bring back coal-mining jobs. Sure, these were lies. But they were lies tailored to citizens in small towns that were getting smaller," wrote LaTosha Brown, the founder of the Black Voters Matter Fund. Trump married his promise of family-sustaining jobs with sharp increases in farm subsidies, which at one point accounted for around 40 percent of total farm income. He also defended Social Security and Medicare, two extraordinarily popular programs that mainstream Republicans had long targeted for massive cuts.[21]

Basically, Trump promised to bring back the post–World War II decades when hard work paid off in a stable life and decent retirement. Of course, he failed to deliver. "He's bragging that he's saving all these jobs. But he's not," a steelworker told Stockman; Trump's erratic trade wars did not help the heartland. But Trump changed the debate. During the Biden administration, demands for "place-based industrial policy"—long out of fashion—emerged in full force and coalesced into Build Back Better, which created large numbers of blue-collar jobs in rural areas and small cities.[22]

Paul Krugman intellectualized liberal condescension in a *New York Times* op-ed responding to Katherine Cramer's work on rural resentment in Wisconsin. Krugman overlooks the history presented above documenting how both Democrats and Republicans ignored rural policy as agribusiness devoured farmers' incomes, confirming that "city people were oblivious to the economic hardships that rural residents face[d]." He ignores "the basic narrative . . . that taxes are high and they must be going somewhere besides rural communities because rural communities are dying." Instead, Krugman depicts rural areas as "takers," pointing to high rates of government redistribution programs in rural areas, with no apparent recognition that accepting government assistance is experienced as humiliation due to the high value placed on hard work and self-reliance. Most strikingly, Krugman asks, "What about rural perceptions of being disrespected? Well, many people have negative views about people with different lifestyles; that's human nature." Can you imagine the reaction if a liberal said the same thing about immigrants or LGBTQ folx? In a later article, Krugman's tone had changed. But he still considered rural voters a "mystery," and he confessed he didn't know how to reach them. But there's no mystery: the Center for Working-Class Politics found that a progressive populist message performed best in rural/small towns, better than the moderate message more popular in urban and suburban areas.[23]

Trump's focus on rural and working-class jobs and honor endeared him to anti-elites. But he added an element that picked up votes of American preservationists: racism. Trump's personal history as a bigot is extensively documented, as is his scapegoating of immigrants and people of color for the ills faced by working people of all races—ills caused not by people of color but by business elites.

In rural areas, racial politics played a role, though it's not as straight-forward as some imagine: one-quarter of rural voters are people of color. In Rust Belts, where Republicans had long purveyed the script that Democrats care only about undeserving people of color, Trump inverted this trope by "showing hostility to minorities while showing regard for white workers." "The Iowa way of life is under siege," he said on the campaign trail. (Meanwhile, Democrats dethroned the Iowa caucuses, points out an outraged Art Cullen, editor of *The Storm Lake Times*). Notes McQuarrie, "For whites, it is a story of the loss of status and 'social honour,' in addition to the loss of material wealth. For African Americans there are elements of this but it is more significantly about the loss of newly won and briefly held material affluence." Black workers were further alienated by mass incarceration stemming from the drug wars under Bill Clinton.[24]

Democratic strategists often note the conventional wisdom in progressive circles that Democrats should give up on rural and Rust Belt voters who are never coming back. This is unrealistic in a political system with winner-take-all elections in districts defined by geography. Democratic strategist Mike Lux's group American Family Voices documents a massive vote shift away from Democrats between 2012 and 2020 in small and mid-size factory-town counties, swamping Democratic gains in big cities and suburbs by a two-to-one margin. Writing off these voters is not an option, Lux points out, because they account for close to half (47–48 percent) of voters in the eight states studied—states that often hold the balance of power in presidential elections.[25]

"Rural people want to share in America's prosperity," noted Bill Hogseth, who ultimately left the Democratic Party in Wisconsin. LaTosha Brown agrees. "The key to winning rural voters is to center their needs with a compelling rural platform—starting with better jobs, higher wages and economic development," she notes. She highlights Benton County in Indiana (pop. 8,650) where wind farm developers paid the county $17 million and spent $33 million on roads and infrastructure, creating jobs for hundreds of construction workers as well as 110 permanent jobs for wind technicians and the like. Lux's group advocates an insistence that corporations and the wealthy pay a lot more in taxes and higher wages, and have less power to crush small business competitors and unions. Lift up labor unions and small businesses (seen as "pillars of their communities") and help rebuild local institutions by maintaining ongoing ties to these communities instead of just showing up a few weeks before the election. Lux, Hogseth, and Brown all stress the importance of showing up. "Progressives have relinquished large swaths of our country to reactionary politicians," Brown argues, whereas many rural voters are gettable. She points out that Democrats lost 11 points in rural areas between 2012 and 2016 but won 6 back in 2018; Democrats made gains in at least fifty-four congressional districts with large rural areas, winning races in upstate New York, Maine, and Alabama.[26]

"When people feel left behind, they look for a way to make sense of what is happening to them," concludes Hogseth. "There is a story to be told about rural America, yet Democrats are not telling it. . . . They want politicians to see a future for rural communities in which food production is localized, energy is cheap and clean, people have good jobs, soil is healthy, towns are bustling with small businesses, schools are vibrant, everyone can see a doctor if they need to." Build Back Better and the Inflation Reduction Act were steps in the right direction, but we need a sustained focus in public policy on creating jobs for people where they want to live.[27]

Such policies are important because the gap between winner-take-all cities and the heartland now yawns so large that moving to such cities has become unrealistic. Big-city wages have flatlined: a janitor moving from the Deep South to Silicon Valley could double his income in 1960 even after accounting for increased housing costs. Today, the same janitor's income would fall 28 percent after accounting for housing costs.[28] At the same time, clerical jobs that used to be a stepping stone to the middle class have disappeared, replaced by software or outsourced to other countries.

Liberals need to stand against inequality between regions as well as between individuals. In Britain, Boris Johnson called this "levelling up" of left-behind regions, which his government described as its "No. 1 policy."[29]

Key Takeaways:

1. Far-right populism is a revolt of rural and Rust Belt areas left behind by the twenty-first-century economy, which has concentrated wealth in a small number of metropolitan areas.
2. This economic system does not fit with political systems that have winner-take-all elections in districts defined by geography (like the US and UK).
3. Condescension and stereotyping of rural and Rust Belt voters adds fuel to the fire of resentment against the Brahmin Left.
4. Progressives need to stand against not only inequality between individuals but also inequality between regions. People want, and deserve, family-sustaining jobs near where they grew up.

Is the Solution to Move to the Center?

*Is it that Black and brown people are not as progressive as some
people want to say they are . . . or do we need to re-examine the
assumptions about what progressive means?*

—Leah Daughtry, Democratic strategist[1]

"Wake up, Democrats," read a 2022 editorial in *The Economist*: "Moving towards the centre ground would not just be a shrewd political tactic, it could
also be the beginning of the cure for American democracy." Influential
American commentators like Ruy Teixeira and Bill Galston agree, arguing
that the only way to counter far-right populism is for Democrats to become "moderates." "The established political theory of victory in Georgia
held that Democrats had hit their limits in Black turnout and that the
key to winning was to regain white support for Democrats from Republicans and, crucially, to position ourselves to be more like Republicans,"
recounted Stacey Abrams. This, of course, was Bill Clinton's strategy in
the 1990s when he "ended welfare as we know it" and adopted neoliberal
policies.[2]

This established wisdom assumes that the only way to bridge the diploma divide is for the Left to connect with noncollege voters in the same
ways the Right has. This is a failure of imagination. The alternative is to
dig deeper and ask some searching questions about what it means to be a
moderate and what it means to be a progressive. Doing so will allow the
Left to forge coalitions that preserve core progressive values by building
bridges to noncollege voters that are very different from the bridges built
by the Far Right.

First, the low-hanging fruit. Some of those scolding progressives and
championing moderates are moderates in the vein of Bill Clinton's "third

way," which combined neoliberal economic policies with cultural policies that appealed to college grads. Clinton embraced three basic elements of neoliberalism. First, he championed free trade, signing NAFTA and endorsing China's entry into the World Trade Organization, paving the way for massive outsourcing of American manufacturing to Mexico and China. Clinton also adopted Republicans' commitment to deregulation. Banking deregulation eliminated the New Deal barrier between commercial and investment banking (the Glass-Steagall Act), paving the way for the Great Recession in 2008. At the same time, Clinton distanced himself from unions and supported legislation that gave tech companies immunity for content posted on social media. This allowed gig-economy companies like Uber to evade New Deal–era worker protections and social media companies like Facebook to become cesspools of falsehood and hate speech. In other words, the third way's brand of neoliberal "moderation" is precisely what got us into this mess.[3]

Ruy Teixeira represents a different call to move to the center. Following the pattern set earlier by Christopher Lasch, Teixeira yearns to turn back the clock to the New Deal coalition.[4]

> The New Deal Democrats . . . were moderate and even small-c conservative in their social outlook. They extolled "the American way of life" (a term popularized in the 1930s); they used patriotic symbols like the "blue Eagle" to promote their programs . . . Roosevelt's politics were those of "the people" (a term summed up in Carl Sandberg's 1936, "The People, Yes") and of the "forgotten Americans." There wasn't a hint of multiculturalism or tribalism. The Democrats need to follow this example.[5]

Teixeira forgets one thing: the New Deal coalition between college-educated liberals like my father and the blue-collar unionized voters arose when college-educated elites were culturally very similar to non-elites. I and others of my generation changed all that in the 1960s and 1970s as we championed equality projects focused on race, gender, the environment, and sexual freedom. Teixeira dismisses these as "boutique ideas about race and gender and the hierarchy and intersecting levels of oppression and all that jazz" or "tribalism." It is not tribal to insist on addressing sexism, racism, and centering potentially apocalyptic climate change. Teixeira stands as one in a long line of white men who dismiss the importance of identity projects without noticing that they're advocating one of their own. They dismiss the importance of those vectors of social inequality that don't disadvantage white men (gender, race) to re-center the vector that does (class). No doubt that does seem most central . . . if you're a white man.[6]

That's what the New Deal coalition did. Returning to those times holds little appeal to myself and other progressives—and, without progressives, Democrats lose a key element of their base. Scolding me and my friends to abandon causes we have dedicated our lives to won't work. I have been a pain in the butt about gender and race for decades; that's the only way women and people of color ever make progress. We are used to being told that we should put our own issues aside, and those of us who are effective don't follow that advice.

Teixeira reminds me of an interaction I had with one of the founders of critical legal studies (CLS), a leftist movement that was ascendent during my early years as a law professor. I was one of the moving forces behind organizing a conference on social class, one of the final CLS conferences in the late 1990s. One of the Great White Fathers of CLS told me condescendingly that he was pleased to see that I had finally realized that class was the most basic of all social divisions and that my little frolics with gender were at an end. I was not amused.

It's telling that Teixeira moved from a perch associated with Democrats (the Center for American Progress) to one associated with Republicans (the American Enterprise Institute). When it comes to the Democratic coalition, he's out of touch. And yet Teixeira is onto something important. He is one of the few commentators today who seeks to explain to the Brahmin Left how their values and priorities are different from those of many noncollege voters.

Research finds that progressive activists are a small percentage of the population that's chiefly white and college-educated. The most complete exploration is in a 2018 report, *Hidden Tribes: A Study of America's Polarized Landscape*. It found that only 8 percent of Americans were progressive activists. They were nearly twice as likely as the average American to have completed college, nearly three times as likely to have a postgraduate degree, and made up the largest share of those from households earning over $100,000. Only 3 percent were Black; 80 percent were white. My colleagues often point to polling that progressive positions are embraced by large majorities, but Democratic strategist David Shor points out that if you look at a "cluster of nine Democratic positions that each poll over

50% individually, you find that only 18% of Americans agree with all of them."[7]

I'm a progressive activist, but I'm also a data devotee—and data shows we are outliers in many ways. Progressive activists are about three times more likely than the average American to say that they are ashamed to be an American and to believe people's outcomes are the result of "luck and circumstance." They are only half as likely as the average American to believe the world is becoming a more and more dangerous place, and more than twice as likely to say they never pray.[8]

Progressive activists aren't into religion, but they are into politics. They are more than twice as likely to list politics as a hobby than the average American. Politics is central to their identities: 74 percent feel a lot in common with other progressives. They report social pressure to conform to others in their group at sharply higher levels (61 percent) than conservatives do (37 percent). Progressive activists are socially tolerant; politically, not so much.[9]

Progressive activists are outliers on a range of issues. They are 2.6 times more likely than the average American to prioritize climate change and 4 times more likely to believe in affirmative action in college admissions and express cold feelings toward gun owners. Another study found that 71 percent of the progressive Left believed that US laws and institutions need to be completely rebuilt because of structural racism, as compared with only 30 percent of "Democratic Mainstays," the largest identified subgroup of the Democratic coalition.[10]

The next most liberal group also is more likely than the average American to be college graduates (48 percent versus 29 percent). Other polling consistently finds that, the more privileged you are, the more likely you are to be liberal. Only 27 percent of Americans with postgraduate education and 31 percent of college grads are conservative, as compared with 42 percent of Americans with no college and 38 percent of those with some college. Over a third of Americans with postgraduate education and 30 percent of college grads are liberal, as compared with less than a fifth of those with no college and 22 percent of those with some college. Other polling finds that "respondents whose parents were highly educated showed stronger preferences for progressive candidates virtually across-the-board." Given the robust association of liberalism and privilege, it seems like an exercise of class privilege to insist that the Democratic Party adhere to every position that I, as a San Francisco progressive, embrace. Note that through-out this book, I recommend messaging but not trade-offs. Here's why: I live in a large and complex country that's not waiting, with bated breath, for some overeducated rando to decide what trade-offs should be made in what contexts. Those decisions will be hard fought again and again within coalitions, and the right answers will differ in different political contexts. My only ask is that those negotiations be conducted in a way that's attuned to the class dynamics involved.[11]

As always, becoming more attuned to class dynamics does not mean ignoring people of color. It's important to keep in mind that progressive activists are overwhelmingly white, and that only 26 percent of Blacks and 28 percent of Latinos identified as liberal in a 2021 poll. Additionally, whites were only slightly more likely (76 percent) than African Americans (71 percent) and Latinos (69 percent) to identify as conservative or moderate. Over 50 percent of Black Americans identified as moderates, a much higher percentage than any other group.[12]

College grads of every racial group are more liberal than noncollege voters of the same group. Overall, college grads were 25 percentage points more likely to identify as liberal than noncollege grads. Racial breakdowns show the same pattern: college grads were 13 points more likely among Latinos, 11 points more likely among African Americans, and 9 points more likely among Asian Americans to identify as liberals, according to data from Gallup and the 2020 Cooperative Election Study. Among Democrats, nearly two-thirds of white college grads identify as liberal or very liberal, compared to 39 percent of Blacks and 41 percent of Latinos.[13]

In this context, it seems like an exercise of racial as well as class privilege to insist that the Democratic Party adhere in every election to every position progressives embrace. Almost 60 percent of respondents in one national survey held a mix of conservative and progressive positions. If progressives want these folks to break our way, we need to engage respectfully and persuade them—not to write off as "moderate" anyone who doesn't pre-agree with San Francisco on every issue.[14]

Culture wars have been carefully designed to tap only some values of noncollege voters: those most compatible with the priorities of the Merchant Right. The Left needs to stop letting the Right define the terms of debate and create a new playbook that taps into those non-elite values that are most compatible with progressive values. Giving in or remaining silent on racial justice and climate change is not the only way to connect with non-elites. A closer look at seven Democrats who won blue seats in red districts in the 2022 midterms highlights the wide variety of ways candidates can connect with voters who are very different from San Francisco progressives. Imposing rigid litmus tests makes no sense: I would far rather have a Democrat who does not agree with me on every issue than to insist on purity with the result that a Republican is elected who agrees with me on virtually nothing.

I did a deep dive for *The Hill* into the seven Democrats (four white, three people of color) who flipped their districts from red to blue in the 2022 midterms, to identify how progressives can appeal successfully to noncollege voters without moving to the center. Each red-to-blue candidate garnered a larger vote share than Biden did in 2020. None was a moderate as defined by Ruy Teixeira.[15]

The conventional wisdom is that the way to forge a cross-class coalition is to focus on economics and avoid cultural issues like the plague. The first half of the conventional wisdom is right (which is why I've spent so much time discussing economics). Every single red-to-blue Democrat made blue-collar jobs a central and insistent theme. "Pro-jobs, pro-fish, pro-family, pro-choice," said Mary Peltola, who won Alaska's congressional seat for Democrats for the first time in fifty years (+20 points as compared with Biden's 2020 vote). John Fetterman, who won Pennsylvania's Senate seat (+4.9 points over Biden's 2020 vote), consistently spoke up for those left behind, dedicating his win "for every small town or person that ever felt left behind, for every job that has ever been lost, for every factory that was ever closed, for every person that works hard, but never got ahead, I'm proud of what we ran on." Marie Gluesenkamp Perez won a House seat in Washington State (+4.8 points) by championing unions, blue-collar jobs, and apprenticeship programs. Gabe Vasquez, who won a House seat in New Mexico, reclaimed the American dream, emphasizing fair wages and affordable health care. Three other white candidates also placed blue-collar jobs and kitchen table economics at the center of their campaigns—Matt Cartwright (+6.8 points), Josh Shapiro (+13.6 points), and Gretchen Whitmer (+7.8 points).[16]

The second half of the conventional advice—to avoid cultural issues like the plague—is wrong. Each red-to-blue Democrat also forged cultural connections with noncollege voters. Whitmer was the most adept at building cross-class coalitions. She's kind of a genius. She championed huge new investments by GM in electric vehicle plants, combining non-elites' focus on jobs with elites' focus on climate change. She brought the first new auto plant to Detroit in a very long time with hiring preference for its mostly Black local residents, combining non-elites' focus on jobs with the Brahmin Left's emphasis on racial justice. She defended abortion rights by arguing that this would help Michigan economically, combining a no-holds-barred issue for the Brahmin Left with blue-collar focus on economic prosperity. She also adopted blue-collar talk traditions ("Fix the damn roads"). She's got what it takes.[17]

Democrats also flipped both chambers of the Michigan legislature in 2022, allowing Whitmer to push a progressive agenda through Michigan for the first time in decades. Democrats, led by Whitmer, also repealed right-to-work laws previously enacted by Republicans, expanded background checks for gun purchases, and enshrined protections for LGBTQ people into state law.[18]

A closer look shows the wide variety of ways Democrats forge cultural connections with noncollege voters. One poll found that 57 percent of Pennsylvania voters said that Fetterman understood the day-to-day concerns of people like them; that's key. "People see John at Costco, at Aldi. He's real and one of them. Even if they might not agree with him on everything," said a Democratic strategist. Note that Fetterman did not back off racial issues; instead, while lieutenant governor, he crossed swords with Josh Shapiro (then attorney general) by championing clemency for mostly Black defendants. (Not saying he's perfect: he's not at all perfect. Just saying that he uses tools others could adapt.)[19]

One strategy is to point out how Republicans use culture wars to distract attention from economic inequality. "Here come the culture wars again," said Cartwright. "And all this is a big distraction from the main play that's going on. The big corporations that got huge tax cuts." Said Gluesenkamp Perez, "I don't know any voters that are still talking about arresting Fauci. Look at gas prices, look at what it's like to get in the housing market. I mean, childcare and workforce participation. These are the things that people really care about in this district. It's not an internet chat room, it's people's lives."[20]

A second strategy is to adopt blue-collar talk traditions. When his opponent complained about the cost of "crudités," Fetterman pounced: "In PA, we call this a . . . veggie tray." He tapped blue-collar traditions of one-upmanship and razzing that ethnographers have documented in mining. Blue-collar Americans highly value language that's unvarnished and direct. Whitmer's "Fix the damn roads" hits the mark.[21]

Another key is to fight Trump's truculent macho with alternative masculinities that also offer adherents different ways to be a "real" man. Fetterman embraced working-class masculinity through dress as well as speech: when his opponent criticized him for not wearing a suit, Fetterman responded, "Wearing a suit doesn't make me any smarter." He abandoned wearing a suit in Congress early in his term. When his stroke impaired his abilities, he tapped a different brand of non-class-specific "decent man" masculinity, when he tweeted: "I had a stroke. I survived it. I'm truly so grateful to still be here today. I know politics can be nasty, but even then, I could *never* imagine ridiculing someone for their health challenges." In sharp contrast with Trump's fragile belligerence, Fetterman offered stoic decency and empathy. Cartwright also tapped "decent man" masculinity when he criticized his opponent by asking who "goes around saying, 'Latinos ruined my town.' Who talks like that? I sure don't."[22]

Another key is to honor small business and working-class people. In his inauguration speech, Shapiro lauded people like "Tim, who did backbreaking work on our roadways for decades," before pointing out that Republicans were trying to take away his hard-won pension and health insurance. Gluesenkamp Perez, who owns an auto body shop with her husband, has commented on the lack of tradespeople in Congress. Small businesses are the most trusted institution in the US. Too few liberals seem to know this.[23]

Tapping respect for hard work is another way to connect with noncollege voters. Vasquez attacked Republican incumbent Yvette Herrell for "using her position to enrich her family rather than standing up for the hardworking people of New Mexico," and defending immigrants as people "who want to work hard . . . to reach their American dream." Don't let Republicans own the American dream; instead, focus less on redistribution and more on who gets what in the labor market. Frame redistribution as universal programs that reward hard work—like Social Security and Medicare, which enjoy robust and abiding support.[24]

Yet another key is to champion issues of concern to non-elites. A great example is Perez's championing of "right to repair" legislation, which Harris also embraced in her 2024 campaign. Farmers are up in arms because companies that produce farm machinery have made it difficult or impossible to repair. "You can't wait three weeks [to fix the tractor] when you've got the harvest coming," said Gluesenkamp Perez. Instead, build a cross-class coalition: coastal elites (and everyone else) want the right to repair their iPhones. Another no-brainer: "The advocacy for legal marijuana is a big thing. It resonates with groups that Democrats struggle with—a lot of the white working class and young men—white, non-college-educated men," commented a pollster on John Fetterman's embrace of that issue.[25]

These candidates sometimes have infuriated progressives. When Gluesenkamp Perez voted against college debt relief, *Slate* published an article titled, "With Democrats Like Marie Gluesenkamp Perez, Who Needs Republicans?" Matt Yglesias persuasively argued that the *Slate* article misrepresented Gluesenkamp Perez's views on abortion and other issues, and raises important questions about whether red-state Democratic candidates should be able to side with the red-state voters they represent. Only about a quarter of voters in her district are college grads; she said she could only support college debt relief if it was accompanied by relief for those who attended vocational school, saying, "It's an issue of respect." Yglesias points out that Gluesenkamp Perez defeated a MAGA Republican and is a valuable Democratic vote on more issues than not in a closely divided Congress.[26]

A look at these candidates shows that there's no one formula, especially given that blue-collar voters highly value authenticity. But the remainder of the book will arm progressives with the tools they need to invent lots of different ways to find authentic connections with noncollege voters—without selling their souls.

The deeper question is whether it's time to reconsider what it means to be a "real" progressive. This is what Leah Daughtry, an African American Democratic strategist, advocated when commenting on Eric Adams's victory in his election as mayor of New York City; Adams won the most Black voters but was not considered a progressive. The implication: judgments about who's a real progressive may reflect white privilege. They may reflect class privilege, too: "Even the terms 'liberal' and 'conservative' seemed to me to divide the world into right and wrong from a largely middle- or upper-middle-class point of view," notes anthropologist Christine J. Walley, who went to Exeter and MIT after growing up in a dying steel town. "It's not just history that's told from the viewpoint of the victors," she noted wryly. "So is the present."[27]

The key move for the Left is to bond with working-class voters through respect. But to do that effectively, we have to respect them. Parts 2 and 3 will pave the way. They explain the parallel universes inhabited by elites and non-elites. We need to start by recognizing that our values reflect our lives, and our lives reflect our privilege—or lack of it.

Key Takeaways:

1. Commentators who argue that bridging the diploma divide requires Democrats to move to the center seek to turn back the clock to a New Deal coalition that won't appeal to today's progressives.

2. And yet those commentators have a point. Progressive activists are less than 10 percent of the American population and trend more educated, wealthier, and whiter than the average American. So insisting that the Democratic Party adhere to every position that I, as a San Francisco progressive, embrace is an exercise of race and class privilege that's inconsistent with progressive ideals.

3. A study of Democrats who flipped seats in House and Senate races in 2022 provides a template for contesting far-right power by stressing blue-collar jobs and forging cultural connections with working-class voters . . . without giving in to racism.

Part II

What's the Matter with Kansas?

In a time when the upper middle class is becoming more isolated socially and geographically from other groups, such isolation fosters a social myopia that makes it increasingly difficult for the college-educated academics and policy makers to see how distinctive a working-class understanding of the world is.

—MICHÈLE LAMONT[1]

In 2004, Thomas Frank famously argued that voters in red America are duped by Republicans into voting against their own self-interest. Frank himself has backed off this view, but his interpretation lives on. "Democrats often lament that so many working-class Americans vote against their own economic interests, by supporting Republicans who try to cut health care programs, school funding and more," remarked *New York Times* reporter David Leonhardt in 2021.[2]

Red-state voters seem less clueless now that they have successfully overturned *Roe v. Wade*, banned affirmative action, enshrined radical gun rights into the Constitution, and changed neoliberal trade policy. Not clueless at all: they've won on issues they care about deeply by aligning with Republicans. The Far Right has put a lot of time and effort into connecting with noncollege grads. The rest of us need to learn how.

To quote one of our most insightful commentators, political scientist Katherine J. Cramer: "Perhaps issues are secondary to identities. . . . Does this person understand people like me?" is the central question that drives electoral politics today. The first step in bridging the diploma divide is cultural competence. Thus this book![3]

In describing the culture of lower-middle-class families, I sometimes use the words *blue-collar* because I'm drawing from a group of studies published in the first decade of the twenty-first century, following about a quarter century during which blue-collar families received little attention. After 2010, studies of blue-collar families tend to focus not on the success stories—on the families who have managed to sustain a settled middle-class standard of living—but on families sliding out of the middle class into poverty and hard living. As always since at least Michael Harrington's *The Other America: Poverty in the United States* was published in 1962—and arguably since the nineteenth century—far more books have documented the lives of the bottom than the middle. But the key class divide for understanding far-right populism is the divide between the Missing Middle and college-educated elites. I hope in this book to bring the insights of ethnographies and narrative sociology into political science, bridging disciplinary divides that feed class blindness.

This section will explore how class is expressed through cultural differences. That's not because economics determine culture—that's simplistic. Rather, each class makes a virtue of the hand they're dealt, creating an internal logic in their tastes for food, fashion, leisure, talk, politics, and much more. This worldview, to quote Bourdieu, "is necessity internalized and converted into a disposition"—"spontaneity without consciousness or will." "The lifeways of a people . . . are the consequence of the conditions to which they must adjust," notes Julie Bettie. Read on to learn how lower-middle-class people forge what society typically sees as their deficiencies into alternative routes to self-esteem.[4]

Why Does the Culture Wars Formula
Work So Well?

[The Far Right] foregrounds real class cultural inequalities in
order to obscure real economic ones.

—Reece Peck[1]

Cultural voting accounts for most of the shift to the right since World
War II. Why do culture wars work so well? Does their prevalence mean
that class no longer plays an important role in politics?[2]

Culture wars are actually an *expression* of class conflict. Sociologists
have recognized since the 1980s that class is not only about economics.
Class scripts are etched deep into our lives, shaping our tastes and sense of
self into systematic cultural differences.

Ignorance of this basic sociological fact has led political scientists to
interpret culture wars as evidence that class no longer matters in contemporary politics. This view is associated most prominently with Ronald
Inglehart, who posited in 1977 that the old class-based politics focused on
material issues was being replaced by "post-materialist" politics focused on
cultural issues.[3]

Only one problem: class isn't only about material issues. Beyond subsistence levels, economics is just one use-case of a larger dynamic: class
conflicts reflect the scrum for social honor.

The desire for status is a fundamental human motive that is as powerful
a motivator as money and power. People vigilantly monitor the status dynamics in their environments because status is integral to personal identity. Part of status is recognition: "acknowledging people's existence and
positive worth, actively making them visible and valued, reducing their
marginalization, and openly integrating them into a group." Americans
who did not graduate from college have lost status, recognition, and social

honor in recent decades. The "dignity gap" between college grads and non-college grads is large—as big as the gap between those in full-time work and those who are unemployed or work only part-time.[4]

Status differentials have been shown to drive support for the Far Right. A study of fifteen European countries found that "moving from medium-high to medium-low status almost doubles the predicted probability of voting for the populist right." The more the subjective social status of a group fell in the prior twenty-five years, the more likely the group was to support the populist right in 2014. Populism is *both* about economics *and* about loss of social status. To quote the most insightful study, by Noam Gidron and Peter Hall:

> Changes in the economy that are disadvantaging male workers without [college degrees] and those living outside big cities have occurred at the same time as shifts in dominant cultural frameworks that attach higher value to college education and urban lifestyles. Developments such as these are likely to depress the subjective social status of people who lack such attributes, creating resentments that parties on the populist right are cultivating.[5]

The first step is to understand some basic cultural differences between middle-status voters and college-educated elites, and how non-elite values make sense in the context of non-elite lives.

Merit and Novelty Versus Morality and Stability

Elites have many sources of status, from Teslas to tasting menus to our understated clothes. But elites' most powerful claim to high status rests on merit. Claiming "merit" is a real power move—one elites can make because they can access the educational opportunities that define merit.

Lower-middle-class people lack both economic capital and also cultural capital—tastes socially defined as "classy." Instead, they value social ties (social capital) and character (moral capital) as evidence of their worth. Sociologist Michèle Lamont, who studied Black and white blue-collar men on the East Coast, found that "keeping the world in order—in moral order, that is—is at the top of their agenda." Their focus on morality helps "workers to maintain a sense of self-worth, to affirm their dignity independently of their relatively low social status, and to locate themselves above others." Lamont found that 49 percent of white and 43 percent of Black blue-collar men used moral references to define success, in sharp contrast with upper-middle-class men, who tended to use socioeconomic success.[6]

A focus on security is integral to keeping the world in order. To quote Lamont:

> They also value responsibility because they are highly dependent on the actions of others. They point out that the physical conditions in which they work and live and their limited financial resources make it difficult for them to buffer themselves from the actions of neighbors, coworkers, kin, and friends. They have no private space at work and live in neighborhoods where houses are set very close to one another. Compared with their professional and managerial counterparts, they can less readily escape crime, drugs, and undesirable people by moving to high-income suburbs.[7]

Blue-collar families are also intensely focused on stability because their fragile hold on middle-class life makes change seem risky. Once when I was going nuts that my husband would not ever change *a single thing ever* in our house, he finally articulated why not: "I associated change with loss." It goes without saying: I associate novelty with creativity.

My husband's father grew up so poor that his family moved from apartment to apartment, staying in each until they got evicted. That made me more sympathetic to his rigid opposition to change. Sociologist Annette Lareau notes that providing comfort, food, and shelter presents for lower-middle-class families "a formidable challenge . . . and they are proud when they can accomplish it." That accomplished, they just want to hold on to what they've got: it's a class-specific form of loss aversion. The sharp downward mobility that's such a common experience for lower-middle-class families in recent decades has only reinforced the sense that change entails loss.[8]

Self-Actualization Versus Self-Regulation

What does keeping the world in moral order mean? Whereas elites are proud of their prestigious jobs, middle-status Americans pride themselves on their hard work. This highlights the moral dimensions of work. It's not just a way of earning money; it's also a way of earning merit, of turning "necessity into pride and servitude into honor," to quote historian Daniel Rodgers. An ethnography found that among working-class people in rural California, "the culture . . . was built around the value of hard work for its own sake, with survival and masculine pride often being its only rewards. Poverty per se was not looked down upon; only poverty in the absence of work." A study of miners observed that "the importance of a work ethic signals one's dignity in a potentially demeaning environment." Here's a truly charming guy named Joe Bageant, in *Deer Hunting with Jesus: Dispatches from America's Class War*:

> Life is about work for the American redneck. . . . For all these people work is an obsession and has been for generations stretching back to the textile mills, the homesteads of the West and Midwest, the immigrant labor mines of West Virginia and Colorado and Montana, the subsistence farms of the South. The forebearers of today's rednecks were people for whom not working meant that their families would starve. Literally . . . The absolute worst thing that rednecks can say about anyone is, "He doesn't want to work," which is generally followed by, "Hell, I don't want to either, but I have to."[9]

Elites prepare their children for a world where having material success and security is taken for granted and the focus is on expressive independence: the ability to think for yourself, to articulate your preferences, challenge authority through logic. "Working-class kids who had really absorbed the rubric of self-development" would face a "terrifying battle" when faced with repetitive and unfulfilling jobs, notes Paul Willis.[10] Here's Mark Cuban:

> When I was in high school and still trying to figure out if and how I could afford to go to college, my mom recommended that I learn how to lay carpet, because she was concerned about my future. Her goal was not that I find fulfillment but that I find stability.

Social psychologists find that middle-status people trade creativity for self-discipline. Makes sense: self-discipline serves you well in pink-, blue-, and routine white-collar jobs; creativity can get you fired when your employer sees you as low in status, with little to offer.[11]

Noncollege grads find honor where they can, belittling professionals as "pencil pushers" who don't really *make* anything. "Hard work pays off because I can look at different jobs I did and say, 'You know what? I built that.'...That shit wasn't built by God," said a thirty-year veteran carpenter. He describes his job almost poetically as "hanging out with your brothers, building America." Farmers are tremendously proud that they feed cities and point out that others are dependent on their important work for food. "One Kansas Farmer Feeds More Than 155 People + You!" said a billboard. Commented Roger Gustafson, "Translation: If we don't do what we do (grow your food), it doesn't matter what you do (type on keyboards)." To quote Tom Vilsack, secretary of agriculture under Obama, small-town and rural people provide

> our food, fiber and feed, and [88%] of our renewable water resources. One of every 12 jobs is connected in some way to what happens in rural America. It's one of the few parts of our economy that still has a trade surplus.[12]

Much of this was news to me and—if you're my modal reader—probably news to you.

While hard-work worship is stronger among blue-collar white men, 59 percent of whom endorsed it, 40 percent of blue-collar Black men endorsed it, too. Lamont found Black men less likely to attribute poverty to bad choices—although later research suggests that African Americans have shifted away from structural, toward individualistic, explanations for inequality. Anthony Flaccavento of the Rural Urban Bridge Initiative, who ran for Congress in rural Virginia, told me a story of a neighbor who came upon him when he was "working up a good sweat" chopping wood. "If my friends could see you now, they'd all vote for you" was the reaction (implicit: despite the fact you're a Democrat). In *Becoming*, Michelle Obama describes how her father never missed a shift in twenty-six years. She highlights why this steadiness was so crucial: "One missed paycheck could leave you without electricity; one missed homework assignment could put you behind and possibly out of college." Growing up in a working-class community, she "learned that planning and vigilance mattered a lot." Middle-status families' insistence on self-regulation may seem heavy-handed, but these families can't count on second chances. In upper-middle-class families, children are encouraged to experiment, secure in the knowledge that any "scrapes" they get into will often pass without a trace. The Missing Middle's insistence on following the rules can impede creativity, social psychologists find, but this may seem worth sacrificing to maintain a foothold in middle-class life.[13]

Children raised to respect authority and rules are "learning to labor." In working-class jobs, workers "are closely supervised and are required to follow orders and instructions," so they bring up children "in a home in which conformity, obedience, and intolerance for back talk are the norm—the same characteristics that make for a good factory worker" or bank clerk. This helps explain why working-class parents display less tolerance for breaking the rules and establish that authority needs to be respected (starting with their own). This helps later: "Oh yeah, the foreman's got somebody knuckling down on him, putting the screws on him. But a foreman is still free to go to the bathroom, go get a cup of coffee," a spot-welder told Studs Terkel.[14]

A 2016 study found that "voters believe that these moral behaviors are the ones that will help them prosper economically." Partly, this is the influence of the American dream; partly, it's just true. Jennifer Sherman found that people of good moral standing got the rare jobs that became available in their rural communities; they could also count on ad hoc community charity if times got tough.[15]

Michelle Obama's father's attendance record was so remarkable because he had, and ultimately died of, multiple sclerosis. He refused to talk about it or go to the doctor. Instead, he "moved with a pained slowness, using an aluminum walker" to go down the three flights of steps to drive to work, "pausing often to catch his breath." Insisting that all was well, he used a motorized scooter to pilot himself between boilers, continuing to take pride in indispensability: he could fix any machine. "His stubbornness was packed beneath so many layers of pride that it was impossible for me to be angry," she commented. "My father loved to be the rock for others"; when he finally had to admit that he was sick, "I was seeing him, I realized, in a moment of pure defeat." Black noncollege Americans are more likely than Black college grads to believe that hard work can get you ahead. More recent data shows that the Latino community is even more committed to hard work, in part a class effect: about 80 percent are not college grads. Progressive activists couldn't be more different: 95 percent believe that no amount of hard work will allow certain people to get ahead.[16]

Hard-work worship influences attitudes toward redistribution in ways that are rarely recognized. To my surprise, 2020 data showed that majorities of all Americans of all racial groups support work requirements for food stamps and that noncollege Americans of every racial group support them more than do college grads of their group.[17]

Pride in perseverance is a cherished blue-collar value that sociologists have long noted. "Workers are acutely aware that 'hanging in there' depends above all on their capacity to work," says Lamont. "Their labor is often painful and time-consuming, underpaid, physically demanding, or psychologically challenging because it was repetitive. Being able to stick to it demands emotional energy and moral fortitude." When she asked blue-collar men to describe a hero, some pointed to their fathers, praising their perseverance and capacity to "keep it together" in the face of adversity. A reporter whose father was a bricklayer described his father as someone who "made a religion of responsibility." A reporter notes that an Ohio auto worker never really liked his job, which was boring. "He worked in the paint shop, wearing two sets of gloves, big plastic boots and a full body apron, while he wielded a sanding tool that smoothed the primer on the surface of the cars. Every night he came home drenched and exhausted. . . . But he was grateful for it." This kind of sacrifice used to be honored, but today, Arlie Hochschild notes, "along with blue-collar jobs, a blue-collar way of life was going out of fashion, and, with it, the honor attached to a . . . pride in endurance."[18]

Conservatives have deftly manipulated Missing Middle voters' worship of perseverance and hard work into the politics of resentment. From the 1970s into the 1990s, the chief trope was the racist story of lazy, entitled people of color collecting welfare. The new millennium substituted another villain: lazy, entitled government workers, with their fat pensions and cushy desk jobs. The first script rechanneled class anger to target government redistribution; the second rechanneled the anger of private-sector workers (who had lost unions, middle-class wages, and employer-financed pensions) against the unions, middle-class wages, and pensions of public-sector workers. Both scripts deftly channeled economic fury away from the business elites.[19]

Non-Elites Cherish Traditional Institutions
That Anchor Self-Regulation

Michelle Obama is what I call a *class migrant*, a term that highlights that changing social class entails many of the same dynamics of loss and reinvention that migrating between countries does. Another famous class-migrant memoir, J. D. Vance's *Hillbilly Elegy*, illustrates why non-elites value traditional institutions so highly.

Vance recounts how he escaped his unstable childhood by joining the Marine Corps, which "assumes that no one taught you anything about physical fitness, personal hygiene, or personal finances." It taught him how to balance a checkbook and healthy eating (he lost forty-five pounds). It was a substitute father: "In the civilian world, your boss wasn't able to control your life after you left work. In the Marines, my boss didn't just make sure I did a good job, he made sure I kept my room clean, kept my hair cut, and ironed my uniforms. He sent an older Marine to supervise as I shopped for my first car so that I ended up with a practical car, like a Toyota or Honda, not the BMW I wanted." The older marine also saved Vance from an exploitative car loan.[20]

Only 7 percent of progressive activists, but 25 percent of Americans overall, believe that attending ceremonies honoring military service members is important to being a good American. The military is the second-most respected institution in the United States (after small business), and many Americans perceive veterans as "more disciplined, patriotic and loyal than those who have not served." Another reason the military is held in such high esteem is that it functions as a reset button for kids not brought up in a stable or orderly environment. When an elite kid wobbles in his ascent to adulthood, parents pay high fees to get psychological help; working-class kids join a church or the military. The military offers not only remedial parenting but one of the only steady jobs with benefits available in areas like the inner-city, rural, and abandoned-factory towns left behind. It also offers to working-class kids what social democracies offer to everyone: affordable health care, subsidized college, financial assistance for childcare, and generous retirement.[21]

Equally important, the military offers honor: it's a highly respected job for people for whom the only alternative may be as a Walmart greeter. When Vance visited home after basic training, the local barber "refused to take my money and told me to stay safe. He had cut my hair before, and I walked by his shop nearly every day for 18 years. Yet it was the first time he'd ever shaken my hand and treated me like an equal."[22]

The military is one traditional institution highly valued by non-elites for the help it offers in maintaining the self-discipline necessary to attain settled living. Religion is another. Two-thirds of Americans who have not completed high school say religion is very important in their lives, as compared with only 46 percent of those with postgraduate degrees. Americans with college degrees are 18 points more likely than Americans with high school education or less to say that believing in God is not necessary to be moral, while six in ten Black Protestants believe it is, even more so than white evangelical Protestants. Lamont found that traditional morality was the single strongest value held by blue-collar Black men and that religious participation was one of the top five. For white men, traditional morality was one of the top three.[23]

Again, Vance's memoir helps us make sense of this. After his father left his mom, Vance credited religion with having changed him for the better, leading him to become the steady family man he became for his second family.

> Dad's church offered something desperately needed by people like me. For alcoholics, it gave them a community of support and a sense that they weren't fighting addiction alone. For expectant mothers, it offered a free home with job training and parenting classes. When someone needed a job, church friends could either provide one or make introductions. When Dad faced financial troubles, his church banded together and purchased a used car for the family. In the broken world all around me—and for people struggling in that world—religion offered tangible assistance to keep the faithful on track.[24]

Religion also offers an alternative source of status to those in lower-status jobs. "I'm successful now because I know Jesus Christ ... I don't put success on a monetary level," a letter carrier told Lamont, comparing himself favorably to his brother (who was a congressman). Said a railroad worker, "There is a certain aura when I walk in. They really listen to what I say, you know. I like that." "We try to be right-living, clean-living people," a former pipe fitter told Arlie Hochschild, who noted that the folks she met in Louisiana talked of "being *churched*" with as much pride as her crowd in Berkeley talked of being highly educated. Everyone needs to be valued.[25]

Hochschild noted that her Louisiana friends were proud of their Christian morality and deeply wounded when it was depicted as homophobic ignorance. A gospel singer told Hochschild how much she loved Rush Limbaugh. Hochschild was initially mystified, then recognized the singer felt Limbaugh was defending her honor: "They think we are racist, sexist, homophobic, and maybe fat." This hurt drives much of the fervor behind culture wars.[26]

Sophistication Versus Straight Talk and Practical Knowledge

Elites value sophistication because it's one way they display their high human capital. Non-elites, instead, value directness and straight talk. Michele Obama's father "didn't like people who were uppity." When Michelle Obama spoke with Iowans, she realized they were like her own family: "They didn't trust people who put on airs." What professionals see as tact and political savvy, blue-collar people decry as phony.[27] A firefighter who left his job as a messenger on Wall Street told Lamont,

> In big business, there's a lot of false stuff going on. People are like, "How are you doing?" And then you turn your back and they are like, "He's a jerk." At least at the job at the firehouse, if you're a jerk, someone is going to tell you you're a jerk.[28]

A car mechanic agreed:

> You know what I hate? Two-face. I can't stand that. You're a fake, you're a fake. Why be a fake? Like with this person, they are snobby, and with this person, they are a regular down-to-earth person . . . Well, if you have to become snobby for them to want to be around you, well, then screw this person.[29]

A pipe fitter decried "shirt and tie types" for "too much politicking." What professionals see as savvy networking, blue-collar guys see as sucking up. "They are jockeying for jobs and worry about whether they are making the right moves and stuff. I feel I don't have to get involved in that." A policeman decried "Barbie and Ken people . . . I just like regular people. I don't try to hang out with doctors or lawyers." Most of the research is on men, but a study of high school girls also found that non-elite girls considered upper-middle-class girls "fake."[30]

"Directness is a working-class norm," to quote one class migrant. These cultural differences help explain why more working-class kids don't go to college. They often feel deeply uneasy there, caught in a no-man's-land where they belong nowhere. And going to college is risky: only 62 percent of students who start college graduate in six years, which leaves them repaying college loans on the salary of a high school graduate. College pays off less even for those first-generation students who graduate: in terms of both income and wealth accumulation, first-generation college students lag behind those whose parents were college grads. And while the college *wage* premium is still high, the college *wealth* premium has disappeared. College grads now owe so much in loans that they often end up no wealthier than those who never graduated. Non-elites are caught in a no-win situation, with low wages ensured if they don't graduate from college, while college has become far from a sure bet.[31]

In conclusion, I offer two points. The first is to reject the false dichotomy between economics and culture that pervades so much of political science and media coverage. It fuels bad political advice, for example, that "economic issues are driving the problems of Democrats in non-metro working-class counties far more than the culture war." This from a strategist I truly respect, and he's right that "our brand is pretty damaged." But it's due to class conflict expressed *both* through economic grievances *and* through culture wars.[32]

The second point is that culture wars don't reflect that non-elites are dim-witted; they reflect elites' failures to understand how blue-collar values reflect blue-collar lives. To quote sociologist Jennifer Hochschild:

> The Democratic party over the past few decades has gotten into the position of appearing to oppose and scorn widely cherished institutions—conventional nuclear family, religion, patriotism, capitalism, wealth, norms of masculinity and femininity, then saying "vote for me." Doesn't sound like a winning strategy to me.[33]

Me either. I don't intend to stop working to make families more inclusive, rein in capitalism, or loosen the grip of gender roles. But expressing scorn for widely cherished values in electoral politics just drives noncollege voters into the arms of a Far Right. When a political candidate advocates a progressive platform using language focused on hard work, loyalty, and freedom, support from moderates and conservatives rises without diminishing support from progressives, a 2019 study found. That's a good place to start.[34]

Key Takeaways:

1. Class is expressed not only through economics but also through cultural differences. Culture wars weaponize class-based cultural differences.

2. College-educated elites pride themselves on their economic and cultural capital (a.k.a. "merit"). The Missing Middle prides itself on keeping the world in moral order and their work ethic. This helps maintain their sense of dignity in a society that devalues them.

3. Elites value novelty and sophistication; the Missing Middle strives for stability and values straight talk.

4. Non-elites raise their kids to maximize their life chances by inculcating self-discipline, a respect for authority, and following the rules—what's needed to thrive in working-class jobs.

5. Non-elites highly value traditional institutions that anchor self-discipline and offer routes to social honor outside capitalism: religion, the military, and "family values" (discussed in the next chapter).

Isn't It Ironic That Red "Family Values" States Have Weaker Families than Blue States?

People can't get or stay married because it takes so much effort to survive. My ex-fiancée said, "You're never around." But I was working to get a better life for us. No one has time for their kids. It's the American Nightmare.

—Thirty-eight-year-old construction worker[1]

"Nine out of the ten worst states for teen pregnancy rates [are] 'red' states. The same can be found for the divorce rate.... Perhaps most amusingly, while blue states watch more pornography per capita than red states, the state that watches the most, by far, is blood red Kansas," wrote Ryan Broderick from BuzzFeed. That 2014 article shows how deeply *What's the Matter with Kansas?* structures liberal narratives. I have often heard liberals deride red states on the grounds that they talk a good game about family values—but blue states enact them. This "red families, blue families" theme stems from a 2010 study by law professors Naomi Cahn and June Carbone, which showed that families are more embattled in red states. When liberals declare themselves amused by red families' high divorce and teen pregnancy rates, they are laughing at poor people. A 2014 study by sociologists Jennifer Glass and Philip Levchak found that red states' high divorce rates reflected the higher percentage of less educated voters, who also have higher rates of teen pregnancy.[2]

Poor families have long had less stable marriages and higher rates of teen pregnancy and nonmarital childbearing. What's new is that these trends have spread to families in the middle. Lower-middle-class families used to have the high marriage and low divorce rates that upper-middle-class families still enjoy; divorce rates among college grads have actually diminished since 1980. But divorce rates for lower-middle-class families have risen sharply, as has nonmarital childbearing: 7 percent of white college grads but over 50 percent of white high school grads have children outside of marriage.[3]

Studies affirm the links with economic woes. Downward mobility predicts stress, alcoholism, depression and marital tension, domestic violence, desertion, child abuse, and "complete disintegration of the family." One study estimated that 40 percent of the decline in marriage rates among Americans twenty-five to thirty-nine is explained by the fall in men's earnings. Another attributed 29 percent of the decline in marriage rates to couples' aversion to having the wife earn more than the husband. Financial instability fuels marital instability, given that the number one thing married couples fight about is money. Teen pregnancy rates are higher in red states not because teens have more sex but because blue states have more abortions; the overruling of *Roe v. Wade* will no doubt exacerbate this. African Americans' marriage rate plummeted when Black men lost out in the early rounds of deindustrialization; whites' marriage rates followed when many white working-class men ultimately met the same economic fate: many women often aren't eager for marriage to someone who can't support at least himself. Conservatives now scold white working-class families for "family dysfunction" just the way they have long scolded Black families. But it's shocking when liberals do, too: William Julius Wilson pointed out long ago that families fall apart "when work disappears." Fully 81 percent of Americans with high school degrees or less believe that "for a man to be a good husband or partner, being able to support a family is very important," compared to 62 percent of college grads. Less educated men are the most likely to believe they should be breadwinners and the least likely to be able to deliver.[4]

Stable marriages have become a class-linked privilege for the few—another of the litany of loss that pinpoints what lower-middle-class people used to enjoy and no longer do. Family values' political allure stems not from families' ability to enact them but precisely because they no longer can. Only 41 percent of the rural Californians in Jennifer Sherman's sample grew up with mothers who worked but by the early 2000s, 83 percent of women in her sample who were married or parents were in the labor force.[5]

The loss of family stability would be painful for anyone, but it's particularly painful for workers because of dynamics surrounding the scrum for social honor. To maintain some sense of personal dignity, lower-middle-class families emphasize the moral and social capital they have rather than economic or cultural capital they lack. This is true across race: Black non-college grads are more conservative than Black college grads, especially on matters of religion and morality.[6]

Social capital refers to the quality of human relationships. "For Tommy and Liza, the good life is to be found not in material success, but in the security of knowing that they have social support, both from their families and the community at large. They can rely on this continued support in part because their choices and lifestyle provide them with high moral capital." As a result, "they are proud of themselves and happy with their lot and well respected in [their community]." Workers, concluded Michèle Lamont, "have a distinct moral code focusing on personal integrity and the quality of interpersonal relationships."[7]

The prerequisite for moral capital is a good work ethic, as we've seen. But that's just the prerequisite: family values are the key. Lower-middle-class families think of themselves as more dedicated to family life than the upper-middle class. A case from the Annals of the National Labor Relations Board provides a vivid example. Thomas Fell held a classic neo-liberal working-class job, selling auto parts (manufactured in China?) at a Buick dealership. Fell's thirteen-year-old son called shortly before the end of the workday, asking his dad to pick him up. His sports practice had ended early, everyone else had left, and he was frightened to be alone at school because someone had fired a gun through the windows the previous week. Fell immediately locked up and left work fifteen minutes early. Later that night, he called to notify his manager, who said he had done the right thing, saying, "Family is number one."[8]

Note that both Fell and his manager embraced a classic blue-collar truism: family comes first. When sociologists Naomi Gerstel and Carla Shows studied EMTs and physicians in Massachusetts, they found that the doctors' wives were expected to shoulder virtually all of the childcare to allow fathers to be virtually always available for work. Physicians tended to define fathering as participation at public events, typically sports. In contrast, the "EMTs emphasized private fathering. . . . They talked about routine involvement in the lives of their children—picking them up from day care or school, feeding them dinner, or staying home with them when they got sick." Some (though not all) EMTs turned down overtime: "I will totally refuse the overtime. Family comes first for me," said one. The EMTs regularly swapped shifts to accommodate family responsibilities, and many liked their jobs precisely for that reason. I joke that, when it comes to feminism, elite men talk the talk but don't walk the walk, while blue-collar guys walk the walk but don't talk the talk. That's one reason why wives of high-earning men are the most likely to take time out of the labor market.[9]

"Blue-collar men put family above work, and find greater satisfaction in family than do upper-middle-class men. Family is the realm of life in which these workers can be in charge and gain status for doing so. It is also a realm of life that gives them intrinsic satisfaction and validation— which is crucial when work is not rewarding and offers limited opportunities," concludes Lamont. "They believe they are different not because their family practices are unusual but because they are more 'traditional' than those of the urban middle class and poor," notes Sherman. "Being 'traditional' and 'family oriented' gives them a sense of their own success in moral terms as opposed to the unattainable economic terms of the American dream."[10]

Those who are seen as having traditional families gain both social and moral capital. Maria Kefalas quotes a Chicago mom comparing her Chicago neighborhood of bungalows favorably to the suburbs where people are "fast-paced, on the go, there was no familiarity with people. Here . . . it's a more close-knit community and people are more involved with their children." Note again her celebration of her social relationships and her sense that upper-middle-class people run around obsessed with work. Research in psychology finds that strong social ties are associated with increased happiness and well-being: "in affluent countries . . . [h]appiness tends to be lower among the very poor. Once comfortable, however, more money provides diminishing returns on happiness."[11]

I know it's annoying to have others say they value family more than you do, but hear me out. Sherman contrasts the rural families she studies with the "self-centeredness of the urban middle class, who are much less likely to sacrifice their own children's material well-being to provide for an extra child in need." Nearly half of the rural people Sherman studied had cared for children not biologically related to them, even when money was tight, with no expectation whatsoever of reciprocity from the child's parents. This expressed their family values and moral worth.[12]

As always, work and family interact in many ways, not the least of which is that keeping an orderly and tidy home is one way people demonstrate their good work ethic. "The state of one's home [is] an outward manifestation of work ethics," notes Sherman. Kefalas's study of blue-collar

"Beltway" (near Chicago) explores how "the neighborhood symbolizes everything its working-class residents value—hard work, honesty, patriotism and respectability." She notes that Mexican Americans were "cautiously welcomed" so long as they showed they were good neighbors "who maintain their property and care for their children." These blue-collar values are expressed through "the care with which they keep their homes clean, cultivate their gardens, maintain their property, and celebrate the nation." Those who don't—which "includes other working-class whites—become the objects of scorn and derision." A white high school boy was deeply offended when a sociologist incorrectly assumed he was from a hard-living family: "Who, them? Oh no, they're white trash."[13]

"Like marriage and children, homeownership thus becomes an act that your neighbors can use to evaluate your moral fiber," notes Kefalas. So it's upsetting that owning a home became close to out of reach after the Great Recession. Thus a rural resident in an area where coastal elites were moving in, raising housing prices, said ruefully, "I might never be able to own property until my parents die." This pattern has become sharply worse since Covid, when elites have moved in large numbers to cheaper Zoom-commuting communities in scenic areas. The growing unaffordability of housing, fed by private equity buying up housing and renting it out after jacking up rents, can be politically volatile. "Owning a Chicago-style bungalow embodied success, security, and achievement," notes Kefalas. Gone with the wind.[14]

All this explains why "lace-curtain Irish" (to quote my mom) are so house-proud and starch-happy. Much more is at stake than dust bunnies. When Kefalas came to Beltway, she "took note of the elaborate lawn decorations, manicured grass, color-coordinated kitchens, fastidiously cared-for American-made cars, and the graffiti-free alleys and streets." The people of Beltway's "ritualistic displays of housepride" signaled a "nearly spiritual devotion" to the two things they "want most to cultivate in their lives": order and abundance. Their "obsession" with having a well-kept home creates a symbolic boundary against disorder and decay. Not having a well-maintained home would make them seem to their neighbors like "white trash," boundary work not limited to white people. Michelle Obama noted that in her "loving and orderly home," her mother "did a ritualistic spring cleaning, attacking on all fronts—vacuuming furniture, laundering curtains, and removing every storm window so she could Windex the glass and wipe down the sills before replacing them with screens to allow the spring air into our tiny, stuffy apartment.... It's because of my mother that still to this day I catch the scent of Pine-Sol and automatically feel better about life." My mom was correct that my husband's family is obsessed with cleanliness but wrong to think that it represented something trivial in their lives. My husband and I now joke about it. His name is Dempsey, so when one of us cleans something that's already clean, we call it *Dempsey-izing* to acknowledge that we are doing emotion-work, not housework.[15]

Stable families signal the "stability and moral fortitude" of adults in control of themselves and their lives, avoiding drug and alcohol abuse and the family violence that about half had grown up with in a study in rural California. In the context of precarity, the creation of a stable family life "was one of his life's greatest achievements," one dad told an ethnographer. Their aspirations are notably modest. "For most, living within a safe rural community and providing a stable and abuse-free environment for their families is proof enough that they are successful parents with traditional values, uncontaminated by the ills of the modern world." They "focus their energies on making sure that their children, and any others in need, are provided with the very basics. Often this does not even mean sufficient food, but simply an abuse-free environment in which to sleep at night and parental figures who will support them in their endeavors." They are not at all focused on whether or where kids in their care will go to college. Instead, their focus is on "keeping your nose clean" and being a "good kid": on morality, not merit.[16]

This is the class logic of culture-wars debates over family values. The appeal of traditionalism is way overdetermined. Social psychologists find a consistent pattern: "individuals with middle status are in fact more insecure and more conforming than those with either high or low status." This makes sense. High-status people don't worry so much about losing status because theirs is so secure; low-status people worry even less because they have so little to lose. Middle-class vigilance to conform is a strategy to avoid losing what they have.[17]

In the 1990s, Lamont found that "high school graduates generally uphold more rigid moral norms than college graduates: they are less supportive of freedom of choice and self-expression, especially in the area of sexual morality, divorce, and abortion." Even today, support for abortion rights is linked to class. Two ethnographies written a decade apart both highlight that pro-life activists tend to be noncollege grads while pro-choice advocates tend to be college grads. A 2022 poll following the *Dobbs* decision found that Americans with postgraduate degrees were 33 points more likely to support legal abortion in all or most cases than noncollege grads. Noncollege voters of every race supported abortion rights at lower rates than same-race college-educated voters do. When non-elites cite elites' devotion to work as evidence of their lack of family values, all too often, abortion becomes a prime example. The narrative (note I'm not endorsing it) is that elites have abortions to protect their precious careers—and that just shows they fail to understand that family comes before work. The data shows this just ain't true.[18]

Noncollege grads also are more conservative on LGBTQ rights. A 2022 poll found that nearly half of Americans with high school or less but only about a quarter of those with grad school opposed gay marriage. As someone who has worked for gender equality my entire life, I don't intend to abandon that quest. But to pursue it effectively, you need to understand how deeply class inflected the family-values debate is. If liberals are going to bridge the diploma divide, we need to take that as a starting point.[19]

Key Takeaways:

1. Economic instability fuels family instability. This happened in Black families after 1970 and to non-elite white families after 1990. Non-elites look back with nostalgia on the stable families of earlier decades.
2. Family instability would be painful for anyone, but it's particularly painful for the lower-middle class because they pride themselves on their "family comes first" ethic and see elites as work obsessed, with ambition tainting their personal and family relationships.
3. "Family values" also reflect "middle-status conservatism": people in the middle of status hierarchies tend to be risk-averse because they have more to lose than the poor and fewer second chances than the rich.

Can't People See Through Trump's Truculent Retro Masculinity?

[Rick Marsh, an autoworker] remembers sitting at home watching a debate between Mr. Trump and Hillary Clinton. . . . Mr. Trump was like a boxer who kept landing punches. It was electrifying. . . . Then Mr. Trump brought up NAFTA, and it was like he was speaking directly to Mr. Marsh. He voted for Mr. Trump, and so did his father, along with just under half the [Ohio auto] workers represented by the union.

—Sabrina Tavernise[1]

The gender gap in politics has been documented since the 1970s and was particularly large in 2016. But the traditional focus is on the gap between the voting behavior of men and women, and the reasons women have increasingly favored Democrats. It's time to shift our focus to men and masculinity. Adept manipulation of masculine anxieties is an essential ingredient in the secret sauce of many far-right figures, from Donald Trump to Jair Bolsonaro to Viktor Orbán to Alternative for Germany's call to "rediscover our manliness."[2]

Telling the story of far-right populism as a story of class-based masculinities is dead easy. In 2016, 64 percent of white noncollege males voted for Trump, followed by 65 percent in 2020, making them Trump's biggest supporters in both election years. Trump's gains among people of color were chiefly fueled by the votes of men. An analysis of the 2022 midterm elections showed that 43 percent of Latinos, but only 34 percent of Latinas, voted Republican. In 2024, the big story was men of color's shift toward Trump. Latinos favored Trump by a 12-point margin (a 32-point shift away from Democrats), while Latinas favored Harris by 22 points.

Trump's support among Black men more than doubled, from 12 percent in 2020 to 25 percent in 2024. Only 10 percent of Black women voted for Trump. "There's a big masculinity component, the Joe Rogan effect," Equis Research's Carlos Odio told me, referring to the tough-guy podcaster "with cross-racial appeal."[3]

Odio also noted how Trump taps Latinos' tradition of "honor-based masculinity." Documenting this is one of my favorite social science experiments ever: researchers had a research associate bump into Northern and Southern men in a hallway and grumpily mutter, "Asshole." Southerners got more upset because they saw this as a challenge to their masculine honor, some threatening to fight it out. Honor-based masculinity remains strong in the South, among Latino Americans, and among Trump voters. A 2020 book, *Trump's Democrats*, summarized Trump's appeal based on honor culture, stressing his "dragon energy," his ability to play "the don" who takes care of his people, and his commitment to America First and Making America Great Again. Trump's aura of aggrieved entitlement reflects that anger in honor cultures is a public performance designed to maintain status.[4]

Politics is one arena in which men enact their masculine identities through the endorsement of politicians, parties, and policies that appear tough, strong, and forceful. Trump's bad-but-bold strain of masculinity excuses men's bad behavior on the grounds that "boys will be boys" (i.e., men are designed for dominance). He taps age-old understandings of virility as a way of using sexual domination of women to negotiate a status hierarchy among men. This explains Trump's obsessive bragging about his brilliance and big hands, and his weird belittling of the attractiveness of opponents' wives. Trump constructs his insults of women and disabled people as courage in taking on "political correctness": he stands up to elites who seek to silence red-blooded men who want to tell it like it is. Even his speaking style connects with blue-collar talk traditions that associate blunt talk with personal integrity. "He doesn't try to sugarcoat things," explained one woman. Media scholars have shown how Fox News connects emotionally with the "NASCAR audience" by using a blue-collar confrontative style and masculinist personalities like Bill O'Reilly, Sean Hannity, and Tucker Carlson. The first two "performed the role of an 'authentic,' blue-collar everyman."[5]

A qualitative study of 2016 Trump voters details their attraction to

Trump's self-presentation as "an icon of manhood: a confident, savvy, and aggressive businessman who had the guts to take on the political establishment." To a one, they praised Trump's willingness to tell it like it is without fear of being labeled politically incorrect, which tapped into a classic theme: that a real man exerts control and resists control by others—John Wayne masculinity. Even those who felt that Trump went too far felt he was a "natural and authentic force that could not be leashed by political correctness." Trump's unvarnished-truth style made him seem more trustworthy: a 2023 report found that more young men trusted Trump than Biden.[6]

Most participants in the qualitative study admired Trump as an "entrepreneur" who got things done even if he bent the rules—Elon Musk masculinity. Other populist leaders also enact masculine tropes. Former Brazilian president Jair Bolsonaro is a prime example:

> The main principle is to defend yourself, your family, your home. We defend guns in the hands of the good people because the bad guys already have guns.[7]

Hungarian prime minister Viktor Orbán "conceptualize[s] the nation in need of security as a family that needs to be protected by a masculine protector," depicting men in the Hungarian army as valiant protectors of white European Christian civilization. These brands of macho appeal when working-class men find "it's increasingly hard for them to feel good about themselves," to quote the ever-insightful Arlie Hochschild.[8]

"Men should be men; women should be women" sexism (a.k.a. hostile sexism) was second only to political orientation in predicting support for Trump in both men and women. Not just white men: hostile sexism strongly predicts Trump voting among the Latino community. Endorsement of both hostile sexism and hegemonic masculinity (a.k.a. macho) predict Trump voting—both in men and women. "A lot of women think that's the way guys should be," noted a masculinity scholar. "They're not begrudgingly voting for Trump, but saying 'He's a real man.' Hegemonic masculinity reflects the ideal that men should be mentally, physically, and emotionally strong, tough, and in control.[9]

Trump, Boris Johnson, Viktor Orbán, and many others embody a truculent form of "protest" masculinity that's deeply resonant in an era of widespread economic anxiety. Ceding masculinity to the Far Right is unwise. The sharp drop in noncollege men's economic fortunes means "more men are leading lonely haphazard lives" (to quote David Brooks): many spend more time underemployed or unemployed, bitter and seeking reassurance that they're real men. Men account for two out of every three despair deaths. No mystery why: all four key components of mature manhood—breadwinner status, homeownership, fatherhood, and marriage—are becoming increasingly unattainable. In response, men double down on aspects of masculinity they can attain—like voting for Mr. Macho.[10]

Non-elite men may try to play off their axis of privilege—being male—to make up for their axis of disadvantage—being working class. The belief that men are socially superior to women "is most likely to matter to men who lack other sources of status," note political scientists Noam Gidron and Peter Hall. "It is perhaps one of the last refuges of the autonomy of the dominated classes, of their capacity to produce their own representation of the accomplished man," observed Pierre Bourdieu. Non-elite men of all races often display a hypermasculine ethos as a way of claiming dignity in the face of the "hidden injuries of class," from NASCAR to rap to lucha libre. Working-class women, understanding men's claims as a yearning for dignity in a society that offers them little, "stand by their man" to support what they, too, see as claims to dignity. One study found that white working-class women were much more likely than college grads to endorse the view that "men should be men and women should be women."[11]

Threat research is the first important lens for understanding how the Far Right weaponizes masculinity. Studies show that when men's masculinity is threatened, they tend to go hydraulic: employed wives of unemployed husbands face greater risks of domestic abuse, as do employed wives who earn more than their husbands. Men who earn less than their wives do less housework, and men told they were less masculine in one study were more likely to sexually harass a female study participant. Social psychologist Robb Willer and colleagues brought men into the lab, had all of them take an assessment, and told half of them that they scored just inside the feminine range while the other half were told they were solidly masculine. The men whose masculine identities were threatened reported significantly greater support for the Iraq War, had more negative views of homosexuality, and were more likely to prefer an SUV and to spend more money ($7,320 on average, to be exact) to buy one than men whose mas-culinity had not been threatened.[12]

Being a man is a cherished identity for most men: a 2023 study found two-thirds of men feel more praised and accepted when they act manly. Cherished—but precarious. Social psychologist Joseph Vandello and col-leagues point out that being a "real" man has to be earned, over and over again. This makes noncollege men's loss of social status particularly pain-ful. And the loss of status is real: as of 2009, the subjective social status of women was lower than that of similarly educated men; by 2014, women noncollege grads felt higher status than their male counterparts in both the US and five European countries. "The relative social status of men without a college education is lower today than it was 25–30 years ago," with some of the most pronounced declines between 2009 and 2014, con-clude Noam Gidron and Peter Hall. Susan Faludi pointed this out as far back as 1999. In districts where Google searches signaled precarious masculinity, Republicans' vote share was higher in the 2018 midterms, an effect researchers tied to Trump.[13]

History provides perspective. The breadwinner-homemaker model, in-vented in the late eighteenth century, was "unattainable for all but the upper and upper-middle-class and an elite minority of the working class" in the nineteenth and twentieth centuries. A man who was a breadwinner with a wife at home was living up to both a gender ideal and a class ideal. That helps explain why, even today among non-elites, "it is still considered the norm and mark of financial success for a woman to stay at home while the man works." Privileged men have alternative sources of social status—but also maintain their breadwinner status. Among married couples in the top 1 percent by wealth or income, 70 percent prioritized men's careers and had a gender-traditional division of labor. Elite families can spout feminism all they want; they let men's salaries do the talking.[14]

For a brief period from roughly 1970 to 2000, many blue-collar fam-ilies could access this social ideal because highly paid blue-collar work meant that their families could get by on only intermittent work by wives. Thus Michelle Obama's mother stayed at home until her kids were in high school, when she went back to work to help pay for tuition—just like my mother-in-law. Because white men had privileged access to blue-collar jobs, the breadwinner ideal was even stronger among non-elite whites. Jennifer Sherman found that 59 percent of the rural whites she talked with said they'd grown up with homemaker moms. "During the forest industry's heyday," she notes, "solid lower-middle-class lifestyle was more commonly achievable without a working wife."[15]

Gone with the wind. The reality changed, but the ideals didn't; both men and women still embrace the provider ideal. Nearly three-fourths of Americans still say it's important for a man to be able to support his family, including 78 percent of Latinos and 84 percent of Black Americans. The lower the education level, the higher the endorsement of the provider ideal: about half of college grads think it's better for children if "one parent" stays home, as compared with two-thirds of those with high school or less and 60 percent of those with some college. One parent? Who are we kidding? said the wife of a laid-off steelworker. "Men have a tendency to identify with what they do. . . . To Al, he was a steelworker. That's who he was." Said another laid-off worker, "I felt like I should be the one out earning money for the family and my wife should be home taking care of her kids, and I just felt horrible." It's non-elite men who feel horrible, not elite ones: elite women actually earn *less* in comparison to elite men than in 1990, whereas non-elite men's wages have fallen so sharply they're now a lot closer to women's than they once were.[16]

Working-class men still want to be providers; many working-class women still want to marry providers. If we look at who earns more, we can see why. While women with degrees have entered traditionally male careers, noncollege women grads typically are stuck in low-paying, pink-collar jobs. One or even two pink-collar jobs means a fragile hold in the middle class (at best); the best defense against downward mobility is a blue-collar job, only 17 percent of which are held by women.[17]

Michèle Lamont found that providing was one of the top three values held by white blue-collar men and one of the top five held by Black blue-collar men. Being "unemployed or underemployed is thus, for many in the working class, not only an economic catastrophe but a moral one."[18]

The loss of non-elites' ability to fulfill the breadwinner ideal is part of what drives the nostalgic deprivation political scientists document. The loss is not just symbolic; it's material. In a society that has steadfastly refused to invest in a childcare system adequate to support two-job families, the alternative to the wife at home is far from ideal. Remember Bailey Hodge, who worked tag team and complained that she had no time to do anything other than sleep and work. She was one of the lucky ones: she had a union job. More common is the experience of Mike, who drove a cab; his wife worked at a hospital. They decided it would be best if she was there during the day and Mike was there at night because "he controls the kids, especially my son, better than I do." So she worked the graveyard shift. "I hate it, but it's the only answer: at least this way someone is here all the time." After her shift, she returned home at 8:30 a.m. to an empty house. Instead of going to sleep, she cleaned the house, did the shopping and the laundry, then finally slept—but only for an hour or two until the kids got home from school. After Mike got home at five, the family had dinner together, and she grabbed another couple of hours of sleep. "I try to get up at 9 so we can have a little time together, but I'm so tired that I don't make it a lot of times"—after all, she'd only had four hours of sleep. By 10:00 p.m., Mike was sleeping because he had to get up and on the road at 6:00 a.m. "It's hard, it's very hard. There's no time to live or anything." No surprise: tag team families have three to six times the national divorce rate.[19]

Sherman details the creativity with which non-elite men redefine the provider role when family-sustaining jobs disappear. Almost every man Sherman interviewed listed hunting and fishing as their favorite hobbies. They were also "the best way for poor men to contribute non-monetarily to his family's basic needs with little loss of respectability." One class migrant noted her aversion to deer meat—associated in my crowd with tasting menus, but in her childhood with unemployment and poverty. "When people don't have money for food, there's lots and lots of food just runnin' around the woods," noted a gamekeeper who cut the locals some slack for hunting to feed their families. Families also relied on unemployment and disability: nearly 40 percent of rural men Sherman interviewed between twenty-one and sixty-four were on disability, nearly twice the rate in the state. She found "a growing incidence and acceptance" of stay-at-home fathers on disability. But this is making lemonade out of lemons: the provider role is so deeply intertwined with masculinity that unemployed men are more likely to be impotent. "I felt like a man again," said a Pennsylvania toll collector when he got a new job after being injured in his prior job as a dockworker. His new job evaporated during Covid, when he was permanently laid off two and a half months before qualifying for a full pension.[20]

Disability is constructed as masculine when disability payments are constructed as the rewards for past, dangerous work. As one thirty-year-old former logger put it, "I don't know if you've ever seen the logging operations, but everything out there is tryin' to kill you. Everything."[21]

Provider—and protector: Lamont found that being a protector was among the top five values for Black blue-collar men; it was a central value for white men, too. Understanding the importance of the protector role starts with polling data that shows that non-elites see the world as a far more dangerous place than elites do. White men without college degrees are more likely (53 percent) than college grads to say that they are very or somewhat worried that they or their families will be the victims of a violent crime, while white women without degrees (62 percent) are much more likely than their counterparts with college degrees (46 percent) to worry about this. Latinos worry almost as much as white women without degrees (63 percent), with African Americans worrying the same as white men without degrees.[22]

"Many of the men I talked to perceive their environment as threatening," notes Lamont. "They believe in the importance of 'not trusting anyone,' and one or two even scolded me for conducting interviews in the living rooms of strangers." An electronics technician said, "I will do anything to make sure my family stays secured. Physically, emotionally, financially . . . If there's something they need, you do it, regardless of the sacrifices you have to make to do it. You do it, no questions asked. That's it." Gun control initiatives trigger anxieties about *both* men's provider *and* their protector roles.[23]

It's easy for elites to look down on the provider and protector as outdated. But these stereotypes still hold tremendous power for both elite and non-elite men. "Even in the world's most gender-egalitarian countries, women tend to prefer men with relatively high income and education," noted Vegard Skirbekk, a population economist. An experiment with a class-diverse sample found that men preferred women who earn less than they do because they saw women who earn more as less likable and less likely to be faithful.[24]

"Where's the boss?" my mother-in-law used to ask me, until I told her in no uncertain terms that no one in our family is the boss. In her generation, men earned the lion's share of the family income so—though they were subordinated at work—at home, they were the boss. A second subtext: to her, it was a privilege to be a homemaker. It gave her pleasure, too, to make her husband feel like he was the boss *somewhere*. "A man's got his pride." This used to be a common saying, now defunct in polite circles as sexist. It *is* sexist but it's still true, whether we admit it or not. It helps explain why high-paid women lawyers drop out of the workforce to support their husbands' careers and why women in blue-collar families mourn the loss of well-paid blue-collar jobs. "I'm voting to save my boyfriend's job," said a white working-class woman to explain her vote for Trump. Both emotional and economic logic drive this. No one wants the person they love to feel humiliated. And working-class women, who still chiefly hold dead-end pink-collar jobs "with no flexibility and no future," often still see good blue-collar jobs held by men as their best hope for a stable, middle-class standard of living. Working-class wives work primarily for the money rather than career satisfaction; this results in more marital tension, which can fuel marital instability that spirals into yet more economic insecurity.[25]

This helps explain why working-class men's marriageability is another casualty of their inability to play the provider role. Marriage rates have plummeted among working-class whites. Black men's marriage rates fell a generation earlier. Men's falling earnings power is one reason for their falling marriage rates: women tend not to marry men who can't provide. By 2014, more young men were living with their parents than with a wife or partner. One in four men in the US was childless at age forty between 2006 and 2010. Yet another humiliation to a group that used to, and still does, pride themselves that "family comes first."[26]

In this context, the common policy prescription that blue-collar men take care-work jobs can only fuel the Far Right. Alas, blue-collar men want what white-collar men have: traditionally male jobs. Reporters who've interviewed me on the topic typically focus on male nurses; one protested that her nephew was a nurse (as is mine). But most pink-collar jobs aren't like nursing: they're low-wage, dead-end jobs, which is one reason men don't want them. It's a recipe for resentment to have college-educated elites (whose men still hold traditionally masculine jobs) tell blue-collar men that the solution to their families' gutted-by-neoliberalism economic prospects is for men to take the low-wage, feminine-coded jobs.

Steve Bannon couldn't think this stuff up. But that's not the only fix Richard Reeves suggests in his influential *Of Boys and Men*. He also suggests giving boys an extra year in the classroom, telling us how he held his middle son back. I'm all for holding kids back if they need it—we held my dyslexic son back when he was in second grade; he now has a PhD in electrical engineering. But I recognize this as responsive to my class-specific obsession on optimizing children's academic potential. It's counterproductive as a solution to working-class economic woes. In many areas of the country, kindergarten is free but pre-K is not; it can cost as much as $10,000 a year. Reeves recognizes the need for free pre-K for working-class kids but doesn't seem to recognize that without it, his proposal would mean they'll be stuck in inadequate childcare for yet another year or that working-class moms (or, less often, dads) will have to take more time out of the workforce in families that need two incomes to survive, much less thrive.[27]

So the plan for addressing the bleak prospects of working-class families is low-paid, pink-collar jobs and to shoulder yet another expense they can't afford? This is just one way class blindness leads to poor public policy. What working-class families need are family-sustaining jobs to address people's desire for dignity, meaning, marriage, and cash. College-educated men—overwhelmingly white—are the only group whose real wages have increased since 1980. Solutions to the problems faced by non-elite men should not be designed to ensure that elite men can reach their potential.[28]

Key Takeaways:

1. Endorsement of traditionalist masculinity is a powerful predictor of MAGA voting in both men and women, and predicts Trump support even more accurately than racism.
2. Politics is one arena where men enact cherished masculine identities. This becomes even more important when the provider role has become unattainable.
3. Threats to masculinity fuel hypermasculine behavior.
4. Far-right figures and followers enact a class-specific "protest masculinity" that's deeply resonant in an era of widespread economic anxiety.

Doesn't the Diploma Divide Just Reflect "Grievance Politics"?

We're voting with our middle finger.

—2016 Trump supporter[1]

Let's begin by noting that anger is not always bad. Feminists have pointed out that rage is often justified in the face of injustice. That's why the Left is often angry: angry about police violence, angry about children in cages, angry about Wall Street. But the Left's anger is coded as righteous. Why is non-elite anger discounted as "grievance"?[2]

Calling something a *grievance* is a rhetorical maneuver that enables you to refuse to engage with the legitimacy of the demand on the grounds that it's being expressed in the wrong tone of voice. This is a common way dominant groups seek to silence subordinate groups. When a colleague in the course of a business disagreement is called an "angry Black man," the speaker is refusing to discuss the business disagreement and shifting attention to the colleague's tone of voice. Social psychologists find that white people tend to see Black people as angry when they aren't angry— just assertive. Calling an assertive Black person *angry* is a good way to undercut their authority and perpetuate inequality.[3]

This is a form of racism documented over and over again. White people prefer Asian Americans who behave in submissive and deferential ways and tend to dislike them when they behave authoritatively: again, the issue becomes whether they have expressed their views in a suitable tone of voice rather than whether their views are worth considering. Known as the *tightrope*, this is an integral part of a pattern of bias that affects women as well as people of color. Women walk a tightrope between being seen as not authoritative enough (and so lacking in competence) or too authoritative, in which case they often are faulted for using the wrong tone: they are difficult, or abrasive, or angry. Tightrope bias signals that someone in a subordinate group does not "know their place."[4]

Progressives have learned not to write off the legitimate demands of women or people of color in this way. Silencing someone on the grounds she's an angry Black woman is readily understood as perpetuating structural racism. It should be equally off-limits to silence Americans disadvantaged by class on the grounds that their demands are "grievances."

The grievance narrative embeds the emotions that anchor inequality: envy up and scorn down, to quote social psychologist Susan Fiske: "Each of us is caught between those whose position we envy and those whose position we scorn. We are comparison machines." Envy combines hurt and anger—again, inequality is humiliating. "The flip side of envy is scorn . . . , [which is] the absence of respect, a lack of attention, a failure to consider." "Scornful powerholders are not only selfish but willfully clueless." People with power are literally worse at reading other people's facial expressions. "Scorn scars the scornful": it's worse for your health even than anger, which itself is unhealthy. It also hurts the scorned: "low status demands a vigilant attention to those with higher status." In other words, cluelessness is an artifact of privilege.[5]

Who is lower in status in the US? No surprise: people of color, especially people of African or mestizo Latino descent, who rank below Anglo whites and Asian Americans. Race is important, but so is class: blue-collar Americans also rank low in perceived competence.[6]

Scorn down involves disgust that blames low-status people for being stupid. "Trump's cultists . . . are beneath contempt and deserve to be demeaned," as Richard Kavesh wrote in a letter to *The New York Times*. Or: "Yes, there are those supporters who have suffered addiction and hardship, but that this might logically lead them to support a criminal and potential dictator who gives no reason for a rational person to believe he would serve their interests is simply a bridge too far . . . [They are] just plain ignorant" (another letter). "I assert that we must clearly call these people out for what they are; selfish, racist bigots like the man they support" (another letter). The casual insertion of racism into a list of classist epithets is even more disturbing. Just Google "Trump supporters are stupid and racist" and you go down a rabbit hole of Reddit threads expounding on the racism theme. It's so popular there's a market for it: an Amazon ad touts a T-shirt with the description "Racist, Crazy, Fraud, Moron, Stupid . . . Know someone who hates Donald Trump? . . . Order today and be that 'thoughtful friend.'" Anti-racism is too important for white elites to casually throw it into a list of classist epithets, implying that it's a working-class problem. It's not: racism affects elites as well as non-elites, as discussed in chapter 14.[7]

White trash was first used in 1833. Shortly thereafter, a character called Ransy Sniffle was considered hilariously funny: "a grotesque character notable for his poor diet, his physical deformities, his laziness, apathy, and low intelligence." Scorn is a dumb move politically. Calling people "deplorables" (Hillary Clinton) or bitter people "clinging" to guns and religion (Barack Obama) or nursing a grievance just plays into the hands of the Far Right. Reece Peck and Anthony Nadler document how Fox News commentators from Bill O'Reilly to Tucker Carlson proposed a deal: that they will stand up for working-class voters against liberal elites who belittle them in return for support for Republicans. Liberals need to remember that every time they reinforce this script, they are empowering the Merchant Right.[8]

The alternative is to defuse class anger by making blue-collar Americans feel both secured and valued. But we've not headed in that direction. "At least in the entertainment world, working-class whites are now regularly portrayed as moronic, while Blacks are hyper-articulate, street-smart, and sometimes as wealthy as Kanye West," noted leftist writer Barbara Ehrenreich. A pivot point was Norman Lear's *All in the Family*, which ran from 1971 to 1979, precisely when the current configuration of distinct class-linked universes crystallized. Lear replaced earlier depictions of blue-collar men as noble (think of the WPA mural in your local post office) with Archie Bunker, who was depicted as narrow-minded, coarse, ignorant, sexist, and racist. Blue-collar men became an accepted brunt of jokes. Homer Simpson epitomized stereotypes of working-class men as fat, ignorant, and boorish alcoholics. Homer works as an inspector at a nuclear power plant at a time when liberals truly hated nuclear power. Noted Ehrenreich, "Presumably, upper-middle-class people generally conceive of these characters and plot lines, which, to a child of white working-class parents like myself, sting with condescension." Populism taps complaints that "we have been shut out of power by corrupt politicians and the unrepresentative elites who betrayed our interests, ignore our opinions, and treat us with contempt."[9]

An important variant of the grievance narrative is one that writes off anti-elitist populist fury on the grounds that it's an expression of *white resentment,* "despair over the loss of their perch in the country's pecking order," to quote a 2016 story in *The Atlantic.* An important source for this interpretation is sociologist Arlie Hochschild's wonderful *Strangers in Their Own Land.* Hochschild's book contains ample evidence of class anger—anger at the cultural disrespect of rural and Southern voters by the Brahmin Left, anger at college-educated bureaucrats who rigorously apply environmental rules to farmers and hunters while applying the same rules leniently or not at all to big business, anger at the death of the American dream. But as insightful as she is—after all, she asked the right questions to elicit this flood of anger—when you look in her book's index, the only class conflict that's reflected is the class conflict between blue-collar people and the poor. Hochschild fails to recognize class conflict between middle-status voters and the Brahmin Left. Instead, she constructs her now-famous "deep story" of whites angered that people of color are cutting in line.[10]

> You are patiently standing in a long line leading up a hill, as in a pilgrimage. You are situated in the middle of this line, along with others who are also white, older, Christian, and predominantly male, some with college degrees, some not. Just over the brow of the hill is the American Dream, the goal of everyone waiting in line. . . . It's scary to look back; there are so many behind you, and in principle you wish them well. . . . You see people cutting in line ahead of you! You're following the rules. They aren't. . . . Who are they? Some are black. . . . Women, immigrants, refugees, public sector workers—where will it end?[11]

Note that economic anxiety is up front of this vivid little scene. Front, but not center: Hochschild enshrines as "deep" not that class anger but the anger against people of color cutting the line. As we have seen, and will explore in greater depth in chapter 13, this narrative aptly captures the viewpoint of American preservationists but erases the existence of anti-elites.

Is it accurate to attribute whites' anger as anger over their loss of white privilege? In a sense, it is. White privilege used to protect middle-status whites from the full brunt of class disadvantage. This meant that whites benefited disproportionately in the decades after World War II from the blue-collar jobs that provided income, and the FHA loans that allowed Americans to build up wealth. When I first started teaching hyper-segregation, the FHA's role in creating it, and resulting wealth gap to my baffled and reluctant law school property class in the 1990s, the ratio of white to Black wealth was ten to one. Today, it's thirteen to one.[12]

That's how I see it because I've studied social inequality for decades, but that's not how working-class white people see it. They compare themselves not to African Americans but to their parents and grandparents. A white man remembered his father saying when he was thirty-five, "'I had a house, and I had five kids or four kids.'... And I'm like, 'Well, Dad, things have changed.'" Indeed, they have: nearly 60 percent of counties in the industrial Midwest, including 69 percent in Michigan and 82 percent in Ohio, have lower median household incomes today than in 1980 when adjusted for inflation. In 1980, white working-class families had not only the house, the car, and washing machine but maybe a boat or a lakeside cabin. Today, many can't buy a home, much less think about luxuries other than "a night at a hotel with a pool," to quote Bailey Hodge—and again, she's one of the lucky few with a union to protect her.[13]

In the US, levels of extreme distress nearly doubled for noncollege whites between 1993 and 2019, with the strongest predictors being unemployment and the state-level decline in manufacturing jobs. These high levels of psychological pain have been accompanied by high levels of physical pain. A 2019 study found that 34 percent of Americans report experiencing bodily aches and pains often or very often, "the highest proportion of any country in the sample." And as if to highlight how capitalism run amok fuels all this, opioid deaths skyrocketed particularly in areas with high loss in employment since 2000. Over two-thirds of overdose deaths from 2000 to 2021 were among Americans without a BA.[14]

In a very concrete measure of racial hierarchy, white Americans used to be happier than Black Americans. Today, the happiness gap has all but disappeared. Black people have gotten much happier since the 1970s because when they compare themselves to their parents and grandparents, they—unlike whites—see progress. This doesn't mean racial privilege has disappeared; the Black-white gap in people's satisfaction with their incomes has not decreased. I suspect that African Americans' greater savvy about structural disadvantage helps them avoid self-blame: Michèle Lamont found that a fifth of white blue-collar men but no African Americans put work at the center of their definition of success. Perhaps this helps explain why the suicide rate among Black men is roughly half that of white men.[15]

Blue-collar whites, we have seen, tend to attribute poverty to moral failings—their own as well as others'. An ethnographer describes a white woman who "does not draw a connection between the rise of free and reduced lunch and the decline of well-compensated jobs and the rise of poorly compensated jobs since the 1980s." Instead, she blames it on "four and five generations that have never had a job." A white auto worker asked, "What am I as a man?" when his job disappeared; being the protector and provider for his daughter was "his worth in the world." When they flounder, whites of both sexes often are looked down upon not only by white neighbors but also by people of color: "People think, 'Hey, you are white. You are privileged. So why do you have so many problems? Maybe you are the problem.'"[16]

This all helps explain the boom in deaths of despair. Drug deaths increased by 73 percent, alcohol-abuse deaths rose by 41 percent, and the suicide rate rose 17 percent between 2013 and 2019; in 2022, suicide was at its highest rate since 1938. Despair deaths rose at a faster rate after the Great Recession of 2008. Nearly all those who died deaths of despair lacked college degrees, and Trump performed best in "counties with the highest drug, alcohol and suicide mortality rates" and those with "high economic distress."[17]

Women in the fragile and failing middle class also have many reasons to be bummed. The only realistic path most had to economic stability—a partner's blue-collar job—is elusive. This often takes a toll on family stability, which can exacerbate the slide to poverty: boys of single moms fare more poorly than those in two-parent families. They exhibit higher levels of disruptive behavior and get suspended from school at twice the rate that boys raised in two-parent families do, found economists Marianne Bertrand and Jessica Pan. The rate of single motherhood among noncollege Americans has risen sharply. Economists David Autor and Melanie Wasserman warn of a vicious cycle, "with the poor economic prospects of less educated males creating differentially large disadvantages for their sons." Economic disadvantage destabilizes families, making non-elites able to fulfill *neither* economic *nor* family ideals. I'd be bummed out, too.[18]

All this has been happening to Black families for much longer, but for white families, it's relatively new. Other than union members, few have a language of class to provide the understanding of structural inequality that's the birthright of many African Americans. A society that understands race but not class as structural exacerbates the hidden injuries of class. "Because they lacked a discourse of class," the high school girls Julie Bettie studied often invoked a discourse of individualism, blaming themselves for their lot in life. They could see the difference that money made, but differences in cultural capital were more obscure to them: their parents valued education but lacked the cultural capital to assist them; talk of their futures made them anxious and depressed, as they were aware that middle-income working-class jobs were unavailable.[19]

All this helps explain the fall in happiness and rise in pessimism among whites. Serious mental distress rose steadily among white noncollege grads from 1997 to 2017. Poorer people have always been less happy than richer ones, but the diploma divide has increased. Black Americans tend to be relatively optimistic; whites, less so.[20]

In 2016, Trump performed better in counties where life expectancy has declined since 1980, and in counties with high rates of economic distress, health distress, and social distress (including marital instability and vacant housing units). Even in 2016, an equalization-of-misery trend was moving people of color in the direction of noncollege whites. Despair deaths among African American and Latino men without college degrees rose between 2010 and 2019: drug deaths doubled, suicides increased by a third, and alcohol-abuse deaths increased by 30 percent.[21]

If people are upset, it's not because they're in the "grip of white grievance." As chapter 2 shows, many people of color also are trending far-right. If people are upset, it's because they've gotten screwed. The fact that Black people used to be—and by most objective measures continue to be—in even worse shape is not a reason to mute the fury of non-elite whites. The solution is not to bring back white supremacy but to forge a multiracial coalition that demands we move beyond the shame of a very rich country with very poor outcomes. The grievance narrative gives free rein to the Merchant Right to bond with non-elite voters through rage. The Left's countermove is to bond through respect. We can only do that if we actually respect them.[22]

Key Takeaways:

1. Dominant groups often refuse to engage with the legitimate demands of "those below" on the grounds that those demands are expressed in the wrong tone of voice.

2. Progressives who have learned not to write off the demands of women as "shrill" or of people of color as "angry" shouldn't write off working-class demands as "grievance." If people are upset, it's because we are a very rich country with very poor outcomes.

3. Anti-racism is too important to be cheapened by casually throwing "racist" into a long litany of class-based insults.

4. Many of the economic woes experienced by working-class whites have been even more acute for people of color—but that's no reason to mute the fury of non-elite whites. The path forward is to build a multiracial coalition that delivers fair outcomes for everyone.

How Can I Respect People Who Deny Facts and Science?

*If we as hillbillies are slow to take the vaccine . . . it's because
we don't trust the pharmaceutical companies nor the
government. Because oxycontin should have been regulated
by the government . . . and Purdue Pharma should not have
made the millions and millions they made off my people.*

—Gwen Johnson, Appalachian woman[1]

The long history of anti-intellectualism in American life has been well
documented but little understood. Since Richard Hofstadter wrote *The
Paranoid Style in American Politics* in 1964, anti-intellectualism has been
conceptualized as a moral failing. This is another example of intellectuals
characterizing disagreements between "those above" and "those below"
as reflecting a character flaw of those below. In fact, resentment against
expertise is part and parcel of class resentment against college-educated
professionals. To quote philosopher Michael Sandel, "Insisting that social
and political problems are best solved by highly educated, value-neutral
experts is a technocratic conceit that corrupts democracy and disempow-
ers ordinary citizens." Lower-middle-class attitudes toward experts were
well summarized by a steelworker, who "has no use for the so-called expert who sits around all day dreaming up new ways to control my life." A
2023 survey of Republican primary voters found that 76 percent of white
noncollege grads and 69 percent of non-grads of color felt that elected
officials should prioritize the common sense of ordinary people over the
knowledge of trained experts, nearly 20 points higher than among college
grads.[2]

This explains the mystery of why the Missing Middle typically ad-
mires the rich but resents professionals. They resent professionals because

college-educated managers, teachers, doctors, and bureaucrats exercise so much control over their lives in ways that are in their face, unlike the ways that rich people do so, which typically are hidden behind impersonal institutions like private equity. Resentment of managers is a good example: they are seen as college kids "who don't know shit about how to do anything but are full of ideas about how I have to do my job." "This one foreman I've got, he's a kid. He's a college graduate. He thinks he's better than everybody else . . . I came here to work, I didn't come here to crawl. There's a fuckin' difference," said a steelworker.[3]

And that's just the start. Teachers may treat working-class kids as dim-witted or in other ways "systematically underestimate the capabilities of less privileged students, discipline them more harshly and provide them with fewer opportunities for high-quality learning." One ethnography condemns "the fundamental underinvestment in those who stay and many who return to rural areas." Upper-middle-class children also are trained to persistently elicit help in ways less privileged children don't—so they get more help. Julie Bettie's wonderful ethnography of white and Latina high school girls in California's Central Valley detailed the terrain of class conflict in high schools, triggered by

> the use of nonstandard grammar, parents who cannot help with homework, who may not know about the distinction between college-prep and non-prep courses, who may not know about college entrance exams, who themselves lack the academic skills to go to college, who might feel they have to de-value themselves and their own lives in the process of encouraging their children to go beyond them, who may wrongly assume that the school will adequately educate their child without their participation, who might desire to avoid the school themselves, because it is a familiar site of failure and intimidation where they are required to interact with middle-class professionals like teachers and administrators.

No surprise that parents' education and income are the best predictors of children's school performance.[4]

Lower-middle-class people's resentment of bureaucrats is part and parcel of their resentment against professionals who exercise so much day-to-day control over their lives. Folded in is what experts call "agency capture," where government agencies end up representing the corporate interests they are supposed to regulate. Conservatives made their usual move: they changed "capture" into the "deep state," transmuting class anger against the Merchant Right into anger against the government. Any attempt to successfully counter the deep state argument needs to understand the class anger that lies beneath it, to acknowledge that agency capture by corporate interests is very real and that it affects the Missing Middle who own businesses or farms or go hunting or fishing. People in Wisconsin resented the Department of Natural Resources as having "little understanding of the practicalities of everyday life in the Northwoods."[5] People in Louisiana said things like this, with "a flash of indignation":

> My nephew used to raise hogs. And you know a hog can stand almost anything. Because of the bad water, my nephew had to cook the slop you fed them. But the hogs got out of the pen and went to drink the Bayou water and died. The health unit came down on my *nephew* for not keeping his hogs away from the bad water, *but they didn't do nothing about the bad water.*[6]

Anger against professionals is understandable: professional roles were invented in the late eighteenth century as a way that middle-class men could claim cultural authority over "those above" (the aristocracy) and "those below" (the working class). Lower-middle-class men may still see expertise as (yet another) class-based power grab designed to rob them of their dignity. Men who endorse traditional masculinity are less likely to consistently wear Covid masks, and 1.5 times less likely to wear them than women. Why? "It's submission, it's muzzling yourself, it looks weak, especially for men." The same pattern can be seen with vaccine resistance. Playing it safe by getting the vaccine contradicts the masculine mandate to "show no weakness," defying experts' warnings signals, "I'm a tough guy, bring it on." A Fox show host derided Biden, saying he "might as well carry a purse with that mask."[7]

Resistance to the authority of science has become part of the identity of rural people, who feel talked down to and ignored by experts. High-income men are more likely than low-income men to feel that scientists share their values. Language criticizing "science deniers" fuels class resentments—and let's not blame less educated Americans for the paltry state of science education in many schools.[8]

Conspiracy theories are often seen as indisputable evidence that MAGA voters are ignorant, irrational, or evil, impervious to facts. Some are. One study looked at people who knowingly shared on social media information they themselves believed to be false, and found they were more likely to harbor a desire to run for political office, to support political violence, and to have positive feelings toward Vladimir Putin, white nationalists, the Proud Boys, and QAnon. They also "displayed higher levels of anti-social characteristics . . . , 'dark' personality traits (narcissism, psychopathy, Machiavellianism and sadism) and paranoia." But these bad actors were only 14 percent of respondents to a national survey.[9]

Many studies attribute conspiracy theories to individual psychological profiles, but it's important to recognize the social dimension. A 2022 study cautioned that "conspiracy beliefs are not merely a product of individual irrationality, but are grounded in, and reflective of, the times that collectives live in." Populism predicts belief in conspiracy theories, presumably because both stem from similar roots, notably a distrust and resentment of elites. A 2022 study found populist anti-elitism related to low political trust, conspiracy thinking, and support for the far-right Alternative for Germany. A 2021 study examined twenty-two Western and non-Western countries to construct a conspiracy index and found 70 percent of the variance accounted for by three factors: 1) people cannot take an active part in the political life of their country, 2) people feel socially threatened, and 3) institutions and authorities are perceived as untrustworthy. I suspect that those who believe in conspiracies might well say that all three describe the United States and some of Europe.[10]

Conspiracy theories are associated with less trust in political institutions, reduced support for democracy, greater endorsement of authoritarian values, and increased support for strong leaders willing to use undemocratic means to achieve desired goals. If democracy hasn't worked for you and your kind for over forty years, maybe it's time to try something different. Conspiracy theories often are cited as evidence that non-elites are irrational; what they really show is that inequality is eroding the social fabric.[11]

A central dynamic is best summarized by the philosopher C. Thi Nguyen: "When people are excited about the conspiracy theory, they note how disempowered they felt before their experience with the conspiracy theory. . . . If you believe in a conspiracy theory, you have total intellectual agency. You don't have to trust others. . . . You can think everything through yourself and then come to a conclusion." It is empowering, in a society that persistently treats you as dim-witted, to "do your own research" and discover a truth hidden to the so-called experts—particularly for people feeling one-down in the scrum for social honor. Conspiracy theories are a "weapon of the weak" that "eases the pain of uncertainty" by enabling people "to regain a sense of order and control in a society that they perceive to be breaking down." Conspiracy theories also are a demand for attention, "allowing for empowerment and a rebalancing of power within an unequal world." Another study found that conspiracy theories "enable believers to defend a fragile ego by perceiving themselves and their groups as important," which certainly helps explain their attraction for the Missing Middle.[12]

And particularly for men: it allows them to regain the masculine agency that's such a central element of masculinity. Elite men need agency to feel whole, too: they still get it through their jobs. Another study found that people lacking agency may turn to conspiracies in an attempt to regain a sense of control, that conspiracy theories are associated with feelings of powerlessness, and that they are prevalent among low-status groups to explain their lack of status. Another study went looking for reasons and found that people with low education are more likely to believe in conspiracy theories as "the result of the complex interplay of multiple psychological factors that are associated with education," one of which was powerlessness. The others were self-identified social class and belief in straightforward solutions. This last factor again reflects blue-collar beliefs that value common sense over book learning. To quote Daniel Markovits, "The middle class increasingly regards elite schools, universities, and professional firms as places that at best indulge eccentric values and at worst impose those values on everyone else—as clubs, dominated by worthless book learning, political correctness, and arrogant self-dealing." "Keep [your horse] in Madison," a man at a horse auction in Wisconsin advised a visiting ethnographer. "That's where they keep all the bullshit."[13]

The same study identified another overlooked driver of populism: it's fun. Nguyen's intuition is that conspiracy theories are related to entertainment. His comments about conspiracy theories are in a book on games that highlights how games provide a reassuring structure (so different from the craziness and unpredictability of real life) where points can reassure you that you're in control and doing just fine.[14] In an insightful article, David French of *The New York Times* deftly describes the "rage and joy of MAGA America."

It's no coincidence that one of the most enduring cultural symbols of Trump's 2020 campaign was the boat parade. To form battle lines behind Trump, the one man they believe can save America from *total destruction*, thousands of supporters in several states got in their MasterCrafts and had giant open-air water parties.[15]

Trump rallies combine rage and fun, complete with Front Row Joes—superfans who follow Trump in the manner of Deadheads. "For enthusiasts, Trump rallies aren't just a way to see a favorite politician up close. They are major life events: festive opportunities to get together with like-minded folks and just *go crazy* about America and all the winning the Trump administration's doing," notes Andrew Egger. Here's a mind-blower: 70 percent of non-white noncollege Republican voters told pollsters in 2023 they thought Trump was "fun."[16]

Conspiracy theories also offer meaning and purpose "by creating an alternative reality that is exciting, attention-grabbing, and spectacular," finds one study, sort of like other kinds of popular entertainment that increase anxiety—scary movies, gambling, bungee jumping. All this rings true to me because of a driver who picked me up at the airport and drove me to Texas A&M, to give a lecture in 2016, exhorting me excitedly throughout the hour and a half ride about how Hillary Clinton and the Democratic Party were running a pedophilia ring out of a pizza parlor in DC. He clearly felt energized by the conversation and enjoyed the social honor he felt his inside knowledge conferred. And I thought: *Oh-my-God-we're-going-to-lose-this-election.*[17]

Another study reported, "We do not find conspiracism to be a product of greater authoritarianism, ignorance, or political conservatism." Instead, what predicted belief in conspiracy theories was a willingness to believe in other unseen, intentional forces and attraction to Manichaean narratives. This reminds me of some friends who see capitalism as the bogey behind every door, providing an explanation for every evil. Not saying that capitalism isn't a powerful force; it's the Manichaean thinking that gives me pause. Other studies confirm that conspiracy theories exist on the Left as well as the Right.[18]

Note, too, that the mainstreaming of conspiracy theories is a symptom of the loss of trust. Polling shows a plummeting of trust in major institutions in the US. No mystery why: inequality.[19]

Conspiracy theories also function like MAGA hats: they "act as calling cards that send clear signals to co-partisans." They help to bond believers in a like-minded in-group. I would argue that this is a powerful driver of Stop the Steal, which is worth analyzing at length. It's truly troubling that nearly 70 percent of Republicans believe something that has been disproven again and again. The key to Stop the Steal is Salena Zito's comment in 2016 that Trump supporters take the former president "seriously but not literally." Stop the Steal's power stems from its ability to help articulate voters' sense of having been robbed: of their futures and of their social honor. Notice that Bernie Sanders uses a similar metaphor when he says the economy is rigged; anti-elites agreed with him, too.[20]

The fact that Stop the Steal is indisputably untrue strikes me as part of its appeal. It's like the Virgin birth. With apologies to those who believe in it, the Virgin birth is just so obviously nonsense. The first argument my parents ever had was about it, the New England WASP and his Jewish wife. It takes a lot to get people to say with a straight face that someone had a child without ever having sex. It risks ridicule, which is exactly what makes it powerful. Someone who embraces these implausible verities has made the decision that belonging is more important than logic—important enough to risk ridicule by ignoring what everyone knows to be true. That's exactly what makes it so powerful as a precommitment strategy. You lose some people who think it's hokum, but the people who bond around an implausible claim are deeply bonded indeed. All this is exaggerated in an era when polarization increasingly makes politics a totalizing identity, when "rather than simply disagreeing over policy outcomes, we are increasingly blind to our commonalities, seeing each other only as two teams fighting for a trophy."[21]

None of this excuses denying the facts or disregarding science. But all of it has important messages for why otherwise-sane people do so. One Trump voter pinpointed the link between class exploitation and lack of attention to facts: "No one that's voting knows all the facts. It's a shame. They keep us so fucking busy and poor that we don't have the time."[22]

Key Takeaways:

1. Anti-intellectualism and resentment of experts are abiding elements of the American class structure. Both represent the class anger of order-takers against order-givers.

2. If democracy hasn't worked for you and your kind for over forty years, you might think it's time to try something different.

3. Inequality predicts low trust, and low trust predicts conspiracy theories, which are a symptom of how inequality is corroding the social fabric.

4. The very implausibility of Stop the Steal is what makes it effective as a bonding tool—that, and that it taps an emotional truth: many people feel ripped off.

Part III

What's the Matter with Cambridge?

One fish asks another, "How's the water?"
The second fish just stares: "What the hell's the water?"

Liberals typically have come to understand (often after reading and reflection) how deeply pervasive racial privilege is. Class privilege is pervasive, too. An integral part of privilege is not knowing that you, yourself, enjoy that privilege. Just as it takes effort to recognize one's racial privilege, it takes effort to recognize class privilege. To loosen the hold of far-right populism will require college grads to understand how their values reflect their lives, and their lives reflect their privilege. Many of the cultural values and political priorities shared by progressives—including me—are class-specific rather than universal.

Class members absorb "class rules as unspoken, socially valid practices that are largely invisible to them," note social psychologists Cecilia Ridgeway and Susan Fiske. They point out that, for Americans, class is an unsettling (or even embarrassing) topic. This is particularly true because of the comfy stories we tell ourselves about meritocracy, equal opportunity, and the American dream.[1]

Elites use three strategies to ease their embarrassment. One is to discount the existence of class on the grounds that they're just the winners in a meritocracy. The second is to blame the victim, seeing "those below" as suffering from "a cultural deficiency . . . a problem of disposition, of not being able to become the right person." The third is to "absolve themselves of blame by transferring it to the *even more* privileged elite." "Elite college students invoked relative language, using phrases such as 'I only have . . .' or 'I am not *that* rich' to describe (and minimize) their privilege compared to others they viewed as above them in the class hierarchy." Only by abandoning these habits can the privileged begin to recognize their privilege.[2]

Over forty-five years of marriage to a man whose father was a factory worker, I have developed what W. E. B. Du Bois called "double consciousness." Du Bois pointed out that Black people need to be able to see things not just from their own point of view but also from the viewpoint of dominant white society. This entails the process of defamiliarization: we need to learn how to see the water we swim in. My double consciousness went into overdrive after Trump's victory in 2016, when I became hyperaware of class, and with seeing things not only from my own viewpoint as a San Francisco progressive but also from a blue-collar point of view. My goal is to help you cultivate double consciousness, too.[3]

Smart People Get Ahead;
Isn't That Just the Reality?

The Challenger School [helps your child] find joy and self-worth through achievement.

          —Ad on KQED, NPR affiliate in San Francisco, 2023[1]

Kids in today's upper-middle class are two to six times more likely than the average teen to suffer from clinical levels of anxiety and depression. Young adults may be ten times more likely to have a major depressive episode than their parents or grandparents.[2]

That sucks . . . but what does this have to do with economic populism? It's the legacy of decades of neoliberalism, which has taken a toll on elites and non-elites alike.

In today's America, meritocracy codes privilege as merit: it posits that elites get ahead because they're more talented and work harder. Meritocracy fills an abiding cultural niche: "those above" have always explained their wealth and status as the outward sign of their better character than "those below." In aristocracies, the explanation was that aristocrats were more virtuous than non-elites. We still find traces of this in everyday language that embeds assumptions that people without money are people without character. *Villain* stems from *villein*, which was another word for a feudal serf. *Mean* originally meant "of poor quality" but now denotes cruelty—a character flaw. *Poor* is used both to mean someone lacking in money and something lacking in quality ("poor show"). *A class act*, on the other hand, is a person of good character. Virtue signaling in the elite continues this tradition by indicating that cultural beliefs and practices common among elites are signs of good character, while cultural beliefs and practices of non-elites are signs of weak or undeserving character. But whereas in aristocracies (up to and including those in early-twentieth-century America), privilege was justified by presumed virtue, today it is justified by the presumed intelligence and hard work of the privileged.[3]

Few know now that the word *meritocracy* was invented in 1958 as a term of derision in a book that linked it with a dystopian future. The word took off in twentieth-century US as a call to free society of class prejudice. Here's a good example: Yale, where my grandfather (class of 1906) slid by with "gentlemen's Cs," was transformed in the second half of the twentieth century into an institution where admission was (supposedly, at least) based much more on talent. Sounds good, but things started to go awry between 1970 and 1990. Meritocracy came to mean something very different, just as inequality started to blossom.[4]

I believe in meritocracy. When I looked for someone to paint my house, I did not hand a paintbrush to the nearest person with a few days to spare. I looked for, and found, someone who had a good artistic sense of what color would look non-trite but also not outré. I was lucky enough to find Mr. Adili, who painted my bedroom this amazing color-without-a-name that I remember to this day even though I moved out of that house nearly twenty years ago. But I remember it because Mr. Adili did something only artists can do: he changed the way I look at the world. I still see that color in sunsets, just before dark: a gray/purple with an undertone of gold. Mr. Adili was not just an artist; he also was a meticulous craftsman whose prep work yielded walls of unbroken smoothness and precision.

This kind of meritocracy is valuable: it denotes a hierarchy in which the person you choose for a job is the person who has the best skill set for that job. Unfortunately, between 1970 and 1990, meritocracy also came to denote a hierarchy of *value*. It came to mean that some skill sets were infinitely more valuable than others and—guess what?—those held by elites were seen as more valuable than those held by non-elites. This ended the period in the 1930s and 1940s when, partly under the influence of communism, the skills of blue-collar men (gender intended) were highly valued, as evidenced by the heroic mythologizing of blue-collar men in many Works Progress Administration murals in post offices across the country.

New Deal cross-class respect was replaced under neoliberalism by the cult of smartness, epitomized by Obama. He praised "smart grids" more than one hundred times and described his policies and programs as "smart" more than nine hundred times. He loved technical policy language, talking not about health care as a human right but universal coverage as "bending the cost curve." Obama talked not about jobs' link with dignity but about "incentivizing" technological development, small business hiring, clean energy, water development, good nutrition, efficient health care delivery, positive school climates, and weatherization programs.[5]

A central tenet of the cult of smartness is that college is the path to success. Not *one* path but *the* path. Note how meritocracy had shifted from meaning a person with the right skill set for the job to a system of value in which only elites' book learning is defined as valuable. "What you can earn depends on what you can learn," said Bill Clinton more than thirty times during his presidency. "If you don't have a good education," said Obama during his presidency, "then it's going to be hard for you to find a job that pays a living wage." In a shocking expression of liberals' inclination to consign anyone who did not attend college to dead-end, low-paid jobs, Obama once said: "One of the reasons that inequality has probably gone up in our society is that people are being treated closer to the way that they're supposed to be treated." "To the liberal class, every big economic problem is really an education problem, a failure by the losers to learn the right skills and get the credentials everyone knows you'll need in the society of the future," notes Thomas Frank. This blame-the-victim argument glosses over the Merchant Right's success in co-opting the share of productivity that a generation before had gone to workers. Full disclosure: Obama's speech at the 2024 Democratic National Convention showed he's changed. "We need to follow the lead of governors like Tim Walz, who said, 'If you've got the skills and the drive you shouldn't need a degree to work for state government.'"[6]

The neoliberal perversion of meritocracy had consequences. One study found that, by 2018, college grads tended to blame less educated people for their social disadvantage. The study also found that college grads in the UK, the Netherlands, and Germany showed more bias against non-grads than against any other stigmatized group tested, including Muslims and people who are poor, blind, or obese. As for the US, the researchers found that American college grads had more bias against and disliked people who weren't college graduates more than any other stigmatized group, including African Americans. "Disdain for the less educated is the last acceptable prejudice," concludes Michael Sandel.[7]

The transformation is remarkable: meritocracy has turned from a call for *freedom from class prejudice* into a *key vector for class prejudice*. This warping of meritocracy led the noncollege educated, no matter how good they were at their jobs, to feel very left out. Franklin D. Roosevelt's economic bill of rights started off with, "The right to a useful and remunerative job." Every man "regardless of station"—that is, regardless of class—was entitled to a job that was not only remunerative but also "useful," meaning that it added value to society. When you think about it, that's what a job's supposed to be: not a totalizing identity, but a way you make yourself useful enough to your fellows that they'll give you money to keep doing it. This struck with the force of a revelation in 2016 when Michael Long sent me an email in response to an election-night essay I wrote explaining why Trump won: "You don't need a college degree, you need to have a skill that people will pay you for. It's as simple as that." Simple, but too often forgotten when the jobs of the college educated are held as deserving more respect and much more compensation than the jobs of the noncollege educated.[8]

This perversion of meritocracy—its transformation into a set of beliefs that recognizes only the college degree and knowledge jobs as a sign of merit—was accompanied by a new college-for-all ideal. That is, just as neoliberal economics were ending the promise that everyone who found a useful job matched to their skills would have a stable middle-class life and social honor, the Left began arguing that everyone should and could get a college education. What a disaster. First of all, it didn't work; by 2010, thirty years into the college-for-all formula, over two-thirds of Americans lacked college degrees, and the percentage was not budging. At a deeper level, the college-for-all formula erased the dignity of all kinds of jobs that are important. "The Democrats have done best with Medicare, Social Security—when what they do helps everyone. They have emphasized college too much," said D. Taylor, labor leader and longtime head of UNITE HERE.[9]

Meritocracy mutated into a habit of belittling many important kinds of work. The degrading of jobs not requiring a college degree is not an inevitable consequence of globalization. Germany is a notable example. Postwar Germany was hyperaware that widespread prosperity was the best insurance against a return to fascism, so they built a robust manufacturing sector that offered sustained access to good jobs for those without university degrees. To this day, many blue-collar workers earn as much or more than white-collar workers. Germany never went down the college-for-all route; instead, they offered social honor and a stable middle-class life for people without university degrees.[10]

The college-for-all ideal was humiliating to noncollege grads, implying they lacked the intelligence, foresight, and/or discipline to do what it takes to succeed. Bad on them. You notice how lack of opportunity is coded as a character flaw? And how meritocracy is functioning to let elites off the hook for robbing non-elites of their right to a middle-class future in the richest country in the world? No surprise that, by 2016, many construction projects were being delayed for lack of plumbers and other skilled workers. Meanwhile, confidence in higher education among noncollege Americans has declined by 25 points since 2015.[11]

College, once celebrated as the great leveler, has become a way to perpetuate class privilege. Thanks again to Raj Chetty's team, we now know that two-thirds of students at Ivy League universities come from the top 20 percent of Americans (by household income). At Yale and Princeton, more students come from the top 1 percent than from the bottom 60 percent. A child from the professional elite is three times more likely to be admitted to a selective private institution than a lower-class white kid with similar qualifications. Not surprising, then, that half of high-earning parents' economic advantage is passed on to their children in the US, more than twice the earnings advantage in Canada, Denmark, Finland, and Norway.[12]

The use of education to perpetuate class privilege starts well before college itself. "The richer a student's family, the higher the SAT score he or she is likely to receive," notes Sandel. Abandoning the SAT and relying only on grades didn't help: after all, grades are influenced by class advantage, too. Affluent parents regularly hire tutors if a kid is struggling. They also pressure teachers to raise kids' grades out of a sense of entitlement or fear over the impact of bad grades on their kids' futures. And strong grade point averages of non-elite students are often suspect because they aren't from the "right" schools or school districts. Meanwhile, elites can afford extracurriculars, which have become a way to get that edge in a ridiculously competitive environment, as more and more kids try more and more desperately to get into the "right" schools. Elite white kids participated in an average of 4.6 organized activities a week; elite Black kids participated in even more (5.2). One ethnographer tried hard to find upper-middle-class kids who did not participate in any organized activities. She found none. Making it to a top school seems so crucial because the winner-take-all sweepstakes has also affected American colleges: the top-earning male college graduate now earns 90 percent more than a low-earning one, up from 70 percent for men and 60 percent for women in 1979. And making it into top schools became much harder: admission rates at the fifty most competitive American universities dropped by 45 percent between 2006 and 2008. At the top ten, admissions have dropped from about 16 percent to 3 percent.[13]

Non-elites pay a steep price for our current perversion of the ideal of meritocracy—but so do elites. Neoliberalism's winner-take-all version of meritocracy is now corroding the quality of life even for elites. In elite families, the pace is frenetic. Parents "rush home, rifle through the mail, prepare snacks, make sure their children are appropriately dressed and have proper equipment for the upcoming activity, find their car keys, put the dog outside, load the children and equipment into the car, lock the door, and drive off." Annette Lareau calls this "the ideology of *concerted cultivation*"; I call it the Great American Speedup in family life.[14]

It's matched by the Great American Speedup in work life. Concerted cultivation is preparation for a life of work devotion. Work hours in the elite increased sharply during neoliberal decades between 1970 and 1990. By the turn of the new millennium, 40 percent of college-educated men and 14 percent of college-educated women worked more than 50 hours a week. "Bankers' hours" and leaving at 3:00 to play golf gave way to extreme schedules displayed as evidence of work devotion. Take just one example: corporate law. In the 1960s, a full-time schedule meant that lawyers billed an average of 1,300 hours a year—about 35 hours a week. Even in the 1980s, corporate lawyers were upper-middle class, but they weren't rich, and the path to law firm partnership was often about six years. Today, law is a profession run by a magazine: *The American Lawyer* list of top law firms, which heavily weights "profits per partner." The result is a winner-take-all arms race in which a few partners make millions of dollars—salaries supported by having the lawyers below them bill as much as 2,300 hours a year, which requires working about 60 hours a week.[15]

Blue-collar workers arguably have their heads screwed on straighter when "they carefully distinguish their own work ethic from what they call overachieving." "If you're going to make it twenty, twenty-five years out here, you've got to pace yourself. I pull my own weight so no one has to cover for me, but I'm not going to break my back for this company," said one blue-collar guy. Upper-middle-class workers have lost sight of this basic truth: their employers want them to overwork so they can make more money off them. Meanwhile, upper-middle-class people "often view ambition, dynamism, a strong work ethic, and competitiveness as doubly sacred because they signal both moral and socioeconomic worth."[16]

Just as parents' outlandish work hours reflect a fear of falling in the winner-take-all economy, so does children's tailorized leisure, which reflects parents' anxieties that children won't "make it" in an economy where the losers really, really lose out. There's an unsettling mixture of parents' concern for kids and parents' striving for social honor. For rural working-class families, notes Jennifer Sherman, children's achievements may be a source of pride, "but they were seldom a main source of the parents' self-worth. More important were the moral achievements of the parents themselves." Compare this with what a Stanford dean called the "competitive over-parenting" of elites, where performance pressure on elite kids is driven by the scrum for social status amongst their parents. I'm not saying I didn't do this; I'm saying I now regret doing it.[17]

The frantic effort to ensure that "every child is above average" extracts tolls on family life that are rarely acknowledged. Moreover, the term *concerted cultivation* veils that it's chiefly mothers who to do it; it's really an "intensive mothering" ideal (to quote sociologist Sharon Hays). Wives sideline their careers to chauffeur children to a complex quilt of activities, leaving both themselves and their children economically vulnerable should they divorce. The Great American Speedup at home frays family relationships. Lareau found tense relationships between siblings, much more so in elite than poor and working-class families. Perhaps this is because, as Lareau also points out, older children's activities determine the schedule for the whole family, which means that younger children often spend their time driving to or killing time at older siblings' travel soccer and music lessons.[18]

The message sent is that achievement is more important than family life. Lareau describes a child who decides to skip an important family gathering because soccer is "more of a priority." Family dinners often fall by the wayside so activities can stretch into the late evening. When social honor demands that every child be above average, the pressure on elite kids becomes hydraulic.[19]

In *Never Enough: When Achievement Culture Becomes Toxic—And What We Can Do About It*, Jennifer Breheny Wallace ties toxic achievement culture directly to "status safeguarding, a term that describes the decades-long project of ensuring that your offspring don't suffer a generational decline in standing." Inequality has gotten so bad that even professional elites' lives are dominated by the fear of falling. This fear is not unrealistic: millennials on average have lower earnings, fewer assets, and less wealth than prior generations had at their age. "Safeguarding generally falls to the mother": it's become the new reason for women to marginalize their careers. Since the 1970s, American parents have doubled the amount of time they spend on kids, with the largest increase on academic activities like reading to children and helping with homework. "When we talk about pressure, perfectionism, anxiety, depression, and loneliness in kids, what we are really talking about is an unmet need to feel valued unconditionally, away from the trophies, the acceptance letters, the likes, and the accolades." More than 70 percent of the young adults Wallace surveyed reported that they thought their parents "valued and appreciated" them more when they were successful in school. More than half thought their parents loved them more when they're successful. To quote one mother in Palo Alto, "Parents say that they just want their kids to be happy, but what they really mean, and their kids know this, is that they want them to be happy like they are, with the prestigious job and the big house." Two prestigious high schools in Palo Alto, the Silicon Valley city adjacent to Stanford, have suffered multiple suicide clusters and ten-year suicide rates four to five times the national average. Tragically, some kids throw themselves in front of trains. One student described the Caltrain morning whistle, heard in classrooms about every twenty minutes, as "like the cannon that goes off in *The Hunger Games* every time a kid dies." This is unspeakably tragic.[20]

Non-elite parents want their kids to succeed in life, too, of course, but typically, the focus is on raising "good kids." Children in non-elite families participate in far fewer organized activities: African American kids average 2.8 activities a week; white kids average 2.3. Non-elites "see adult life as hard and pressured, and want their kids to spend time happy and relaxed before the pressures of life set in." Lareau notes that elite children's lives are so structured by adults that kids often feel disoriented and unsure of themselves when they have unstructured time. In contrast, she describes non-elite Tyrec who "needs no adult assistance to pursue the great majority of his plans." His group of neighborhood friends "functions without adult monitoring [so] he learned how to construct and sustain friendships on his own," something elite kids often depend on their mothers to do. Tyrec's informal play allowed him "to develop skills in peer mediation, conflict management, personal responsibility, and strategizing." She observes: "Tyrec learned important life skills not available to [upper-middle-class] Garrett. He and his friends found numerous ways of entertaining themselves, showing creativity and independence." The pressure-cooker environment in elite homes often strikes non-elites as off. "I just kept thinking these kids don't know how to play," commented a nanny from a self-described "hillbilly" family. While acknowledging that all the activities might pay off "job-wise," Lareau's poor and working-class informants expressed reservations. "He must be dead-dog tired," said one. "I think he doesn't enjoy what he's doing at the time," said another woman, laughing ruefully.[21]

To me, treating non-elites as intelligent, insightful people with their heads screwed on straight can help heal not only American politics; it can help heal a society where even elites' lives are being distorted by ever-spiraling inequality. Among other things, class blindness impedes elites' ability to see the costs kids pay for the Great American Speedup.

I made all the predictable mistakes myself—that's why I believe it's so important that elites back off competitive over-parenting. It's time to listen to the less privileged Americans who never stopped trying to just raise good kids.

Key Takeaways:

1. Under neoliberalism, meritocracy changed from the principle of rewarding excellence in any field into a claim that only elite jobs reflect merit. This transmuted a call for freedom from class prejudice into a key vector for class prejudice.
2. The college-for-all ideal was flawed by its erasure of the social value of many blue-, pink-, and routine white-collar jobs. It also was a failure: two-thirds of Americans lack college degrees.
3. College, once celebrated as the great leveler, has become a way to perpetuate class privilege.
4. Neoliberalism not only gutted the futures of many in the Missing Middle; its winner-take-all ethic has placed elite children under hydraulic performance pressures that non-elites see as unhealthy—and they're probably right.

It's a Battle Between Sophisticated Global Citizens and Parochial Ethno-Nationalists, Right?

"Open" meant the free flow of capital, goods and people across borders. To object in any way to that was to be closed-minded, prejudiced and hostile to cosmopolitan identities.

—Michael Sandel[1]

Sometimes a look can say a lot. I was living in Leiden, a university town in the Netherlands, trying to buy a bike because in the Netherlands, you're not a person without a bike. I went to a bike shop, where I greeted the shop owner in English. I thought nothing of it: every single Dutch person I had ever met addressed me in English, except for one who assumed I was German.

The shop owner responded very differently. He gave me a look that combined shame, anger, and Dutch good manners. He told me in Dutch that he didn't speak English. In a split second, I understood what it's like to be left behind in the Netherlands, to feel shamed by speaking your own language in your own country. And I understood why educated Dutch elites had been told in no uncertain terms that they needed to speak Dutch rather than English during official ceremonies. When I received an honorary degree, my hosts apologized profusely that much of the ceremony would be in Dutch. Speaking Dutch in the presence of a foreigner struck them as bad manners; the shop owner's anger and shame suggested to me an attitude toward elites that made me worry that the Far Right would gain strength in the Netherlands. It has: in 2023, far-right populist Geert Wilders and his PVV party won a thirty-seven-seat plurality in the legislature.[2]

A second snapshot comes from the US. In *Hollowing Out the Middle: The Rural Brain Drain and What It Means for America*, Patrick J. Carr and

Maria J. Kefalas studied kids in rural areas, painting a vivid picture of the different dispositions of those who leave, those who stay, and those who come back: the Achievers, the Stayers, and the Boomerangs. Teachers lavished attention on Achievers like Rose, who grew up so poor her "winter boots consisted of plastic bread sacks wrapped around last year's shoes." But her academic talent meant that she became a teacher's pet; she soon recognized that "different rules applied to her than to the town's privileged sons and daughters. 'I mean, I could always do anything. I didn't, but I got away with stuff that I know I shouldn't have, and that the other kids couldn't have.'" With her teachers' support, she went on to college and moved on to a "new life of upscale comfort and privilege in the D. C. suburbs."[3]

The Stayers have quite a different experience. "Stayers do not drift off course in school without the complicity of adults. When they skipped class, no one came looking for them, and when they didn't turn in their homework, their parents shrugged their shoulders and told them to find a job." Overwhelmingly male, Stayers typically worked twenty or thirty hours a week on top of attending school, so they were puzzled that their teachers saw them as lazy. "Work was something I was raised to do," said one, but working hard and playing by the rules no longer paid off: "What were solid, middle-class jobs a generation ago have now become barely subsistence." "There's no ladder to climb," said Dave, aged twenty-five. These men want what their fathers had: masculine dignity through hard work.[4]

The third group in rural areas, the Boomerangs, are predominantly women. Typically, they complete two-year programs at vocational schools or community college, only to return when they find "the values of the world beyond do not match up with what they believe to be important." Melissa, aged thirty, explained that she dropped out of her premed program at the University of Iowa because "it was very intimidating. . . . I didn't like college; it was a whole bunch of what I wasn't used to. I was used to small-town Iowa . . . And this was little rich kids from Chicago . . . and that just didn't fit my lifestyle. And it was a lot more open-minded than I was used to in terms of ideals and people and clothing and everything." Note that Melissa defined her discomfort in part by reference to class ("rich kids"). She returned home, married a guy from the adjacent county, and became a bank manager.[5]

Madeline Spencer was another Stayer who tried out college for a year before returning home to get a community college degree in medical administration. "Maybe if I had grown up in a big city, like Minneapolis," she said, she would have wanted to pursue her original degree in accounting, but "I don't want to even try to be a Superwoman. I'd rather hang out with the kids on the floor." Like other Stayers, she felt the pull of traditional gender roles.[6]

Many deep insights into American politics can be derived from *Hollowing Out the Middle*, but for now, I want to focus on one: "The Stayers don't long for change and adventure," note Carr and Kefalas. Scholars have found that people who migrate tend to differ from those who don't in two personality traits: extroversion and openness. Extroverts, who feel comfortable in groups of strangers, are more likely to move within their own state. People high in openness to new experiences are nearly twice as likely to move to a new state. Low openness, in contrast, gives individuals a taste for "stability, familiarity, inherited wisdom, satisfaction in the done thing and a wariness of change."[7]

Notice the terminology. *Low openness* could be called a "preference for stability." It's not, perhaps because college-educated people named this category. What they value is openness; a preference for stability is coded as a deficit in openness. Stability, of course, is precisely what's valued by the Missing Middle. Elites' intense focus on self-development and sophistication translates into a strong cultural preference for novelty. A taste for the novel and artisanal is a way of displaying sophistication, whether it's hiking in Bhutan, watching avant-garde theater, or eating bugs and grasshoppers on a Mexico City food tour. After around 1970, this taste for novelty and edginess meant that the working-class anchors of stability (faith, family, and patriotism) came to be seen as unsophisticated, as hippie counterculture was co-opted into an enactment of class status. "Highly educated, curious, ironic, wittily countercultural," to quote David Brooks, who called the post-hippie elite the *bobos*: bourgeois Bohemians. Think Steve Jobs, Elon Musk, and all the other billionaires who fancy themselves rebels. This turn of mind is epitomized by a mug advertising *The Nation*, which boasts the lettering "Insubordi(nation)." For elites, insubordination is interpreted as fearless self-actualizing—thinking for yourself. For non-elites, it's just another way to get fired.[8]

Those who leave differ from those who stay (to quote the title of Elena Ferrante's novel about class) in cultural as well as psychological ways. Elite culture's celebration of self-actualization means that bobos place a higher value on expressive individualism than community, as documented in a series of studies by social psychologist Nicole Stephens. She and Hazel Markus found that telling first-generation college men that the car they wanted was also chosen by someone else made them like it *more*, whereas telling elite men the same thing made them like it less. Non-elites' prefer solidarity over individualism because life and safety can depend on fellow workers in blue-collar jobs. "We've got to watch out for each other first," said one miner. "We are supposed to support each other, not tear each other down," said another. This is the cultural value unions sculpt into labor solidarity; too often, in political science scales, it shows up as conformity, a lack of individualism, or, worse, a tendency toward authoritarianism.[9]

Rural residents are higher in communality than city dwellers. Rural Organizing found that 89 percent of rural respondents agreed with this message: "In small towns and rural communities we believe in looking out for each other, whether we're white, Black or brown, tenth generation or newcomers." Ethnographers find the same. Remember Tommy and Liza for whom "the good life was not in material success, but in knowing they have social support, from their community."[10]

All this translates into place loyalty. A 2017 study found that more than two-thirds of whites without college degrees still live in their hometown or within a two-hour drive from it. *Trump's Democrats* explained the deep appeal of one of Trump's mottos, America First. In all three towns, "the identity of [their] citizens cannot be easily divorced from the town itself." "When a big company comes in, I always try to have them sign an agreement [to hire local citizens]." Loyalty to place includes loyalty to country. "I've always kinda been a made-in-America person . . . [If] I'm looking at a bucket made in Wisconsin for $8, you know, and a bucket made in China for $5.50, I'm going to buy the eight-dollar bucket. There is just something in my soul that tells me, hey, I'm going to do that." This sentiment has been incubated in unions: "And if you were a union member and went to the union hall in a Toyota, you might get your ass beat," one man recalled. A union member told his sister when she bought a Honda, "It's not American-made. You're just sending jobs someplace else." During the period when elites in both parties embraced unfettered free trade, "the American public remained stubbornly protectionist" until Trump changed both parties' positions to bring them back in sync with public opinion.[11]

Place loyalty fuels both patriotism and nationalism, which are higher among non-elite Americans than elites. Americans with only high school eduction or less are twice (30 percent) as likely as those with postgraduate education (16 percent) to think the US is the best country. The Brahmin Left's disdain for this brand of patriotism is an example of class parochialism. Non-elites are proud of being Americans for the same reason elites aren't: everyone stresses the highest-status categories they belong to, which is why elites are so proud they are global citizens (a.k.a. members of a globalized *elite*.) But for non-elites, being American is one of the few high-status categories they inhabit. A 2020 poll found that being American was an important part of the identity of 79 percent of Americans with (at most) high school degrees, but only 43 percent of predominantly college-educated progressive activists.[12] Fully 40 percent of those with high school or less said that displaying the flag was important to being a good American, compared with only 24 percent of post-grads.[13]

Michèle Lamont notes the importance of patriotism to blue-collar men: "Workers are busy keeping moral order not only in their home and neighborhood but also in the world at large. Notably, these themes never emerged in the interviews I conducted with managers and professionals." Patriotism is particularly highly valued in rural regions: "Service is important for rural folks, country is important, patriotism is important," said former secretary of agriculture Tom Vilsack. Progressive activists are again outliers on the question of whether "America is a better country than most others": only 8 percent strongly agree, compared with 81 percent of Americans in general.[14]

Place loyalty also reflects class-based differences both in social honor and in the organization of intimacy. Elites' social honor stems from their jobs, so it's portable from Boston to Berlin to Mumbai. Not so for non-elites, who are offended by efforts to have their work define their identity. I've often told the anecdote of returning to my husband's high school reunion, where—forgetting the rules of the game in Rust Belt Waterbury—he asked one of his former classmates, "What do you do?" The classmate got visibly angry and very close and said loudly, "I SELL *TOILETS.*"

To elites, work offers honor. Non-elites prefer to hang out with people who understand that they're not just the toilet guy. My brother-in-law still hangs out in the same bar, with the same friends he went to high school with. When we happened into it one evening, we recognized a depth and density of social bonds that is lacking in our lives. We've lived life as an elite that grows up and flies away.

Place loyalty also reflects non-elites' organization of intimacy. "In the working class, the world of reciprocal invitations, spontaneous or organized, is restricted to the family and the world of familiars who can be treated as 'one of the family,'" notes Bourdieu. Working-class parents expect children to remain in their social networks, unlike elites who expect kids to fly the coop. Notes sociologist Marjorie DeVault, "working-class families live relatively close to their relatives and spend a large part of their social time with kin. Husbands and wives often have separate social groups, and their friends tend to be local people they have known for many years." They "are often immersed in tight networks of sociability, in part because their extended family often resides within a few miles (the children appear to spend considerable time visiting cousins)," reports Lamont. She describes close connections among relatives in poor and working-class families, noting that adults "speak daily with their brothers and sisters and their parents."[15]

Typically, elites have broad "entrepreneurial networks" of acquaintances, while non-elites have smaller "clique networks" anchored by deep relationships. These networks play economic as well as social roles. Neighbors and relatives help non-elites get access to good jobs; when my husband got his summer jobs, it was through a woman his mom knew at the unemployment office. He joked his mom had friends in low places.

Today, most non-elites are reluctant to move for a better job because that's very risky in their world. They stick close to home because a small network of family and friends they've known forever sustains them both economically and emotionally. That network provides childcare, eldercare, help fixing the car—necessities of life they can't take for granted. Equally important, that network offers blue-collar families something not provided by their less-than-prestigious jobs: respect. The respect point is important. So is the fact that non-elites' clique network protects families with limited disposable income from the low quality of the services they could afford to buy: one study found that childcare quality is poorest for the Missing Middle.[16]

This helps explain why non-elites are so reluctant to move: You need to find not just a job (or two jobs for many families), but jobs that pay so much more that you'll still come out ahead even after paying for childcare and eldercare you got for free in your hometown. The ways the twentieth-century attenuated family ties have received a lot of attention, but the ways late-twentieth-century economic changes enhanced family ties often get overlooked, perhaps because this pattern affects non-elites more than elites.

Even then, you can't move. The gap between winner-take-all cities and the heartland now yawns so large that moving to the city has become unrealistic. Real wages for noncollege grads in big cities have actually fallen: recall that a janitor who moves today from the Deep South to Silicon Valley would see his after-housing income fall 30 percent.[17]

You often hear that elites are comfortable anywhere while non-elites aren't. This is a theme of David Goodhart's influential *The Road to Somewhere: The Populist Revolt and the Future Politics*, which posits a dichotomy between Somewheres and Anywheres. But that's not quite true. The reality is that the Boston-Berlin-Mumbai crowd feels no more comfortable in rural Kansas than blue-collar Americans feel in hipster Brooklyn. It's truer to say that non-elites often are place loyal to their own hometowns, while elites can feel comfortable anywhere—as long as it's in another superstar city. Here I think of Ezra Klein admitting that he realizes that his algorithm always sends him to cafés that look alike, whether he's in Tokyo, LA, Berlin, or Beijing. Is this more cosmopolitan or just a different set of parochial preferences?[18]

And yet the truism that elites are cosmopolitan helps explain why it is so easy for them to forget the left-behind areas of their own country. A dramatic illustration is "effective altruism," beloved of cryptocurrency entrepreneur Sam Bankman-Fried. Throughout the nineteenth and into the twentieth century, elites focused on building civic institutions in their own cities. Effective altruism says that philanthropy should take a global perspective, guided by where the money will have the most impact, aka poor countries. But the result is to defund local institutions. Effective altruism is the darling of the financial elite set, who also played a central role in gutting regional businesses by loading them up with debt only to institute "cost savings" in the form of pay cuts and layoffs and the selling-off of assets that left factories shuttered. We need to get more cosmopolitan about what we consider cosmopolitan.

Key Takeaways:

1. Place loyalty and patriotism reflect that while elites place a higher value on expressive individualism, non-elites place a higher value on solidarity and community.

2. Place loyalty reflects the material conditions of non-elite lives, which rely on relatives, neighbors, and friends for many services elites buy on the market.

3. Non-elites' social honor is not highly transferable because it's based on personal relationships rather than impersonal degrees or pedigrees.

4. Everyone stresses the high-status categories they belong to. Non-elites are patriotic because that's one of the few high-status categories they can claim.

Aren't the College-Educated
Just More Enlightened?

In this house, we believe:
Black lives matter
Women's rights are human rights
No human is illegal
Science is real
Love is love
Kindness is everything

This yard sign epitomizes the feeling rules of the Brahmin Left, who establish their moral bona fides by expressing empathy for the struggles of African Americans, women, and immigrants. (Feeling rules govern how one *should* feel.) Note that class privilege is left out. Adding fuel to the fire is the message that anyone failing to embrace these sentiments is ignorant ("Science is real") and so morally flawed they don't believe in either love or kindness.[1]

I understand that this sign is coming from an idealistic place, but every time I read it, I hear echoes of my beloved German-Jewish grandmother scoffing at her rabbi husband's Russian-Jewish congregation as "those peasants." This attitude persists. Remember the Louisiana woman who said she *loved* Rush Limbaugh because she felt he was defending her against liberals' insults.[2]

Feeling rules that mandate empathy for immigrants but disdain for non-elites of one's own country are bound to backfire. Not only do they hand a loaded gun to the Far Right; they hurt precisely the groups we progressives care about, by sculpting class anger into fury against immigrants, women, and people of color. Remember how you hated "teachers' pets"? Having someone in power lift up one person or group but leave others behind pits the less powerful against one another.

The sign's message is that the family inside has enlightened views and that anyone who disagrees with them is unenlightened. But isn't that true? How could anyone not prioritize the plight of vulnerable refugees?

Here's where to start: recognize that feeling rules are social conventions. An insightful exploration of this idea is by historian Thomas Haskell, who asked why, given that people had been enslaved for millennia, did slavery come to be seen as immoral quite suddenly in the eighteenth century? Haskell pointed out that we all draw arbitrary boundaries around our ambit of social responsibility.

> As I sit at my desk writing this essay, and as you, the reader, now sit reading it, both of us are aware that some people in Phnom Penh, Bombay, Rangoon, the Sahel, and elsewhere will die next week of starvation. They are strangers; all we know about them is that they will die. . . . Why do we not go to their aid? It is not for lack of ethical maxims teaching us that it is good to help strangers. Presumably, we all subscribe to the Golden Rule, and certainly if we were starving, we would hope that some stranger would care enough to drop his daily routine and come to our aid. And yet we sit here.[3]

Haskell points out that "the limits of moral responsibility have to be drawn somewhere and that the 'somewhere' will always fall far short of much pain and suffering that we could do something to alleviate." Before the middle of the eighteenth century, enslaved people fell outside that ambit of social responsibility, so that "even the most scrupulous and compassionate men and women did not feel obliged to go to the aid of suffering slaves."[4]

We live in a world in which seven hundred million people face chronic hunger and millions live in places torn apart by violence. Non-elites don't see those suffering people as within their ambit of social responsibility.[5] To quote just two:

> We are drowning right now. Our vets are homeless. There's one out of every five American children starving right now. And Clinton wants to open the floodgates and let everybody else in.[6]

> In America we have hungry, we have veterans, we have mental illness, we have so many problems in our own country that we at this point in time just can't be concerned with, I feel bad, but . . . our country's in dire straits financially.[7]

"I feel bad, but ..." This shows an awareness of the Golden Rule, but also the sense that the 281 million migrants worldwide aren't their responsibility in a country that's failing to protect the vulnerable inside its own borders. True, many immigrants are fleeing countries due to conditions created by US foreign policy. But I suspect that lower-middle-class people are unlikely to feel that past geostrategic mistakes by political elites take precedence over their blue-collar focus on the needy in their own communities.[8]

A study of Silicon Valley entrepreneurs, surveyed in 2017 when they were still virtually all Democrats, helps explain lower-middle-class impatience with elite attitudes toward immigration. The entrepreneurs were overwhelmingly in favor of immigration, but they also were dead set against unions and government regulation that would protect their workers. It's easy to see why a working-class person would think these entrepreneurs were not enlightened at all: they supported immigration because they rely on immigration of computer scientists to work in their companies and of nannies and gardeners to care for their kids and estates. You don't have to read many stories of exploited Tesla workers to recognize that those workers were outside these entrepreneurs' ambit of social responsibility. So were the many so-called independent contractors and freelancers who form up to over 40 percent of the tech workforce, sometimes doing the same jobs as employees—without the health and retirement benefits that are essential to a middle-class life.[9]

Perhaps you're thinking, *But that's not me.* But the house sign with which this chapter begins draws its residents' ambit of social responsibility the same way, to include immigrants but not the lower-middle-class people who struggle on the margins of the economy and who voted for Trump. Progressive activists have very cold feelings toward Trump voters. This sentiment is widespread and deeply embedded in elite common sense. Maladroit politicians make it explicit, as when Hillary Clinton said, "You know, to just be grossly generalistic, you could put half of Trump's supporters into what I call the basket of deplorables. Right? The racist, sexist, homophobic, xenophobic, Islamophobic—you name it. And unfortunately there are people like that."[10]

The problem isn't merely that she said it; the worse problem is that it reflects feelings common among the Brahmin Left. When Trump won in 2016, Bette Midler tweeted that West Virginians are "poor, illiterate, and strung out." She's right: 90 percent of counties with persistent poverty are rural, and opioid addiction is concentrated in rural areas . . . but since when did liberals start making fun of poor people? Midler later apologized, but such sentiments are heard far too often. Comments in *The New York Times* call rural people "angry illiterates," "country bumpkins," "not capable of logic," and "rural leftovers [who] are dying out anyway." "Rural America, you didn't get left behind—you chose not to keep up," said SundaeDivine, a Trump-basher with 111,000 Twitter/X followers. Comments like these are easily weaponized on social media to reinforce the narrative that liberals look down on rural and noncollege voters.[11]

The assumption that liberals are enlightened and that those who disagree with them are dinosaurs who are dying off anyway shows up not just in snarky social media but in the work of influential academics. A preeminent example is the "backlash" thesis of Pippa Norris and Ronald Inglehart, which posits a dichotomy between "libertarian" and "authoritarian" values. The arc of history, Norris said on the Ezra Klein podcast, bends toward libertarian values, "like a tide which is moving in a single direction" as those who disagree are dying out. This thesis has been extraordinarily influential, both in political science (their book has been cited over four thousand times) and in the popular press—despite the fact that its methodology has been roundly criticized.[12]

The backlash thesis is distorted by class blindness. "Class identities weakened," opined Pippa Norris in her interview with Ezra Klein, but that's not what her data shows. She codes people as "authoritarian" if they "believe it's important to behave properly," that "people should do what they're told," that "tradition is important," that "it's important to live in secure surroundings," and that government should secure people from threats.

These are not anti-democratic sentiments; they represent the survival strategies of non-elites. They value rule following because that's what it takes to succeed as order-takers in blue-, pink-, and routine white-collar jobs. They value tradition both as an aid to self-discipline and as a source of social honor. They value safety because they can't take it for granted the way elites can. They're more likely than elites to experience the world as a dangerous and uncertain place because, for them, it often is. And believing that kids should be well-behaved is not the same as supporting "authoritarian values that threaten the liberal norms underpinning American democracy," to quote Norris and Inglehart.[13]

Political science scales that denigrate non-elites are not uncommon. A prime example is a 2018 article that found that "neurotic traits positively predicted share of Brexit and Trump votes, and Trump gains from Romney." Those neurotic traits included depression and anxiety, which were higher among the economically precarious people who supported the Far Right for a simple reason: economic precarity makes people anxious and bummed out. Calling far-right voters neurotic turns economic precarity from a social justice issue into a personality defect.[14]

A large literature claims to link authoritarianism with working-class parenting styles. This linkage goes back to Theodor Adorno in the 1950s, when Adorno, a member of the Frankfurt School, linked strict parenting styles with economic hardship. That link has been lost.[15]

A particularly dramatic example is work by linguist George Lakoff, who has been influential in political science. He contrasted "strict father" and "nurturant parent" values. "Strict father" values stress self-discipline, hard work, respect for authority, and being well-behaved—precisely what order-takers teach their children so they can succeed in the best jobs available to them. "Nurturant parent" values stress that children be "fulfilled and happy in their lives," develop their "potential for achievement and enjoyment," and "explore the range of ideas the world has to offer"—precisely what order-givers teach their children so they can succeed in the best jobs available to them.[16]

What's most striking about Lakoff is how he chooses sides: "I should say at the outset that virtually all of the mainstream experts on child-rearing see the strict father model as being destructive to children. A nurturant parent is preferred." No wonder: Lakoff associates the "nurturing parent" style with someone for whom "love, empathy and nurturance are primary," who has "a lifelong relationship of mutual respect, communication, and caring" with their children. Is it just me, or did he just say that working-class parents don't share fundamental human virtues like love and empathy and lack lifelong caring relationships with their children? Here's a working-class mom describing what it means to be a good parent: "Just taking the time to ask your child, you know, how was your day, and what do you think about this? . . . You know, just sort of taking the time to let them know that they matter to you." Sounds like nurturance and empathy to me.[17]

Lakoff's "nurturant parenting" is a singularly self-congratulatory description of the concerted cultivation practiced by elites. Lakoff overlooks entirely the performance pressures incident to competitive parenting. If Lakoff recognized his scale as a scale of class privilege, I doubt he would take such a smug tone. Once again class blindness allows the casual translation of class privilege into moral superiority.

Norris and Inglehart's backlash thesis has been received uncritically because it provides an explanation for why populism has arisen not just in the US but also throughout Europe. But there's an alternative explanation: far-right populists filled the representation gap by appealing to the Missing Middle voters with liberal economic views and conservative social views. The second reason the backlash thesis is popular is that it affirms elite "common sense" that their beliefs will inevitably triumph "almost like a tidal pattern. Of course, every generation is more liberal, more tolerant, more open than the one that came before it," and liberals need not worry about leftover authoritarians who are dying out anyway. "We hypothesize that socially liberal values are spreading through intergenerational population replacement and demographic shifts," assert Norris and Inglehart serenely. To quote political strategist Michael Podhorzer, "Confirmation bias is a hell of a drug."[18]

Key Takeaways:

1. Feeling rules that mandate empathy for immigrants and people of color but scorn for non-elites sculpt class anger into anger against immigrants and people of color.
2. Non-elites' place loyalty shapes how they define their ambit of social responsibility. No one includes everyone they *could* help within the scope of those they *should* help. Elites and non-elites draw that line differently.
3. The deplorables narrative—that non-elites are morally flawed—is embedded in scales and interpretations that are influential in political science and popular culture.

Aren't Elites Just Less Racist?

One marker of having progressive politics is displaying
oneself as antiracist, and this can, at times, unfortunately
manifest as a demeaning of and distancing from white
working-class people, who are constructed as stupid and
racist.

—Julie Bettie[1]

Racism still pervades virtually every area of American life, and the post–
George Floyd era in which anti-racism is seen as nonnegotiable is an
important step forward. That said, too often, college-educated elites dis-
place blame for racism onto less elite whites. However, racism is a white
people problem—not a working-class problem. We need to stop using
anti-racism as an excuse for snobbery. MDs, PhDs, and MBAs don't score
lower for implicit racial bias than high school grads do. But styles of racism differ by social class: college-educated whites who pride themselves
on merit see people of color, and Blacks in particular, as lacking in merit.
Noncollege-educated whites who pride themselves on morality see people
of color, and Blacks in particular, as lacking in morality. Imagining racism
as a simple on-off binary is a mistake: one reason it's so persistent is that
it's shape-shifting, providing rich cultural resources for people to use in
the scrum for resources and social honor.[2]

Working-class racism has been extensively documented. In 1977, Paul
Willis's classic study noted how working-class men's sense of white superiority softened the blow of the hidden injuries of class. In the 1990s,
Michèle Lamont found that 60 percent of white-collar workers and
63 percent of blue-collar workers used racist logic or arguments. Their
"work ethic and the defense of traditional morality are the main criteria

white workers used to place themselves above Blacks." Lamont quoted one white worker:

> Blacks have a tendency to . . . try to get off doing less, the least possible . . . to keep the job, where whites will put that extra oomph in. I know this is a generality and it does not go for all, it goes for a portion. It's this whole unemployment and welfare gig. A lot of the Blacks on welfare have no desire to get off it.[3]

Lamont also found workers who were convinced that African Americans lack family values. Said a pipe fitter, "I could have ended up stealing cars and stuff too if I wanted. I was brought up better than that . . . I think they have less family values." In the 1990s, white workers blamed African Americans for the same conditions that now undermine white workers' families, for high rates of nonmarital childbearing and family breakup, attributing those conditions to lack of character instead of economic stress. There's even some evidence that in the UK racism has diminished among white elites while growing among non-elites: a British study found that overt prejudice against people of color had declined among managers and professionals (to 20 percent in 2013 from 33 percent in 1991) but increased (from 20 percent to 41 percent) among unskilled manual workers. When Working America organizers interviewed Trump voters in 2017, "they heard deeply troubling characterizations of immigrants and people of color, and felt that on this issue more than any other, a real sense of menace has been injected into the national debate."[4]

Do I find all this disturbing? Definitely. One Trump voter said immigrants "come over here, populate like rabbits and are trying to enact sharia law across America."[5]

It would be insane to deny the deep and pervasive influence of racism on American politics. But my perspective is shaped by my decades of studying racial bias in professional workplaces. Around 2012, I started studying how gender bias played out in professional workplaces. What I did was simple: every time I met a truly savvy woman, I would ask her for forty-five minutes of her time. Then I recited my seven-minute summary of forty years of studies on gender bias and asked her if any of that sounded familiar (96 percent said yes).

But after close to a hundred interviews, I realized that I was a typical white woman: because my networks were largely white, and so were my subjects. I realized that I was producing yet another study not of gender but of white women. So I contacted my cherished friend Kathy Phillips, a well-known social psychologist who died tragically young, who recruited her then student Erika V. Hall to interview women of color. We were interviewing science professors as part of a National Science Foundation grant to help advance women in science.

Many white people's racial awakening occurred after George Floyd's murder, but mine occurred when I was reading those interviews in 2013. One woman, after hearing the seven-minute summary of the patterns of bias, burst into tears; she was so upset, Erika offered to end the interview. Another common reaction explains why: just this year, a woman of color again told me, when I asked whether any of that sounded familiar, "All of it. You just described my life." Both white women and women of color reported, overwhelmingly, that they experience gender bias, but key differences emerged. Women of color reported startling levels of disrespect. A Latina in environmental engineering reported that her professor made her take an extra course to ensure she was qualified, and "went as far as knocking on my head and saying, 'Is there anybody there?'" Black women in particular reflected a tone of bleak isolation and startling levels of disrespect. One recounted how a colleague who was supposed to be reviewing her teaching for faculty promotion sat in the back row loudly discussing with students how she would never get tenure. More recently, a Latina in tech told us, "No matter how much a company advertises they are diverse and open to opportunities for minority women, it's not true . . . From my experience in the workforce over 12 years, it's a lot of extra work we have to do just to get respected and viewed for other roles."[6] Said another Latina:

> I was outperforming, and they said, "We're going to hire a contractor to help you. She's going to report to you. You're going to train them. It'll be great." [After a company reorganization] they gave a white woman, the person that I had trained, . . . they gave her my job, and then six months later they gave her my promotion.[7]

A super-brilliant, highly accomplished Black medical school professor who had graduated from Harvard at age twenty had a mentor tell her, "You know, you're smarter than you look." ("This meeting is over," she said, and walked out.)

What these stories told me is that racial bias is not confined to the working class; it occurs frequently in professional and managerial settings, too. Bias against immigrants also emerges in sharp focus. "Every e-mail that I wrote, I spell checked it, and I read it three times before sending it out because if I made a typo or if I made a mistake, it was seen as not being skilled enough or that my English wasn't that good, as opposed to it just being a typo," said an Indian woman. Many Latinas and Asian American women are treated as "forever foreign" even when they're not. "I should speak good English," said an Asian American scientist dryly. "I grew up in Pittsburgh."[8]

In that initial study, at Erika's suggestion (she's now tenured at Emory's Goizueta Business School), we added a quantitative component to our research. A decade later, that early survey has turned into a ten-minute survey called the Workplace Experiences Survey. Nearly twenty thousand people have taken it, across many different industries and in three different countries. Gradually, the survey's focus morphed from studying gender to studying how the experience of gender bias differed by race, to studying both racial and gender bias. Our findings confirm that elites' version of racism faults people of color for lack of merit.

The most obvious way this occurs is through prove-it-again bias, my shorthand name for many different competence-based patterns. Higher-status groups are seen as more competent. This plays out robustly by race in professional workplaces. Across samples from different industries and different companies, typically about one-third of white men, but roughly half to three-quarters of people of color report having to prove themselves more than their colleagues. Again and again, we find that Black women report the highest levels of prove-it-again bias. Over three-quarters of Black women scientists reported having to prove themselves more than colleagues with similar education and experience. Both men and women are affected: "Others are judged on their potential. I have always— always—had to show demonstrated results," a Black former CEO told me. Said a Black lawyer, "White associates are not expected to be perfect. Black associates . . . have one chance, and if you mess up that chance, look out." In architecture, only 8 percent of white men, but about a quarter of Black women, have had their accomplishments dismissed as luck. "You can try to ignore it just to keep your sanity and move on, but the biases that are there are prevalent. And closing your eyes to them will not make them disappear," said an Asian American woman geologist.[9]

All this has very concrete consequences. One famous study found that "Jamal" needed eight additional years of experience to get the same number of callbacks as "Greg"—despite their identical résumés. Another experiment sent memos with mistakes to law firm partners and found that the (heavily white) partners found twice as many of the mistakes in memos with Black-sounding names as in those with white-sounding names. Mistakes were also more costly for African Americans than for white men, more often leading to formal reports of incompetence or recommendations that the offending attorney be fired. "When I went up for promotion, [questions were asked about] whether or not I would continue to be doing the things I was doing once I got full professor. I had never heard that kind of comment ever expressed in deliberations. It was a double standard," said a Latina professor. Note that prove-it-again bias is just one of five different patterns of workplace bias.[10]

In study after study, we also find that workplace systems—from hiring to performance evaluations to compensation and on and on—are seen as sharply less fair by people of color than white men. Our study of women of color in tech found that these perceptions of fairness, along with the patterns of bias, accounted for 65 percent of the variation in feelings of fairness, 59 percent of the variation in people's intent to stay in their workplace, and 67 percent of the variation in career satisfaction. That study compared women of color to white women; each of those numbers would probably be quite a bit higher had women of color been compared with white men.[11]

Responses are also sobering if you just ask people of color about racism. Typically about half of professionals of color report it, and about two-thirds of Black ones. I've been gathering this data nonstop for over a decade, so you can imagine my surprise when I read article after article displacing blame for racism onto lower-class whites. Remember that in 2016, one segment of Trump voters (American preservationists) was deeply racist and highly motivated by racism, but that another segment (anti-elites) expressed about the same warmth toward people of color as Clinton voters. In part, this reflects that elite modes of racism typically involve unspoken and unconscious assumptions that white men are more competent in elite jobs supposedly based on merit.[12]

This is not the kind of racism picked up by the racial resentment scale, which is "by far the most common instrument used to measure racism in political science research." That scale measures whether whites are seen as higher in "self-reliance, work ethic, obedience and discipline," to quote the scale's inventor. As we've seen, these values all map tightly onto the cultural dispositions of blue-collar Americans, so it's not surprising that noncollege grads express higher levels of racial resentment than college grads.[13] The core racial resentment scale contains four items:

1. Irish, Italian, Jewish, and many other minorities overcame prejudice and worked their way up. Blacks should do the same without any special favors.
2. Generations of slavery and discrimination have created conditions that make it difficult for Blacks to work their way out of the lower class.
3. Over the past few years, Blacks have gotten less than they deserve.
4. It's really a matter of some people just not trying hard enough: if Blacks would only try harder, they could be just as well off as whites.[14]

What this scale really measures is whether one attributes African Americans' current disadvantages to structural or individual reasons. As we have seen, ethnographies often find that blue-collar whites embrace individual, not structural, causes. Thus when Nicholas Kristof interviewed his old high school buddy Bill Beard, whose life was derailed by drugs and who ended up seriously assaulting a store clerk in a robbery gone wrong, Beard took full responsibility. "As long as you have the mental capacity to know right from wrong, it's your own damn fault" if you get into trouble, Beard told Kristof. "You can't blame anyone else. It's ludicrous, who else is there to blame?" Kristof notes that this "no-excuse personal responsibility narrative" can be highly motivating: "It's often a pillar of efforts to overcome addiction."[15]

The blame-the-victim narrative is often seen as emblematic of racism. That's true when it's used only against people of color—but often, it isn't. Whites blame the victim when judging other whites. Scholars have pointed out that self-blame is a coping mechanism: "The more victims blame themselves . . . , the better they coped" because it gave them a sense that they could control their destinies. In another column, Kristof describes his "pal Mike," another white man whose life went off the rails who ended up dying homeless on the street. "He didn't want to work," said his ex-wife. I can see how this makes sense to her: other men persevered against similarly steep odds and didn't leave their wives holding the bag, supporting kids on low-wage jobs. It also may make sense to some people of color. While a majority of Democratic primary voters thought hard work is no guarantee of success, a majority of Black voters believed that most people can get ahead if they work hard. Latinos express respect for hard work more than any other group; they also are the least likely to attribute where they are today to luck and circumstance (19 percent). Ian Haney López found that similar proportions of African Americans, Latinos, and whites found "dog whistle" racist messaging convincing; blaming the poor for their own plight is a classic part of dog whistle politics. I'm not saying that blaming the poor is never racist; it is when people of color's poverty is blamed on their lack of character while white people's poverty is not. But when everyone's poverty is blamed on lack of character, it's not racism; it's the process by which the lucky discount the influence of their luck.[16]

Just as there are structural reasons why non-elites will tend to score higher on racial resentment scales, there are structural reasons why elites will tend to be more focused on race than class. Elite Blacks tend to work in majority-white environments; I have described the ubiquity of racial bias they encounter day after day.

And I haven't even discussed a second strong pattern of bias that affects people of color. The technical name is *prescriptive bias*, and it reflects that a much broader range of behavior is accepted from white men than from people of color. White men can behave in authoritative ways without comment, but Black men who do the same often are criticized as "intimidating"; white people often see African Americans of all genders as angry when they behave authoritatively. "When you have a stance about how you will and will not be treated, you're an angry Black woman," said another woman in tech. Thus both men and women of color often walk a tightrope between being seen as too authoritative and so as having personality problems—or not authoritative enough and so lacking in leadership potential. Most of the research is on (white) women, but our data suggests this pattern may be strongest for Asian American women. This, of course, makes office politics much more complicated—meaning that people of color have to be *both* more technically competent *and* more politically savvy in order to succeed: "When I do say something, you have a problem with the way I say it. When I don't say anything, then you have a problem that I'm not saying it," said another Black woman in tech.[17]

These kinds of racism lead privileged people of color to focus on race as the most important social division. One reason higher-income Blacks are more likely to experience discrimination due to race than low-income Blacks is because they operate in more integrated environments. The same may be true of Latinos: increased education increases Latinos' sense of a linked fate. Less affluent people of color, on the other hand, typically live their lives among other people of color and tend to see poverty as their chief day-to-day concern (class, not race). This helps explain why a flip occurred when elite Blacks began to be able to enter white workplaces circa 1970. Before then, poor Blacks were more likely than elite Blacks to report discrimination; after the 1970s, reported Jennifer Hochschild in 1995, "well-off African Americans see *more* racial discrimination than do poor Blacks, see less decline in discrimination, expect less improvement in the future, and claim to have experienced more in their lives. By the 1990s, poor Blacks were four times more likely than more affluent ones to identify by class than race." Working-class people, particularly working-class Blacks, are more likely than their middle-class counterparts to identify strongly with their class group. In sharp contrast, well-off Blacks thought that race mattered more than any other factor named and were more likely to see discrimination as Blacks' most important problem. This was still true in 2019, when college-educated Blacks were more likely than Black non-college grads to believe that discrimination had negatively affected their ability to succeed.[18]

The class-linked linked-fate patterns also hold for Latinos; as noted in chapter 2, college-educated Latinos are more likely to share a sense of linked fate. "Racism is not something that people deal with here in Starr County because everybody's brown," noted a former mayor in Texas. "Climate change isn't something they feel. They prefer bread on the table."[19]

Just as many white women I know are convinced, absolutely convinced, that gender is the most important social division, many professionals of color feel the same about race. There's a pattern: people tend to focus on the axis of social power that disadvantages them—the same reason why working-class white men tend to focus on their class disadvantage, not their gender and racial advantage. Understanding the situated nature of what we "see with our own eyes" can help make us more supple in seeing the same phenomenon through different, non-mutually-exclusive lenses.

Keep in mind, my conclusion is *not* that racism plays no role in driving far-right sentiment. Scapegoating minorities, whether it's Jews and immigrants in Europe or immigrants and people of color in the US, is an abiding ingredient in the far-right formula. Trump's racism is deeply attractive to an important segment of Trump voters (American preservationists) and shockingly not a deal-breaker for anti-elites. My point is not that anti-elites are pure as the driven snow but that elite whites shouldn't use the racism of less privileged whites as a mute button. White Americans—of all classes—need to work on racism. Privileged Americans—of all races—need to take responsibility for addressing class disadvantage.[20]

Which is more important? It depends on context. Unlike race, which is *always* influential in the workplace, class origin is important in some industries but not others. In high-social-capital fields like corporate law and real estate investing, we find that first-generation white men sometimes report levels of belonging and culture fit *lower* than people of color. That's not proof that class is more important than race; it proves that to create a level playing field, you need to address *both*. Where class is important, it's vital not to ignore it—and doing so will hurt people of color. That's because two-thirds of first-generation professionals are people of color.[21]

I remember how, when I was on a book tour giving a talk at Harvard's Kennedy School about how hard it is to be a class migrant, a young Black woman came up to me afterward in tears. She expressed her gratitude and said that no one—*no one*—had ever talked about this before and that her class origin was painful and ever present in her professional journey. This means that an initiative to help people of color will fail if it fails to actively address both their disadvantage based on race and their disadvantage based on class. In workplaces as well as in politics, caring about class disadvantage and caring about racial disadvantage are not mutually exclusive. We need to care about both.

In case you're interested, it's totally possible to make concrete year-over-year progress on eliminating racial and gender bias in professional workplaces. In one ninety-minute training, we drove down an important form of bias against women of color from 27 points to 0 and decreased a key measure of prove-it-again bias against women of color by 24 points. (We use women of color as the key metric because typically they encounter the most bias.) In aggregated data from two companies, we sharply decreased the tendency of people of color to be faulted for personality problems on their performance evaluations, by 19 points. Men of color in a consumer goods company were getting a *lot* more negative personality comments; we fixed that, too. At a tech company, we found that white men were getting hired with lower ratings than any other group; we decreased bias against women of color by 7 points in just a few months' time.[22]

Class and race interact in another way, too. When white elites fail to listen to white non-elites, guess who pays the price? The people of color targeted by far-right populism.

Key Takeaways:

1. Racism is well documented among lower-middle-class whites— but also is commonplace among elites.
2. Styles of racism differ between elites and non-elites. The popular racial resentment scale tends to pick up working-class styles, but overlook elite styles, of racism.
3. White Americans—of all classes—need to work on racism. Privileged Americans—of all races—need to take responsibility for addressing class disadvantage.

Part IV

The Path Past Far-Right Populism

Winning an argument is actually a terrible way to change someone's mind . . . People are far more likely to be persuaded when they feel seen and heard, when they feel their own argument has been fairly presented, and if they are confronted by a story.

—RACHEL HELD EVANS[1]

I'm not an expert in public health, or LGBTQ rights, or immigration, or climate change. Yet I strongly believe that understanding the class dynamic in American politics will help us make progress on each of these important goals. This section provides a road map for doing so.

One structural factor that impedes progress on these issues is the news media. It's not just Fox, or social media, or lies. It's something subtler. In 1971, reporters ranked below electricians, right above factory foremen and carpenters, in prestige. Today, mainstream journalism is dominated by graduates of elite colleges: a 2018 study found that more than half of the staff writers at *The New York Times* and *Wall Street Journal* attended one of the top twenty-nine most elite universities. But it's not just reporters; it's elite "common sense." The highly educated are in some ways the most insular group. We need to get outside our class bubble.[2]

No doubt people who are truly expert in each of these areas can do a better job of using existing knowledge to build cross-class coalitions. My goal is to arm and inspire them to do so.

Of Covid and Playground Design:
How Class Blindness Distorts Public Policy

[In the US] our level of Covid anxiety is higher, especially in communities that lean to the left politically.

—David Leonhardt[1]

There are two farmers markets near my home in San Francisco. Before the pandemic, I went to one on Saturday, next to a highway, in a working-class neighborhood. In 2021, after the CDC gave the green light on no masking outdoors, I returned. I immediately realized I didn't feel comfortable there: too many people, too close. So I switched to the Sunday market in a more upscale neighborhood. I didn't like it as much, but there, people kept their distance.

And then it hit me: this was about class. Many of the customers at the Saturday market are working-class immigrants—you see headscarves and hear a lot of Chinese—who have more pressing worries than hypervigilance about health. Customers at the Sunday market shared my attitudes toward risk. This hunch was confirmed when, long after vaccines were widely available, I went to a farmers market in Berkeley, very upper crust. This was months and months after the CDC said there was no need to wear a mask outdoors, but virtually everyone wore a mask. Actually, not true. Virtually every shopper wore a mask. No farmer did.

Elites' extreme risk aversion can distort public policy in ways large and small. A small but important way is playground design. In upper-middle-class neighborhoods, gone are the merry-go-rounds where my brothers and I twirled until we were dizzy. Gone the seesaws. Gone the metal-pipe jungle gyms. US playgrounds are now so risk averse that children are actually at more risk of injury. Children naturally seek out rough-and-tumble play—climbing to heights, moving their bodies at high speed—so they can learn about risks and coping with fears. As Ellen Beate Hansen Sand-seter, a Norwegian early-childhood researcher, told *The New York Times*, "When we prevent them from doing these things, they get bored, and are tempted to perform rash stunts like turning somersaults on top of climbing frames and standing on the shoulders of others on the swings." Another study found that children have fewer injuries in British playgrounds, de-signed with a more balanced approach to risk. Children there are also more physically active and stay at the playgrounds longer.[2]

"Imposing too many restrictions on children's outdoor risky play hin-ders their development," writes Mariana Brussoni of the Department of Pediatrics at the University of British Columbia. A risk-deprived child is more prone to obesity and decreased learning, perception, independence, and judgment. Play deprivation contributes to a reduced sense of personal control and enhances other characteristics associated with anxiety and/or depression. "The goal should not be to eliminate all risks, but to control risk," Brussoni concludes.[3]

So why do we design playgrounds this way? Brussoni and others link today's extreme risk aversion to the same high levels of parental anxiety that fuel the concerted cultivation model of child-rearing found among college-educated Americans and discussed in chapter 11: competitive over-parenting. "[O]ver-directing, over-protecting, or over-involving ourselves in our kids' lives. We treat our kids like rare and precious botanical speci-mens . . . while running interference on all that might toughen and weather them." In *Small Animals: Parenthood in the Age of Fear*, Kim Brooks describes "our culture's obsession with safety" and "fixation on risk avoidance." Com-menting on one mom's obsession with "speech therapy, occupational ther-apy, baby monitors all over the house," Brooks notes tartly, "I'm afraid to fart." In *The End of American Childhood*, historian Paula S. Fass critiques elite parents (herself included—and I did it, too) as "increasingly fearful that the slightest deviation will ruin their children's carefully prepared path." Precar-ity has pushed elite parents to unhealthy places.[4]

Supersafeism as a class-based phenomenon goes beyond parenting, and it deeply shaped the US Covid response. One easy way to see this is in news coverage. Given that most reporters are elites whose attitudes toward risk tend to mirror those of their class, it's not surprising that news coverage of the pandemic in the US emphasized risk. One study by three economists found that coverage in major US media was more pessimistic (91 percent) than in scientific journals (65 percent). There were 15,000 story mentions of increases in caseloads, but only 2,500 mentions of decreases: a six-to-one ratio. Nor was average media negativity on Covid correlated with actual case counts. Stories describing Covid caseloads as increasing outnumbered those describing caseloads as decreasing by a factor of 5.5 even during periods when new cases were declining overall. The most popular Covid stories in *The New York Times* were 1.5 standard deviations more negative than the mean. The researchers concluded that the negativity of stories responded to reader demand: "Our results suggest that U.S. major outlets publish[ed] unusually negative Covid-19 stories in response to reader demand and interest."[5]

Coverage in major US media outlets was dramatically bleaker than coverage abroad. "Overall, we find that relative to other media sources, the most influential U.S. news sources are outliers in terms of the negative tone of their coronavirus stories and their choices of stories covered," found the economists quoted above. The difference between media coverage on Covid inside and outside the US was not subtle. When 91 percent of US stories had a negative valance, only 54 percent of stories in major media outlets outside the country were negative. The same pattern held for stories on school reopenings: 90 percent were negative in the US for reopening schools as compared with 56 percent elsewhere.[6]

Major US outlets did not begin covering the progress toward a vaccine until April, two months after the first coverage in the UK. Even then, the story downplayed as "incredibly small" the likelihood that the vaccine would be available anytime soon, instead emphasizing "caveats from health officials and experts downplaying the optimistic timeline and past success of the Oxford researchers." News coverage about vaccines in American media was "45 percentage points more likely to be negative" than coverage outside it, including coverage of Pfizer's positive stage-three trial result. Dr. Monica Gandhi, an American infectious disease doctor and epidemiologist, notes that American media's intense focus on "how to stay safe during the holidays" in 2022 (an entire year after the vaccines were available) "may have led the public to think that our widely available vaccines weren't effective."[7]

Conservatives understood that non-elites might feel differently. That's why politicians like Florida governor Ron DeSantis and Virginia governor Glenn Youngkin gained a lot of support from noncollege grads by standing up against shutdowns of schools and the economy. "When Democrats focused their Covid messaging solely on healthcare without talking about the economy, it exposes them to GOP attacks. We were right to shut down the economy and mandate masks, but we also needed to make clear that was because we stood for getting the economy, schools and stadiums open ASAP."[8]

Not all reporters got it wrong. Finally, deep into the pandemic, David Leonhardt, a journalist at *The New York Times* whose understanding of class dynamics is astute, politely pointed out that liberals' supersafeism diverged from the science. After quoting a British expert who said the worst was over, Leonhardt was politic: "I know that many Americans feel differently. Our level of Covid anxiety is higher, especially in communities that lean to the left politically." His tribe; nonetheless, he soldiers on to highlight the small risks of Covid for the vaccinated: "That risk is so close to zero that the human mind can't easily process it. My best attempt is to say that the Covid risks for most vaccinated people are of the same order of magnitude as risks that people unthinkingly accept every day, like riding in a vehicle."[9]

Supersafeism turned the response into a culture war that distorted objectivity on both sides. A December 2020 poll found that Democrats overestimated the risks for young people more than Republicans did and overestimated the likelihood of severe harm after infection. The point is not that Democrats were always wrong or that Republicans were always right but that neither side consistently followed the science. The vaccines were a triumph of science, but some liberals downplayed their benefits. Indeed, "there is abundant evidence that the most liberal Americans are exaggerating the risks to the vaccinated and to children." Democrats younger than forty-five said that the virus posed a greater risk to them than to those older than sixty-five—"which is inconsistent with scientific reality but consistent with younger Democrats' more intense liberalism." Leonhardt also notes, "Many liberals feel deep anxiety about Covid's effects on children—even though the flu kills more children in a typical year and car crashes kill about five times as many."[10]

The fallacy of supersafeism is that life isn't about *eliminating* risk: otherwise, one could never drive, or ski, or even dare to eat a peach. "Rather than eliminating the risk of Covid, you've got to manage the risk," said Elizabeth H. Bradley, a public health expert and president of Vassar College. "If you really go for minimizing the risk, you're going to have unintended consequences to people's physical health, their mental health, their social health. It's Public Health 101." Not surprisingly, countries where policy was driven by Public Health 101, rather than culture wars, made very different decisions and had better outcomes.[11]

Dr. Gandhi points out that it was known very early (by February 2020) that Covid poses low risks for children: the infection fatality rate is 1 percent for adults over fifty but 0.005 percent for children. Most children are sick for only six days at the most, with long Covid in children very rare. Studies from Germany, France, Ireland, Finland, Australia, Singapore, the US, and Israel all suggested that transmission between children in schools is uncommon, but as of March 2021, "much negative news coverage relied on inaccurate modeling data" that exaggerated the spread from children. Studies from Australia, Ireland, and the Netherlands found that school-children were not the primary driver of adult Covid cases in schools. Instead, adult staff members brought Covid in from the community; one study estimated that Covid was 37 percent lower in schools than in the community during the same time frame. Dr. Gandhi's assessment: staff and students were safe in school during Covid even before vaccines became available and regardless of the hygiene measures taken, and certainly by April 2021, when nearly 80 percent of teachers had received one dose of the vaccine. She published nine pieces with other public health experts on why schools should be reopened once vaccines were available. They were largely ignored. Closures were longer in blue than red states; in San Francisco, schools were remote for nearly eighteen months. Dr. Jennifer Nuzzo (now at the Brown University School of Public Health) warned of the dangers of extended school closures as early as March 2020, followed by experts in the US, the UK, Italy, and Hong Kong. All were ignored in the US. Negative health effects ranged from weight gain and children missing health screenings and vaccinations to increased suicide rates and child abuse. All came to pass, as predicted, as *The New York Times* summarized in March 2024.[12]

What did the Covid response look like in a country that followed the science? Denmark closed down in March 2020, at a time when it had only moderate infection rates, but manufacturing remained open throughout the pandemic to mute the impact on the economy. Everyone else was "asked to sacrifice to protect elders and the economy," Social Democrat Rasmus Horn Langhoff told me in an interview. He was the party's spokesman on health policy during the pandemic. At every stage, he stressed, decisions were driven by a cost-benefit analysis that included impacts on the economy. Part of the strategy across Europe was to prioritize programs that provided funding for employers to keep workers on the payroll in areas of the economy that had been shut down. In the US, by contrast, the chief focus was on stimulus checks and unemployment compensation, not job retention. As a result, Americans lost significantly more jobs during Covid than Europeans. Moreover, among advanced industrial democracies, the US had the third largest gap in job loss between workers with and without a college degree. Only 19 percent of Americans with high school or less and 29 percent of those with some college said they would likely continue to get paid if a shutdown lasted at least two weeks, as compared to 53 percent of college grads and 65 percent of Americans with postgraduate education.[13]

Closures, of course, also affected schools and day care centers in Denmark, but again, both costs and benefits were part of the equation during decision-making. Langhoff emphasized that school closures were "not good for children at all" nor for the economy, because "the Danish workforce is very dependent on women," so it was "very important to get the children back in school as soon as possible."

It's not that supersafeism doesn't exist in Denmark. Indeed, the prime minister, the Social Democrat Mette Frederiksen, said she would not accept anyone dying from Covid if the government could prevent it, and that the priority was public health and eliminating risks. Crucially, the public health service (Statens Serum Institut, or SSI), was in charge of Covid policy. It weighed the costs and benefits of a shutdown.[14]

This cost-benefit approach meant that Denmark was the first country in Europe to reopen day care and primary schools. Day care reopened just five weeks after lockdown, on April 20, 2020, as did primary school through fifth grade. More evidence of thoughtful rational planning: graduating high school students also returned in person. Upon the advice of the SSI, the government announced that the youngest children would reenter society first because SSI's scientific model showed that young children were the least susceptible to the virus and the government wanted parents to be able to work effectively from home. Classrooms were reorganized so that desks could be at the recommended two meters apart, which meant that only half the students could fit; the other half were taught in temporary quarters, including tents. (Here in sunny California, I kept asking myself, why not tents?) Children washed their hands at least every two hours, and teaching timetables were changed to keep learning to small groups. School hours were shortened (8:00 a.m.–1:00 p.m.), with emphasis on outside projects and socializing. "There is an increased focus on well-being. We're not putting the academic needs second but we're thinking differently about it," said one primary school principal.[15]

Despite the early opening, Denmark's infection rate remained stable. (A CDC study found no significant difference in case rates between counties that opened school by December 2020 and those that didn't; studies out of Norway, Australia, South Korea, and Italy also found no spikes when schools opened.) The SSI's Kåre Mølbak said his mathematical model had found that only 1.8 percent of children had probably been infected with Covid as compared with 10–11 percent of adults: "That's why we do not have such a big concern about children." Within three days of reopening, only half of students had returned to school, but by the third week, 90 percent were in school and 66 percent were in day care. The Delta variant brought a second shutdown in the fall of 2020, but it was relatively brief. When local outbreaks occurred, either a classroom or school would shut down briefly and then reopen: "A lot of schools sent the children home at some points, but not for long. That was the price of reopening earlier," Langhoff told me, "two steps forward, one backward." Denmark avoided the strategies that led to continual disruptions in the US even after students finally returned to in-school instruction, including weekly testing of asymptomatic kids, quarantines, and mandatory masking after vaccines became available.[16]

"We were laying railroad tracks while running the train," Langhoff stressed. "I know some of the rules might seem a little silly," and it was "not easy, but we accepted this cannot be pretty." Supermarkets remained open, but bookstores were closed, so supermarkets started selling a lot of books. Bookstores were furious. "We had that debate, and we explained that the alternative was to shut down supermarkets, since it was not feasible to reopen every store." During the pandemic, the government was "historically popular," he said. By March 2023, 82 percent of Danes were fully vaccinated. In the US, the vaccination rate was only 68 percent.[17]

It's not just Denmark. Chile's vaccination rate in March 2023 was 93 percent. "Governments in South America have generally not faced the kind of apathy, polarization and conspiracy theories that left much of the United States vulnerable to the highly contagious Delta variant," noted *The New York Times*. A 2021 study found that only 65 percent of US respondents said they would get vaccinated, making Americans far more vaccine-hesitant than those in developing countries, where 80 percent of residents wanted the vaccine. Vaccine opposition in the US was the second highest in the world, behind only Russia.[18]

Here's the irony: supersafeism turned the pandemic into a culture war that made people less safe. The US had a higher mortality rate than at least nine other high-income countries, even though those countries shut their schools far more briefly (50 percent shut in the US versus 13 percent in other countries during the period between February 2020 and March 2022). Not only was the overall vaccination rate low in the US overall, it was 1.25 times lower in red counties, making hypervigilant elites in adjacent blue counties more vulnerable to Covid. And now that public health has been infected by a culture war, it's likely everyone will be even less safe when the next pandemic hits because trust in US public health authorities cratered and has yet to recover, along with trust in the government, public schools, and the news media. Faith in public health authorities fell particularly steeply among the less educated and African Americans. This was not inevitable. Trust both in government and in science in the Netherlands increased over the pandemic.[19]

The negative effects that have received the most attention are the long school closures, especially in blue states. Pre-2020 pandemic planning recommendations by the Centers for Disease Control and Prevention (CDC) and the World Health Organization suggested brief closures of up to four weeks. In blue states like California, Oregon, and Washington, and in Democratic-controlled states, such as Illinois, New Jersey, and Virginia, many schools were closed much, much longer. School closures, especially long ones, had devastating long-term effects that jeopardized many important progressive goals. For one thing, they contributed to an exodus from public schools, making this vital democratic institution still more embattled than it already was. In the 2020–2021 school year, about one-quarter of US students were chronically absent, up sharply from 15 percent before the pandemic; absenteeism rose more sharply in states with long school closures. The 2021–2022 school year showed a slight improvement, but chronic absenteeism was still double what it had been before the pandemic in some states like California and New Mexico. In 2022, national test results in both math and reading for thirteen-year-olds hit the lowest levels in decades, with Black and Hispanic students more likely to have attended schools that stayed remote for longer often having the greatest learning losses.[20]

A 2021 study found that remote learning worked worst for racial minorities, children in poverty, and children who speak English as a second language. A report from an institute at Harvard found that high-poverty schools suffered large losses in achievement when learning was remote. A June 2020 estimate was that if remote learning lasted a year, low-income students would end up losing 12.4 months of schooling. Forty-six percent of low-income parents reported that their children faced at least one of the following obstacles to learning: 1) had to do schoolwork on a cell phone, 2) unable to complete schoolwork due to lacking computer access at home, or 3) had to use public Wi-Fi due to unreliable internet connection at home. "We find that school closures have a large, persistent, and unequal effect on human capital accumulation," noted a 2022 study that reported the deficit as 5 percent in the most affluent communities but 30 percent in the least. A 2023 study found good news—most students were catching up—and bad news—students in poor districts weren't.[21]

"By summer 2020 school reopening had become politicized, with the progressive left aligned firmly against it. This should be surprising, for we've seen that progressive principles pointed in favor of reopening. Why then did school closures become a flagship value for the left?" asks Shamik Dasgupta, a philosophy professor at Berkeley.[22] Progressives weren't at their best: their reflexive hypervigilance overrode their concern for social justice. We need to handle the next pandemic differently. A class lens can help by allowing elites to gain some sober distance from supersafeism so that we can begin to change the culture-wars frame before our next public health crisis hits.

Key Takeaways:

1. The same neoliberal forces that spur conspiracy theories among Americans without degrees spur supersafeism among college grads: an unrealistic insistence on eliminating rather than controlling risk.
2. The lack of a class-competent approach to Covid produced poorer outcomes in the US than in many other countries: lower vaccination rates, higher mortality rates, and higher rates of learning loss and job loss.
3. Public health authorities need to take class-based resentment against experts into account when designing the next pandemic response.

Nothing Is as Dangerous as
a Man Without a Future
(Even If You Offer Universal Basic Income)

*Too often, those who champion the working class speak only of
social safety nets, not the jobs that anchor a working person's
identity.*

—Farah Stockman[1]

Nothing is as dangerous as a man without a future: such men supported
the Nazis in the 1930s, and they provide the core support for far-right
populists today. Populists understand men's sense of aggrieved loss when
jobs disappear and how the disappearance of provider status is felt as a disappearance of dignity. "If I won the lottery I would still work," a school ad-
ministrator told an ethnographer, "because that's how I get my self-esteem."
No jobs, no self-esteem. Donald Trump gets this, so he promised to provide good jobs for noncollege grads constantly in 2016, 2020, and 2024.
Democrats, on the other hand, assumed that voters would reward them
for "going big" on new redistributive programs during Covid—stimulus
checks, paid leave, and the child tax credit. That assumption proved wrong.
Why?[2]

The bad news is that support for redistribution by the government is
much weaker in the US than in most other industrialized countries. The
good news is that far more Americans believe that something has gone
seriously wrong with a labor market where the rich are paid too much
and everyone else is paid too little—and they support government interventions to change that. Americans support labor market interventions—
"predistribution"—at far higher rates than they support government
redistribution. Especially noncollege grads: "Less educated voters appear
to prefer a less market-based and more interventionist economic program
that aims to promote domestic employment and wages," concluded a 2023

National Bureau of Economic Research working paper. The researchers estimated that nearly half of Democrats' loss of less educated voters over the past several decades can be directly attributed to Democrats' focus on redistribution instead of predistribution. Nearly half: that's a lot.[3]

Liberal elites favor redistribution more than non-elites. Across eleven European countries, among supporters of leftist parties, "those with higher levels of education show *more* support for redistribution than those with less education." In the US, middle-income Americans are 5 points more likely than upper-income Americans but 20 points less likely than low-income Americans to say that government should provide more assistance to people in need. On universal basic income (UBI), middle-income Americans oppose it at levels much closer to the rich than the poor (59 percent). Most astonishing, only 39 percent of those without high school degrees favor a 70 percent tax rate for those earning over $10 million, as compared with nearly two-thirds of college grads.[4]

In other words, there's a major disconnect: middle-income Americans favor predistribution much more than redistribution, but elites favor redistribution much more than predistribution. Recall the study of Silicon Valley entrepreneurs that found strong support for higher taxes to support redistributive welfare policies, but much lower support for unionization and regulation that would help American workers—and threaten Big Tech's bottom line. Support for UBI offers social virtue without changing a business model where up to one-third of Google workers are "fissured workers" working for staffing companies, typically at lower pay, with fewer benefits. Labor economists estimate that "gigification" accounts "for a quarter to a third of the increase in wage inequality since 1980." Janitors are now twelve times less likely to be employees than in the 1950s and 44 percent less likely to have employer health insurance. Outsourced security guards earn on average 24 percent less than those who are employees. This is justified by the ideology that companies should keep to their "core competencies," which is just an excuse to screw non-white-collar workers (and increasingly, many white-collar ones).[5]

The nigh-universal assumption is that bridging the diploma divide just means focusing on "kitchen table" issues. Inflation is the ultimate kitchen table issue; liberals' failure to spot its political consequences early on was a serious misstep. In 2022, inflation was causing serious problems for up to 42 percent of Americans without college degrees but only about a quarter of college grads. Car loan delinquencies were higher in early 2023 than at the peak of the Great Recession, with credit card delinquencies at their highest rates in a decade.[6]

As important as kitchen table politics is, it only scratches the surface. Truly understanding class dynamics in American politics requires understanding a cultural dynamic few outside of sociology have ever heard of: between hard living and settled living.

Remember blue-collar pride in persevering and the hard-fought battle to remain employed, pay the rent, and raise kids who keep their nose clean? The alternative is "hard living." To quote J. D. Vance:

> I knew even as a child that there were two separate sets of mores and social pressures. My grandparents embodied one type: old-fashioned, quietly faithful, self-reliant, working hard. My mother and, increasingly, the entire neighborhood embodied another: consumerist, isolated, angry, distrustful.[7]

While hardworking families insist on order and self-discipline, hard-living families tend to drugs, heavy drinking, and marital instability. Vance's memoir describes this dynamic. His mother was a "partier" with serious alcohol and drug addictions, impulse-control issues, suicide attempts, child abuse, and a series of unsavory boyfriends. Her signature move was demanding that Vance provide clean urine so she could pass a drug test. Vance was raised chiefly by his grandmother, a classic pattern in hard-living families. Vance lionizes his grandmother while heaping scorn on his hard-living mom. Vance's father represents settled living, with his "modest house on a beautiful plot of land," a stable marriage, and a family life of "almost jarring serenity." No one drank, and everyone went to a Pentecostal church. "The church—especially the Pentecostal church—offered hard living folks one possible channel for making the transition to settled living," notes the book that named the hard-living versus settled-living dynamic, *Hard Living on Clay Street*.[8]

Vance heaps scorn on his neighbors on welfare. "As one who works hard, is 'settled,' is worthy, and yet still claims the hillbilly mantle, he wishes to clearly distinguish himself from those who represent the other side of each of these dichotomies: lazy, hard living, unworthy, 'white trash,'" notes law professor Lisa Pruitt. This sentiment is widespread: Jennifer Sherman found that people accepting food stamps could expect to be ridiculed at the cash register due to the "strong social disgrace around unemployment and welfare receipt"; welfare is associated with laziness and poor moral character. This explains why Biden's American Families Plan, which contained the wish list of my crowd of care work advocates (paid family leave and subsidized childcare) polled much stronger among college grads than non-grads. Only 28 percent of Americans supported making the child tax credit implemented by the Covid-related American Rescue Plan permanent, with support for making it only temporary or eliminating it higher among the working and middle classes than among the upper class. A Latina in her late thirties acknowledged that the tax credit money was "really beneficial" but added, "It could also coddle people that don't want to work and are playing the system."[9]

All this is part of the deep structure of inequality. To quote psychologist Susan Fiske, "Low-status groups face a conflict between favoring their in-group and living within a system that devalues it, so they show more ambivalence toward their own group than high-status people show toward theirs." When a community is stigmatized, individual members have two choices. Either they conclude that the stigma is unjustified and throw their lot in with their communities, or they distance themselves with the belief "I'm not like *them*." Thus Michelle Obama's grandfather was galled by the "young black men—the 'boo-boos,' he called them—whom he perceived to be hanging uselessly around the neighborhood, giving Black people everywhere a bad name." I call this *strategic distancing*. "I'd been taught self-sufficiency was everything," noted Michelle Obama. Yet she has also worked for racial justice her whole life: African Americans adopt strategic distancing far less than whites do. Michèle Lamont found that 70 percent of white—but only 40 percent of Black—blue-collar men chose "irresponsibility" as something they disliked. Black people are sharply more supportive of redistributive programs than Americans in general, partly because of their "there but for the grace of God go I" ethic.[10]

Lamont also found a cultural difference between the US and France, with Americans far more likely to blame the poor: half of blue-collar and two-thirds of white-collar Americans had a negative view of the poor, as compared to only 7 percent of white-collar and 37 percent of blue-collar French. Lamont found Black blue-collar men more like their French counterparts than their American white counterparts in their understanding that inequality is deeply structural. Slavery will do that: clarify that disadvantage reflects oppression, not character flaws.[11]

Progressives tend to read any reference to "hard work" as racial coding. This captures an important dynamic. A key way Republicans played the

race card during and after the Civil Rights Movement was to character-
ize redistributive programs as rewarding "welfare queens." "Government
welfare was presented as the principal mechanism for stealing the pro-
ductive majority's wealth and property, with the racial minorities being
portrayed as society's chief parasitic menace," to quote one commentator.
Studies show that whites' opinions about welfare in the early 1990s were
strongly linked to their feelings about African Americans in general, and
an assumption they had a poor work ethic, a history aptly explained in Ian
Haney López's *Dog Whistle Politics*.[12]

Racism plays a role, but let's get it right: the racism is the assumption
that Black people (all of them?) are lazy; that's different from the dislike
of laziness in anyone. When white people use hard-work worship to fault
white people, it's not racism—it's a class dynamic that stems from non-
elites' determination to "turn servitude into honor." This spans race: recall
that Latinos are particularly strong believers in hard work. Hard-work
worship is peculiarly American: over three-fourths of Americans, but less
than half of French and Japanese, think people can succeed if they work
hard.[13]

The "hard working" vs. "hard-living" dynamic deeply shapes attitudes
toward government redistribution. Kathryn Edin's wonderful study of
Earned Income Tax Credit recipients found "the implied condemnation
of less virtuous others is nearly ubiquitous among those who have had any
experience with government aid." A Latina single mother of three said, "I
didn't want to end up like everybody else, just sitting on welfare, getting
welfare. . . . I could have sat on my behind and got the food stamps and
the MassHealth, but my mother was like, 'No, you're not going to. You're
going to get up and get a job and support your kids.' So I just didn't have
the luxury of being able to sit on my ass." As income inequality has risen,
low-income voters' support for government redistribution has *diminished*.
Americans with postgraduate education are outliers: about two-thirds believe that government should do more to solve problems. Only about half
of less educated groups do.[14]

Hard-work worship explains why work requirements are supported
by majorities of every class and racial group of Americans. It also helps
explain why work requirements are more popular with noncollege voters than college grads. An analysis of Cooperative Election Study data
by Third Way found that white, Hispanic, and Asian noncollege voters
(67 percent / 64 percent / 60 percent) were more likely than same-race

college grads (53 percent / 60 percent / 57 percent) to support such requirements; Black college and noncollege voters supported them at the same rate (58 percent versus 57 percent). I find it shocking that so many think their fellow Americans should go hungry, but it's a fact of life. Pretending it's not there won't make it go away.[15]

The hardworking/hard-living dynamic runs deep. Remember Tommy and Liza? They scraped by on her two part-time jobs and his seasonal work. They relied on family, and Tommy's willingness to "set aside [his] pride" and not to be picky about what he will and won't do. They take pride in not accepting welfare, disability, or food stamps—nothing except unemployment insurance, which they saw as "earned and deserved." "I'm not really into handouts," Tommy said.[16]

Trump understood this. "You better vote for me, I got you so many damn car plants," he said during a rally in Michigan in 2020. "And we're going to bring you a lot more." This was a lie: Michigan had 66,500 fewer factory workers in July 2020 compared to a year earlier, and during Trump's presidency, the US lost 154,000 factory jobs. Though he lied, he understood what people cared about. "I'm super-Mexican but just the way he wanted to keep jobs here and the way he wanted to promote the economy that was something admirable," said a 2020 Trump voter.[17]

There are many ways progressives can leverage hard-work worship. Americans were widely upset about supply chain disruptions during Covid, which raised awareness of the need for supply chain resilience. This can be leveraged into a demand for industrial policy to create good jobs at home. So can widespread support for apprenticeship programs, which 86 percent of Americans support. It makes sense to combine college debt relief with apprenticeship programs because only 20 percent of white voters, 30 percent of Latinos, and 41 percent of Black voters view college debt relief as a priority, according to a 2023 poll.[18]

Predictable race and class patterns in support for redistribution emerged in polling on Biden's expansion of the childcare tax credit during the pandemic. Support was much higher among African Americans (72 percent) than any other group; support was only 41–54 percent among Latinos and noncollege whites. Later, support for making the tax credit permanent without a work requirement was also low: only 28 percent of Americans supported it. White college grads were the only group whose support exceeded 50 percent. Tellingly, describing the credit as helping working parents cover the costs of raising a child instead of as a poverty program sharply increased support among Latinos. Progressives need to make hard-work worship work for them, because the Far Right will keep using that norm against them.[19]

Another crucial message is that a job is about far more than money. Martin Luther King understood this. "One day," he told striking sanitation workers in 1968, "our society will come to respect the sanitation worker if it is to survive . . . for if he doesn't do his job, diseases are rampant. All labor has dignity." To quote Farah Stockman, "Some people have begun to talk about 'universal basic income,' a naked admission that a significant portion of the American people no longer fits into the economy. That might be part of the solution. But it's far from clear that a government check can replace what people get from a good job. . . . [Jobs are] a place of identity, belonging, and redemption."[20]

MLK's message that blue-collar jobs have dignity has been lost, resulting in a 49 percent drop in the application rate for young people seeking jobs in the trades in 2022 as compared with 2020. "For a long time, our society has not talked favorably about the skilled trades," said the study's author. "We've instead encouraged students to all go to college, all go to four-year institutions, graduate, go out into white-collar jobs." Said a labor economist, "We have to recruit people to do these things or else our bridges are going to fall down." Bridges matter. So do votes.[21]

Trump's focus on blue-collar jobs changed both Republicans and Democrats. Democrats had not centered concerns about unions or blue-collar jobs for decades when President Joe Biden prioritized passing two pieces of legislation designed to spur the development of manufacturing and construction jobs: the Inflation Reduction Act (IRA) and bipartisan Infrastructure Investment and Jobs Act, projected to create "four million jobs per year" over a ten-year period. Biden tried to make sure his blue-collar bet worked politically: 80 percent of the investment from the IRA is going to counties where college graduation rates are lower than average. Biden in effect resuscitated "industrial policy"—the government providing incentives to spur private industry, which had fallen into disrepute under neoliberalism with the tagline, "The government shouldn't be choosing winners and losers." Antitrust laws also have a crucial role to play in reining in the power of big corporations: here again, Biden made progress.[22]

Progressives need to learn to frame their arguments in a way that taps *into* hard-work worship rather than fighting *against* it. The key message, which progressives should be proclaiming from the rooftops—early, often, incessantly—is that we need to return to an economy where hard work pays off in a stable, middle-class living. To quote an unemployed mother of three from Youngstown, Ohio:

> At this age, we should be so much further along. For two people who worked all their lives, the only way to have the American dream is to hit the lottery. That's the new American dream . . . I'm not asking for wealth, just comfort. I want to pay my bills, pay for my children's education, and put a little money aside.[23]

Americans' belief they can get ahead by working hard plummeted from 76 percent to 53 percent between 2001 and 2012; in 2018, it stood at 63 percent. Importantly, this is a wedge issue for the GOP: low-income Republicans are 19 percentage points more likely than high-income Republicans to agree that hard work and determination are no guarantee of success. Unions are crucial, and support for unions is higher than since 1965: 71 percent of Americans approved of unions in 2022. Democrats need to return to the fervent defense of unions they abandoned under neoliberalism.[24]

Americans may be skeptical about redistribution by the government, but there is widespread belief that the labor market is rigged. Even before Occupy Wall Street, half to two-thirds of Americans believed that income differences were too large and rejected the explanation that this was necessary for prosperity. Polling consistently finds that 70–86 percent of Americans believe that the rich are paid too much, a view shared across racial groups. They also believe that skilled and unskilled workers are paid too little.[25]

Liberals won't give up on government redistribution, of course, but they need to stop making believe that the settled-living versus hard-living dynamic doesn't exist. This brings us back to UBI. Silicon Valley elites have a hard time understanding why something as eminently logical as universal basic income should outrage people, but this just shows their ignorance of a central reality of American politics. If you get up every day and go to a pink-collar job with little pay and lots of sexual harassment, or a blue-collar job with lots of monotony and high risk of injury, the idea of paying for other people not to work is truly irritating. Elites' identities are typically so intertwined with their work roles that they cannot imagine anything more than a short period of being "funemployed," which is why universal basic income seems so perfect: they can take that time out after their start-up died to work on the Next Big Thing.

UBI also has rigorously documented benefits for poor people, who can finally pay their bills *and* the rent (oh, the luxury). But that's not how it looks to the Missing Middle. To quote Janice, an eighty-one-year-old Trump voter from Columbus, Ohio, "The poor folks don't pay taxes, the rich can afford them, and [the middle] gets the short end of the stick." I personally believe that UBI won't happen—and that it will provide a powerful talking point for the Far Right.[26]

Another implication of the settled-living versus hard-living dynamic concerns means-tested programs that are targeted tightly to the poor. In Europe, support for redistribution is much higher among the middle class than in the US, probably because most programs aren't means-tested—instead, they are universal, like Social Security. You get social security no matter what your income.

Means-tested programs that target the poor exacerbate opposition to redistribution, for a simple reason best summarized by a blue-collar home-maker: they pit the have-a-littles against the have-nots. "The taxes go to the poor, not to us . . . The middle-income people are carrying the cost of liberal social programs on their backs," said another homemaker. Means-tested programs produce "benefits cliffs" that mean that people who earn even one dollar above the cutoff lack access to the program. For example, in Kansas a family of four is eligible for Medicaid if it earns $39,900 but not if it earns $39,901.[27]

Middle-income voters also are most likely to feel that government should provide less or the current level of support for people in need (71 percent) and least likely to believe that government should provide more (28 percent). Support for making Biden's pandemic-related child-care tax credit permanent was lowest among lower-middle-income non-college voters. When that tax credit ended it broke my heart. When it was eliminated in 2022, child poverty more than doubled.[28]

Liberals often support means testing to "target the most vulnerable." Economists often favor it as efficient. But programs targeted to the poor result in benefits that are stingy and stigmatized: TANF, public housing, and subsidized childcare all are good examples. Liberals have not caught on that making redistributive programs means-tested is a logical move for the *Right*—not the Left. Get with it: political scientist Theda Skocpol pointed this out in the 1990s. Tim Walz got it: he purposely designed

Minnesota's free school lunch program to avoid stigma and create widespread political support for it.[29]

A great example concerns social housing in Vienna. Unlike in the US, where people are kicked out of public housing if they earn too much, in Vienna, someone in "social housing" can stay forever. This means that social housing has the stability of mixed-income groups, rather than being chock-full of families hyper-stressed by poverty. This also means that middle-class people not only live in social housing; they also support it politically. When you compare that to what happened to public housing in America, it becomes readily apparent that insisting on means testing is a recipe for hurting the poor and eroding the long-term political prospects for redistributive social programs.[30]

In sharp contrast to means-tested programs, Social Security and Medicare have become the "third rail of American politics." Why? Simple: Social Security is understood as a benefit earned from one's history of hard work. To some extent, that's a fiction, given that it's funded out of current revenues. But it was designed from the beginning as something you "pay into," which highlights the importance of this messaging when designing redistributive programs in the US.

It's time to stop having the Far Right be the only ones aware of the settled-living versus hard-living dynamic in American politics. Once liberals savvy up, they can begin to tap into the widespread support for greater equality in the US. When shown pie charts illustrating the distribution of wealth in the US and Sweden (but not identified by country!), 92 percent of Americans preferred the Swedish distribution of income, where the top quintile holds 36 percent of wealth (as opposed to 84 percent in the US).[31]

Liberals need to stop assuming that government redistribution to the poor is the key way to alleviate inequality. Instead, what Americans want—the poor, the professionals, and the Missing Middle—are stable jobs, with benefits, that pay enough to sustain a stable middle-class life for everyone, regardless of race or education level. The key message is that "People who play by the rules shouldn't lose the game," to quote a key architect of the Earned Income Tax Credit (EITC). Blue-collar jobs are crucial, but they're just a start. "All they want is a three-bedroom, two-bath cinderblock house," said a friend from Atlanta, but after the 2008 Recession, "they can't get one." The key for Democrats in the US and for leftists abroad is to signal incessantly—and deliver—on the modest expectations of noncollege grads.[32]

Universal Basic Income goes in exactly the wrong direction. Programs that provide benefits "earned" through work command more robust political support with far less stigma than programs not linked with work. The Earned Income Tax Credit is an outstanding example: it grew into the nation's largest antipoverty program for eligible families, offering recipients both more self-respect and far less government intrusion than other anti-poverty programs. This basic political fact needs to be more widely appreciated. Of course, in order to work, people need childcare—that goes without saying. It's illegal to leave young children home alone.[33]

The best way to keep economic issues at the center of coalition building is to connect blue-collar families' economic pain with the pain of college-educated Gen-Zers who increasingly see their access to a solid middle-class life blocked, too. There is widespread agreement on what it takes to be middle-class: a 2024 *Washington Post* poll found that roughly 90 percent of respondents agreed that being middle-class meant having a secure job, the ability to save money for the future, afford an emergency $1,000 expense without debt, pay all bills on time without worry, have health insurance, and be able to retire comfortably—but just 35 percent of Americans were middle class according to that definition. The poor, of course, don't qualify; nor does most of the Missing Middle; but increasingly, neither do many college grads. Well-being "is about being financially stable. It's not about being rich, but it's about being able to take care of your everyday needs without stressing," said an HR employee in Indiana. "I like the feeling of not living on the edge of disaster . . . [but] I'm still one doctor's visit away from not being [at my fullest economic potential], and pretty much most people I know are." Note that both these folks are probably college grads.[34]

The college wage premium has diminished over the last two decades; now what's needed is a graduate degree. Though college grads still have sharply higher earnings than noncollege grads, going to college no longer predictably enhances wealth. Average college debt among graduating seniors who had taken out student loans more than doubled between 1986 and 2008. College students today graduate with an average of nearly $20,000 in debt, while those who continue into graduate school average $45,000 in student loans. Salaries are lower, too. While high school grads' incomes have fallen more (from $42,630 to $29,647 in 2002 dollars), college grads' typical earnings slid from $52,087 to $48,955. The result is that many Gen Z college grads are putting off buying homes and having children because they are unable to accumulate enough wealth to do so.[35]

The diploma divide has received the most attention, but there's a divide among college graduates, too. Inequality has risen between the top 1 percent and the median household. Remember that top-earning male college graduates earn 90 percent more than low-earning ones, up from 70 percent in 1979. An increasing number of male college grads end up in medium-skilled jobs, and a surprising number of both male (19.4 percent) and female (14 percent) college grads earn *less* than the average high school graduate. The winner-take-all economy has meant that even many college grads from solid universities are unable to afford the house, the childcare, the car, the vacations, and the security associated with the upper-middle-class life they felt was promised them. "Millennials are less well off than members of earlier generations when they were young, with lower earnings, fewer assets, and less wealth," concluded a 2018 study by the Federal Reserve Board. Today's millennials are only half as likely to own a home as compared to young adults in 1975 and have 300 percent more student debt than their parents had.[36]

This inability to launch is a relatively recent development in the US, but many parts of Western Europe have long seen high rates of un- and underemployment among the young. As of 2022, double-digit numbers of youth aged fifteen to twenty-four in France (18 percent), Italy (24 percent), and Spain (30 percent) are unemployed; in the US, the number is 11 percent. This highlights the potential of forging a coalition among blue-collar voters infuriated by the loss of family-sustaining jobs for non-college grads and college grads who are frustrated economically, too.[37]

Another key pain point is housing prices, which have spiraled out of control for a variety of reasons, one of which is that private equity has bought up so much housing starting during the Great Recession of 2008 (subsidized, of course, by the carried-interest deduction). By 2030, "institutional investors may control 40% of U.S. single-family rental homes." This highlights the need not just to focus on blue-collar jobs but to forge a coalition around kitchen table frustrations shared by the Missing Middle and the Brahmin Left. The clear path to doing this is to link working-class woes with those of Gen Z in superstar cities who can't afford to buy a house—the key to wealth transmission for all but the very rich. Kamala Harris wasted no time in doing this after she became Democrats' nominee in 2024: she immediately started talking about the price of housing.

Young people in developed countries are more pessimistic about their futures than young people in less developed ones, with US young people more likely than those in any country surveyed except Cameroon to say that family wealth and connections play as big a role as hard work does in determining success. In the US and five other rich countries, only about a third of young people said they thought their children would be economically better off than their parents.[38]

"It sucks to be 33," said *New York Times* economics reporter Jeanna Smialek on *The Daily*, explaining why millennials are putting off having children—because they have had a harder time than prior generations getting into college, getting jobs, and buying a house. In 1960, 77 percent of women and 65 percent of men had the traditional accoutrements of adulthood by age thirty: they had finished school, become financially independent, left home, married, and had a child. By 2000, only 46 percent of women and 31 percent of men had.[39]

Part of the problem is that geographic and income maldistribution have gotten so acute that it's impossible to own or even rent for many college-educated Gen-Zers in superstar cities. Between 1995 and 2002, median rents rose by more than 50 percent in nearly all the largest metropolitan areas. In San Francisco, rents rose 76 percent. Both of my own children moved away from San Francisco, in part because neither felt they could afford to buy a house here. A 2023 poll found that housing placed second only to inflation as a cause for concern among eighteen-to-thirty-four-year-olds. That's not surprising, given that rents have climbed about 22 percent between 2019 and 2023, during a period when the key index of home prices rose 46 percent. Just check out the TikTok videos where people compare how long it takes to save up for a house now as compared to the past.[40]

Again, we need an economy where anyone willing to work hard can achieve a middle-class life—college grads as well as noncollege grads. That's not too much to ask of one of the richest countries in the world.

Key Takeaways:

1. In the US, support for government *redistribution* is weaker than in most other industrialized countries. Much stronger support exists for *predistribution*: labor market interventions powered

by the belief that the rich earn too much and everyone else earns too little.

2. Means-tested redistribution programs pit the have-a-littles against the have-nots. This translates into a lack of political support, leading to programs that are stingy and stigmatized.

3. Class-competent messaging requires understanding the dichotomy between settled living and hard living—and that jobs offer not just money but social honor.

4. The path forward is to link the economic woes of the Missing Middle with those of younger college-educated voters struggling to buy houses, afford childcare, and find good, stable jobs.

Understand Why Demography Wasn't Destiny

For me, the choice . . . is between maintaining democracy and eroding it, between defending bodily autonomy and surrendering it, between racism and egalitarianism. But I'm careful not to project my framing onto other Black people, careful not to assume that my priorities are theirs.

—Charles Blow[1]

Too often, the assumption among progressives is that all people of color are progressives; ¡*Ojalá*! Many aren't, or aren't consistently.

Recall that, among Democrats, nearly two-thirds of white Americans identify as liberal or very liberal, compared to 39 percent of Blacks and 41 percent of Latinos. Polling in 2023 found that non-white Americans without degrees were the group least likely to think abortion should be legal. The diploma divide also emerged on gay marriage; 63–67 percent of noncollege respondents supported it, compared with 76–82 percent of college grads. Polling in 2024 found support for a pathway to citizenship for undocumented immigrants currently in the US is only 1 point higher among non-whites without degrees than among same-class whites (36 percent versus 35 percent). It's not surprising that Latinos and African Americans are sometimes more like white Americans without degrees: remember that 79 percent of Latinos and 72 percent of African Americans didn't graduate from college.[2]

Another example: racial justice rhetoric is unappealing to many in the multiracial coalition that progressives seek to forge. Ian Haney López found that a "call out racism" message alienated about two-thirds of Latinos. Instead, he recommends messaging that addresses Latinos as an equal and valued part of the American whole. "The pushback against a racial justice message was so strong in the focus groups that when we crafted and tested messages in a national survey, we omitted that frame" from their polling, Haney López reported. Its unpopularity surprised him, he told me. "Even in a progressive state like California, the persuadable middle found the racial justice frame . . . significantly less convincing than color-blind economic populism and all nine of the race-class messages. . . . In short, the research suggests that the racial justice message loses persuadable voters, potentially by a lot."[3]

Conservatism among people of color is a huge topic not often studied by academics, so my discussion will be impressionistic. My goal is to provide enough background to spur creative thinking on how the Left can build bridges to people of color by better understanding their complexity. There's a lot on Latinos and quite a bit about African Americans. The same is not true of Asian Americans, perhaps because they are only 6 percent of eligible voters, and 55 percent are concentrated in five states, four of which vote reliably Democratic in presidential races. Thus my focus will be on Latinos and African Americans. The bottom line is that assumptions of racial homogeneity can impede progressives' ability to fully process that people of color aren't invariably progressive—an insight that's crucial for building multiracial cross-class coalitions.[4]

Let's look first at African Americans, who are less uniformly liberal than is often assumed. In fact, Blacks who vote or lean Democratic are the least likely Democrats to identify as liberals. Generation matters: as noted before, one poll found that Black voters under forty-five shifted 22 points toward Republicans between 2018 and 2022.[5]

Though Black Americans also are much more likely than any other group to see addressing racial issues as a key concern, only 28 percent saw it as their top priority in 2024, trailing economic issues by 11 points. This makes sense: the Black-white pay gap shrank more in the boom decades after World War II than it did since the passage of the civil rights laws of the 1960s.[6]

Black Americans differ from other groups in their attitudes toward police and the criminal justice system. Only about 60 percent say police treat them fairly, dramatically lower than any other group, and a higher percentage of African Americans than any other group have a desire for major changes in policing and criminal justice reform. That does not necessarily mean they want less policing. In 2022, Black Democrats were twice as likely as white Democrats to say reducing crime should be a top priority. A 2022 survey found that nearly three-fourths of white liberals but only about half of Blacks supported defunding the police and shifting resources to social services. Another poll found that a third of whites who leaned or voted Democratic favored increasing police by 10 percent even if that meant fewer funds for other public services while half of Blacks agreed—more than any other racial group.[7]

Blacks who vote or lean Democratic also express more support for increasing the number of border patrols (63 percent) than do their white (47 percent) or Latino (50 percent) counterparts. They also are much more likely (30 percent) than white (15 percent) or Latino (22 percent) counterparts to support increased spending on border security, including building a wall.[8]

Black voters also differ from Democratic primary voters on climate change issues. Among Democrats, they are the only group (60 percent) to support increasing fossil-fuel production and exports of natural gas, in sharp contrast to their white (36 percent) or Latino (43 percent) counterparts. They are also the least likely group (26 percent) to say that climate change is an extremely important issue—half as likely as their white and Latino counterparts.[9]

In some good news for Democrats, Black Americans place by far the highest priority of any racial group on helping the poor: 70 percent support it, compared with half of Latinos and about a third of whites and Asian Americans. Digging deeper, polling in 2021 found that roughly 60 percent of Blacks believed that Democrats do better at managing the economy, creating good-paying jobs, creating opportunity, and helping people get a raise; Latinos and Americans in general were in the 30s for each question.[10]

But it's easy to exaggerate how much Black voters agree with college-educated liberals. While a majority of Democratic primary voters thought hard work is no guarantee of success, a majority of Black voters believe that most people can get ahead if they work hard. As has been discussed, though a deep literature links suspicion of redistribution to racism, people of color sometimes articulate the same suspicion. "You've got people out there that have got five, six and seven kids and they get Social Security and they get Section 8 and they get utility checks and they get food stamps," said an African American woman. "When you sit there and you abuse the system . . ." She trailed off, and her Latina friend piped up, "Welfare." This sentiment is less common than among whites, however, because affluent African Americans vigorously monitor one another's commitment to the poor.[11]

African Americans are more likely than whites or Latinos to believe that the wealthy create jobs and prosperity for everyone. Corey Fields's important study of Black Republicans, chiefly men, found that many were attracted by Republicans' insistence on the empowering possibilities of entrepreneurship and hard work, which some linked with Black nationalism. (You read that right: Republicans attracting Black nationalists.) The Republicans Fields studied were typically college grads; more recent polling found that, though Black working-class respondents were strongly drawn to candidates with an economic populist message, other Blacks were not.[12]

The rightward shift of Black voters is concentrated among Black men—if the electorate were composed of Black women, we would probably be living in a social democracy. "Black men are both Black and they are men," mused Ben Jealous, outgoing president of People for the American Way and former president of the NAACP.

> For many white working-class men, the things that primarily matter are getting a good job, looking forward to a better job, having a strategy to make sure that the kids can work or whether or not the kids go to college. The reality is there are a lot of Black men with the same primary concerns.[13]

Trump's bad-but-bold masculinity also plays a role. The endorsements of famous rappers Ice Cube, Lil Wayne, and Lil Pump are emblematic. "In the rap world, Trump has long been an avatar for ostentatious wealth. He was seen as a boss and a self-promotional hustler—basically, most rappers' idea of a rich person," commented a reporter.[14]

And it's not just a few rappers. A 2023 study found that "Black men were . . . most likely to agree with the Man Box," defined as "a restrictive, dominance-driven view of manhood" perhaps due to "historical threats and violence from police, white-majority workplaces, racist exclusion from social spaces, and unjust incarceration [that may make] . . . hypermasculine ideas . . . a way to survive." Also fueling male support is Trump's enactment of masculinity. "From many Black male perspectives, the Democratic Party is perceived as weak," says Charles Cherry, president of an advertising and marketing firm. "And that's why you've got some brothers who appreciate Trump, even as bad as Trump has been."[15]

There's also some evidence of a diploma divide. Recall that "most

Blacks report having more in common with their social class than with their racial group, and that Blacks who self-identify as working class are particularly likely to do so." Just like less educated whites, working-class African Americans sometimes are more conservative than college grads are. Black college grads gave consistently liberal responses at about twice the rate as older Black noncollege grads did (27 percent). Sixty percent of Blacks with high school degrees or less believe that government is almost always wasteful, compared with only 46 percent of Black college grads. Black college grads are also 20 percentage points (86 percent) higher than those with a high school degree or less (66 percent) to say that immigrants strengthen our country. Black college grads are 12 points more likely than those with at most a high school degree to say that hard work can get you ahead.[16]

Another way Black voters often disagree with progressives concerns religion and religious-inflected social issues. Black voters are more likely to be pro-life than Democrats overall. By two to one, they think that believing in God is necessary for good morals, while Democratic primary voters disagreed by the same margin. Over half of Blacks associate with Black Protestantism, and nearly half of Latinos identify as Catholic—the two groups with the strongest ties to religion. Nearly half (45 percent) of Blacks identify as born again, much higher than whites (26 percent) or any other group. Blacks also are the most likely to attend services regularly (35 percent). Religiosity affects attitudes toward cherished progressive projects like equality for the LGBTQ community: in 2018, over 60 percent of Black Protestants said that homosexual sex is always wrong, the same percentage as evangelicals.[17]

Social conservatism does not have a large effect on Black Americans' voting behavior, but progressives should not delude themselves: Democrats' positions on social issues consistently reflect the beliefs of predominantly white progressive activists, not people of color. Black people, particularly non-elites, are more conservative on some major issues.[18]

By far the most has been written about Latinos' shift right: it has become clear that Latinos aren't monolithic. Florida has flipped Republican in part because its Latino community includes so many fervent anti-communists whose families fled Castro's Cuba or Venezuela under Hugo Chavez or Nicolas Maduro. Socialism means something very different to them than it does to Bernie Sanders. "We're Cubans. We come from a dictatorship—we don't want any of that here," said one voter. In Florida, Trump won 46 percent of the Latino vote in 2020, an 11-point improvement compared to 2016. "There were Trump flags all over Miami"; "they've created an identity," one Democratic pollster lamented. "I have heard this president stand behind the mic and boast of how proud he is of Hispanic working Americans, how we are the backbone of the economy of this country," said a Florida Trump supporter. He felt that Trump "has really put Hispanic voices on the table and let us talk to America about the issues that we face, the things that we need."[19]

But it's not just Latinos in Florida. While Cubans shifted toward Trump the most in 2020 (13 points), Latinos of Mexican origin shifted toward him 6 points, and Puerto Ricans by 9 points.[20]

What most shocked Democrats in the 2022 midterms was the widespread defections from Latinos in border areas in South Texas that are former Democratic strongholds. In the border towns of McAllen and Laredo, Trump improved his 2016 results by more than 23 points in 2020. "Aside from our Mexican heritage, much of South Texas has ... demographic similarities to some of the more conservative strongholds and white communities in the state," said nine-term Democratic congressman Henry Cuellar. Many Texas Latinos see themselves as white: in one county with one of the highest concentrations of Latinos in the country, 96 percent of census respondents were Hispanic, and nearly 99 percent identified as white. (In sharp contrast, in Salinas, California, a mere 37 percent of Latinos identified as white.) Many Texas Latinos see the Border Patrol, law enforcement, and gas and oil jobs as desirable paths to the middle class. "For our community, all the good work is in the oil lines," said one South Texas voter. "Growing up, my dad used to take me to work in the oil fields. It was a white man's industry," said another Texas Latino. "Today it is us Latinos." In Texas, Republicans hold a "15 point lead over Democrats on being the party most associated with 'hard work,' and an eight point lead on supporting small business owners."[21] Republicans adeptly leverage this into opposition to government regulation.

But it was not just Florida (where Trump gained 14 points) and Texas (9 points); in 2020, Trump also gained in Wisconsin (9 points), Nevada (8 points), Pennsylvania (6 points), Arizona (5 points), and Georgia (4 points). Precincts in New York City with at least 75 percent Hispanics swung 25 points toward Trump.[22]

Both region and generation matter a lot. A large nonpartisan 2022 survey found Latino voters evenly split between the parties in the South, while Democrats led 62–24 among Latinos in other parts of the country. In 2016, among foreign-born Latinos, those with college degrees were 12 points *less* likely than those without to identify as Democratic; by contrast, US-born Latinos with degrees were 10 points *more* likely than those without degrees to do so. By the third generation, Latinos' diploma divide is in the same direction as whites': college grads are 15 points more likely than noncollege grads to identify as Democrats. Latinos without degrees don't tend to identify as Republicans; instead, almost half (44 percent) identify as independents—they are 16 points more likely than college grads to do so. What Republicans offer is the chance to work hard and get rich. "Democrats have lots of real reasons they should be worried," noted one strategist. Latinos "look at us and say: we believe we work harder, we want the opportunity to build something . . . , and why should we punish people who do well?" As has been noted, Latinos are particularly strong believers in hard work; they were 23 points less likely than Blacks to believe that Democrats do a better job of respecting and rewarding hard work, and 13 points less likely to support taxing big business and the rich at sharply higher rates. Latinos and Asian Americans are the most likely to believe they can achieve the American dream.[23]

Sometimes the issues that attract Latinos and Latinas differ. Polling in 2022 found that Latinas were much more concerned than Latinos about abortion rights (34 percent versus 22 percent), while Latinos are more concerned about crime (14 percent versus 10 percent)—there's the protector and provider again. It's crucial to understand "how much Latino men identify with being a provider—earning enough money to support their families is central to the way they view both themselves and the political world." Some Latinos also respond to bad-but-bold masculinity. Said a Latino who doesn't support Trump of those who do: "They're the Billy Badasses."[24]

In the 2020 elections, the Latino community was very focused on economic issues. To quote Susie Martinez, Democratic state legislator and head of the Nevada chapter of the AFL-CIO, "We want to be safe in our homes. We want a good job. We want housing, so we can rest. We want pensions, so we can retire with dignity. That's what people want. That's the American dream." A survey found that over 70 percent rated jobs, the economy, health care, and the coronavirus as issues that were "very important" to them; no other issues were even close. Republicans clued into this: Republicans in Texas were "knocking on every single door and telling people that ... if they don't vote for Trump, they're going to be [jobless and] homeless," said a Latino Texan activist. "Everybody is looking for all the reasons" for Biden's decline in popularity, noted the political research firm Equis's Carlos Odio; "with Latinos, it's like the suspect is there holding the smoking gun and it's always the frickin' economy." Polling in 2021 found that only roughly a third of Latinos believed that Democrats do better at managing the economy, creating good-paying jobs, creating opportunity, and helping people get a raise—similar to the percentage for the overall sample, which was 75 percent white.[25]

One reason for Trump's relative success in 2020 was that his anti-immigrant rhetoric from 2016 was replaced with a focus on the economy. Among swing Latino voters and focus groups, Equis found that approval of Trump's handling of the economy affected vote choice, with persuadable Latino voters impressed by Trump the businessman. To quote one: "Biden was acting like he wanted to do a complete shutdown. Trump wanted to reopen the states, return to normal." The path to economic stability for many is to own a small business, and Republicans pointed out in 2020 how much pandemic shutdowns hurt small businesses. Again, Latinos express respect for hard work more than any other group.[26]

The key for progressives is to express respect for small businesses and hard work and to stress government's important role in ensuring that hard work leads to a stable, middle-class life—while recognizing, warned Odio, that Latino voters may be concerned about government spending. Yet, like African Americans, Latinos express strong support for some redistributive issues: in 2023, 92 percent wanted Medicare to be able to negotiate lower prices on prescription drugs for all Americans, 80 percent supported closing corporate tax loopholes, and 72 percent supported canceling student debt for those earning less than $125,000 a year.[27]

Another important theme is family. Odio points to polling that "named family as the number one motivator in their lives. Its impact is felt in every aspect of people's priorities around the election, resonating much more strongly than ideas of community, and driving the question, 'Who is protecting me and my family?'" Note that this theme can be tied both to economic issues and to social issues such as gun safety and safe access to abortion, particularly given polling that many Latinos oppose the overturning of *Roe v. Wade* and support increased gun control. Republicans have won some Latino votes presenting themselves as protecting religion and law and order, opposing abortion rights, and being patriotic. "*Dios, patria y familia,*" was the campaign slogan of Republican Mayra Flores, who won a special election House seat in 2022. Among Democrats, 41 percent of Latinos believe it is necessary to believe in God to be moral, compared with only 11 percent of white Dems.[28]

On social issues, generation matters a lot: only 18 percent of first-generation Latinos never attend church, compared with 40 percent of second-generation and 46 percent of third-generation Latinos. Only 41 percent of first-gen Latinos believed abortion should be legal in 2022, as compared with 59 percent of second-gen and 62 percent of third-gen Latinos.[29]

Latinos are more likely than any other group to support a path to citizenship for immigrants (83 percent), but progressives also can't assume that all Latinos embrace their values on immigration. Astonishing to me: 51 percent of Latinos supported Trump's "Remain in Mexico" policy in 2022. The Far Right's divide-and-conquer strategy has made inroads. "Our parents came in a certain way—they came in and worked, they became citizens and didn't ask for anything," said a forty-eight-year-old Latino Texas rancher. "The people coming now seem to be less willing to work and are more dangerous compared to how it used to be," said a Texas pastor. "They don't want the American dream." Latino Trump supporters are attracted by the claim that unregulated immigration will hurt them economically. "Illegal immigration hurts employment as far as wages are concerned. And who are the people who get hurt? People at the bottom . . . And many times that is still the Hispanics," said a founder of Border Hispanics for Trump. There's also a sense that Trump will help address the homelessness and human trafficking that can come in the wake of large-scale immigration.[30]

Some Latinos are convinced when the Far Right links immigrants with crime: a 2024 poll found that nearly half said the migrant situation at the border was leading to more crime. Latinos over fifty had the same likelihood as non-Hispanics (59 percent) of saying that the increase of migrants at the border is leading to more crime.[31]

Assimilation into whiteness is an established path in the scrum for social honor, with each wave of immigrants famously scorning the next wave. There's a growing consensus that Democrats need to learn a lot more about Latinos and to build lasting relationships. And perhaps most of all, show up. Trump and his surrogates do, both in Florida and Texas. Democrats, less so, is the widespread sense of Democratic operatives I and others have spoken with. One local organizer bemoaned the lack of outreach and resources: "what did we expect was going to happen?"[32]

Key Takeaways:

1. College-educated progressives often assume people of color are more liberal than they actually are.
2. African Americans trend more conservative than white liberals on climate change, religion, some social issues, defunding the police, and immigration.
3. Latinos aren't monolithic. They trend more conservative than white liberals on issues like hard work and whether Democrats do better in handling the economy. Family and small business are cherished values.
4. Generation matters. Younger Black voters shifted 22 points toward Republicans between 2018 and 2022, and third-generation Latinos without degrees are a lot less Democratic than first-generation Latinos.

Understand the Flaws in the Conventional Wisdom That MAGA Is About Racism and Status Anxiety, Not Economics

Status threat, not economic hardship, explains the 2016 presidential vote.

—Diana Mutz[1]

For a couple of years after Trump's election in 2016, there was a flood of attention to class dynamics in American politics. This ended abruptly in 2018, with studies that purported to show that far-right populism is not about class, but about whites' fears that their traditionally dominant status is being threatened by people of color. Emblematic of this shift was a 2016 *Washington Post* op-ed titled "The education gap this year wasn't about race." This adeptly summarizes the zero-sum narrative: if populism is about race, it's not about class. This narrative remains so influential that many won't tackle class blindness without an explanation about why this argument is flawed. This chapter pinpoints the flaws by focusing on the two influential studies: "Beyond Economics: Fears of Cultural Displacement Pushed the White Working Class to Trump," a 2017 joint study by the Public Religion Research Institute (PRRI) and *The Atlantic* magazine, and a 2018 academic article by political scientist Diana Mutz.[2]

These studies' flawed assumptions are a threshold problem. One is that class is about economics and only economics, an assumption that causes all the ways class is expressed through cultural difference to be understood as proof that populism *isn't* about class rather than proof that it is. The general public is overly influenced by economists unaware of the thirty years of ethnographies documenting that class is expressed through culture as well as economics.

A second threshold problem is confusion caused by different uses of "working class," as evidenced by the 2017 *Washington Post* op-ed titled

"It's Time to Bust the Myth: Most Trump Voters Were Not Working Class." Progressives often use "working class" to describe the poor, which is what this op-ed does: it points out that the poor didn't vote for Trump and that many of the rich did. That's true: the poor voted Democratic if they voted at all, and rich Republicans voted Republican. But none of this disproves the point that Trump attracted not just the Merchant Right but also middle-status voters in routine jobs.[3]

Beyond threshold difficulties lie deeper problems. The zero-sum narrative misunderstands how race and class interact in far-right politics—as well as the relationship of class and race to status anxiety and cultural displacement.

Racism Drives MAGA Voting . . . but Class Does, Too

Racism does drive support for far-right populism. There's no doubt about that. One study calculated a 60-point increase in Trump support when moving from people assessed by the survey to be least racist to those assessed as most racist. But that doesn't mean that all far-right voters are motivated chiefly by race and racism; only that racists now very predictably vote with the Far Right.[4]

Let's unpack this step by step. First, we'll look at the evidence that the Merchant Right intentionally uses racism to build support among non-college voters. Next, we'll examine the evidence that this has been a successful strategy. Finally, we'll untangle why the solid evidence that racism predicts votes for Trump does not mean that all Trump voters are racist.

First, the evidence that the Merchant Right intentionally uses racism. There's a lot of it. Elites have used racism since at least the 1670s to pit Black and white non-elites against each other to ward off an interracial working-class coalition capable of challenging elite power. An early well-documented example is Bacon's Rebellion of 1676–1677, when a combination of indentured, enslaved, and free African Americans allied with European indentured servants to rebel against the governor of Virginia. In the aftermath of the rebellion, Virginia elites drove a wedge between non-elite whites and Blacks by enhancing white indentured servants' rights at the same time as they wrote a virulent form of slavery into the law for African Americans. Pro-slavery advocates insisted that slavery guaranteed equality among whites: John C. Calhoun explained to John Quincy

Adams that "slavery was the best guarantee to equality among whites. It produced an unvarying level among them. It not only did not excite, but did not even admit of inequalities, by which one white man could domineer over another." Of course, this was untrue. Instead, this "wages of whiteness" strategy only served to deflect attention from poor whites' exploitation by rich whites.[5]

Fast-forward to the 1970s, when Republicans were looking for a way to revitalize the GOP. They saw an opportunity to win the then solidly Democratic South after President Lyndon Johnson signed the civil rights acts of the 1960s. Political scientists and historians have amply documented this "Southern strategy," and Ian Haney López has documented how it evolved into dog whistle politics after open racism fell out of fashion.[6]

Political scientist William Marble nonetheless found low correlations between white voting and racism in the 1990s. The relevance of race began to increase around 2004; by 2020, white noncollege and college grad voters placed around the same weight on race. "Over the course of several decades during which both Republican and Democratic office holders were mostly ignoring distress and discontent, a few political entrepreneurs—notably including Steve Bannon and . . . Donald Trump—developed scapegoat stories," notes the Institute for New Economic Thinking. The relevance of immigration, often intertwined with racism, began to increase around 2008 and was especially large in 2016. Four different measures of racism—racial resentment, racial animosity, white identity politics, and opposition to anti-racism—all are highly predictive of Trump support and/or voting.[7]

Despite his long personal history of racism, Trump's speeches in his first campaign depicted him as standing up for African Americans, describing them as a group that needs to be "celebrated and cherished" because they work hard for the country, arguing that they need "protections from 'illegal' immigrants and the violence in inner cities." This changed when an openly racist Unite the Right rally in Charlottesville, Virginia, led to the murder of a leftist protester. Trump's famous statement "There were good people on both sides" followed by his subsequent tweets of white-supremacist content and refusal to distance himself from them began his path of bringing white supremacy into the mainstream.[8]

The wages-of-whiteness strategy is alive and working well with a key segment of far-right voters: the American preservationists. This 20 percent of 2016 Trump voters were 30–50 points higher than any other Trump voter group to say that race was important to their identity, 10–20 points less likely to have warm feelings toward minorities, and 20–50 points more likely to say that being born in the US was very important to being a real American.[9]

Who were these preservationists? Only 15 percent were college graduates. They were only half as likely to be employed full-time and the most likely to be underemployed, with 19 percent reporting being unable to work due to a disability.

The Far Right has convinced this group that their dim prospects stem from the fact *they are white*. In fact, it's because they are *working class*: similarly situated people of color, and particularly African Americans, lost more manufacturing jobs than whites did and have persistently higher rates of un- and underemployment.[10]

This is the group of voters that gives rise to the persistent finding that racism strongly predicts far-right voting. Perhaps most influential is the work of political scientists John Sides and Michael Tesler. In "How Trump Lost and Won," they and coauthor Lynn Vavreck credit racial attitudes, not economics. "This educational divide in whites' support for Clinton against Trump disappeared after racial attitudes were taken into account—suggesting that differing attitudes towards ethnic minorities in less-educated white voters were a key reason for the educational split in voting."[11]

Writing in *The Washington Post*, Sides and Tesler attribute the rise of Trump to "white identity and grievances." They point out that, in 2016, whites who think it's extremely likely that "many whites are unable to find a job because employers are hiring minorities instead" were over 50 points more likely to support Trump than those who don't, and that white independents and Republicans whose white identity was extremely important to them are 30 points more likely to support Trump. Another prominent scholar, Lilliana Mason, found that racial animus in 2021 predicted future support for Trump but not for other Republicans. Some studies that document that racial attitudes are the strongest predictor of votes for Trump explicitly discount the importance of social class; others just ignore it.[12]

Racial attitudes indeed are the strongest predictor of Trump voting . . . but they are not the reason Trump won. How can one explain this apparent contradiction?

The source is what I call *regression confusion*: regression analysis predicts which group is most likely to vote for the Far Right; the confusion comes when it's used to support an assumption that every Trump voter fits that profile.

Sides, Tesler, Mason, and many others use regression analysis to identify the strongest predictor of far-right voting. What they find is that the relationship between vote choice and racial attitudes began to grow in the backlash against Barack Obama's presidency and was stronger in 2016 and 2020 than in prior elections. The effect is huge: in a study of primary voters, they found that support for Trump grew consistently at each step of a 17-point scale measuring white identity, from 2 percent at the bottom of the scale to 81 percent at the top. Racist voters more and more consistently veer right; the least racially resentful voters increasingly vote Democratic.[13]

And yet this does not explain Trump's victory. Trump won because he carried not only the most racially retrograde voters but also a much larger group of voters with moderate racial attitudes. In fact, "among white Republicans, the largest increase in net Republican votes between 2016 and 2020 actually came from the least racially resentful," concludes an important 2023 study. If you compare net Republican votes for Trump in 2020 to Romney votes in 2012, you find that "Trump's support grew the most, relative to prior Republican candidates', among whites with relatively moderate racial resentment scores." This finding is in a rigorous, highly mathematical study that concludes that there are simply too few highly racist voters to explain Trump's victory, especially since "between 2012 and 2016, the number of people who scored at the high end of the racial resentment scale declined significantly."[14]

Still, it's highly disturbing that Trump's racism was not a deal-breaker. Moderate resentment scores—damning with faint praise. But recall that anti-elites' racial attitudes did not differ from those of non-Trump voters by one common measure of racism.[15] The point is not to deny the role of racism but to acknowledge that racism retains a hold on many Americans, both elite and non-elite. The solution is to keep working to eliminate racism in both elites and non-elites; for elite whites to use racism as an excuse to discount the legitimate economic grievances of non-elites does not help accomplish this. Regression confusion has become one means of doing that. We need to distinguish between who is *most likely* to vote for the Far Right—American preservationists who will never be part of a progressive coalition—from other people who also voted for the Far Right but could be brought into an interracial progressive coalition if we play our cards right.

Do Cultural Displacement and Status Anxiety, Not Economics, Explain MAGA?

The second piece of the zero-sum narrative is that MAGA is about status anxiety and fear of cultural displacement, not economics. This section discusses two studies, by Diana Mutz and the PRRI/*Atlantic*, that have been extremely influential in crystallizing this conventional wisdom.

The first problem is that these studies mismeasure economics. Mutz, for example, found that those whose incomes declined between 2012 and 2016 were more likely to support Trump. She interpreted this as "status threat." But isn't a reduction in income an economic concern? Mutz also looks at voters who lost a job, who were negative about their current economic situation or felt they have lost ground due to trade. She's not looking at the right group of voters: workers still hanging on to routine jobs but worried and waiting for the other shoe to drop. The PRRI study also looks at the poor, not the Missing Middle: it found that white non-college voters "who reported being in poor financial shape predicted support for Hillary Clinton." But there's a deeper problem. It's been known for decades that economic insecurity—the sense that the best years for Americans are over—is what predicts support for populists, not whether voters feel they personally are in good shape financially or feel the economy is. The question that most accurately predicted who would vote for Ross Perot in the 1990s was: "When it comes to the availability of good jobs for American workers, some say that America's best years are behind us. Others say that the best times are yet to come. What do you think?"[16]

The PRRI/*Atlantic* report's own focus groups reflected precisely these kinds of anxieties, which we saw with the Hodges' experience in chapter 3. To quote one focus group member:

> The middle class can't survive in today's economy because there really isn't a middle-class anymore. You've got poverty level, you got your 1%, 2%. You don't have a middle class anymore like you had in the 70s and 80s. My dad

started at Cinco making a buck 10 an hour. When he retired he was making $45 an hour. It took him 40 years, but he did it. Can't find that today; there's no job that exists like that today.[17]

Economic anxiety came through in survey data, too. White college-educated Americans were about three times as likely as noncollege Americans to say their financial circumstances had improved. Only 14 percent of noncollege grads said things had improved for them. Nearly two-thirds of college grads but less than half of noncollege grads believed the American dream is still a reality. Noncollege grads were 22 points more likely than non-grads to say America's best days are behind us. It's disheartening that progressives at PRRI and *The Atlantic* include all this and yet discount the influence of economics.[18]

The second problem with these two studies is how they measure cultural displacement/status threat. Mutz concludes that "evidence points overwhelmingly to perceived status threat among high-status groups as the key motivation underlying Trump support. White Americans' declining numerical dominance in the United States together with the rising status of African Americans and American insecurity about whether the United States is still the dominant economic superpower combined to prompt a classic defensive reaction among members of dominant groups." She supports her thesis that Trump voting represents "racial/global status threat," by pointing out that people who embraced Trump's views on trade and China tended to support him, which explained the greater mass appeal of Trump in 2016 relative to Mitt Romney in 2012. But this reflects that the middle-status voters who trend far-right have seen with their own eyes what's confirmed by economists: globalization helped Chinese workers at the same time that it hurt many workers in advanced industrial democracies. David Autor documented that those affected by the China shock did indeed veer toward Trump.[19]

Mutz notes her assumption that globalization is mutually beneficial to countries that participate. This conventional wisdom reflects neoclassical economics' obsession with GDP—and its lack of concern with how GDP is distributed. People aren't impressed by increased GDP if they feel the new wealth has only helped the haves further enrich themselves at the expense of the have-nots.[20]

Mutz also acknowledges research showing that "to the extent that immigration is perceived as threatening by Americans, scholars find that it is due to the increased economic burden Americans believe immigrants place on the social welfare system rather than a threat to white status." But isn't that evidence that these Americans are driven by (perhaps misplaced) economic considerations, not racism? In fact, attitudes toward immigration intertwine economic anxiety with racism (as will be discussed in chapter 25). Mutz does not disentangle any of this. She merely throws in immigration attitudes as the third measure of her "racial/status threat, not economics" thesis.[21]

The PRRI study states right up front that attitudes about race were not significant in predicting Trump support among noncollege whites, who are "roughly as likely as Americans overall to believe many minority groups face substantial discrimination in society." Regression analysis also showed support for deporting non-documented immigrants strongly predicted Trump voting, but that's the American preservationists again: overall, support for a path to citizenship for non-documented immigrants among noncollege whites was "only slightly lower than support among the general public" (63 percent). It's ironic, then, how the PRRI report helped crystallize the common sense among progressives that racism, not economics, explains MAGA.[22]

A key data point used to show that "fears of cultural displacement" are what drive MAGA is that "white working-class voters who say they often feel like a stranger in their own land and who believe the US needs protecting against foreign influence were 3.5 times more likely to favor Trump than those" who didn't. Nearly half of noncollege voters (but only a quarter of white college grads) felt that "things have changed so much that I often feel like a stranger in my own country." This finding begs more questions than it answers. Do these noncollege grads feel like strangers because they feel out of sync with elites' liberal cultural values? Or because they yearn for the days when patriotism was a value shared by elites and non-elites? Or because they feel minorities are threatening white supremacy? The PRRI report interprets this "stranger in my own land" question as evidence of racism, linking it with fear of foreign influence. These were different questions on the survey, but they are lumped together to pave the way for the interpretation that both are evidence that MAGA really stands for *Making America White Again*. This is contradicted by other evidence in the report, notably that noncollege whites were about as likely as Americans overall to believe that many minority groups face substantial discrimination and that nearly 60 percent believed that immigrants should be allowed to become citizens if they meet certain requirements, only slightly lower than the general public.[23] Don't get me wrong—the American preservationists are definitely there: 87 percent of those who supported increased deportations voted for Trump, as did 70 percent of those who said that discrimination against whites is a serious problem. But don't fall prey to regression confusion: the fact that racists have flocked to the Far Right doesn't mean that all far-right voters are driven chiefly by racism.[24]

The irony is that, though these studies don't show it, it's very likely that far-right voters are higher in status anxiety than non–Trump voters. As mentioned before, classic research documents "middle-status conservatism." People in the middle of status hierarchies are higher in status anxiety than "those above" or "those below." Again, high-status people don't worry so much about losing status because theirs is so secure; low-status people worry even less because they have so little to lose. Middle-status people have a class-specific form of risk aversion—what leftist writer Barbara Ehrenreich called the "fear of falling." Inequality fuels status anxiety in other ways, too, "as people worry more about being evaluated under more intense competition."[25]

The Mutz and PRRI studies have been so effective at reinforcing the deplorables narrative that progressives often refer in an offhand way to the "fact" that racism, not economics, drives the Far Right. The deplorables narrative serves as a mute button to ensure that the Left doesn't hear or attend to the economic and social anxieties of the Missing Middle. This is an ideal scenario for the Far Right. The solution is not to deny the very real influence of racism in American politics. It's to have the Left provide an alternative channel for the fury and anxiety the Far Right has learned how to channel so effectively. "There was a time when a man could work 40 hours of honest labor and let his wife stay with the kids, own his home, give children the choice of whether or not to go to college. But something has happened," said Will McMillan, a forty-eight-year-old union electrician. People like this won't shut up. Nor should they.[26]

Key Takeaways:

1. If a voter is racist, that's a strong predictor he or she will vote for MAGA.
2. But there aren't enough of those voters to explain Trump's

success; he also attracts a much larger group of voters with moderate racial attitudes.

3. Though Trump voters tend to be higher in status anxiety, this isn't necessarily proof of racism; it reflects that middle-status people trend higher in status anxiety than "those above" or "those below."

4. Studies that have been widely influential in supporting the thesis that MAGA reflects racism, not economics, often mismeasure economics and/or racism.

Talking Across Class Lines

*Who gives a shit if the majority of Hispanics don't know or
use Latinx.*

—César Vargas, Latino Rebels newsletter[1]

My crowd of social justice warriors is fond of specialized language. We
coined the term *care work* to highlight that child-rearing and eldercare
are *work*, not just the natural emanation of the female soul. Lesbians in
the gay rights movement pointed out that the movement was named
for the term used for gay men, so the accepted term became first *lesbian and gay*, then *lesbigay*, then *LBGT*, then *LGBTQIA+*. The motivation
is idealistic: the hope that neologisms can help deconstruct the way a
certain distribution of power is invisibilized by language. *Latinx* reflects
this tradition by eliminating the unspoken male norm of *Latinos*, which
is used to refer both to men and to everyone, erasing the existence of
women. It's troublesome in the same way that referring to all people as
"mankind" is. But in our intense focus to deconstruct racial and gender
hierarchies, we have ignored the class signals this language sends. Non-
elites hear not social justice but sophistry: that elites love language games
and lack common sense. That's why terms like *Latinx* are off-putting:
40 percent of Hispanics found the term offensive, and only 3 percent
use it. I read this as a class effect: remember that nearly 80 percent of
Latinos lack college degrees. Only about a third of progressive activists
think that political correctness is a problem, but between two-thirds and
100 percent of all other groups do. This in-group orientation has costs.
"It's hard to build a coalition while constantly correcting how people
talk," notes Emily Bazelon. "Symbolic fights distract elites while doing
nothing to address economic hardship." Americans focus on virtue more

than non-Americans—okay, but let's not pursue virtue by policing class-parochial language.[2]

Sadly, liberals are 2.4 times as likely as conservatives to fail to use arguments tailored to their audiences, an experiment found. The message of parallel universes has not gotten through. Non-elites hear language policing as people telling them they're dowdy and dim-witted. This is the class dynamic that far-right politicians tap through attacks on "woke" and "political correctness." "Today's most popular, secular conservative media tell an overarching story of conservatism as an identity facing the threat of stigma from liberal elites," notes media scholar Anthony Nadler. He interviewed people in southeast Pennsylvania who rely on conservative news sources and found almost everyone "told me they think that liberals see conservatives as reprehensible people whose beliefs are fueled by racism, homophobia, sexism, greed, and other moral failings." These feelings stemmed from experiences on social media but also from stories on conservative news shows. "From Fox News commentators to conservative talk show hosts to popular online right-wing outlets like *Daily Caller* and Breitbart, there's one motif that audiences will find repeated endlessly: Liberals and leftists see conservatives—and their communities—as suffering from deep moral failures, and they want to shame and even humiliate them." A white woman in her forties told Nadler that liberals think "if you're conservative, you don't care about the environment. You hate gays, lesbians, transgender." An African American in her sixties said that, even though she had become disillusioned with the Republican Party, she was upset that liberals assumed religious and conservative people are "uneducated and unreasonable." A white man in his sixties was offended when he saw clips on Fox News in which liberal reporters referred to anti-lockdown protesters as "rednecks" and "fascists." Recall the Louisiana gospel singer we met in chapter 6 who felt that Rush Limbaugh was standing up for her. Nadler met someone who "trusts Limbaugh to punch back, and it gives him a sense of relief to have such a fighter in his corner."[3]

Progressives need to call out racism and homophobia, but they also need to stop displacing blame for these and other social ills onto one social group. One-third of the groups Katherine Cramer spoke with in Wisconsin felt that public decision-makers in metropolitan areas held negative stereotypes of rural residents as "hicks," "country bumpkins," "rednecks," and the like; one group called itself the "Mediocre Redneck Coffee Klatch." Anthony Nadler astutely notes that far-right provocateurs "agitate an identity threat, then defend and counterattack." It doesn't help when influential people call "MAGAworld" irrational, "not grounded in reality," in *The New York Times*.[4]

Class-based insults betray key progressive values. The clearest example was in the coverage of *White Rural Rage: The Threat to American Democracy*. To quote Tom Schaller, one of the book's coauthors, on MSNBC:

> Rural white voters are the most racist, xenophobic, anti-immigrant and anti-gay demographic group in the country. They are also the most conspiracist group, . . . [who] don't believe in an independent press, free speech . . . , the most white nationalist [and] most likely to excuse and justify violence as an acceptable alternative to peaceful public discourse.[5]

Wow. This is a classic example of stereotyping. To quote one tweet in response, "Racism exists everywhere, it is not only in rural towns. What a perfect way to alienate MORE voters by calling them every stereotype in the book." What Schaller *means* is that the prevalence of these patterns is greater among rural white voters, but what he *says* tars every member of that group. Can you imagine the reaction on MSNBC if someone said that Black people are more violent, citing as evidence the high incidence of inner-city gun violence?[6]

In addition to open insults, progressives give off many unintended signals of class privilege. Media scholars explain that class is expressed though different "taste cultures." Reece Peck highlights this through his comparison of *The Rachel Maddow Show* (on MSNBC) and *The O'Reilly Factor* (Fox News' long-reigning top show). A 2009 *O'Reilly* promo began with smoke swirling as if from an explosion while capital letters read "THE ULTIMATE IN CONFRONTATION TV. A REAL VOICE FOR THE LITTLE GUY. LOVE HIM. HATE HIM. HE'S CLEARLY NUMBER ONE." "As Donald Trump's 2016 presidential campaign so spectacularly demonstrated, lacking credentials, expressing rage, having poor taste and 'bad manners,' and following one's gut can be positively spun as signs of 'ordinariness' and 'authenticity.'"[7]

Conservatives have taken the time to learn non-elites' taste in culture. The hit show *Yellowstone* is a good example. *Yellowstone* has a message: You are enviable. You, right where you are, have something everyone else wants. This makes you richer than them, and more real. 'Every millionaire I know wants to be a cowboy,' a developer says in the pilot. 'Authenticity's the one thing money can't buy.'" Conservatives know this stuff. Liberals should learn it.[8]

Folks, this ain't that hard to do. "I'll fight to make more sh*t in America," said John Fetterman in a 2022 campaign ad. Fetterman, as usual, goes bad-but-bold. "He's a man who could pass as a Hells Angel," noted a *Politico* reporter in April 2021. *People* magazine said, "He looks like a bad guy from central casting or, at least, an intimidating bouncer." He's received massive publicity about his nine tattoos listing the name of every person who died by violence during his tenure as mayor of Braddock, Pennsylvania. Fetterman's deftness at sculpting cultural metaphors was lost on his Republican opponent, Mehmet Oz: "He's kicking authority in the balls," said Oz, not seeing that this is part of Fetterman's appeal. Fetterman's an equal-opportunity transgressor: progressives were not amused when he announced in 2024 that he was not a progressive due to dissatisfactions with progressive positions on Israel and immigration.[9]

Democrats' 2024 vice-presidential candidate Tim Walz showed very different ways of connecting with non-elite "taste culture." Like Fetterman, he embraced legislation of interest to blue-collar guys: the nation's strongest right-to-repair law and legalization of recreational marijuana. Equally important, he did so with a personal style perfectly calibrated to connect with the values of rural and working-class America. "You can tell those flannel shirts he wears don't come from some political consultant. They come from his closet and they have been through some stuff," said Barack Obama (making sure we understood that by *stuff* he meant *manure*). Walz loves straight talk: "In Minnesota, we respect our neighbors in the personal choices that they make. Even if we wouldn't make the same choice for ourselves, there's a golden rule: Mind your own damn business." His liberal use of "damn" and "hell"—"These guys are creepy, and yes, weird as hell"—reflects an old-fashioned rural talk tradition: these words are far too dowdy for my crowd in San Francisco. Walz also embraces the blue-collar "don't complain" norm: "If there's one thing I hope folks across the country recognize and take away from what we're doing here in Minnesota, is it's amazing what you can accomplish when you stop complaining about corporations going 'woke' and start giving a damn about real people and real lives." Note how he both deftly calls out "complainers" and decries culture-wars hoopla as a distraction. Walz is the equal of Fetterman in his savvy use of blue-collar repartee to deflate people: "Like all regular people I grew up with in the heartland, J.D. studied at Yale, had his career funded by Silicon Valley billionaires, and then wrote a bestseller trashing that community." Walz uses food as a class marker, too: "Look, my mom and dad and those people I grew up with, they taught me some things in those communities: show generosity toward your neighbor, work for a common good. They also taught us, and this is for all the people outside of Nebraska, they taught us that chili and cinnamon rolls is the most perfect culinary combination in the country." Walz also said Vance would call a runza a hot pocket. (Google it: a runza looks to me like an empanada in a hot dog roll.)[10]

Walz displays everyday rural and blue-collar masculinity: stories abound of fixing cars, pulling cars out of snowbanks, working on a farm, joining the military as a way of enacting reverence for a father who served, being the best damn shot in Congress but too humble to brag about it. Walz is as focused as Trump on displaying masculinity. He just displays Decent Midwestern Dad masculinity instead of bad-but-bold.[11] But many progressives prefer a Rachel Maddow. Peck explains how Maddow epitomizes upper-middle-class style in an ad published about the same time as the O'Reilly ad. Maddow is shown wearing a hoodie and thick-framed glasses, kneeling on the carpet, frenetically marking up documents. Brooding classical music plays in the background with an overdub by Maddow saying, "News is about stories. It's about finding all the disparate facts and then finding their coherence. Doing this right takes rigor and a devotion to facts that borders on obsessive." Subsequent scenes show Maddow writing out ideas on a whiteboard as if she is teaching a seminar.[12]

This enacts a very specific class script: the cult of busy smartness. Democratic politicians enact this script out a lot. "I have a plan for that," Elizabeth Warren said famously, again and again. I'm impressed she does, but many noncollege voters don't feel she's talking their language. Democratic operatives keep begging Democratic candidates to campaign in poetry and govern in prose. To quote Stacey Abrams and Lauren Groh-Wargo, "Too often, Democrats [turn] a legitimate message into an unclear or overstuffed manifesto."[13]

Producers at Fox coach both hosts and guests to perform blue-collar scripts, which producers call being "ordinary" and "authentic." "It doesn't matter if Bill O'Reilly is really a blue-collar hero as long as he can play one on television," wryly noted a Salon columnist. How true. Fox News hosts use working-class slang and sports references, and lean close to the camera for emotional effect, enacting outrage against elites. "Do you know how many American families are being affected, their livelihoods are being drilled because of this recession ... Why don't we just kick the American worker in the teeth?" shouted one host as the camera caught his vicious air-kick. The outrage in question was Obama's bailing out American car manufacturers during the 2008 recession. By enacting a blue-collar aesthetic, the Merchant Right seeks to bond with blue-collar men to convince them to oppose saving blue-collar jobs? That's bold.[14]

In sharp contrast, *The Daily Show* and its many spinoffs enact a white-collar cultural style. Ironic sophistication is key to all these shows, flattering their audience as viewers who can see beneath illusion to the reality below. The fictional anchorman Stephen Colbert enacted on *The Colbert Report* from 2005 to 2014 was the ultimate enactment of ironic sophistication, allowing the viewer to feel an inside-the-velvet-rope coziness that they got the joke.

Sincerity, often viewed by elites as corny and unsophisticated, is highly valued by non-elites, who see it as a sign of character. Michèle Lamont found that 75 percent of workers were "critical of those above for being self-centered and ambitious, lacking in sincerity, and not concerned enough 'with people.'" Recall John Fetterman saying his blue-collar hometown was an "irony-free" zone.[15]

Here's the deep structure. Traditionally, elites distinguished themselves by displaying a taste for high culture, coded as high-class taste; low culture was coded as low-class. This was still true in 1979 when Pierre Bourdieu wrote *Distinction*, his path-breaking analysis of how class is expressed through cultural difference. Since then, elites have embraced plastic flamingos, garish Halloween decorations, and many other low-brow cultural artifacts as a sign of sophistication—so long as the embrace is ironic. In other words, the high/low distinction distinguished elites from non-elites before the 1980s, while irony performs the same function today. Thus even if elites like precisely the same cultural artifacts as non-elites, non-elites remain "those below" because they don't like those artifacts with the requisite irony.[16]

This doesn't mean that working-class talk traditions are plodding and inarticulate. Fetterman's much-admired social media prowess taps into blue-collar men's tradition of razzing, described in detail in Jessica Smith Rolston's excellent book on coal mines. Repartee and one-upmanship help forge close work bonds in dangerous jobs where workers rely on one another for personal safety. Fetterman and his ad campaigns delighted in this one-upmanship against his opponent Mehmet Oz, notably hiring *Jersey Shore's* Snooki to do a video ribbing Oz for being a carpetbagger who moved to Pennsylvania to run for senator: "Personally, I don't know why anyone would want to leave Jersey . . . I know you're away from home, and you're in a new place, but Jersey will not forget you and I just wanted to let you know I will not forget you and don't worry because you'll be home in Jersey soon. This is only temporary." The video got over 2.5 million views. Fetterman's Twitter feed consistently taps this tradition. "To any same-sex couples in Tennessee, it would be my pleasure to travel to your beautiful state and officiate your wedding. DM me," he said in response to the governor of Tennessee's signing of the bill allowing public officials to refuse to officiate at same-sex weddings.[17]

In the rare instance when progressives note the importance of cultural style, it's often to comment that Democrats appeal to voters based on facts and logic whereas Republicans appeal based on emotions. "This election, Republicans tended to reach people and connect at an emotional level and Dems tried to connect with people at an intellectual level," said a national media correspondent. High-status groups often justify their privilege by depicting lower-status groups as emotional, not logical. (Women have been on the receiving end of this forever.) In fact, both parties seek to persuade their intended audiences by reaffirming cherished identities. Democrats affirm the identity of college-educated voters by sending the message that "you are thinking people who understand the ins and outs of policy design." Political scientists find that people with higher levels of education tend to have more consistent policy views and that policy influences their votes more than those with lower levels of education. So if you want to send the message that you only care about the one-third of Americans with college degrees, definitely keep talking on and on about policy. The Kamala Harris campaign showed signs of having heard this message by finally—but still too little, too late—campaigning in poetry even if they intended to govern in prose.[18]

Bill Clinton, the last Democratic presidential candidate to be a first-generation college student, hired David Kusnet as a speechwriter because of his book *Speaking American*. Clinton embraced his role as "explainer in chief," but his class sensitivities meant that his missteps were rare.[19] One simple thing is to recapture respect for working people from the Far Right. To quote Trump in the 2016 cycle, "While my opponent slanders you as deplorable and irredeemable, I call you hard-working American patriots

who love your country and want a better future for all of our people. . . .
Every American is entitled to be treated with dignity and respect in our
country." Germany's Olaf Scholz picked up votes from the Far Right by
criticizing meritocracy and emphasizing cross-class respect, influenced by
political philosopher Michael Sandel: "Manual laborers don't deserve less
respect than academics," he said. The Labor Party found its way back to
power in Norway with the slogan, "It's the ordinary people's turn now."
American politicians need to do this, too.[20]

At a subtler level, they need to understand how references to food
and leisure send unintended class messages. "Anybody gone into Whole
Foods lately? See what they charge for arugula?" asked Barack Obama
when campaigning in Iowa in 2008, where only a quarter of residents
were college grads. "I don't know what it is," a hospital clinic assistant told
a reporter. "Maybe it's a Hawaiian thing." It wasn't a Hawaiian thing; it
was an upper-middle-class thing. Howard Dean was decried as a "latte-
drinking" elitist. Michael Dukakis got into trouble over Belgian endive.
Beware: food is a class code. Elites signal sophistication by adopting
new and novel foods; the settled working class celebrates its settledness
through abundant portions of the tried-and-true. Think Olive Garden,
not Chez Panisse.[21]

Leisure is class-marked, too. A picture of John Kerry windsurfing was
intended to signal youthfulness and vigor; instead, he signaled class privilege. Barack Obama was ridiculed for his poor bowling score. We all know
that leisure is class-marked, but liberals need to really take that in, say,
when we make trade-offs between keeping public land as wilderness and
allowing off-road vehicles.[22]

Quite a different set of insights on talk traditions stems from studies
of rural and working-class voters. The Rural Urban Bridge Initiative, after
pointing out that "Democrats can win rural voters," recommends themes
that will now sound familiar. "Democrats should focus on the value of
work and the pride people take in their work, including many blue-collar
occupations." Stress the importance of bread-and-butter issues, practical
problem-solving, and "down-to-earth language," warning that "candidates
who come across like career politicians, policy wonks, or finger-wagging
scolds strongly alienate rural people." Be humble and candid: the standard
advice to "pivot" when asked a hard question plays poorly with plain-
spoken rural people.[23]

Research by the Center for Working-Class Politics and *Jacobin*, a left-wing magazine, about how to appeal to working-class voters also stressed the importance of focusing on bread-and-butter issues. They compared "woke messaging" (Message A) that "borrows rhetoric from Alexandria Ocasio-Cortez and Ayanna Pressley" and "combines identity-focused, activist-inspired language with a call for social justice" with "progressive populist" messaging focused on jobs (Message B).[24]

> ### A.
> The people closest to pain should be the people closest to power. In Washington, the wealthy and the privileged make the rules, but if you're poor, or an immigrant, or a person of color in America, then you know how hard it is just to survive in this country. We need courageous leaders who will protect the most vulnerable, fight for justice, and make transformative change.

> ### B.
> This country belongs to all of us, not just the superrich. But for years, politicians in Washington have turned their backs on people who work for a living. We need tough leaders who won't give in to millionaires and the lobbyists but will fight for good jobs, good wages, and guaranteed health care for every American.

Message B polled better than Message A among key demographics, including rural/small-town voters, blue-collar voters, and voters who identified as working class. Sections of the working class that prefer woke messaging—including Democrats of color—also responded positively to progressive populist messaging. The effects were substantial: a progressive populist who named jobs as their day-one priority won 63 percent support, whereas a woke progressive who named racial justice as their day-one priority garnered only 49 percent support.[25]

Their findings did not show that Democrats need to distance themselves from racial justice—which is, of course, nonnegotiable. But it matters how one talks about it.

> Our findings suggest that struggles for racial justice over the past decade have had such a profound effect on contemporary liberal political thinking that discussions of race and racism on the campaign trail are no longer political liabilities among working-class voters.[26]

Survey respondents didn't care about the race or gender of candidates, but they did care about class: in swing states, progressive populist candidates who were teachers or construction workers are preferred by nearly two-thirds of working-class voters, notably higher than any other message/occupation grouping (including veterans).[27]

How you talk about race matters a lot. Note that Message A mentions three vectors of social inequality—race, poverty, and immigrant status—but leaves out social class. Not surprisingly, this is a turnoff for Americans advantaged by race but not class. No surprise, then, that Message B polled better among low-education whites. Woke language played worst for those who weren't supervisors; the group that liked it best was the upper-middle class. The common progressive incantation that [fill-in-the-blank disadvantage] is "worse for people of color" is very often true. Yet that formulation reinforces Tucker Carlson's narrative that "the ruling class's 'obsession with race' and 'equality' creates a world that favors the rights of people of color and discriminates against you."[28]

Leaving out the vector of social disadvantage that affects non-elite whites also will exacerbate their tendency to deny that disadvantage is structural, which they already do much more than Black Americans. Needless to say, this will ultimately hurt people of color, women, and the poor.[29]

A prominent Democrat with deep knowledge of how to construct cross-class coalitions is California congressman Ro Khanna, who represents Silicon Valley. Khanna has impeccable progressive credentials: he cochaired Bernie Sanders's campaign. After Trump's victory in 2016, he organized Silicon Valley entrepreneurs to go to the South and Midwest to explore partnerships to revitalize the Rust Belt. And he knows how to speak American. What he advocates is "a new economic patriotism."

The story matters as much as the policy. And the story is the rejection of neoliberalism. For forty years, we made a mistake. Frankly, it was both parties. Now we need to be a nation that reclaims economic self-sufficiency and economic leadership. We'll make sure the U.S. is preeminent. Having an aspirational vision for America is really powerful. In a sense, the new economic patriotism is a blend of culture and economics. We need to show we believe America is the greatest country in the world. It's O.K. to root for the home team.[30]

Khanna gets it on so many levels. That progressives need the power of narrative. That neoliberalism haunts them. That place loyalty is a crucial part of the story: "National policymakers, to our peril, have ignored the destabilizing of local communities. For that matter, we have overlooked the extent to which Americans' sense of fulfillment is tied to where we live." That people don't want to be taken care of; they want to be empowered to take care of themselves. That masculinity is a tidal pull: jobs can give "more Americans pride in restoring their communities with many important customs intact and respect as breadwinners for their families, making it harder for narratives of resentment to take hold." The importance of hard-work worship and demands for dignity: "Until all workers reap the benefits of their hard work and are treated with dignity, the promise of the digital age remains unfulfilled." That many Americans want precisely what Khanna's parents emigrated from India for: "It's a very simple story, about having worthwhile job opportunities, high-quality education and health care, and better job prospects for one's kids."[31]

Key Takeaways:

1. Liberals, progressives, and liberal media often reflect upper-middle-class "taste cultures," while conservative media embrace blue-collar taste cultures.
2. Liberals, progressives, and liberal media sometimes stereotype non-elites as ignorant and/or deplorable in ways inconsistent with progressive values.
3. Specialized language (e.g., Latinx) often is heard by non-elites as class condescension or upper-class affectation.
4. Liberals are less than half as likely as conservatives to connect their arguments with their audiences' values.
5. The common formulation that a given social ill affects "especially Black and brown people" inadvertently sends the message that the speaker doesn't care about working-class whites experiencing similar problems.

Redirect Anti-Elitist Anger

There are two populist messages: #1. Left populism: they're robbing you blind. #2. Right populism: they think they're better than you. Progressives should stick with #1 and not fall into #2.

—David Kusnet, chief speechwriter for President Bill Clinton[1]

Americans hear a lot about elites—but chiefly from the Far Right. An analysis of *Tucker Carlson Tonight* from 2016 to 2021 found that he used the term *ruling class* in 70 percent of the episodes: the *ruling class* wants to "control you"; they want you to just "shut up and obey." "He frames nearly every topic on his show as a 'ruling class' plot, from gun control to marijuana legalization to Covid-19 restrictions."[2]

In sharp contrast, only about 20 percent of 2022 congressional TV ads by Democratic candidates running in competitive districts critiqued economic elites in any way whatsoever. "The mainstream Democratic Party's tendency to avoid naming corporations as bad actors, whether pharmaceutical companies or big banks, is politically disastrous," argues Deepak Bhargava in a 2024 paper.[3]

In a recent shift, Democrats in 2024 abruptly embraced anti-elitism with a bang. At the Democratic National Convention in 2024, Michelle Obama decried Trump as a product "of the affirmative action of generational wealth" who had enjoyed the "grace of falling forward" while claiming to be a victim. She was speaking for ordinary people, she said: "If we bankrupt a business or choke in a crisis, we don't get a second, third or fourth chance. If things don't go our way, we don't have the luxury of whining or cheating others to get further ahead. No. We don't get to change the rules so we always win. If we see a mountain in front of us, we don't expect there to be an escalator to take us to the top." Barack Obama chimed in: "Here's a 78-year-old billionaire who has not stopped whining about his problems since he rode down his golden escalator nine years ago." (Clearly they had a metaphor-reinforcement pact.)[4]

Tim Walz used anti-elitist rhetoric, too: "[Kamala Harris] worked at McDonald's, like so many of us growing up took jobs to get by. The funny thing to me is can you picture Donald Trump working the Mc-Flurry machine?" In the same speech, Walz praised Harris for standing up against "corporate greed" and accusing Trump of trying to "rig the economy for the ultrarich by punishing the middle class. Raising costs on you" to give his rich friends a tax break. Kamala Harris had her own version of anti-elitism, with her constant reminders that she stood up for the people of California against big banks, after the Great Recession. All this marked an end to an era when the Far Right had a near-monopoly on anti-elitism.[5]

The potential upside to using anti-elitist rhetoric is considerable. In a follow-up to their 2021 study, *Jacobin*, YouGov, and the Center for Working-Class Politics found that "us-versus-them populist language appeals to working-class voters of all parties." "Working-class respondents, especially manual workers, favor candidates who pit 'Americans who work for a living' against 'corrupt millionaires' and 'super-rich elites,' while other occupational groups exhibit no discernible distaste for them." Republican donors are sophisticated enough to understand the need for anti-elitist rhetoric. Democratic donors need to be, too.[6]

Populist anti-elitism reflects anger against three different types of elites: business elites, political elites, and cultural elites. The Far Right typically targets cultural and political elites; the Left needs to redirect the anger toward economic elites, acknowledge the failings of political elites, and learn how to avoid making themselves the target of anger against cultural elites. Prior chapters have focused on how to defuse anger against cultural elites. This chapter will focus on political and economic elites.

Trump deftly taps the anger against political elites. One analysis showed that in the 2016 cycle Trump invoked political elites twice as often as even Bernie Sanders (who did so quite a bit). A 2020 study found that less educated Dutch felt politicians were "blind or indifferent to the lives of 'common people,'" that they lacked integrity because they "'beat about the bush,'" and that politicians looked down on them." The Far Right populist party became the largest party in the Dutch House of Representatives in 2023.[7]

Less often does the Far Right take aim at economic elites. Liberals should do so, to tap Americans' growing sense that Big Business is out of control. Twenty years ago, fewer than half of Americans said they were dissatisfied with the size and influence of major corporations; today, 74 percent are. The Harris campaign started out using anti-elitist rhetoric, but backed off it, reportedly for fear of alienating Wall Street. A bad mistake. This left Trump as the only candidate using anti-elitist rhetoric, and Harris with a muddied message on economics.[8]

Resentment against corporate power is a wedge issue among Republicans: lower-income Republicans are nearly 20 points more likely than upper-income ones to believe that corporations have too much power. Another wedge issue: nearly three times as many low-income Republican voters and leaners, and about twice as many middle-income ones ($30,000–$100,000), believe that hard work is no guarantee of success as compared with just 12 percent of rich Republicans. Beliefs that the economic system unfairly favors powerful interests show a similar pattern: about a third of rich Republicans believe this compared with roughly half of middle-income ones. Working-class Republicans are even more supportive than wealthy Democrats are of raising taxes on the wealthy (over $250,000), another wedge issue that has received startlingly little attention.[9]

Working America organizers found that the key is to give people new information instead of telling them that what they think is wrong. Organizers talked with one voter caked in mud just after getting off his construction job who was "upset to hear that Trump might roll back safety regulations, as he had once been injured on an unsafe work site. He was also upset to hear about Trump's tax policy, saying 'That wasn't what he promised.'" Organizers also found many voters unaware of Trump's efforts to roll back overtime pay. They were shocked: "Trump is not taking care of regular, everyday working Americans as he promised he would." A third of Trump swing voters disapproved of his plan to cut taxes on the rich and programs like Meals on Wheels in 2017.[10]

A 2023 study found that hypothetical candidates who explicitly called out economic elites and raised the voices of working-class people were preferred by 7.2 points among working-class respondents (defined by occupation), especially manual workers—without alienating non-working-class respondents. A 2024 study found that Democratic candidates in 2022 performed significantly better when they used anti-elitist campaign messaging. Recall that the sense of being deprived economically increased support for Trump by 41 points. It's baffling that only the Far Right is consistently tapping into this.[11]

Populist rhetoric is particularly strong—more so than moderate rhetoric—among those who make less money, are manual laborers, not supervisors, and those who identify as working class. Even non-Democrats, who are generally much cooler toward progressive politics, supported a progressive populist who focused on jobs 53 percent of the time.[12]

One reason it's so important for progressives to tap economic anger early and often is that far-right populism also taps anger against political elites: the sense of being deprived of political influence increased support for Trump by 23 points. One reason many Trump voters trust him is precisely because he's a wealthy businessman who (the theory goes) will not enrich himself, unlike a conventional politician. Another insightful analyst points out that Trump enabled Rust Belt whites to exact revenge on "the political class that had silenced the Rust Belt as it was dismantled." The Left needs to acknowledge the failings of political elites in embracing a neoliberal agenda that jeopardized the economic futures of many in the fragile and failing middle class.[13]

In yet another example of zero-sum thinking, many who center class argue against focusing on race and racism on the ground it's too divisive. I find this advice shockingly impolitic and misguided. Progressives should never forget that people of color vote Democratic at much higher rates than whites do.[14]

The key is not to minimize the importance of racism but to deconstruct why dog whistle populism works and to counter it effectively. Steve Bannon is remarkably open about his strategy: "The longer they talk about identity politics, I got 'em." Conservatives at least since George Wallace have worked hard to intertwine white working-class anger against elites with racism through the claim that the Brahmin Left favors people of color over hardworking whites. Just one example: during his 1990 senatorial campaign, Republican Jesse Helms ran an ad that showed a pair of white hands crumpling up a job rejection letter with a voiceover explaining that the job was given to a less qualified minority.[15]

What's recognized too rarely is Bannon's distinctly twenty-first-century riff on the dog whistle tradition. His goal is to have liberals talking about racism—the racism of the white working class—because he recognizes how effectively that drives those voters into the arms of the Far Right.

The conventional wisdom is to fall silent about racism. Given the persistence of structural racism, that's unethical. It's also ineffective, given Democrats' reliance on voters of color. "No Democratic resurgence is possible based on a game plan that expects racial justice movements to set aside their core concerns." Instead, we "should learn from the populist protest," urges Michael Sandel, "not by replicating" its racism and xenophobia "but by taking seriously the legitimate grievances with which these sentiments are entangled." The question, to quote critical race scholar Ian Haney López, "is *how* the Left should engage Black folks and other people of color," not *whether* they should.[16]

There's a formula for doing this, developed by Haney López. His key contribution is simple but profound: to point out that dog whistle politics is a strategy that's being used to divide the white workers from workers of color in order to help people see how racism is being used as a weapon of the rich. "If you can convince the lowest white man he's better than the best colored man, he won't notice you're picking his pocket," to quote Lyndon Johnson.[17]

This is the core of Haney López's brilliant "race-class narrative." It's the springboard for a message liberals should be sending every day of the week. Far-right populism is basically a one-trick pony: its only move is to take economic anger and direct it away from the Merchant Right, toward people of color and the Brahmin Left. Every single day, progressives need to direct it back, pointing out what the Far Right is doing, linked with the message: *We know you're too smart for that.* Instead of responding to dog whistle populism with a judgy condescension (*You're so racist*), the Left needs instead to respond with respect (*The Far Right thinks it can manipulate you because they underestimate your intelligence, but we don't*). To quote a white participant in a focus group in Ohio: "I think that racial division is something that is pushed by those in power. It's a way to keep us arguing. It's a way to oppress people, keep them uneducated."[18]

Let's start with a prominent example where progressives walked straight into Bannon's racism-as-bait trap: the fury over Oliver Anthony's song "Rich Men North of Richmond." (His real name is Chris, by the way.) Anthony's life epitomizes what the working class is pissed off about. He's a high school dropout who had worked at a paper mill in North Carolina that he described as a "living hell." He fractured his skull in 2013, forcing him to move home to Virginia. Ten years later, he was living in a camper on his farmland in North Dinwiddie, Virginia, struggling with alcoholism and depression. He worked selling industrial equipment, which meant he spoke with thousands of other blue-collar workers. "I've spent all day, every day, for the last 10 years hearing the same story. People are SO damned tired of being neglected, divided and manipulated."[19] So he wrote a song about how they're wasting their lives away working "overtime hours with bullshit pay." He goes on to decry the state of the world for "people like me and people like you," with young men "puttin' themselves six feet in the ground"—despair deaths—because "this damn country keeps on kickin' them down."

Chapter 3 of this book, in poetry. You'd think the Left would elevate him, but no: Fox News did. Why? Because the song also contained lyrics about "the obese milkin' welfare," saying that if you weigh "300 pounds / Taxes ought not to pay for your bags of fudge rounds."

Many on the Left saw these lines as a racist dog whistle. So the Left didn't just ignore the song. They *hated* it. It is progressive dogma that any negative reference to welfare is racist, ignoring that whites are judgmental toward white as well as Black welfare recipients. This doesn't make this judgmentalism attractive, but it certainly complicates the story that this is all about racism. While some people of color no doubt saw the song as racist, others posted online tributes that saw it not as racist but as speaking truth to power about economic exploitation. As the song hit number one on the Billboard Hot 100, progressives lost a major opportunity to direct its pain and anger onto the Merchant Right paying the bullshit wages that Anthony complained about.[20]

Anthony is a poet, not a political theorist: he taps the explanations for bullshit pay floating around in his environment. The Left's leap to condemn Anthony as racist was overdrawn: he's pointed to other songs where he defended the poor as exploited. On the disturbing "milkin' welfare" line, Oliver said that it "references a news story about adolescent kids in Richmond missing meals in the summer because their parents can't afford food and they can't access cafeteria food. Oliver noted that 30 to 40 percent of food stamp "purchases are on snack food and sodas. That's not the fault of those people. Welfare only makes up a small percentage of our budget. If we can fuel a proxy war in a foreign land but can't take care of our own people; that's all the song is trying to say; the government takes people who are needy and dependent and makes them needy and dependent." His economic critique even took on Big Tech, when he decried the internet as "hours wasted, goals forgotten, loved ones sitting in houses with each other distracted all day by technology made by the hands of other poor souls in sweatshops in a foreign land." On divide-and-conquer strategies: "Just for us to all sit here and do this stupid shittiness that we do every day that keeps us all beat down and divided. That's what I want to see stop."[21]

Republicans have been astute in embracing artists as mouthpieces. They did so with Merle Haggard's "Okie from Muskogee," and they tried to do so with Anthony, too. It didn't go well. When Republicans played the song in a Republican presidential debate, Oliver commented, "It was funny seeing my song in the presidential debate, because I wrote that song about those people, so for them to have to sit there and listen to that, that cracks me up. . . . That song is written about the people on that stage and a lot more, too, not just them." Notes an online comment, "The left sees 'Rich Men North of Richmond' as a rebuke of their policies, but the rebuke is for both parties."[22]

The "Rich Men North of Richmond" debacle highlights how effective the racism-as-bait strategy is in subverting the Left's ability to tap into the economic anger of non-elites. Luckily, there's a formula for reversing this process. The race-class narrative combines three elements:

- Demand government help provide economic opportunity and stability for all Americans.
- Call out "wealthy special interests who rig the rules in their favor"[23] and sow division to distract us.
- Invite people who work for a living to join together across racial lines to get what they deserve.

Let's take these elements step by step.

The first element we've already discussed; just one more word here. The term *economic justice*, which resonates so deeply with me, has been infected by successful right-wing propaganda. Anthony Flaccavento of the Rural Urban Bridge Initiative explained to me, "Most working-class folks I know, and even more so in rural areas, now associate 'justice' with 'social justice,' which in turn is nothing more than another word for socialism and various other conceits of the elite class." He suggests terms like prosperity, bootstrapping, and self-reliance.[24]

What worked for Haney López was language that taps hard-work worship. "Minnesotans work hard to provide for our families." Note that this does *not* say or imply that the poor should be thrown to the dogs. Other effective language is to speak up "for the middle class, and those seeking to enter it." No doubt there are other formulations.[25]

The second step is to call out the Merchant Right. To quote United Auto Workers President Shawn Fain at the 2024 Democratic National Convention, "Trump is pushing divide-and-conquer tactics of the rich ... They want to blame the frustrations of working-class people ... to keep the focus off the one true enemy, corporate greed." Or, to quote Kamala Harris in the 2024 presidential debate, "You know, I do believe that the vast majority of us know that we have so much more in common than what separates us, and we don't want this kind of approach that is just constantly trying to divide us, and especially by race."[26]

Not surprisingly, Haney López's research found that formulations like "wealthy special interests who rig the rules" and "the greedy few" polled better than phrases like "the wealthy few." We now know why: many in the Missing Middle admire the rich and seek to be like them. That's why it worked better to do what Oliver Anthony did: he didn't talk about *low* pay; he talked about *bullshit* pay. Someone who's bullshitting you is dissing you and ripping you off—not an honorable entrepreneur who's rich because he worked hard and built a successful business. This is just what Haney López's polling found: "When it comes to class consciousness, it seems many Americans believe they belong to the not-yet-rich class," so rather than attack "the rich," "respondents were far more comfortable faulting people for ill motives." Another variation: "My opponent ... wants to pit us against each other in order to gain power for himself and kickbacks for his donors."[27]

The third element is the call for people to join together across racial lines to contest the power of greedy elites. "Whether white, Black or brown, fifth generation or newcomer, we all want to build a better future for our children." How does this differ from both anti-racism and color-blind liberalism? One challenge is that "among many of those insisting that the Left must frontally address race and racism, there is a lot of anger." Haney López continues, "Those demanding attention to racism have to be thoughtful about when and how to call people in or out." "It's true," he acknowledges:

> those in the middle—most whites and most people of color, too—filter the
> world through stereotypes and racist ideas. It's also true, though, that they

simultaneously hold progressive racial ideals. The job ahead is not to start from scratch in educating the broad middle about racism but speak to the anti-racist convictions they *already* embrace.

Many people of goodwill *both* participate in perpetuating and benefit from structural racism, *and* hold sincerely held progressive racial ideals. Many Americans across class appreciate being called upon to be their better selves: Haney López found those surveyed to be more enthusiastic about progressive policies when they were told that all racial groups would benefit.[28]

Haney López found through polling that the race-class message "trounced" racial fear messaging. Race-class messaging could be the difference between winning and losing among voters who initially agreed with a racial dog whistle message. "In a match-up between a Republican dog-whistle message, a Democratic color-blind economic message lost, but a Democratic race-class message won. Moreover, there was a remarkable 25-point jump in net approval." Race-class messaging also performed better than color-blind economic messaging: "Whites, African Americans, and Latinx all found the race-class messages more convincing than colorblind economic populism, and by similar margins." That makes sense, because the race-class narrative combines economic populism with anti-elitist language that highlights how economic elites have been pitting workers against each other.[29]

Haney López found this message to be more effective than either a message that focuses exclusively on social class or a message that focuses exclusively on racial justice. The race-class narrative calls out the chief weapon the Far Right has used to sculpt economic and cultural anxieties into racism and then takes concrete steps to sculpt those anxieties into a united demand for an economy that supports a middle-class standard of living for noncollege voters.

Recent research finds that not all messages that reference both race and class interests are equally effective. The race-class messages must simultaneously call out racial division *and* highlight shared interests.[30]

The race-class narrative reclaims anti-elitism for the Left, contesting the Far Right's harnessing of anti-elitism into anger against political and cultural elites, and redirecting that anger against the Merchant Right. That in itself is a huge contribution.

Social psychology explains why the race-class narrative works. It contests the Far Right's deployment of in-group favoritism: the very human instinct to favor one's own, often described as "like likes like." In-group favoritism is pervasive. What's malleable is how one defines one's in-group. Unions define your in-group as other workers, which explains why survey data shows that union membership lowers racial resentment and increases support for policies that benefit African Americans. After 9/11, "racial identities became less salient as the shared American identity prevailed, at least temporarily. . . . We all have multiple, flexible identities that depend on context." Remember the advice of the Working America organizers: give people information they don't have and let them draw their own conclusions. A social psychology experiment found that providing noncollege whites with information on rising income inequality led to an increased understanding that people of color and other lower-status groups also have a harder time getting ahead.[31]

The race-class narrative shows that priming class solidarity is not inconsistent with a sustained focus on decreasing racism. No surprise. After all, that's precisely what Martin Luther King did in the Poor People's Campaign of 1968. "Equality means dignity. And dignity demands a job and a paycheck that lasts through the week." From his lips to God's ears.[32]

Key Takeaways:

1. Too often today, the Far Right taps class anger without an effective response from the Left. It's political malpractice to cede anti-elitist rhetoric to the Far Right.
2. The Far Right typically targets cultural and political elites; the Left needs to redirect the anger toward economic elites, acknowledge the failings of political elites, and learn how to avoid triggering anger against cultural elites.
3. The Left needs to stop falling into the rhetorical traps set by the Far Right. The race-class narrative does so by calling out the Far Right's use of racism as a divide-and-conquer strategy and redirecting anger where it belongs: onto economic elites that have substituted precarity for stability.

Therapy's Expensive, but Praying Is Free

What do you call a Jew in California? A Buddhist.

Progressives' attitude toward religion means they make a lot of unforced errors. Religion provides for many non-elites the kind of intellectual engagement, stability, hopefulness, future orientation, impulse control, aspirations to purity, and social safety net that elites typically get from their careers, their therapists, their politics, and their bank accounts. Fun fact: the effect on self-reported happiness of moving from never attending religious services to attending weekly is comparable to the happiness effect of moving from the bottom to top income quartile—and, unlike therapy, it's free.[1]

Progressives' skepticism is understandable. In 2020, 84 percent of white evangelicals' votes went to Donald Trump despite his long history of unethical behavior. "If the rapture had occurred," joked Ralph Reed of the Faith & Freedom Coalition, "Donald Trump would have lost by the worst landslide since George McGovern." Evangelicals voted for Trump by a margin of nearly five to one. For whites, being an evangelical is a better predictor of far-right voting than being a noncollege grad, the influential Democratic strategist Michael Podhorzer points out. A "strong taproot" of white evangelical Christianity was whites' abandonment of public schools to avoid desegregation, flocking to private schools associated with their churches. Evangelicals also joined Catholics in leading counter-feminist and antiabortion movements. "For the Republican Party, long seen as the party of big business rather than labor, embracing the pro-family movement's positions enabled it to claim to be the champion of the family without championing programs designed to protect jobs and wages."[2]

Polling shows that progressives have very cold feelings toward evangelicals; only NRA members and Trump supporters are viewed more unfavorably. Yet polling also suggests that caricatures of evangelicals as uniformly reactionary are exaggerated, as such stereotypes always are. By 2021, 35 percent of evangelicals were in favor of gay marriage, including a majority (56 percent) between the ages of eighteen and thirty-five. If you believe that some people are inherently gay, it follows that being gay is randomly distributed throughout the population, which means there are gay fundamentalists. The winning strategy is to say: "We understand you are gay *and* that you are fundamentalist, and we accept that you're both—unlike the fundamentalists, who insist on making you choose." This is not to say that most evangelicals will abandon the Far Right. Indeed, some Trump supporters began identifying as evangelicals only during his presidency; for them, it seems that being an evangelical is an expression of politics, which has become their "master identity," to quote political scientist Ryan Burge.[3]

Another cause of progressives' reluctance is the ugly, well-documented intertwining of religion and racism. But critics often forget that religion is not the only major American institution whose history is intertwined with racism. So is baseball, which long excluded Black players; so is the Constitution. We don't throw out baseball or the Constitution: we reinvent them, cleansing out racist elements so we can continue to watch a game and have a democracy. We can decry those elements of any religious tradition that are racist without writing off religion altogether. Don't forget that the abolitionist movement in the US grew out of the Second Great Awakening.[4]

You may have the impression that religion is waning. That stems from reports that belief in God is at "a new low" or that the "nones"—people who do not affiliate with any religion—are now the largest group. Beware: the "new low" is that now only 81 percent of Americans believe in God—that's still a very high number. And fully one-third of the nones say religion is at least somewhat important in their lives, 15 percent go to services at least once a month, and over a quarter pray every day.[5]

Changing Brahmin Left attitudes toward religion is crucial for healing class divides. In the US, less education means more religious belief; more education equals less. Pew Research found that 81 percent of Americans with high school degrees or less say they are religious, compared with 58 percent of college grads. Two-thirds (66 percent) of high school dropouts say religion is very important in their lives, 19 percentage points higher than college grads. Two-thirds of noncollege grads but only 55 percent of college grads believe in God "with absolute certainty." Fully 40 percent of college grads but only 28 percent of those with some college say they are neither spiritual nor religious.[6]

Rates of attendance at worship don't follow the same class pattern, which can confuse commentators. It makes sense to me because I have studied unstable scheduling in hourly jobs. Many people in blue- and pink-collar jobs work schedules that change every day and every week, often on only a few days' notice. Combined with two-job families and no adequate childcare, this makes family scheduling a nightmare.[7]

While non-elites are more religious, the "textbook atheist [is] an upper-educated, upper-class white guy living in an urban or suburban area," notes Burge. Atheism embeds elites' preference for novelty and display of high human capital through sophistication; the message is, "I'm a fearless deep thinker who doesn't blindly follow tradition." The new atheists, who are highly critical toward religion and turn instead to science, are more than 90 percent white and have double the educational attainment of other atheists. Also disproportionately college-educated are the nearly one-third of Americans who say they are "spiritual but not religious." Some are those Buddhists in California, who embrace meditation as a heuristic that is helpful in accessing spirituality and inner peace without dwelling on elements of Buddhism they find unhelpful, unattractive, or implausible. That's a tolerance intellectuals often don't extend to the religious traditions of low-human-capital Americans. (One example: in Japan you need to pay for a new burial name for your dead parent; if you don't pay the local temple enough, they'll give a second-rate name, which can carry a "heavy stigma.")[8]

The 6 percent of Americans who are atheists are very different from the 22 percent of Americans who are nones, who don't identify with any particular religion. They are the least educated religious group: only 25 percent have college degrees, and 60 percent make less than $50,000 a year. They "feel left out, left behind, lost, and disconnected from the larger society," notes Burge.[9]

For families holding on for dear life to settled middle-class life, religion offers many resources. We saw in chapter 6 how it offers a source of social status independent of one's human or financial capital accumulation, as well as the self-discipline required to sustain a settled middle-class life.

For many, religion provides the kind of reset button elites might get from therapy. Remember J. D. Vance's dad, who stopped partying and became a settled family man once he converted to Pentecostal Christianity. Surgeon General Vivek H. Murthy highlights that religion reduces risk-taking behaviors. After Vance moved into his dad's house as a teenager, "I don't know that I had ever felt so content, so completely unworried about life and its stresses." Vance ultimately left his dad's church, which was rigid in all the predictable ways, but his memoir shows many ways religion protects non-elites from their disadvantaged market position.[10]

Most concretely, being part of a religious community can give members access to both jobs and a safety net in an economy where the larger community—inexcusably—fails to do so. This is important because high levels of social capital (a.k.a. social relationships) predict economic mobility, according to a study by Raj Chetty and coauthors. Studies find that religious attendance was associated with higher levels of social integration and social support. Social support comes in many forms, whether in the form of emotional support, a car when yours broke down, or cash to tide you over till payday; religious people are more likely to donate money.[11]

Religion provides resources for resilience. When upper-middle-class kids go off the rails, the family sends them to therapy—an expensive luxury. The average cost of therapy is $100–$200 per session. Therapy is expensive, but praying is free. Religious people generally have better mental health than the general population, with the link more pronounced in the less educated. Highly religious people are twice as likely to say they are very happy as the least religious. Support from fellow believers helps offset depression associated with financial difficulties, thereby improving health outcomes. A stronger sense that God is in control is associated with greater life satisfaction, greater optimism, and greater feelings of self-worth. Three-fourths of US adults believed in God-mediated control in 2008. Seventy-seven percent believe that God has protected them, which is particularly precious because society hasn't. Arlie Hochschild spoke with Jackie, who described a "moment of transformation." Hochschild asked how she felt: "Clean, beautiful. I believe that, for the first time, I saw in the mirror how He saw me. He showed me *who I am to Him*." In a society that too often treats non-elites with little respect, God offers a refuge of dignity and self-worth.[12]

At best, religion also helps adherents cultivate habits of mind that positive psychology has documented are conducive to happiness. While the assertion that "God doesn't send you anything you can't handle" is objectively untrue—people succumb to drugs, despair, and suicide every day of the week—positive psychology documents that optimism leads to better health, through immunological robustness and health-promoting behaviors. Optimism also predicts grit, perseverance, effective coping, and good choice of goals. It enhances cognitive performance by promoting effective problem-solving. Also, not surprisingly, it promotes positive mood and good morale, both of which lead to better health outcomes. "When there is room for doubt, people should fill that gap with hope," advises Christopher Peterson, who has a long history of work on positive psychology. Having God on your side is one heuristic for accomplishing that. Hope combines the expectation that things will go your way with a sense you can make it happen.[13]

Another habit of mind that correlates powerfully with happiness is gratitude. Gratitude predicts happiness. Try it: listing three good things that happened to you every day has a lasting impact on happiness. People assigned to pray for four weeks reported higher gratitude at the end of the study than controls, even those assigned to pray for their partners as compared with those assigned just to think positive thoughts about their partner. Prayers associated with thanksgiving and related topics are associated with higher levels of self-esteem, optimism, and life satisfaction. Religion also may well help with grit: when God's on your side, it's easier to keep your nose to the grindstone in an economy that's rigged against you—the famous opiate of the masses. Another study delved deeper and found thankfulness associated with reduced risk for both externalizing disorders (e.g., alcohol, nicotine, or drug dependence and antisocial behavior) and internalizing disorders (e.g., major depression, anxiety, etc.). General religiosity, forgiveness, the feeling that God is involved in your life, and that God will judge all decrease externalizing disorders.[14]

At worst, of course, religion just makes people more frightened and bummed out, when people assume a vengeful God or that God personally intended for you to get that terminal cancer in retribution for your past sins. But this is a minority view: about 13 percent of white men and 8 percent of Black men see God in terms of sin and punishment. Such "negative coping" was inversely associated with overall quality of life, as was distrust and skepticism about God's presence. Again: we need to find some way working-class whites (especially men) can learn from Black

Americans to see structural disadvantage, instead of then heaping blame on themselves for their failure to achieve the American dream. [15]

Being part of a religious community also helps Americans avoid what Surgeon General Murthy called America's "epidemic of loneliness." To quote Murthy, "Religious or faith-based groups can be a source for regular social contact, serve as a community of support, provide meaning and purpose, [and] create a sense of belonging around shared values and beliefs." Church members are much more likely than nonmembers to volunteer in their communities at least a few times a year (47 percent versus 23 percent), to talk to someone they don't know well (64 percent versus 54 percent), and to attend a local community event (60 percent versus 41 percent). Going to church helps create and sustain a social network that aids in emotional and practical support. Personal connection and close relationships have a strong association with happiness, so it's no surprise that frequent church attendance is related to less distress and depression and greater happiness, life satisfaction, and self-esteem. Anticipated support from one's co-religionists may be even more important than support itself. In a recent trenchant book, *Rust Belt Union Blues*, Theda Skocpol argues that evangelical churches and gun clubs have replaced many of the civic and social functions formerly held by unions. I wish unions still held that role: not only do unions help people see their lot in life as unfair; they also help them change it.[16]

The literature on the links between religious belief and both mental and physical health is vast: over 1,200 studies had been published as of 2001. A rigorous study found that "after adjustment for age, sex, race, and chronic medical conditions, churchgoers had a 46% reduction in all-cause mortality." Religion has been documented to improve outcomes in open-heart surgery, prostate cancer, arthritis. The all-cause mortality study measured decreased stress, resulting in over a seven-year increase in life expectancy for people in general (and fourteen years for African Americans) who went to church at least once a week.[17]

Worrying about whether religious doctrine is "really" true is what Ludwig Wittgenstein would call *a category mistake*. Religion is a tool for living. "If you're watching your community lose population and collapse, but your church is still strong and the life of the community is centered around that, well then, you know you'd better be paying attention to that," said Barack Obama.[18]

We need to get more sophisticated about sophistication. "I kept waiting for that, like, the dig—right? The cutting joke that was going to somehow eviscerate this religious person . . . Because that's what we're sort of used to seeing," said NPR host Rachel Martin in interviewing Jeff Hiller of HBO's *Somebody Somewhere*.[19] Martin was surprised because, on NPR, guests who identify as believers are rare; the "cutting joke" is far more common.

> MARTIN: It's just treated so gently in the show. Like, it's not treated with derision. . . . It's just a part of who he is as a fully re-alized human being.
> HILLER: Exactly. 'Cause I know so many queer folks who are members of faith communities. And, in fact, that's where they found their people, their family, their found family. And I know so many churches that are basically the only voice of social justice in their communities. They're—that's where you go if you need food. That's where you go if you need help on your rent. You know, I think, in pop culture, when you see church, you just think, oh, it's going to smoosh down the gay people.[20]

To me, elites' focus on whether Christian claims are literally true is an ever-so-Christian obsession with doctrine—one not shared by most world religions. "I often say that as a social scientist, the least consequential part about religion is the belief piece," Burge told me. Other traditions aren't similarly hung-up. "For a Japanese person it is completely normal to bring a newborn baby to a Shinto shrine for a blessing, have a Christian-style wedding and a Buddhist funeral. The reason is that in Japan, religions are often seen as being defined by their rituals and practices, not so much by their doctrines." They don't worry so much about which is "true": they see religion as a way of organizing emotions, marking major life events, and a way of keeping in touch with one's culture, just as many liberal Jews do. Think of religion as a heroic gesture to create meaning in a meaningless universe; Camus would be proud.[21]

Religion has such staying power because it's useful for cultivating op-timism and gratitude, for bonding people together in networks of mutual support, for encouraging healthy habits, and more. Look, I'm as upset as everyone else I know when *holier-than-thou*-ers try to impose variants of Christianity we abhor on us and everyone else, up to and sometimes in-cluding eliminating the barrier between church and state. I intensely dis-like the "holier than thou" power move, whether it's from religious zealots or the political hobbyists I'll discuss in the next chapter. Here's my credo: the righteous are always flawed, and the flawed are often righteous.

That said, let's stop using racism, ruralism, and religion as media for class condescension. That's inconsistent with our commitments as progressives.

Key Takeaways:

1. Changing elite attitudes toward religion is crucial to healing class divides: in the US, the more educated believe in religion less and the less educated believe in religion more.
2. Religion offers non-elites the kind of social status, hopefulness, resilience, and social safety net that elites get from their career potential, their therapists, and their bank accounts.
3. The textbook atheist is a college-educated white man. Progressives' often-dismissive attitude toward religion is politically costly and inconsistent with their ideals.

Understand How We Won the
Gay Marriage Battle: Rinse and Repeat

When moral values, family, and tradition are the main axes along which you define your own and your community's strengths, the agenda that stresses these issues more will be the one that resonates better.

—Jennifer Sherman[1]

If conservatives turn everything into a culture war, what's the antidote? Commentators like Ruy Teixeira argue that liberals should moderate on social issues. That doesn't make sense to me. After all, in 1996, only 27 percent of Americans supported gay marriage; twenty-six years later, 71 percent did. Progress on LGBTQ rights is the single most powerful social inequality victory of my lifetime. How did we accomplish it? By being immoderate: to quote historian Laurel Ulrich, "Well-behaved women seldom make history." Being a pain is the only way to change deeply resilient social power differentials.[2]

But it matters a lot *how* you're a pain. Some leaders in the gay rights movement in the 1990s advocated for gay marriage, but many saw their goal as a broadscale attack on the institutions that organize intimacy: marriage and monogamy. They saw marriage as patriarchal and "would have preferred a different battle . . . : Queer family politics . . . emphasized legal protection for a variety of relationship forms" and the "complete sexual liberation for all people." "The majority of the movement leaders wanted the legal protections you get by virtue of marriage but didn't much care what it was called, and in many cases would rather it not be marriage," said my colleague Matt Coles, who was one of the architects of the strategy that won gay marriage when he was the director of the ACLU's Center for Equality.[3]

Most movement leaders weren't marriage enthusiasts. The push for marriage "really came from, for lack of a better word, from ordinary folks, with the most overwhelming support for marriage coming from people of color and low-income people." One of the early marriage cases in Hawaii, Matt told me, involved "people who wanted to get married, and they went to the ACLU, they went to Lambda Legal, and they went to the National Center for Lesbian Rights and we all turned them down, saying, 'Oh wow, the courts are not ready for this, society's not ready for this.'" Eventually, around 2004, leaders decided they needed to push for marriage because "whether we think going for marriage was the ideal thing to do or not doesn't matter anymore. The other side's using it to clobber us."

Matt told me that he began to understand the push for recognition of gay relationships after he and others helped pass a domestic partnership law in San Francisco. "It took effect on Valentine's Day, and the San Francisco county clerk called me up and said, 'All right, we've got to get this organized.' I said, 'Well, you know, my work is done—this is your job.'" But he helped her prepare anyway as she put desks with heart-shaped balloons in the rotunda of San Francisco City Hall to process the crowd that had come to tie the knot. Then they had anyone who signed up assemble in the board of supervisors chamber, followed by a "grand march" down the staircase. Matt's thoughts:

> I said I want nothing to do with this, and I'm not even going to hang around for it because I thought it performative. But I stood there and watched, and a couple of things leapt out at me. The people coming down the stairs were not doctors and lawyers; they were ordinary, average people. I looked at their faces and said to myself, "I get it now. It's the prom and the wedding ceremony and everything rolled into one. They're finally able to say, 'Mom, yeah, I got married.'"

The push for marriage, he realized, was coming not from leadership but "from our people. . . . I think the community wanted marriage because they were less focused on legal protections and more focused on the institution: the social, symbolic enactment of bonding in the family. . . . Marriage was the universal expectation, and our people wanted in." To quote my husband, many people don't want to smash the hegemony. They just want to join it.

Matt got his bosses at the ACLU to put up money for focus groups around the country, led by the Belden Russonello media relations firm. The focus group leader asked, "What does marriage mean to you?" "Somebody, and I can even picture one guy who did this in Chicago, said, 'Commitment,'" Matt told me. "Everybody around the table agreed: commitment. And that happened in every single focus group." Some were quite conservative but "coalesced around the sentiment that if gay people made the same commitment, then they should be entitled to the same protections." "People raised when you and I were"—Matt and I are both in our seventies—"didn't believe gay people have real relationships. They were tawdry, shabby little things." But what the focus groups "told us was [that] the key to changing the way Americans thought about this was to show them not so much the consequences of discrimination as to show them the commitment."

Commitment: that's why a perfect case to establish the principle of gay marriage was *United States v. Windsor*. The named plaintiff was Edith Windsor, whom Matt initially thought was a terrible choice because she was wealthy: the core issue involved payment of $363,000 in estate taxes. But Edith's story epitomized commitment and care: she and her partner had been together for forty years, and for the last twenty, her partner had been slowly declining and in terrible ill health, and Windsor had cared for her in sickness and in health. "The case said we are committed to each other and we're going to take care of each other for the rest of our lives. That's what marriage means to America, and that's what our constituency wanted."[4]

Gay marriage was a rare social movement that actually listened to non-elites and tapped the moral intuitions of ordinary people. If you look at the document that Matt drafted in 2005 to summarize what LGBT advocates thought, "Winning Marriage: What We Need to Do," it acknowledges, "Many people in the LGBT community would have preferred not to have made marriage a leading issue now. Many would have preferred to have addressed the legal and social recognition of same-sex couples with different tactics and/or different conceptual models." But by 2008, a forty-page guide for advocates, *Talking to the Movable Middle About Marriage*, acted on the realization that "rights talk appealed to liberals" but what appealed to those the movement needed to persuade were "love, commitment, fairness, and freedom."[5] Listen where they ended up in a Lambda Legal brief in a 2006 case:

Marriage remains a dream for many Americans, including the four plaintiffs, a vision of what can be for two people and their family, with commitment, love and patience . . . Plaintiffs want to marry their unique partners, to have and to hold them, under the shelter of New Jersey's marriage law, until death do them part.[6]

This dramatizes the strategy of shifting from an equality frame and an emphasis on the material consequences of marriage to an emphasis on commitment, child-rearing, and the symbolic dimensions of marriage—on the desire to join marriage rather than to change it.[7]

Jonathan Haidt's work provides the backstory that explains why abandoning the legalistic equal-rights strategy worked so well. Haidt launched his work as a corrective to the decades of studies that mischaracterized working-class realism about their need to respect authority (so they don't get fired) as "authoritarianism." Haidt starts from the assumption that conservatives are good people with different values. In a common formulation of Haidt's work, liberals' morality is built on *individualizing foundations* that center fairness, autonomy, and protecting the vulnerable from harm, whereas social conservatives' morality is built on *binding foundations* that center respect for authority and adherence to the rules, roles, and traditions of the community.[8]

Haidt's message of mutual respect is welcome. He rejects the decades-old conventional wisdom that

conservatives are conservative because they were raised by overly strict parents, or because they are inordinately afraid of change, novelty, and complexity, or because they suffer from existential fears and therefore cling to a simple worldview with no shades of gray. These approaches all had one feature in common: they use psychology to [make it] unnecessary for liberals to take conservative ideas seriously because these ideas are caused by bad childhoods or ugly personality traits. I [have] suggested a very different approach: start by assuming that conservatives are just as sincere as liberals.[9]

Admirable. He's forging a language of cross-class respect. Individualizing foundations track the intuitions of elites focused on expressive individualism: "liberals like adventure" and value "equality, engage risk, prefer new experiences, and support independence," notes Susan Fiske. Binding foundations track the intuitions of the lower-middle class, with respect for 1) authority and rules that allow them to survive as order-takers, 2) communities that protect them from a market economy that leaves them vulnerable, and 3) traditional institutions that anchor their self-discipline and self-respect in the scrum for social honor.[10]

Connecting these dispositions to their class locations offers an important insight: it's not just that some individuals favor binding foundations while others prefer individuating ones. Each is part and parcel of a class-based parallel universe. Haidt's moral foundations theory helps heal class blindness: it "has been groundbreaking in the way it expanded the moral domain to consider the roles of loyalty, authority and purity," in contrast to prior theories that recognized only the individuating foundations cherished by elites. He also offers two crucial insights: the best way to persuade people is to use their native tongue—and to communicate respect.[11]

The architects of the gay marriage campaign didn't consciously set out to use binding foundations to manipulate class dynamics, but that's where they ended up. They identified whom they needed to persuade; then they listened and connected their message with the moral intuitions of their audience. They did not pander to emotions rather than logic, although later commentators sometimes described them as having "moved beyond polling and focused on expanding their understanding of the emotional motivators that inhibited movable middle voters from supporting same-sex marriage." Again, it's not that one side is emotional and the other logical. Both sides reinforce cherished identities: elites' cherished identity is that they are intelligent people who follow logic, non-elites' is that they keep the world in moral order. Both frames appeal to emotions by flattering and reassuring their adherents.[12]

Polling documents the rarely noted class dynamic surrounding gay marriage. In 2003, college grads supported it at a rate 18 percentage points higher (44 percent) than noncollege grads (26 percent). A decade later, overall support had grown, but the class gap hadn't shrunk: college grads still supported it at a rate 18 percentage points higher (76 percent) than those with high school or less (58 percent). A decade after that, in 2023, overall support had grown again, but the class gap remained: 78 percent of college grads supported gay marriage compared to 67 percent of non-college grads.[13]

Not surprising, then, that framing gay marriage as a demand for fairness-defined-as-equality didn't increase support. Instead, the movement in effect embraced what Haidt calls the sanctity/degradation frame by communicating that gay relationships weren't "tawdry, shabby little things" but committed relationships that deserved the sanctity of marriage. Liberals typically would shy away from the sanctity frame as icky. Gay marriage advocates didn't do that: instead, they colonized it and flipped the script, positioning gay folks as good people who wanted commitment and the sanctity of marriage. This is an important lesson going forward. Shying away from conservative frames just leaves their compelling power uncontestedly in the hands of conservatives.

Gay marriage advocates adeptly tapped working-class moral intuitions in other ways, too. Instead of relying on experts (lawyers) speaking about rights, they tapped authority figures respected in blue-collar circles (a.k.a. validators): clergy, grandparents, older veterans. These spokespeople didn't make arguments about why their audience should accept homosexuality. Instead, they used a cross-class talk tradition: storytelling. They used "elements of narrativity—the creation of characters, construction of a storytelling arc and the depiction of conflict being resolved." These "journey stories" featured family members and friends telling the story of how they changed their minds. The focus was not on persuasion or deliberation but on identification. These stories tapped blue-collar traditions of loyalty to family and friends, with the message, "I was taught that homosexuality was wrong, but now I see that my gay friends and family need and deserve the same chance at a happy life that I have . . . The speaker did not argue that homosexuality was good" but that supporting gay marriage meant supporting family and friends who sought to be good people living a settled family life. The focus was not on sexual self-fulfillment but family values: gays weren't looking for ecstasy in a San Francisco bathhouse but for a settled life in Pittsburgh, "implicitly refut[ing] the stereotypes of hypersexuality associated with gay men."[14]

Not surprisingly, a social psychology experiment found that defending same-sex marriage by emphasizing that "same-sex couples are proud and patriotic Americans" who "contribute to the American economy and society" worked better among conservatives than emphasizing fairness. This was part of a series of experiments testing out Haidt's theories that also involved universal health care, military spending, and English-as-the-official-language policies. The experiments found that political arguments framed to appeal to the moral values of those targeted for persuasion were more effective than those that weren't—but that almost three-quarters of both liberals and conservatives typically were guided by their own moral intuitions, not those of their intended audience. The advantages of matching one's audience's moral intuitions were substantial.[15]

A different paper by Robb Willer found that framing progressive economic goals as binding rather than individualizing increased support—but that progressive candidates tend to use individualizing language, which convinced conservatives that progressives did not share their values. Take heed.[16]

Too often, inside the Beltway, the question of how to connect with the working class is treated as purely a messaging issue. Note that the LGBTQ rights movement did not merely manipulate its working-class audience through clever messaging; they changed their policy direction. This required ceding two types of power. The first was the power to insist on the native language of the Brahmin Left (freedom and self-actualization) in favor of the native language of their working-class audience (sanctity and family values). But that's not all the movement did. It also ceded the power to insist on what the movement's priorities should be. Purists were not pleased.[17]

Is this inexcusable defeatism, or is it an admirable ceding of elite power in the name of winning the larger battle of making concrete progress toward the overall goal: acceptance of LGBTQIA+ people as ordinary human beings? To me, this kind of pragmatism doesn't mean giving up on long-term projects like contesting patriarchy; it just means recognizing that these are long-term projects, often best achieved through shorter-term steps by connecting with the moral intuitions of your audience. Don't those moral intuitions reflect patriarchy? Sure they do, so flip them, to tap the power of patriarchy to subvert patriarchy. Do you want to perform purity or get shit done?

After the Supreme Court ruled that the Constitution mandated states to recognize gay marriage, the Right did what the Left too rarely does. "We knew we needed to find an issue that the candidates were comfortable talking about. And we threw everything at the wall," said Terry Schilling, president of the American Principles Project, a conservative advocacy group. "What has stuck is the issue of trans identity, particularly among young people."[18]

First, they tried trans bathrooms: laws requiring people to use the bathroom of the gender they were assigned at birth. But support for that evaporated when a North Carolina ban was repealed after it cost the state billions due to boycotts from sports leagues, corporations, and musicians.

Then they shifted the focus to kids and recognized that they'd hit gold both in the public and philanthropic spheres, attracting thousands of new donors mostly making small contributions. "In many ways, the trans sports ban was the test balloon in terms of how they can frame these things," said Nadine Smith of a liberal group in Florida. "Once they opened that parents' rights frame, they began to use it everywhere."[19]

Why? While gay marriage advocates had carefully chosen plaintiffs who looked like "normal" men and women (or, as we would say in the gender biz, who performed hegemonic masculinity and femininity), trans folks' liminality fascinates elites who embrace novelty—but not to working-class folks who cherish masculinity and femininity as social ideals they can attain. The focus on kids also allowed conservatives to tap the parents' rights frame that had become a channel for class anger during Covid school shutdowns.

It made sense for the Right to try to drag the Left onto this terrain; it didn't make sense to allow ourselves to be dragged. "If you get your jollies or you get your voters excited by bullying gay and trans kids, you know, it's time for a new line of work," said John Fetterman in a campaign stop: notice how he flips the "leftists aren't doing right by kids" into "right-wing bullies are cruel to kids." Then colonize to the parental rights frame, Matt Coles suggested after criticizing cynical politicians trying to build political careers off bullying vulnerable schoolkids, and identify as the *real* issue whether earnest, decent parents in a tough situation can do what they decide is best for their kids.[20]

Then pivot. Pivot? What to? One candidate is to leverage hard-work worship to point out that a gay couple can be married on Tuesday, then fired for being gay on Wednesday, centering the argument that these are just people—many of them working class—who want to support their families. A 2022 poll found that 80 percent of Americans support anti-discrimination legislation for LGBTQ people. Trans people often suffer job discrimination.[21]

One thing's for sure. After the gay marriage campaign was so successful in convincing Americans to view LGBTQIA+ folx as just folks, anti-LGBT hate crimes jumped 19 percent in 2022, and anti-trans bias jumped over 35 percent. I don't have all the answers, but I care deeply about LGBTQ rights. I'm trying to help the Left figure out how to stop being dragged into culture wars fought on terrain carefully sloped to give us an uphill battle.[22]

All this brings us to a deeper question: What's the purpose of politics anyway? For some, leftist politics has become a hobby, argues political scientist Eitan Hersh. "A third of Americans say they spend two hours or more each day on politics. Of these people, four out of five say that not one minute of that time is spent on any kind of real political work. It's all TV shows and podcasts and radio shows and social media and cheering and booing and complaining to friends and family." Hersh compares the hobbyists to sports fans rooting for the home team. It's not about organizing victory; it's about venting, exulting, despairing. Emotion. The Americans who report consuming the most news typically report belonging to zero organizations; 68 percent never attended a single meeting about a community issue. "The population that is informed enough and cares enough about politics to follow the daily news is mostly disengaged from participation in political and community endeavors."[23]

Who are the hobbyists? Predominantly, they're college-educated, white, and more likely to be men. Blacks, Latinos, and noncollege grads who were interested in politics were three times more likely to report that part of the time they spent on politics was spent actually volunteering; women spend more time, too. "Political hobbyism is found in all circles, but it's mainly a problem for people who are well educated and on the political center and left." Hersh found that Americans who are white, college-educated, and interested in politics were 60 percent more likely to identify as Democrats than Republicans. "Political hobbyism on the left also stands in sharp contrast to the most successful recent political movements, which have been on the right—the right-to-life movement, the gun rights movement—which were developed around chapter-based, local organizations with thousands of volunteers."[24]

Note that political hobbyism reflects that elite ur-goal of self-actualization. One way of heightening the drama is to turn everything into a moral issue. For Democrats (but not independents or Republicans), being a news-junkie hobbyist predicts your feelings of moral conviction. For Rachel Maddow, fueling moral outrage is in her job description no less than that of name-your-villain on Fox News.[25]

Instead, if you view politics as about getting shit done, compromises are part of this particular language game. To quote the leftist organizing guru Marshall Ganz, "You have to know how to arise passions to fuel the fight and then how to cool everyone down so they'll accept the deal on the table. . . . You have to control and direct the passion, or else it can burn down everything you've worked so hard to build."

Key Takeaways:

1. The conventional wisdom that the way to connect with non-elites is to "moderate" on social issues ignores a key fact: the only way deeply embedded social hierarchies ever change is when advocates are a pain in the butt.
2. The most successful redistribution of social power in my lifetime—the fight for gay marriage—occurred because movement leaders listened to what "our people" wanted and connected movement goals with priorities and messaging that appealed to non-elites.
3. Research shows that the way to persuade people is to speak the moral language that feels comfortable to *them*, instead of the moral language that feels comfortable to *you*.

Deploy Alternative Masculinities
to Build Support for Vaccinations,
Sane Gun Policies, and More

The left will need to find a better way to talk to men; half of the population is far too many people to abandon to the would-be strongmen of the far right.

—Liza Featherstone[1]

Rear Admiral Henrique Gouveia e Melo carries himself with military bearing even on Zoom. That's where I interviewed him in November 2021 to discuss his stunning success in leading Portugal's Covid response, which yielded a death toll thirty times lower than in neighboring Spain.[2]

The rear admiral's career prepared him for work under stress. He has logged more hours than any serving Portuguese naval officer, at one point commanding two submarines at once: he would return to eat a meal on shore before taking the other sub out to sea. He captained a frigate and led the European Union's maritime force.

How did he get 85 percent of Portugal's population vaccinated in just nine months? He deftly deployed a widely respected masculine script: the military man. His example illustrates what I would propose as an abiding truth: the only effective antidotes to claims of masculinity are competing claims of masculinity.[3]

Gouveia e Melo was the government's second choice. Its first was a bank manager and politician who was removed after allegations of fraud, Eva Falcão told me. She was chief of staff of the Portuguese Ministry of Health during the pandemic. Gouveia e Melo "is the face of our success," she said. "The goal was to depoliticize the process, so it was run by the military. Everyone respects that it would be run with integrity." The rear admiral was well known because he had led the effort to fight the devastating wildfires

Portugal experienced in 2017. "Everyone knew the military follows orders and won't hesitate to enforce the rules," Falcão noted.

When Gouveia e Melo's appointment was announced, he wore his navy whites, but soon he switched to camouflage. When I interviewed him a few days after I spoke with Falcão, he told me he always appeared on TV in his "war uniform" to send the message that Portugal was at war with the virus: "We have entered into a war, a war that affects the Portuguese people. The enemy is this virus, which will attack our lives, not only our health and our economy but all of modern life." He explained:

> I used simple rhetoric of two sides. The virus is the enemy versus the community; there is no neutral side. If you believe you are on a neutral side, you are an instrument of the virus and have become the enemy. You don't vaccinate just to protect yourself and your family but also to protect the community.

He sent the message that "you won't be vaccinated in a forcible way," instead explaining people's choice "in a very logical way":

> It's a matter of time, but you will get the virus. What do you prefer? By virus or by vaccination? If by virus, it's very dangerous, not predictable, and you don't know the outcome. Out of every five hundred people, one will die. That's one option . . . The second option is vaccination. It's medically safe, and the chances of dying are one in a million. What side? One in five hundred or one in a million?

"Another argument I used a lot," he said, was

> if you believe in crazy ideas like the world is flat, the injection will put a ship inside of you, that Bill Gates wants to control you by injection, I'm sorry, but I have to inform you that you are living in the twenty-first century not living in the twelfth century. . . . In the twenty-first century you have to believe in science and in things that are true and not lies spread in a bubble . . . not crazy information spread by some countries that want to disrupt our country. I won't say the name, but it starts with R.

Notice how deftly he enacts the military man: he's apolitical, so he doesn't name Russia—but he knows his enemy when he sees it, so he can name Russia. Dr. Fauci could never pull that off. Nor could Fauci call out pandemic conspiracy theorists this way without coming off as condescending, because Fauci was enacting a different script of masculine authority—the expert—that inevitably triggers class resentments. It feels very different to blue-collar folks to be called out by a rear admiral than by a physician. "I am a very simple naval officer," Gouveia e Melo told me.

> I have spent too much time underwater and had too much time to think. That was the trick—to communicate clearly what were good attitudes towards the vaccine. . . . They did not attack me as a politician, because I am not a politician. . . . I was independent and very credible in the eyes of public opinion.

Perhaps you're wondering whether enacting masculinity really mattered. The rear admiral thought it did: when an anti-vaccination group held a demonstration trying to block the door of a vaccination center, "I went through them in my military uniform without any protection with all the TVs there," he told me. "They were calling me a killer and a murderer. In a calm way, I said, 'The killer is the virus. The murderer is the virus,' on national TV, so the people could see logic and calm versus this crazy lunatic group shouting. . . . That day, I won the war." His security detail wanted him to enter through the back door because there were no police at the site. He replied, "I am officer of the [Navy]. I will never enter through the back door. I will go through these persons to show the strength of my ideas. I thought a lot about my messaging: clear, simple, direct words."

Gouveia e Melo was hyperaware he was talking across class lines: "I used vocabulary that a simple person can understand but that the cultural elite also will understand." His time in the military taught him this. "The strength of the submarine is in the weakest link, not the strongest link . . . In a society, there also are people who are weak, who need help. Take them into account. . . . If you don't take care of the poor, the poor will transmit the virus to the rich. . . . You have to talk to these classes." Why was he so sensitized to this? I asked. He grew up partly in Angola, he said, where "my father and mother made me play with all the kids, even the poor kids. It taught me the biggest lesson of my life . . . A life is a life. No rich lives. No poor lives. Take care of all lives."

What does it mean to have insight into class dynamics? It means this. Given anti-elitist resentment of elites, we should have spotted the spoiler potential of class dynamics from the start of the pandemic. They're certainly evident now. A 2021 poll found that about a quarter of white college grads, but roughly 40 percent of white men without degrees, agreed with people's decisions not to get vaccinated. African Americans without degrees were closer to college grads (26 percent), while Hispanics without degrees were in the middle (30 percent). Class-based masculinities show up strongly in mask-wearing: less than a quarter of noncollege white men said they always wore masks, compared with about a third of college-educated white men, and about half of Blacks and Hispanics.[4]

Is it disheartening to me as a feminist that masculinity is the cross-class language that worked? Yup: I'm not a masculinity junkie. But neither am I a fan of death—of handling a pandemic with such class blindness that the US ends up with a much higher death rate than other wealthy countries, and with poor Black, brown, and white kids falling even further behind, exacerbating already excruciating inequality. The Denmark example is important to show that we should have opened schools earlier, but Portugal's Covid success may hold more lessons for the US than does small, homogeneous Denmark. In a future pandemic, what we need is not someone like Fauci (much as I, personally, adored him). We need someone who can enact a form of masculine authority with cross-class appeal. All that points to the military; so does the fact that getting people vaccinated is the type of logistical challenge the military was built to deliver on. And don't forget: the military is the second-most trusted institution in the country.[5]

In this and so many other contexts, the Left needs to mobilize masculinity because the Right now owns this extremely valuable real estate pretty much uncontested. Trump's "anti-establishment masculine swagger" has cross-class appeal. Bad-but-bold is a masculinity where only one man can be the Man, and Trump displays it by humiliating women and other men and gaining sexual conquests. Elon Musk has eleven children with three different women; Trump brags about grabbing pussies. Both apparently cheat on everyone, from wives to workers, and see it as a sign of their oh-so-uncontrollable macho. Bad-but-bold has a particularly strong hold in the working class, as Paul Willis's sublime *Learning to Labour* detailed in 1977. Willis points out that blue-collar schoolkids—"the lads"—enact a protest masculinity that expresses disdain both for the self-regulation of settled working-class men and for middle-class schools that try to teach them to be order-takers. Willis points out that the lads' embrace of bad-but-bold masculinity makes them feel powerful at the same time as it consigns them to working-class jobs.[6]

This is not a masculinity popular with progressives, nor with me. But it's a powerful masculinity: the Far Right thrives on bad-but-bold. Gouveia e Melo understood its choreography when he confronted the anti-vax protesters and enacted a masculinity that was not bad but was equally bold, calling their bluff. This is not a dance a scientist can convincingly do.

In 2024, the Biden campaign inadvertently strengthened Donald Trump's hand by constantly decrying him as dangerous. This losing strategy was abandoned when the campaign transitioned to Kamala Harris. Arguably what got Tim Walz the Democratic vice presidential nomination was his insight that the most effective response to bad-but-bold masculinity is to ridicule Trump as "weird." This is Charlie Chaplin's strategy in *The Great Dictator*, in which Chaplin depicted Hitler as laughable. Not surprisingly, this emperor-has-no-clothes strategy deflated Mr. Macho and drove Trump nuts, throwing him off his game (a tactic Harris used again in her debate with Trump). At the Democratic National Convention, Barack Obama joined in, making fun of Trump by calling him "a guy whose act has, let's face it, gotten pretty stale," and calling out Trump's obsession with the size of his crowds while communicating through hand gestures (This big? Or this big?) that Trump was concerned about the size of something altogether different. Obama also very adeptly tapped into the blue-collar norm of not whining when he described Trump as a billionaire who had not stopped whining since he inaugurated his 2016 campaign. "It has been a constant stream of gripes and grievances that's actually been getting worse now he's afraid of losing to Kamala." Michelle Obama joined in: "who's going to tell him that the job he's currently seeking might just be one of those 'Black jobs' (referring to Trump's frequent comment that immigrants 'take Black jobs')."[7]

In Walz, Democrats found a masculinity maestro. He put meat on the bones of Decent Guy masculinity in a way I've seen no other politician do as effectively. Chapter 5 described the way he so adeptly tapped into class-specific masculinities: the straight-talking guy who wears flannel shirts, eats runzas, fixes cars, gets cars out of snowbanks. But there's more: Walz stressed his successful completion of masculine roles that confer honor for men without fancy degrees: football coach, and Command Sergeant Major (I didn't know that was the highest rank enlisted personnel could reach but I feel confident most people do in heartland communities where military service is commonplace). Walz wants us to know that he's proud that the team he helped coach won a state championship, although he says it with suitable humility, since bragging would violate another blue-collar speech norm. At the Democratic Convention, he had his whole team march on stage, stuffed into their high school jerseys. The crowd went wild, and America saw that celebrating Ordinary White Guys is something both parties do. Decent Midwestern Guy combined with that sharp blue-collar take-down of elite pretensions is a powerful model to use against bad-but-bolds, who are a dime a dozen [Trump (US), Boris Johnson (UK), Bolsonaro (Brazil), Silvio Berlusconi (Italy), and Orbán (Hungary)].[8]

When tragedy struck with Fetterman's stroke in 2022, he leveraged his bad-but-bold cred into another accepted masculinity, enacting the stoicism and perseverance that's so highly valued by working-class men. He also intertwined his bold-but-bad aesthetic with a Decent Family Man life. In a tweet sweetly titled "Date night," a photo shows his wife elegantly dressed while Fetterman is in his signature black shorts and a hoodie . . . with a tuxedo stenciled on. There's blue-collar humor again, poking fun at white-collar conventions and pretentions.

Fetterman also plays the provider. When he was mayor, Fetterman played the don who takes care of his people, tapping into a masculine ideal that used to be owned by Democratic bosses. "He's available to take kids to get a driver's license—and pay for it," noted *Rolling Stone*. He and his wife, Gisele, opened a "store" that gives away diapers, clothes, and other goods. "The archetypical political boss—like the ideal working-class father and husband—is a provider and protector," wrote Stephanie Muravchik and Jon A. Shields in *Trump's Democrats*. This helps explain why working-class voters are less troubled than many more elite ones about Trump's alarming mixture of public and private. Obviously, I wouldn't advocate corruption, but how is it that the Right gets to own the provider ideal, while social redistribution policies are demonized as the "nanny state"? There's a long line of research showing that redistribution programs are coded as care, which predictably creates higher levels of support among women than among men. Why can't we learn to design and code these programs as supporting men's ability to provide for their families—or better yet, people's ability?[9]

Fetterman and Walz have much to teach progressives; their brand of masculinity holds broad cross-class appeal. Polling found that 51 percent of Democrats, 52 percent of independents, and 68 percent of Republicans agreed with this statement: "All they care about is looking tough, looking strong. For me, masculinity is taking care of people—your family, your community—and making sure that you actually stand for something." The same polling tested this quote, too: "We've kind of confused what it means to be a man, what it means to be masculine. You've got this trope out there that you've got to be tough—and angry—and lash out to be strong. It's just the opposite . . . Strength is how you show your love for people." *Three-fourths* of both Democrats and Republicans agreed. We need a lot more of this type of research into masculinities that center "pro-activeness, agency, risk-taking and courage, but with a pro-social cast," to quote Christine Emba's insightful essay, "Men Are Lost. Here's a Map Out of the Wilderness."[10]

Which brings us to guns. American gun owners are overwhelmingly male, and many studies explore the relationship between gun ownership and masculine identity. One of those amazing masculinity threat experiments found that when men were told they ranked lower in masculinity, they showed significantly more interest in owning firearms. A 2020 study found that views about men's dominance were "about as important as party iden-tification" in determining men's views of gun control—wow, that's strong indeed. There's also a class dynamic: an analysis of 2020 CES data showed that noncollege grads of every racial group are more likely than college grads to support making it easier for people to obtain concealed-carry permits: among whites, the gap is 13 points, 12 points among Asian Americans, 10 points among Blacks, and 3 points among Latinos.[11]

Working-class masculinities are at work, linked with economic anx-iety. Several different studies all have "substantially the same findings: when the number of households in which married men, but not married women, lose their jobs rise so, too, does the number of firearm background checks." A 2020 study concludes, "It scarcely matters whether the economic threat to men is experienced directly or indirectly; in either case, increases in relative unemployment among men are correlated with increased sales of firearms." Gun dealers know this, of course: in 2020, just hours after Kyle Rittenhouse was acquitted after shooting two protesters during anti-racism protests, a Florida gun dealer published an image of him brandish-ing an assault rifle, headed, "BE A MAN AMONG MEN." Revolting.[12]

We saw in chapter 8 that when rural men lose breadwinner jobs, some use their guns to fulfill the provider role by hunting and fishing to provide food for their families. Men denied the ability to see themselves as providers may also double down on another cherished masculine role: the Protector. "When men can no longer credibly claim to be providers, the protector role takes on extra significance" as "an alternative way of performing masculinity," notes the 2020 study. A 2023 Pew survey found that 91 percent of gun owners cited personal safety or protection as the major or minor reason they own a gun, followed by hunting (52 percent). A study of Texas men with concealed carry permits found that they stressed the need to protect their families. A 2015 study also found that gun owners in deindustrialized Michigan reconstruct their masculine identities by assuming the protector role.[13]

Predictable racial dynamics emerge: a 2017 study found that white men facing economic threat become more likely to say that guns provide moral and emotional empowerment and that they can solve societal problems. White men may well stress the need to protect their families from others who are imagined as men of color. But, given inner-city gangs and crime rates, few would deny that subordinated Latinos and African Americans also turn to guns to reestablish manhood when provider status eludes them.[14]

Effective gun legislation also requires understanding elements of gun culture that constitute basic cultural competence for persuading the target audience. Katherine Cramer found that rural people in Wisconsin felt that, unlike city folk, "they understood how to hunt and fish and knew what it was like to really interact with nature." Barack Obama presumably drew on his Kansas roots when he noted, "If you've grown up and your dad went out and took you hunting, and that is part of your self-identity and provides you a sense of continuity and stability that is unavailable in your economic life, then that's going to be pretty important, and rightfully so."[15]

We've been so focused on Obama's status as the first Black president that we've lost sight of the fact that a key part of his success was that he understood—and knew how to connect to—white working-class voters: a Wisconsin Obama voter saw Clinton as having "her nose is turned this way . . . she's not just an average person" while Obama was "down to earth." Guns were a part of this. Obama critiqued "how we talk about issues. . . . To act like hunting, like somebody who wants firearms just doesn't get it—that kind of condescension has to be purged from our vocabulary."

Just one example is Maureen Dowd's takedown of Sarah Palin's world-view: "You're either a pointy-headed graduate of Harvard Law School or you're eviscerating animals for fun, which she presents as somehow more authentic." I'm fine if Maureen Dowd prefers that someone else eviscerate animals for her, but turning that into a blanket denunciation of people who own guns will be perceived as a class insult. Most gun control advocates wouldn't do this, but it's a good example of how random comments by the Brahmin Left can undercut movements they support. The Right knows how to tweet that kind of stuff.[16]

Thus far, only Third Way moderates have explored more culturally competent messaging. "Democrats and gun-control groups had approached the debate consistently in a way that deeply, almost automatically alienated a lot of gun owners," said Jonathan Cowan, now president of Third Way but formerly of Americans for Gun Safety (AGS). AGS advocated messaging stressing that Democrats respect Second Amendment rights and won't take people's guns away, but advocating gun safety and responsible gun ownership. "How the Gun-Control Movement Got Smart," announced Molly Ball in *The Atlantic* in 2013, with high hopes that the new messaging would take off.

I'd never heard of AGS, so it struck me with the force of a revelation a full decade after its founding when anti-violence advocate Jackson Katz pointed out to me how gun control advocates play into far-right hands when they frame the issue as "gun *control*." This is a perfect foil for far-right promises to stand up for the autonomy and independence of "real men" who resist being "controlled."

Remember blue-collar resentment of order-givers, and how order-takers make up for it by enacting independence outside the workplace? In the early years of my marriage, it took me a really long time to understand why my normally conscientious husband always made us late for dinner parties. Then I read Pierre Bourdieu, who pointed out how blue-collar gatherings were informal, with people coming and going and no one held to a schedule—so unlike the bourgeois dinner party with its tight control of time and space. That's when I realized: it's a way his blue-collar dad enacted manly independence. His blue-collar mom accepted his making everyone late to preserve manly dignity corroded by the hidden injuries of class. This explains why the first step toward effective gun control is to stop calling it *gun control* and start calling it *gun safety*.[17]

We need to adopt culturally competent framing. After all, who's really depriving men of the ability to protect even their kindergarteners? Fanatics who put guns in the hands of bitter, angry (white male) high school kids. While we've made great strides in protecting children from car accidents, "the opposite is happening with firearms," noted Dr. Rebekah Mannix. "It's getting worse, and kids are dying at higher rates"—up 18 percent in the decade before 2021. We've created a society where fathers literally can't protect their own five-year-olds, perhaps the most fundamental traditional duty of a father. Not to mention mothers.[18]

I can already hear the critique: college-educated liberals may well be reluctant to fight toxic masculinity with alternative masculinities, because they see the future as gender nonbinary. I fully embrace that goal. But remember Jonathan Haidt: use the rhetoric that will persuade your audience, not the rhetoric that will persuade you. The fact is that we aren't gender nonbinary at the moment. The path to a less-gender-binary future is to get out there and work for a less-gender-binary future—not to hobble our ability to fight Covid and enact sane gun policies. Because here's the brutal fact: if we don't tap into people's cherished identities—including class-based masculinities—we know who will.

Key Takeaways:

1. Masculinity is valuable real estate currently owned, pretty much uncontested, by the Far Right. This is an untenable situation.
2. Because masculinity is a cherished identity for most men (and many women), the only way to fight toxic masculinities is with alternative, honorable masculinities.
3. Understanding working-class masculinities can improve pandemic response, enhance the prospects for sane gun policies, and much more.

Talk About Solutions—Not the Causes—
of "Extreme Weather"

*Elites are talking about the end of the world; we are talking about
the end of the month.*

—Yellow Vests protester in France[1]

I remember flipping through a copy of the Sierra Club's magazine perhaps
a decade ago and being surprised by a story about a Midwestern farmer
who expressed gratitude that hosting a wind farm on his land had given
him the cash flow to make his farm economically viable again. *Wow*, I
thought, *that's smart*. This was back when policy debates about climate
change were polar bearsy, and policy was dominated by an enthusiastic
embrace of carbon taxes.[2]

Climate change is a far more polarized issue in the US than abroad
because it has become associated with culture wars: in 2021, a lower
percentage of Americans believed in the climate emergency than people
in Japan, Italy, France, Russia, Egypt, and Australia. On-the-ground organizers probably are familiar with everything I say here; my goal is to
reach the average college-educated environmentalist who has not spent
years in the field learning what works. Reducing the gap between Everyman and those on the front lines will help ensure that Everyman—and
woman—does not inadvertently help Big Oil turn climate change into
a culture-wars issue.[3]

For decades, policy approaches to climate change were dominated by
carbon taxes and cap-and-trade emissions trading systems. In good neoliberal fashion, the idea was to let the markets solve the problem in the
most efficient way possible, by increasing the cost of emissions. This makes
eminent sense because it corrects the market failure that makes emissions
artificially costless—but it ignores important political realities. Despite

some notable successes at the state level, these market mechanisms made it just too easy for massive, wealthy, and powerful fossil-fuel companies to frame climate change initiatives as involving more taxes and fewer jobs. These approaches were never popular politically even in countries without our lethal culture-wars dynamic, probably because both carbon taxes and (less plausibly, but still enough to carry political heft) cap-and-trade are easy to caricature as "let's make energy more expensive" policies.[4] To quote an article in *Nature Climate Change* (citing seventeen studies):

> Carbon taxes have been rejected in referenda and elections, have been reversed after political backlash, been opposed by a substantial proportion of the public and generated political controversy whenever debated across advanced democracies. Scholars have identified diverse barriers to public acceptance of carbon taxes, including perceptions that the policy will not reduce emissions, that it is too costly, that it is regressive and that it might undermine economic prosperity.[5]

These sentiments were bound to resonate in an era of declining standards of living for many in the fragile and failing middle class. The "more taxes" frame disserved climate change action during an era that saw a "colossal drop" in the public's inclination to favor higher taxes.[6]

The Merchant Right effectively undermined early bipartisan support for environmental issues through the narrative that environmental gains would come at the expense of blue-collar jobs, which was sometimes true and remains so. This placed climate change in culture-wars territory, a shift made easier because environmentalism has been commodified into a way for elites to claim and display social virtue without concerning themselves with issues of inequality. From Teslas to Whole Foods, both the Merchant Right and the Brahmin Left display their commitment to climate through expensive consumer goods, with non-elites sometimes scornfully referring to Whole Foods as "whole paycheck." This association of environmentalism with elite consumerism strengthens the Far Right's claim that environmentalism is the plaything of the elites who need not care about jobs and gas prices. I think of the Inn at Newport Ranch north of Mendocino, California. It's eco-everything and charges $1,500 a night.[7]

When elites display their social virtue in this hollow way, the association of environmentalism with elitism becomes convincing. The far-right Finns Party decried climate change initiatives as "an elitist approach that hurts the working class." Particularly problematic are policy approaches that raise costs for people who are already economically pinched, like President Emmanuel Macron's gas tax that so infuriated the Yellow Vests protesters. Alternative for Germany weaponized a recent law that requires many Germans to replace fossil-fuel boilers with heat pumps, with the anti-elitist argument that "government has no business in how people heat their homes." In the US, the association of environmentalism with elitism is reinforced by fights over public lands.[8]

Blue-Collar Jobs Aren't in the "What I'm Willing to Sacrifice" Box

Turning this situation around requires starting from a simple fact: blue-collar workers prioritize the economy more strongly than white-collar workers do, and they are typically worried about job loss. And there's no denying that effectively addressing climate change threatens some high-paying fossil fuels jobs. *The New York Times* interviewed a worker who was laid off after fourteen years at an oil refinery in Contra Costa County, California. Like so many other blue-collar workers, he survived by depleting his pension and withdrawing most of his 401(k) early. Early in 2022, he moved to Roseville, California, to work at a power plant, only to be laid off again after four months. He ended up working as a meal delivery driver before landing a job at a chemical plant, where he makes seventeen dollars an hour less than he did at the refinery and is barely able to cover his mortgage.[9]

This is what the energy transition feels like for some: same old, same old, getting screwed. One reason Latinos in southern Texas swung for Trump in 2020 was their concern that Democrats threatened valued blue-collar fossil-fuel jobs. Same situation with coal miners. What turned West Virginia from bright blue to bright red was the withering of the only realistic path to settled middle-class life for many noncollege grads: the coal mines. West Virginia has some of the highest rates of opioid use and other social disfunction due to coal mines shutting down.[10] Remember Hillary Clinton's famous gaffe about shutting down mines? Here's what she actually said:

> Instead of dividing people the way Donald Trump does, let's reunite around politics that will bring jobs and opportunities to all these under-served poor

communities. So, for example, I'm the only candidate who has a policy about how to bring economic opportunity using clean renewable energy into coal country. *Because we're going to put a lot of coal miners and coal companies out of business, right, Tim?* [My italics. Representative Tim Ryan (D-OH) was in the audience.] And we're going to make it clear that we don't want to forget those people. Those people labored in those mines for generations, losing their health, often losing their lives to turn on our lights and power our factories. Now we've got to move away from coal and all the other fossil fuels, but I don't want to move away from the people who did the best they could to produce energy that we relied on.[11]

She was quoted out of context—outrageously so. Still: forewarned is forearmed. Any liberal needs to understand how to avoid the italicized sound bite in the age of social media.

Addressing climate change has high salience for college-educated Democrats, but low salience for the typical voter: it ranked only fourteenth in voters' (and noncollege voters') list of top priorities in a 2022 survey. The economy, in sharp contrast, typically emerges as noncollege voters' top concern or near it. A 2023 poll found that majorities supported many climate change initiatives, though it also found that college grads supported virtually all by 7–10 points more than those without degrees.[12]

As always, the best defense is a good offense: turn the blue-collar-job argument from a weakness into a strength. Activist Saul Griffith and Jesse Jenkins, a Princeton professor who played a major role in developing President Biden's Inflation Reduction Act (IRA) of 2022, are crucial figures in transitioning away from neoliberal "let's make energy more expensive" strategies. Jenkins and Griffith shift attention away from the *causes* of climate change to the *solution*: to rewire America, which will require a World War II level of investment to create twenty-five million new jobs (according to Griffith; Jenkins quotes a more modest figure). Jenkins is admirably adept at the class politics of climate change, epitomized by his tweet describing the IRA, which made the single-largest investment ever in energy and climate, as "billion-dollar corporations and people who have been cheating on their taxes paying for all of us to get cheaper, cleaner energy and manufacture clean energy technologies in America."[13]

Importantly, the IRA's focus was not simply on addressing market failures but on building long-term political support for climate initiatives by intertwining those goals with goals cherished by blue-collar workers. Biden's messaging highlighted that the bill would create jobs in all zip codes, with benefits to areas left behind. Wind turbine technician (median pay: $56,200) is the second-fastest-growing occupation in America: environmentalists have now learned to talk about this constantly and should continue to do so. The IRA also channeled a lot of money to communities dependent on fossil fuels. This is not the kind of cost-efficient solution beloved of economists, but it's effective legislative sausage-making. The IRA's approach represents a welcome shift to counter the climate-versus-jobs narrative. "A push for environmental legislation to restrict the use of fossil fuels must engage the thousands of union workers employed by industries reliant on those energy sources," observe Stacey Abrams and Lauren Groh-Wargo.[14]

"Pollution? I don't talk about it much with friends," a Louisiana woman told Arlie Hochschild. "This whole town operates off of oil. So I could be talking to two moms whose husbands work in the plants. They think government regulation will hurt jobs, or stop new plants from coming in."[15] Here's the fact: we all do lots that's inconsistent with our climate change concerns. For example, my generation of environmentalists would never, ever have considered having more than two children; just unthinkable because we were influenced by the link between larger population and larger environmental impacts. In subsequent generations, many placed that outside the "things I do to protect the earth" box.

These boxes are, in some sense, arbitrary. College-educated environmentalists need to respect the fact that many non-elites don't put blue-collar jobs into the sacrifices-I-am-willing-to-make-for-climate-change box. "Certainly no Louisianan I talked to liked pollution," noted Hochschild, but "oil brought jobs. Jobs brought money. Money bought a better life—school, home, health, a piece of the American Dream."[16]

It's important for environmentalists to adopt a tone of sincere regret that coal and oil are contracting as industries: about nine hundred thousand workers were still directly employed by fossil-fuel industries in 2022. By stressing the need to protect workers' interests while the economy transitions to the next generation of blue-collar jobs, let's make this a battle between the Right and the Left over who *really* has workers' backs.[17]

I'm not saying it's a slam dunk: once construction is complete, wind and solar farms typically require few operators, and clean energy jobs don't necessarily offer comparable wages or require the same skills laid-off fossil-fuel workers have. "We've heard the same things over and over and over again going back to JFK," said Phil Smith, chief of staff of the United Mine Workers of America. Pay attention to whether renewables will offer as many jobs as fossil fuels did in a given local area and to whether the new jobs will require the same skills as old jobs did.[18] Sometimes they will: offshore wind farms require skills similar to those required on oil platforms; geothermal draws on the same skill sets required in fossil-fuel jobs; coal is waning in Wyoming, but there's phenomenal wind farm potential.[19]

But sometimes they won't. Environmentalists need to stress they will when that's true and have some answers when they won't. Too often, I have heard that new jobs are a-comin' without attention to the fact that skills are different, compensation and benefits are worse, and that insulation installation in Georgia holds no appeal for Louisiana oil platform workers. Don't assume people will move: many won't, and they'll be angry at you for suggesting they need to. Yet again, decades of neoliberalism—with liberals' complicity—privatized profits while imposing risks and costs onto workers. This has created a deep well of skepticism that creates a Sisyphean task for climate change activists.

It's not as if environmentalists are unaware of the distributive issues. The environmental justice movement has been around for decades, but its chief focus is on environmental racism and the widespread citing of highly polluting land uses in or nearby poor communities of color, with disastrous results for human health. This focus is vitally important—but it is not a substitute for a focus on blue-collar jobs and income for hard-strapped farmers. As always, it's not a zero-sum game: adding a focus on the middle does not preclude a focus on the poor; adding a focus on class does not preclude sustained attention to dismantling racial hierarchies.

Connect with the Moral Intuitions of Your Audience

Katharine Hayhoe, a Christian evangelical and climate scientist at Texas Tech, points out that more than 70 percent of Americans believe climate change is occurring and the vast majority are worried about it. But they are influenced by messages (from both the Left and the Right) that addressing climate change "will involve pain, a complete repudiation of their lives, or both." She points out that "a lot of the news outlets are doubling-, tripling- or quadrupling-down on fear-based messages because they think more fear is going to make more people pay attention. What they don't realize is this: Most people are already worried. And if you're already worried but you're not activated, more fear is not going to activate you." What will work instead is connecting with the values of the people you are trying to persuade.[20] Here's Hayhoe:

> It's really a matter of showing people that they are already the perfect person to care *because* of who they are, and that climate action would be an even more genuine expression of their identity. . . . Someone who loves the birds at her backyard feeder might become an advocate for renewable energy when she learned how dangerous climate change has made the songbird migration. Hunters might push their representatives to fund highway wildlife corridors and protect forest habitats.[21]

Jonathan Haidt's point again: use messages that connect with the audience you seek to persuade. An analysis of environmental messaging found that it's typically grounded on liberal moral foundations and that conservatives' support for environmental legislation increased when it was framed in terms of conservative values like purity rather than liberal values like harm. This is different from the common contention that environmentalists should stop talking about moral commitments and talk only about economics. My point is different: environmentalists should try to connect with the moral intuitions of the people they need to convince.[22]

Place loyalty is a key value that can be mobilized to fight climate change. In rural areas, tap into farmers' loyalty to tradition and locale—and their need for cash. Use farmers as messengers to the effect that "I can no longer grow what my grandfather grew on this land." In coastal and fire-prone areas, point out that insurance companies are already changing underwriting habits due to fires and floods exacerbated by climate change. In other words, Big Business is making sure it doesn't get stuck with the bill, sometimes at the same time as Big Business is significantly responsible for—and for denying the reality of—climate change. Some areas that have been built upon will soon be vulnerable to flooding and other climate-related disasters. Anti-environmental forces no doubt will try to frame this as the government trying to deprive landowners of their hard-earned property. Environmentalists need to frame this as a defense of taxpayers, who will get stuck footing the bill again and again for rebuilding.[23]

Environmentalists also need to tap into blue-collar patriotism and anxieties about China. Point out that solar cells were first developed in America, but then China stepped in with huge subsidies and stole the market out from under us. We need to invest now to make sure the same thing doesn't happen with electric vehicles and wind turbines. The Inflation Reduction Act took a step in the right direction by providing subsidies only for cars built in the US despite the fact that this will slow the rate of EV adoption because of the limited number of manufacturers who can currently fulfill this requirement (unless it doesn't; relationships with allies mean this "Made in America" requirement has been considerably watered down). Insisting that EVs be built in the US will burden US consumers because American manufacturers don't make low-cost EVs, at least yet. But it's time to recognize that, politically, empowering Americans as consumers often needs to take a back seat to empowering Americans by giving them good jobs.[24]

A second crucial move is to tap into the widespread support for renewable energy. A study of red-state Indiana found that 94 percent of respondents wanted more solar energy; 88 percent wanted more wind energy. Younger Republicans (78 percent) are dramatically more likely than older ones (53 percent) to prioritize renewables. People greatly overestimate the percentage of power we now get from renewables, so they need to know it's still small—but could be much higher within ten years with the right investments. Also, it's important to ensure that communities where wind farms are located aren't expected to shoulder many costs—including the simple cost of change in an environment where many have stayed put precisely to avoid it: that's a cost. Recent work by Christiana Ochoa details the challenge and proposes a model to help ensure that wind farms don't turn into yet another culture-wars issue.[25]

Polling shows that tying climate change initiatives to cleaning up pollution is promising. The Indiana study found widespread concern over air pollution from coal, oil spills, and industrial accidents. Solar and wind are widely seen as clean and emissions-free. Another fact that should be on every environmentalist's lips: an all-electric energy system will mean lower rates of asthma, heart attacks, and strokes. Let's not overlook the health effects of extreme heat on many kinds of blue-collar jobs, from landscaping to roofing and more. "Democrats talk about climate justice in abstract terms that are not relevant," said Representative Marie Gluesenkamp Perez. "When it's 117 degrees outside, I can't work [in my family's auto shop]. I can't pay my mortgage." That's the ticket.[26]

Last but definitely not least, climate change action needs to make sense at a household level. Environmentalists during the cap-and-trade era sometimes were a bit blasé about higher costs, on the theory that no one should get to externalize the costs of pollution onto others. I get that, but remember that two-thirds of low-income American and 40 percent of middle-income ones—but only 18 percent of the affluent—worry about being able to pay their bills at the end of the month. Politicians now get this; the Inflation Reduction Act subsidizes heat pumps and home up-grades. In fact, household-level changes could deliver 40 percent of the IRA's carbon emissions reduction. Saul Griffith's calculations suggest that the average American household could save roughly $1,900 a year in an all-electric economy. Again, persuade blue-collar people with arguments that resonate with the logic of blue-collar lives.[27]

Activists' Language Can Feel Unpersuasive at Best and Insulting at Worst

Climate change activists need to think carefully about their language. Alas, the term *climate change* has been so thoroughly demonized and politi-cized that it's not the best frame for persuading people who don't already agree on the need to decarbonize. "Focusing instead on the 'energy tran-sition' that is necessary over the next decade can communicate the need for change without stepping on the land mine that has been created by anti-climate messaging over the last few decades," Michael Vandenbergh suggested to me. Again, focus on jobs, jobs, jobs and the better health (less asthma and fewer strokes) that the new energy economy will bring.[28]

And then there are the insults. Calling people *climate deniers* will often be perceived as college-educated professionals yet again condescending to those without degrees, attributing their different preferences to dim-wittedness. Instead, embrace as a working assumption that people resis-tant to effective climate change measures are concerned about jobs and costs. For the same reason, avoid *climate crisis*. It is a crisis, but that doesn't mean that calling it one won't have negative consequences for the envi-ronment: that phrase again intimates that anyone who is not on board is at best an idiot and at worst in need of serious psychotherapy. Instead, talk about "extreme weather," advises Hayhoe.[29]

Do I find it irritating not to be able to call a crisis a crisis? Yes, I do. But what we face is truly a crisis, so I'm willing to change the way I talk if that will deflate the Far Right and increase our chances of an effective energy transition. Take a tip from a Montana farmer who believes unequivocally that climate change had damaged his barley crop—but back at the bar with his friends, dropped the taboo words "climate change" in favor of "erratic weather" and "drier, hotter summers."[30]

Folks, we don't have any more time to waste. We need class-competent climate change messaging without further delay. I have a grandchild; I want her to grow up in a world that's not embattled and searing hot.

Key Takeaways:

1. Environmentalism can be caricatured as a plaything of the rich because it's been commodified into a way elites can claim and display social virtue without concerning themselves with inequality.
2. Climate change is a far more polarized issue in the US than abroad because it has been turned into a culture-wars issue.
3. There are many ways to make climate change initiatives appealing to non-elites—by tapping place loyalty, patriotism, resentment against economic elites, and the need for a new generation of blue-collar jobs to replace jobs in contracting industries.
4. Avoid language like *climate deniers*: this insults the intelligence of people for whom climate change is less of a priority than it is for progressives.

Reframe the Immigration Debate
to Tap Working-Class Values

I believe in amnesty for those who have put down roots and lived
here, even though some time back they may have entered illegally.
                                                    —Ronald Reagan, 1989[1]

"Nativist, anti-immigrant attitudes are the most important predictor of
voting for the populist radical-right," concludes a study of seven European
countries. An earlier study found that no far-right populist party performed well in elections without mobilizing grievances over immigration.
In the US, anti-immigrant sentiment is a strong determinant of Trump
voting. These findings are fueled by class differences. In November 2023,
noncollege voters were 15 percentage points less likely than college grads
to say Democrats were closer to their views on immigration. Place also
plays an important role. Rural residents are nearly three times more likely
than city folk to say that immigrants are a burden on the country and also
much more likely to say that immigrants don't share their values.[2]

I do not pretend to be an immigration expert. My hope is to explain
the class dynamics underlying the immigration mess, to explain why some
common arguments are not persuasive, and to suggest some alternatives
that might be.

Why Does Anti-Immigration Rhetoric
Work So Well for the Far Right?

Immigration fits beautifully into the politics of distraction. Immigrants
are faulted for stealing jobs and driving down wages, deflecting blame for
workers' falling standard of living from the Merchant Right onto people
of color. Culture-war dynamics also deflect anger away from economic

elites onto immigrants and cultural elites in three other ways. First, immigrants upset noncollege grads' preference for stability and similarity (a dynamic exacerbated when immigrants' defense is structured around elites' preference for novelty and diversity). Second, undocumented immigrants clash with order-takers' belief that since they have to follow the rules, others should, too. Finally, when progressives indulge in name-calling, they trigger anger over elite condescension. "It's really easy to show up in any small town anywhere and look at how people react to change and decide that it all belongs in this bucket of prejudice," noted Ira Glass after *This American Life* (*TAL*) conducted over one hundred interviews in Albertville, Alabama. "But, in Albertville, it was hard to parse out just how much was prejudice and how much was just people dealing with something new. That was real, also."[3]

The first way to counter these culture-wars dynamics is a familiar one: call out the politics of distraction. "Nobody stays awake all night worrying about the southern border. They worry if their kid is going to relapse, if they are going to lose their house. That's when people listen," said Marie Gluesenkamp Perez in 2023 on *Pod Save America*. I suspect that some people do stay up at night obsessing about the southern border. The Left needs to reach the ones who don't.[4]

Next, let's address racism. Whites' attitudes toward immigration are and have always been intertwined with racism: Trump opined that the US needs fewer immigrants from "shithole countries" and more from Norway. Not subtle. Nonetheless, few would claim that blue-collar Americans are more racist now than thirty years ago, but when Michèle Lamont interviewed blue-collar men in the New York metropolitan area in the late 1990s, most were largely indifferent to immigrants. "To the extent that workers referred to immigrants in interviews, they often described them in positive terms," she found, as hard workers with family values. In the early 1980s, only 20 percent of Americans did not perceive immigrants as "basically good, honest people," with higher figures for undocumented immigrants. Ronald Reagan went so far as to offer a broad amnesty to people who had entered the country illegally. What changed? One change was increased economic insecurity: when people are pessimistic about the economy, they are more likely to endorse restrictionist immigration policy preferences; in the 1990s, the blue-collar slide was not yet in full swing. Once again, economic anxiety fuels racism.[5]

Regression analysis shows that people who are racially resentful are very likely to oppose immigration. But beware of regression confusion: the fact that racists oppose immigration does not prove that everyone who opposes immigration is an irredeemable racist. For some people—the American preservationists—the racism is front and center. Again, my goal is to build bridges to a different group: the anti-elites.[6]

Understand Why Macroeconomic Arguments Aren't Persuasive

Tons of research documents immigrants' positive effects on the economy. Many studies document that immigrants enhance the GDP. A recent Congressional Budget Office study documented that high rates of immigration will help boost GDP by $7 trillion over the next decade. Another found that immigrants contribute about $100 billion annually to greater Boston's gross domestic product. Immigrants do indeed grow the economy.[7]

A large literature explores whether immigration has driven down wages and/or crowded Americans out of jobs they would otherwise have. A 2017 National Academy of Sciences report cited research finding that wages fell in regions that received more immigrants. On the other hand, there's substantial evidence that cuts the other way. Giovanni Peri and a coauthor found for 2000–2022 a "small positive effect on wages of non-college natives and no significant crowding out effects on employment." A study of 1995–2007 found small negative impacts on men without high school degrees, particularly in the four states with the highest immigration (California, Florida, New York, and Texas)—but these are not the middle-status voters who flock to the Far Right. The subject is complex, and scholars' conclusions require complicated modeling that takes into account that immigrants consume goods and services and found businesses, all of which create more jobs and increase tax revenues. The CBO study mentioned above found that immigration boosted tax revenues by about $1 trillion, and the Massachusetts study predicted increases in state and local tax revenues in Massachusetts by $2 million for every one thousand new immigrant workers. Immigrants have also been credited with helping tame the US inflation rate and avoid recession (because more workers produce more stuff, and inflation occurs when too few goods chase too many dollars).[8]

It's frustrating when anti-immigrant forces ignore the substantial evidence of the positive economic effects of immigration. "I have almost given up writing about this type of research," *Boston Globe* columnist Marcela García remarks bleakly when she discusses three new studies documenting immigrants' positive economic contributions.[9] She muses:

> Stressing the economic gains newcomers bring rarely makes a dent in their strong anti-immigrant sentiments. I don't know that there's anything one can say to this crowd—the "what part of illegal don't you understand?" crowd—to change their hearts and minds. Has anything ever worked to persuade them? Are they all irreparable xenophobes?[10]

Note the name-calling.

Why doesn't data like this persuade noncollege voters? Again, increases in GDP don't impress people who have not gotten their fair share of that increase. And the secondary effects of immigration on new job creation, new tax revenues, and the like rely on complex modeling precisely because they are not easy to untangle—and believing in them requires a trust in expertise the Missing Middle currently lacks.

In addition, in ways that are rarely understood, many anti-elites aren't impressed with macroeconomic arguments because they have "seen with their own eyes" immigrants' negative impacts. *This American Life's* case study of Albertville illustrates this better than any ethnography.

Albertville attracted a poultry processing plant after World War II. "Everybody knew the chicken plant was good pay, benefits, retirement, a decent job if you didn't finish high school," said Miki Meek of *TAL*. Jobs were plentiful: "People joked that you could quit one plant in the morning and get hired by another plant in the afternoon." That changed when hundreds of Mexican workers started coming to Albertville in the mid-1990s due to an economic crash in Mexico.[11]

Basically, blue-collar Americans looked on as employers exploited poor foreigners to undercut the economic prospects of American workers. *This American Life* quotes one worker saying that she makes more in the poultry plant than she did as a teacher in Mexico: "Here, what I earn makes me upper-middle-class" in Mexico. The American workers' logic was that if immigrants hadn't been available, employers would have had to offer Americans what they had had before the Mexicans showed up: plentiful jobs that offered a lower-middle-class standard of living for those without college degrees.[12]

The racial politics are complex: the belief that immigrants take jobs from Americans is much higher among Black (51 percent) than white Americans (28 percent). Between 1980 and 2005, 40 percent of immigrants to the Midwest were Latino. The South was also affected: soon jobs weren't so plentiful in Albertville because Latino applicants started lining up at 2:00 a.m. for any openings.[13]

> Lots of local workers said it wasn't long before management seemed to prefer the new Latino workers—thought they were better workers. . . . Latino didn't want to do anything that could make them lose their jobs—didn't complain, didn't make a big deal about injuries. This is true even for the documented workers.[14]

This American Life quoted a Latino worker saying that they didn't really know their rights, and besides, they kept quiet because they had hungry families to feed. Employers recognized they could abuse workers with impunity, not just by bringing in vulnerable undocumented workers but also at times paying below minimum wage and hiring child labor, so they expanded their operations in Albertville. Tyson Foods quadrupled in size; another factory added two hundred jobs. "If there hadn't been a flood of new foreign workers to take those jobs, the companies might have had to pay more to attract employees to the plants. But that was not a choice they ever had to make," notes Ira Glass.[15] Another point of contention was that most Latinos didn't join the union. Alabama is a "right to work" state— really a right to freeload. State law allows workers to opt out of paying union dues and still get the benefit of a union contract. The plants went from being 80–95 percent unionized, one labor leader estimated, to much lower union density. Once unions lost their power, "you were at [the company's] mercy." It should be said that the relationship between unions and immigrants is complex; although immigrants sometimes undercut unions, at other times, they join them to gain relief from exploitation: Justice for Janitors, which has organized largely undocumented immigrants, is just one example.[16]

But in Albertville, residents were distressed. Said a resident who voted for Hillary Clinton, "You know, you need to hire Americans. You know, there are people out there that wants jobs. But there, for many years, they just quit hiring Americans." Democrats were unresponsive, so other voices arose.[17] A 2004 ad by the Coalition for the Future American Worker featured an inflatable dummy getting punched over and over, with the following voice-over:

> How much longer can Iowa workers be the punching bags of greedy corpo-
> rations and politicians? First, meatpackers replaced Iowans with thousands
> of foreign workers. Next, wages were cut almost in half. Now, politicians
> want new laws to import millions more foreign workers and give amnesty
> to illegal aliens. Tell the candidates no more foreign workers and no am-
> nesty for millions to be here illegally.[18]

A barrage of complaints, including from the Iowa Federation of Labor, led the ad to be pulled. What happened in Albertville happened
throughout the South and Midwest, "as a new breed of [meat]pack-
ers gutted the unions that had existed for many years in the old-line
plants, slashed wages and benefits and" instituted speedups that sharply
increased injury rates.[19]

This is just one US example. Another from Europe: in 2017, shortly
after Britain's vote to leave the EU, two British professionals both decried
Brexit and belittled Leavers' fears of foreign competition. "Have you done
house renovations lately?" I asked. Both had and had been pleased with
their Polish contractors, whose bids were much lower than those of their
British competitors.

All this helps explain why non-elites often believe that immigration
is intertwined with a fall in their standard of living. *This American Life*'s
labor economist found what some others have found: that immigration
helped grow the economy, but workers without high school degrees
earned less—about $1,200 less than workers in adjacent counties without
large immigration flows. But this decrease was small compared with the
overall wage decrease incident to automation and neoliberal policies that
corroded protections for unions, gutted antitrust enforcement, and subsidized outsourcing. One worker at the Albertville chicken factory was
earning $11.95 an hour in 2017 after working at the plant for forty-four
years—only half of her 1974 take-home pay in real dollars. The overall
$1,200 decrease attributable to immigration works out to about 5 percent
of the overall decrease. That's exactly what another economist found as a
general rule: that immigration accounts for 5 percent of the increase in
wage inequality between 1980 and 2000.[20]

"Meatpacking is a well-known exception" to the general rule that immigration does not drive down wages or take jobs from US citizens, David Dyssegaard Kallick of the Immigration Research Initiative told me in an interview. But it may have had an outsize effect on attitudes toward immigration in rural areas. As noted before, rural residents are nearly three times as likely as city folk to say that immigrants are a burden on the country (42 percent versus 16 percent). Meatpacking is what many rural people have seen on the ground. They often mistake correlation for causation—a mistake graduate students make all the time. One worker didn't: "No, I wasn't mad at Latinos. I was mad at management. They were scheming, conniving, taking shortcuts to get [the Mexicans] in. I'm mad—I'm not mad. I'm upset. I'm hurt really."[21]

The challenge for the Left is to connect with this sentiment. Otherwise, the Far Right owns this turf. Jeff Sessions, later Trump's attorney general, decried "big greedy businesses who hire illegal workers, and hiring those numbers by the tens or hundreds of thousands, will pull down the wages of American citizens. Why would we do that? Why don't we take care of our American workers?" It's so cynical: Sessions twice voted against comprehensive immigration reform.[22]

Yet in 2022, voters in battleground states still trusted Republicans (48 percent) more than Democrats (40 percent) to handle the immigration issue, and over a third (36 percent) of Latinos said they were more likely to support a candidate who says the "southern border should remain closed to asylum seekers until the border crisis is resolved."[23] The good news, though, is that effective messaging shrank Republicans' advantage to just 2 percent.

Connect with the Working Class Through Working-Class Values

The key is to connect with anti-elites through working-class values: helping family farms and small business, patriotism, "family values," and hardwork worship.

The first step is to talk with family farmers whose crops are rotting in the fields because they are unable to find workers. Use farmers as spokespeople to say that most immigrants take jobs Americans don't want: hard labor stooping in fields all day. Show strawberries rotting in the fields and farmers being driven into bankruptcy (and, alas, sometimes suicide). Polling in 2022 by Hart Research Associates in battleground states and congressional districts found that voters supported a path to citizenship for farmworkers by two to one.[24]

Second, talk with small business owners struggling to keep afloat for lack of workers. In 2023, New York City faced a labor shortage of 10,000 bar and restaurant workers. Point out what's happened in Britain, where Brexit led to severe labor shortages: by June 2022, there was a shortfall of 460,000 workers, including a 3 percent deficit in wholesale and retail employment. Link these numbers with narratives of small-business owners who can't get dishwashers. Remind people who's taking care of grandma—there's a labor shortage of 70,000 nurses and 40,000 home health aides. The labor shortage includes doctors: rural areas rely heavily on foreign-born doctors. Hart Research polling found that 57 percent of battleground voters support granting temporary legal status and work permits for undocumented workers in critical industries facing labor shortages. While you're at it, remind people that immigrants start businesses at much higher rates than Americans. "This is what Latinos do. We open small businesses," to quote Senator Catherine Cortez Masto of Nevada (D-Nevada). Hart polling found that 67 percent of battleground voters agree that immigrants play a positive role in keeping businesses fully staffed up and open.[25]

Patriotism can be tapped in several ways. Immigrants prop up our fertility rate, which is below the 2.1 children per woman replacement rate needed to keep a developed economy's population stable. Immigration and immigrants' relatively high birth rate are the only thing that stands between the US and a sharp population decline that would have negative consequences for American power abroad and the economy at home, which is what low-immigration, low-birth-rate countries like Korea and Japan now face. Social scientists have long warned of an era of labor scarcity; it's here.[26]

Also, point out that immigrants are patriotic, as patriotic as Americans in general: 71 percent of immigrants and 73 percent of native-born Americans agree that "generally speaking, America is a better country than most countries." Only 46 percent of progressive activists would choose to live in the US if they could live anywhere in the world—but 79 percent of Latinos would. Latinos share some blue-collar values for a simple reason: they are less likely than the general population to be college grads.[27]

Another blue-collar value, "Family comes first," dominates in Latino communities. Over two-thirds (67 percent) of swing voters in battleground states said a "very serious concern" was that Republicans support separating immigrant families and putting children in cages. Remember Carlos Odio's point that family is the strongest motivator in Latino lives.[28]

Hard-work worship, so central to American blue-collar culture, is yet another point of cultural connection between immigrants and the Missing Middle. Remember that Latinos express more respect for hard work than any other group and are least likely to attribute where they are today to luck and circumstance.[29] Hart Research found this message performed well:

> Like most of us, immigrant families value hard work, self-reliance, and contributing to our communities, and we need an immigration system that is secure, accessible, and grows our economy.[30]

The key is to connect immigrants with working-class values, as did an Iowa billboard that depicted an extended Latino family of grandparents, parents, and four children, including a baby, at a family occasion (perhaps the baby's baptism), with the caption, "Welcome the Immigrant *You* Once Were." "The subtext was clear: today's immigrants are no different from your family members who traveled by train and wagon to build a life in the prairie a hundred years ago. Hardworking, religious, and devoted to family, they share your values." Haidt again.[31]

Contest the Far Right's Ownership of "What Don't You Get About Illegal?"

Another key dynamic of the immigration debate is that the Far Right makes a big deal of pointing out that immigration without papers is illegal, tapping order-takers' insistence on rule following. Thus, *This American Life* found that locals resented immigrants flouting the eighteen-year-old minimum age rule when they heard coworkers planning their quinceañeras. Of course, many immigrants also broke immigration law, but refugees typically didn't, which is why the Far Right regularly lumps together refugees (who have a legal right to enter) with immigrants (who don't). It's also why Republicans were so eager to keep the "illegals" argument alive in 2024 that they refused to support a bipartisan immigration reform bill that gave them nearly all they had demanded (much to the consternation of progressives).[32]

It's time to stop letting the Far Right own the "What don't you get about illegal?" argument by redirecting the anger against immigrants and refugees back where it belongs: onto political and economic elites. Political elites cynically rejected the opportunity to both gain control of our borders and create a path to citizenship for many people who have lived, worked, paid taxes, and contributed to our economy for years: 60 percent of swing voters in battleground states said it was a very serious concern that Republicans were trying to deport law-abiding immigrants who have lived in and contributed to the United States for many years. Who's really to blame for making it impossible for immigrants to play by the rules? The key message: "Look at the bill of goods elites are trying to sell you. We know you're way too smart for that."[33]

Another way to flip the "law abiding" script is to point out that far-right political elites aligned with economic elites don't want to regularize immigration status for undocumented workers because that makes it easy to exploit both them and native-born workers. The only real way to protect the wages of native-born Americans is to regularize immigrant workers' legal status. And point out that *employers* also are breaking the rules by hiring people without papers. A particularly egregious example: in 2002, Tyson executives were indicted for paying smugglers $100 to $200 to recruit undocumented workers to work in fifteen poultry-processing plants in the South and Midwest.[34]

Avoid Arguments That Appeal to Elites but Alienate Non-Elites

I value immigrants for the diversity they bring and the way they enrich American culture. But this frame aligns immigrants with elites' taste for diversity over similarity, novelty over stability. The Brahmin Left celebrates diversity and difference: that new restaurant with authentic Ethiopian food, the celebration of Día de los Muertos, Chinese Lunar New Year, Cinco de Mayo. At diversity days at school and at work, immigrants' unique cultures are celebrated, as they should be. But when talking with the Missing Middle, it's important to stress similarity: that immigrants quickly become as American as apple pie or bagels or pizza. Or spaghetti, which my New England WASP father (b. 1915) used to refer to as *ethnic food*.

Here's Haidt again: reframe our arguments to tap our intended audience's values of similarity and stability. Lamont found blue-collar Americans "less concerned with [immigrants'] moral character than with their lack of desire to assimilate." "You're in my country. You come to me, to my business, speak my language," said a tin factory foreman. "Why do I have to learn your language to communicate with you? My family learned English."[35]

By the second or third generation, immigrants "are often indistinguishable from native-born Americans in their cultural, social, and political preferences." "When immigrants first began to arrive in Perry [Iowa], few would've anticipated that within 20 years Hispanic and Anglo families would treat one another as relative equals or that immigrants would be incorporated so deeply into the life of this small community," notes an ethnographic study. Work by Raj Chetty finds that "Hispanics are on an upward trajectory across generations and may close most of the gap between their incomes and those of whites"; unlike African Americans, Latinos have relatively high rates of intergenerational income mobility. Children of Mexican parents who were raised at the 25th percentile reach, on average, the 50th percentile in adulthood. Mexican immigrants show the fastest assimilation of any group as measured by the names parents give their kids. A sociology professor notes, "The names immigrants give their children go through three stages: from names in the original language, to universal names, and finally to names in the destination-country language. Accordingly, I would expect a decline in the name Jose." That's exactly what another sociologist found.[36]

Assimilation is rapid by other measures, too. Second-generation immigrants are more likely (77 percent) than native-born Americans (69 percent) to say they are proud to be an American. Fully 90 percent of Americans—whether native or foreign-born—agree that it's very or fairly important to speak English. The Left has perhaps been reluctant to stress all this, but if it really cares about immigrants' welfare, we should get over it. It's not that difficult to say that we should respect the diversity of Americans' heritage while also pointing out that immigrants do, in fact, assimilate.[37]

Another misstep is rhetoric that takes sides in the culture clash between metro and retro described in chapter 12. The settled lower-middle class is deeply place loyal and community-minded. *This American Life* interviewed a local woman who joked that she bonded with an immigrant because both were "outsiders": he from Mexico; she from a town twenty-five minutes away from Albertville. Depict immigrants as working-class people with working-class values. And recognize that immigrants sometimes break rules without meaning to, upsetting settled understandings in formerly homogeneous communities. An example: Remember the obsession with having a well-kept home with a tidy yard as a way of distinguishing a settled working-class family from "white trash"? In Albertville, Mexicans at first were chiefly single men, who piled into houses with predictable results.[38] Said one resident:

> Well, you have a car parked right in the front yard, you can see where they've destroyed the grass that's been on it because of all the traffic on it. You can see garbage cans sitting right in the front door, trash scattered on the yard. You see this next house. You've got one, two, three, four, five, six cars sitting in it.[39]

Longtime residents were worried that immigrants would drive down property values. A brothel opened in a trailer park where many immigrants lived; the town had never before had a brothel. Lower-middle-class people concerned with keeping the world in moral order were unsettled. Before you judge them, keep in mind that the upper-middle class doesn't live with brothels close by. Locals eventually explained that they expected grass, not beaten-down dirt, in front yards, and the immigrants followed the rules once they knew them. This is not the kind of issue the upper-middle class commonly has to cope with.

At a deeper level, deriding as unsophisticated or racist anyone who lacks a globalist outlook just helps the Far Right. YouGov in Britain presents this statement: "Britain has changed in recent times beyond recognition, it sometimes feels like a foreign country, and this makes me feel uncomfortable." Only 16 percent of college graduates agreed, compared with 41 percent of noncollege grads. Just as elites need to talk—and think—about religious people differently, the same holds true for people who prefer rootedness and continuity over novelty and change. Understand that change can be very scary for the fragile middle class, a fear only reinforced by forty years of declining economic prospects. Liberals often gloss over immigrants' preferences for traditionalism or treat them gently, recognizing that immigrants have different needs—but then harshly judge native-born Americans with similar preferences. For non-elite locals and immigrants alike, heritage and tradition reflect imagined communities to which many people are deeply attached.[40]

The standard progressive attitude toward immigration is driven by the rhetoric of human rights, either through legal language or (more often) through human interest stories that highlight with empathy the plight of immigrants and refugees. Stories on NPR have a persistent focus on the tragedies that drove immigrants away from home (typically gang or other violence), immigrants' vulnerability in chaotic border towns, searing stories of family separations, and people whose lives are torn apart. These heart-wrenching stories land with me because of my ties to Venezuela, where I lived the happiest years of my childhood and which is now a total, tragic mess. But that's just the point: I feel closer to immigrants from Latin America than to farmers in Kansas. To lower-middle-class Americans who are place loyal and patriotic, that feels like a betrayal of the imagined communities most precious to them.[41]

I fear these stories are counterproductive, particularly when linked with feeling rules that mandate empathy for immigrants paired with scorn for working-class whites. Case in point: in 2024, Mika Brzezinski on *Morning Joe* decried white rural voters as a threat to democracy, while introducing authors who laid out "the fourfold interconnected threat that white rural voters pose to the country. . . . They are the most racist, xenophobic, anti-immigrant, anti-gay geo-demographic group in the country." This kind of talk places a target on immigrants' backs.[42]

Key Takeaways:

1. Anti-immigrant fervor is the most important predictor of far-right voting because immigration marries economic anxieties with cultural anxieties.
2. Proof that immigration helps the GDP is not persuasive to people who have been left behind and who "see with their own eyes" that increased immigration has been accompanied by lower wages and fewer unions. *Accompanied* is not *caused*, but that needs to be explained, in a respectful way.
3. Highlight that immigrants typically are working-class people

with working-class values of patriotism, family, and hard-work worship—and that most assimilate within a generation.

4. Flip the "law abiding" script by pointing out that economic elites don't want to regularize immigration status for undocumented workers, because that makes it easy to exploit both them and native-born workers. The only way to avoid this is to provide legal status.

Conclusion

Our politics are being driven by middle-class people's fear of falling into poverty. We need to stop scolding people for being afraid, or for expressing their fears the wrong way. We need to listen to them.

—Mark Cuban[1]

During Ted Kennedy's first run for the Senate when he was thirty, his opponent pointed a finger at him and accused him of never having had a full-time job. The next morning, back when Democrats used to do this as a matter of course, Kennedy showed up outside a factory to greet workers as they came off work at 6:00 a.m. A burly ironworker came up, extended his hand, and said, "Kennedy, I heard what they said about you last night. You never worked a day in your life." Kennedy said something like, "I guess you're right." "Let me tell you something," the worker shot back. "You haven't missed a damn thing."[2]

Kennedy did something simple: he listened, and acknowledged his privilege. Not that hard, and it made for a genuine connection. "We're going to talk about what people will listen to," he said once. "You have to get them listening by talking about what they're interested in, before you can start trying to persuade them about other matters."[3]

The Far Right's formula has been to listen and then provide an explanation for the flood of pain and frustration it hears. I firmly believe it's the *wrong* explanation, but here's the point: you can't fight a vivid and compelling explanation without an alternative explanation.

Mused Arlie Hochschild, "They were victims without a language of victimhood." Julie Bettie continues the thought: "Because class is unarticulated, they have only individual characteristics to blame ... their status as a consequence of the fact that they and/or their parents are just 'losers.'" Said a

Mexican-American high school girl, "I mean, they're white. They've had opportunity. What's wrong with them?" A society with a robust understanding of structural racism combined with a blindness to class dynamics is bound to have an angry and alienated white working class. This opens the door to a far-right coalition based on "multiracial whiteness"— between people who are seen as indisputably white, and people of color who aspire to be seen as white—tapping the same kinds of angers in working-class people of color as it taps in noncollege whites.[4]

The Democrat who was most successful in recent times at doing what Ted Kennedy did was Barack Obama: Obama fared far better among working-class Midwestern voters than the Democratic nominee before or after him. He had dreams of his father, but it was his grandparents from clueless Kansas who raised him in their apartment from the age of ten. Obama overcame "my biggest boneheaded move": trying to explain to the San Francisco donor class that small-town voters in Pennsylvania "bitter" over lost jobs "cling to guns and religion or antipathy to people who aren't like them."

Not for nothing was Obama raised by an anthropologist. He took pains to connect with the natives on their own terms and used all the right moves when campaigning in small towns. He started out with validators— "getting respected surrogates to stand up and say that Obama is a guy you can trust"—just what rural activists recommend today. He bonded through religion, saying, "This is a nation of believers, and I'm one of them." A reporter on the campaign trail noted that the president of the mineworkers' union "preached as if he were at a revival, putting Obama's early years into a framework that southwestern Virginians could understand . . . 'Moses was a community organizer! And yes, Jesus was a community organizer!'" Obama talked about creating more jobs for local students "so when they graduate from college those kids can stay here and live in Lebanon instead of having to go and work someplace else." He understood the role that gun ownership played in rural areas, too.[5] Obama also was hyper focused on countering the Fox News narrative.

If I were watching Fox News, I wouldn't vote for me, right? Because the way I'm portrayed 24/7 as a freak! I am the latte-sipping, New York Times–reading, Volvo-driving, no-gun-owning, effete, politically correct, arrogant liberal. Who wants somebody like that . . . People want to know that you're fighting for them, that you get them.[6]

Some of the ways Obama chose would not be my ways: defending coal and what sounded like a sweeping defense of "Second Amendment rights." But he understood that part of American politics was working hard to connect to decent people living in a parallel universe.[7]

College-educated voters' values and preferences currently dominate the Democratic Party in the US and many parties on the Left in Europe. How much will we have to give up to win back the Missing Middle? Like everyone else, there are some issues I would never trade off and other issues I could compromise on. But since I'm not queen of the universe, I'm not sure that's of interest. Trade-offs will be hard-fought within coalitions—as they should be. They will depend heavily on context—as they must. The point is to ensure the trade-offs are made in a way that is class-competent so that multiracial progressive coalitions can yield wins toward a more progressive future. We can't reach that so long as class remains the unfashionable inequality, one not mentioned in polite company.

"I have given up my efforts to help the Democrats," an influential friend told me. "I tried for many years, and all it got me was accusations of being on the right." I joke that the subtitle of this book should have been *I'll Never Have Lunch Again in San Francisco*. Remember that progressive activists report very high levels of pressure to conform in ways this book does not. Don't murder the messenger because you'd prefer to live in a world where everybody embraced your values and your politics. I wish that, too. But we are supposed to be the ones who face facts. In 2024, Donald Trump built the cross-class interracial coalition Democrats dream of. To quote Ezra Klein, they can respond with "contempt or curiosity": with more disdain for the deplorables or with a genuine curiosity about why noncollege voters are unhappy with the Left.[8]

I am not just proposing a change in messaging. I am talking about that but also something much deeper: a changed relationship between noncollege voters and the Brahmin Left. I'm well aware this won't be easy. Therapy never is, and I'm proposing family therapy for the body politic. Good therapy insists you open yourself up to seeing that you are perhaps not as perfect, and perfectly well intentioned, as you thought you were. It forces you to see yourself as others see you, warts and all. Not pleasant—but eyes open wide see better than eyes half-shut.

Acknowledgments

This book has a lot of endnotes—you may have noticed. I'm forever grateful to Ryan Malek-Maple for his tireless work to track stuff down, writing the endnotes in one citation format, rewriting them in another citation format, then consolidating them into one endnote per paragraph so as not to overwhelm you, the reader. Please join me in thanking him for his deep insight, his amazing work ethic, and his sheer stick-to-itiveness.

I was truly blessed by awesome research assistance in helping me navigate five very different types of sources: polling data, political science, sociology, social psychology, and media studies. Olivia Andrews helped shape this project at the beginning, with her patient and endless investigations into polling data. She's going to make an amazing lawyer. Naomi Yang is equally brilliant, and I owe the title and much of the search behind the religion chapter to her. Other staff at the Equality Action Center, which I direct, helped with the book, and with the meeting of the Bridging the Diploma Divide Working Group in November 2023: Henrique Ferreira Menezes and Kallen Beier. Thanks to Henrique, too, for help with Portuguese, and to Raafiya Ali Khan, for answering random questions with her usual efficiency. Thanks also to Kaytlyn Fleming, who printed out approximately eight linear feet of photocopies to make up for my carpal tunnel problems. As always, thanks to my librarians, who found so many needles in so many haystacks: Hilary Hardcastle and Tony Pelczynski.

I am indebted to all the members of the Diploma Divide Working Group for helping me focus and sharpen my thinking: Matt Barreto, Jean Bordewich, Kathy Cramer, Corey Fields, Susan Fiske, Anthony Flaccavento, Justin Gest, Saida Grundy, Jackson Katz, Michèle Lamont, Karyn Lacy, Celinda Lake, Ian Haney López, Hazel Markus, Daniel Markovits, Leslie McCall, Anthony Nadler, Mara Ostfeld, Reece Peck, Lisa Pruitt,

Cecilia Ridgeway, Michael Sandel, Jennifer Sherman, Robb Willer, and Representative Ro Khanna. Thanks, too, to those who are helping me develop the New Class Bubble Quiz: Karyn Lacy, Rachel Korn, Andrea Dittmann, Reece Peck, Nicole Stephens, and Jennifer Sherman.

Thanks to the Rockefeller Foundation for a month spent at the Bellagio Center, where I laid the foundations of this book.

I am particularly indebted to those who took time out of their very busy lives to give me interviews and/or read parts of the draft and give me feedback. My colleague Matt Coles, who was generous with his reminiscences about the gay marriage battle and read that chapter with close attention to detail and accuracy. My colleague David Owen read the climate change chapter not once but *twice*, surely above and beyond the call of duty. Ryan Burge responded generously to a cold-call email, giving me almost immediate comments on the religion chapter. Michael Vandenbergh and Jane Miller gave me extensive and thoughtful comments on the climate change chapters. David Dyssegaard Kallick gave me extensive comments, and invaluable guidance, in navigating immigration debates. Shauna Marshall suffered the frustration of reading the race chapters very closely and having her computer eat her comments up! Sonu Bedi invited me to Dartmouth to give my very first talk on the book. Both he and his colleague Dean Lacy gave me extraordinarily insightful comments on several chapters. Fergus Bordewich invariably answered my SOS requests about nineteenth-century history. Many thanks, too, to Alexandra Mitukiewicz, who carved out time to update the statistics defining the poor, the professionals, and the Missing Middle in chapter 1, and to Dr. Di Di of Santa Clara University, for giving me a quick, insightful introduction to the sociology of religion.

Jonathan Haidt stepped up to provide me an early blurb for the book—while he was on a European book tour and not answering email . . . but he answered mine. Many thanks, too, to Arlie Hochschild. I have been deeply influenced by her brilliance, her humanism, and her unwavering support. This book would not exist but for my agent, Roger Freet, who saw me through the process while dealing with a serious health challenge—he was always there for me. Elisabeth Dyssegaard, my editor, was a pleasure to work with and saved me from any number of missteps. Many thanks to them for the title and subtitle to this book; not my strong suit.

This book also would not exist but for my husband of forty-six years, James X. Dempsey, who patiently helped me talk through the arguments in this book again and again even when he disagreed with me. He also spent a lot of time giving the book a very close reading and expert editing. His generosity never ceases to enrich my life. I love you very much. Thanks, too, to his mother, Ruth, who was always there for me when I was raising my kids. She died at 101 while this book was in process, leaving a big hole in my life.

Notes

Introduction

1. **Quote:** Plaut, V. C., Thomas, K. M., Hurd, K., & Romano, C. A. (2018). Do color blindness and multiculturalism remedy or foster discrimination and racism?, p. 200. *Current Directions in Psychological Science,* 27(3), 200–206. https://doi.org/10.1177 /0963721418766068; **seven words:** Kraus, M. W., Park, J. W., & Tan, J. J. X. (2017). Signs of social class: The experience of economic inequality in everyday life, p. 424. *Perspectives of Psychological Science,* 12(3), 422–435. https://doi.org/10.1177/1745691616673192.

2. **Inequality:** Gethin, A., Martínez-Toledano, C., & Piketty, T. (2022). Brahmin left versus merchant right: Changing political cleavages in 21 Western democracies, 1948–2020. *The Quarterly Journal of Economics,* 137(1), 1–48. https://doi.org/10.1093/qje/qjab036; **white and nonwhite noncollege:** Astrow, A. (2021, May 2). The college degree conun-drum: Democrats' path forward with noncollege voters. *Third Way.* https://www.thirdway .org/memo/the-college-degree-conundrum-democrats-path-forward-with-non-college -voters.

3. **Top two quintiles:** Podhorzer, M. (2022, April 10). The congressional class reversal. *Week-end Reading.* https://docs.google.com/document/d/1S0RH8sqV33BzLLA6V1tXmwL MbmGhoEcVEhA8Fg7aiL0/edit?_hsmi=240137472&_hsenc=p2ANqtz-9LFTPUffA FrlHo1qXrmnLoldowdsdjOyw680aOJ3vFZDbHyzbyCWIfqyYlkjXWYvH5eOFuQO YGc5Kkm2zJYOElNP0Fpx5_ekJsiM2LRIYsrOL1Fxk&pli=1#heading=h.gjdgxs.

4. **Not just the US:** Hall, S. (1988). *The hard road to renewal.* Verso; **striking parallels:** Gethin et al., 2022, 1–48.

5. **Class conflict:** General Social Survey. (2021). National Opinion Research Center (NORC). https://gss.norc.org/.

6. **Three European countries:** Kurer, T. (2020). The declining middle: Occupational change, social status, and the populist right. *Comparative Political Studies,* 53(10–11), 1798–1835. https://doi.org/10.1177/0010414020912283; **did better than their parents:** Chetty, R., Grusky, D., Hell, M., Hendren, N., Manduca, R., & Narang, J. (2017). The fading Amer-ican dream: Trends in absolute income mobility since 1940, p. 398. *Science,* 356(6336), 398–406. https://doi.org/10.1126/science.aal4617; **sharp declines:** Chetty et al., 2017, p. 403.

7. **First quote:** Leonhardt, D. (2023). *Ours was the shining future: The story of the American Dream,* p. 264. Random House; **neoliberalism, see also:** Gerstle, G. (2022). *The rise and fall of the neoliberal order: America and the world in the free market era.* Oxford University Press; **second quote:** Scheiber, N. (2021, May 13). Middle-class pay lost pace. Is Wash-ington to blame? *The New York Times.* https://www.nytimes.com/2021/05/13/business /economy/middle-class-pay.html; **more than three-fourths:** Mishel, L., & Bivens, J.

(2021, May 13). Identifying the policy levers generating wage suppression and wage inequality. *Economic Policy Institute.* https://www.epi.org/unequalpower/publications /wage-suppression-inequality/.

8. **Rust Belt and Trump:** Baccini, L., & Weymouth, S. (2021). Gone for good: Deindustrialization, white voter backlash, and US presidential voting. *American Political Science Review,* 115(2), 550–567. https://doi.org/10.1017/S0003055421000022; **Brexit:** Neal, S., Gawlewicz, A., Heley, J., & Jones, R. D. (2021, April 19). Don't forget the countryside: Rural communities and Brexit. *LSE Blogs.* https://blogs.lse.ac.uk/brexit/2021 /04/19/dont-forget-the-countryside-the-social-impact-of-brexit-in-rural-communities -must-not-be-overlooked/; **rural Far Right in Europe:** Mamonova, N., & Franquesa, J. (2020). Populism, neoliberalism and agrarian movements in Europe. Understanding rural support for right-wing politics and looking for progressive solutions, p. 710. *Sociologia Ruralis,* 60(4), 710–731. https://doi.org/10.1111/soru.12291.

9. **Most famously:** Frank, T. (2004). *What's the matter with Kansas? How conservatives won the heart of America.* Metropolitan Books; **changed his tune:** Frank, T. (2016). *Listen, liberal: Or, what ever happened to the party of the people?* Metropolitan Books; **broke with traditional Republicans:** Rappeport, A., & Parlapiano, A. (2016, May 11). Where Trump breaks with the Republican Party. *The New York Times.* https://www.nytimes.com/interactive/2016/05 /11/us/politics/where-trump-breaks-with-the-republican-party.html.

10. **Slammed Walmart and Uber:** Fox News. (2018, August 30). *Tucker: There is nothing free about this market* [video]. *YouTube.* https://www.youtube.com/watch?v=u8gqHnCB3Qg; **gained more Democratic viewers:** Griffing, A. (2022, February 2). Who is the most watched host in all of cable news for young Democrats? Tucker Carlson. *Mediaite.* https://www.mediaite.com/tv/who-is-the-most-watched-host-in-all-of-cable-news-for -young-democrats-tucker-carlson/.

11. **Twice as much weight:** Bartels, L. M. (2006). What's the matter with What's the Matter with Kansas?, p. 214. *Quarterly Journal of Political Science,* 1, 201–226. 10.561/100.00000010; **at higher rates:** Bartels, 2006, p. 207; **"representation gap":** Hall, P. A., & Evans, G. (2019). Representation gaps: Changes in popular preferences and the structure of partisan competition in the developed democracies. In Annual Meeting of the APSA, Washington, DC. https://scholar.harvard.edu/files/hall/files/hallevans2019apsa .pdf.

12. **Quote:** Peck, R. (2019). *Fox populism: Branding conservatism as working class,* p. 124. Cambridge University Press. https://doi.org/10.1017/9781108634410; **Bourdieu:** Bourdieu, P. (1984). *Distinction: A social critique on the judgment of taste* (R. Nice, Trans.). Harvard University Press. (Original work published 1979).

13. **Politics of distraction:** Ferguson, T., Page, B., Rothschild, J., Chang, A., & Chen, J. (2018). The economic and social roots of populist rebellion: Support for Donald Trump in 2016, p. 7. Institute for New Economic Thinking Working Paper Series (83). https: //papers.ssrn.com/sol3/papers.cfm?abstract_id=3306267.

14. **Typically know less:** Galinsky, A. D., Magee, J. C., Inesi, M. E., & Gruenfeld, D. H. (2006). Power and perspectives not taken, p. 1068. *Psychological Science,* 17(12), 1068– 1074. https://doi.org/10.1111/j.1467-9280.2006.01824.x.

15. **"Master identity":** Graham, R., & Homans, C. (2024, January 10). Trump is connecting with a different type of Evangelical voter. *The New York Times.* https://www.nytimes.com /2024/01/08/us/politics/donald-trump-evangelicals-iowa.html.

16. **High levels of resentment:** Hooghe, M., & Dassonneville, R. (2018). Explaining the Trump vote: The effect of racist resentment and anti-immigrant sentiments, p. 528. *PS: Political Science and Politics,* 51(3), 528–534. https://doi.org/10.1017/S1049096518000367; **2024:** CNN. (2024). *Exit polls: National results - General election - President.* Retrieved from https://www.cnn.com/election/2024/exitpolls/ national-results/general/president/0: **moderate resentment:** Grimmer, J., Marble, W., & Tanigawa-Lau, C. (2022). Measuring

the contribution of voting blocs to election outcomes, p. 1. https://doi.org/10.31235/osf
.io/c9fkg; **anti-elites and American preservationists:** Ekins, E. (2017). The five types of
Trump voters: Who they are and what they believe, pp. 6–7. Democracy Fund Voter Study
Group. https://www.voterstudygroup.org/publication/the-five-types-trump-voters.

17. **Hegemonic masculinity:** Vescio, T. K., & Schermerhorn, N. E. C. (2021). Hegemonic
masculinity predicts 2016 and 2020 voting and candidate evaluations. *Proceedings of
the National Academy of Sciences*, 118(2), e2020589118. https://doi.org/10.1073/pnas
.2020589118.

18. **Elite hyper-individualism:** Stephens, N. M., Townsend, S. S. M., & Dittmann, A. G.
(2019). Social-class disparities in higher education and professional workplaces: The role
of cultural mismatch. *Current Directions in Psychological Science*, 28(1), 67–73. https://doi
.org/10.1177/0963721418806506; **helicopter parenting:** Cui, M., Hong, P., & Jiao, C.
(2022). Overparenting and emerging adult development: A systematic review. *Emerging
Adulthood*, 10(5), 1076–1094. https://doi.org/10.1177/21676968221108828.

19. **Plurality of values:** Brooks, D. (2024, February 15). The cure for what ails our democracy.
The New York Times. https://www.nytimes.com/2024/02/15/opinion/democracy-good
-evil.html.

Part I: Aren't You Sick of Losing Elections or Just Scraping By?

1. **Pat Buchanan:** Greenfield, J. (2016, September). Trump is Pat Buchanan with better
timing. *Politico*. https://www.politico.com/magazine/story/2016/09/donald-trump-pat
-buchanan-republican-america-first-nativist-214221/; **Ross Perot:** Mughan, A., &
Lacy, D. (2002). Economic performance, job insecurity and electoral choice. *British Journal
of Political Science*, 32(3), 513–533. https://doi.org/10.1017/S0007123402000212; **Hungary:** Pawlak, J., & Than, K. (2022, April 3). Orban scores crushing victory as Ukraine
war solidifies support. Reuters. https://www.reuters.com/world/europe/hungarians
-vote-orbans-12-year-rule-tight-ballot-overshadowed-by-ukraine-war-2022-04-03/;
Poland: Cienski, J. (2023, October 17). Poland election results: Opposition secures win,
final count shows. *Politico*. https://www.politico.eu/article/poland-election-results
-opposition-donald-tusk-wins-final-count-civic-platform-pis/; **Italy:** Farrell, R. (2022,
October 3). Migrants in Italy face uncertainty after far-right prime minister's win. ABC
News. https://abcnews.go.com/International/migrants-italy-face-uncertainty-prime
-ministers-win/story?id=90916653; **Finns Party:** Bubola, E., & Lemola, J. (2023, June
16). Conservatives poised to lead Finland in coalition with hard right. *The New York Times*.
https://www.nytimes.com/2023/06/16/world/europe/finland-finns-party.html; **France
presidential:** Henley, J. (2024, July 4). French elections: What is the Republican Front—
and will it head off National Rally? *The Guardian*. https://www.theguardian.com/world
/article/2024/jul/04/french-elections-what-is-the-republican-front-and-will-it-head
-off-national-rally; **France EU parliament:** Chrisafis, A. (2024, June 9). 'We're everywhere now': National Rally members toast EU elections success. *The Guardian*. https://
www.theguardian.com/world/article/2024/jun/09/were-everywhere-now-national-rally
-toast-eu-elections-success; **Geert Wilders:** *Politico* Staff. (2024, May 15). Watch out
Brussels, Geert Wilders' new Dutch government is coming. *Politico*. https://www.politico
.eu/article/geert-wilders-eu-netherlands-governing-agreement-right-wing-ruling-coali
tion-party-for-freedom/; **Austria parliamentary election:** Shamim, S. (2024, September
30). Austria election results: Far-right FPO wins, what's next? Al Jazeera. https://www.
aljazeera.com/news/2024/9/30/austria-election-results-far-right-fpo-wins-whats-next;
Austria EU election: Murphy, F. (2024, June 9). Austrian far right says EU vote win gives
it momentum for national race. Reuters. https://www.reuters.com/world/europe/polling-
based-forecast-says-austrias-far-right-wins-eu-vote-2024-06-09/; **Alternative for Germany:** Poll of polls: Germany—national parliament voting intention. (2024, August 12).
Politico. https://www.politico.eu/europe-poll-of-polls/germany/.

Chapter 1: Is There Really a Diploma Divide?

1. **Quote:** Cuban, M. (2020). Foreword, in J. C. Williams, *White working class: Overcoming class cluelessness in America*, p. xv. Harvard Business Review Press. (Original work published 2017.)

2. **Mary Kaptur:** Metzger, B. (2023, March 27). This 40-year veteran lawmaker shows top Democrats one eye-popping chart revealing her party's problem winning over the working class. Business Insider. https://www.businessinsider.com/marcy-kaptur-chart-working-class-districts-top-democrats-2023–3.

3. **Still represented:** Podhorzer, M. (2022, April 10). The congressional class reversal. *Weekend Reading.* https://docs.google.com/document/d/1S0RH8sqV33BzLLA6V1tXmwL MbmGhoEcVEhA8Fg7aiL0/edit?_hsmi=240137472&_hsenc=p2ANqtz-9LFTPUff AFrlHo1qXrmnLoldowdsdjOyw680aOJ3vFZDbHyzbyCWIfqyYlkjXWYvH5eOFu QOYGc5Kkm2zJYOElNP0Fpx5_ekJsiM2LRIYsrOL1Fxk&pli=1#heading=h.gjdgxs; **Biden and Clinton:** Cohn, N. (2021, October 8). How educational differences are widening America's political rift. *The New York Times.* https://www.nytimes.com/2021/09/08 /us/politics/how-college-graduates-vote.html; **27 percent of Biden's:** Igielnik, R., Keeter, S., & Hartig, H. (2021, June 30). Behind Biden's 2020 victory, p. 9. Pew Research Center. https://www.pewresearch.org/politics/2021/06/30/behind-bidens-2020-victory/; **Democrats or Democratic leaners:** Changing partisan coalitions in a politically divided nation, p. 51. (2024, April 9). Pew Research Center. https://www.pewresearch.org/politics/2024 /04/09/changing-partisan-coalitions-in-a-politically-divided-nation/; **2024:** Baharaheen, M. (2024). 10 things we know about the election so far, The Liberal Patriot, https:// substack.com/home/post/p-151479505 strong: Abbott, J. (2024). Understanding class dealignment, p. 82. *Catalyst*, 7(4). https://catalyst-journal.com/2024/03/understanding -class-dealignment.

4. **2016 exit poll:** CNN. (2024). Exit polls: National president. (2016). CNN. https://www .cnn.com/election/2016/results/exit-polls; 2020 exit poll: Exit polls: National results. (2020). CNN. https://www.cnn.com/election/2020/exit-polls/president/national-results; **doubling the diploma divide:** Tyson, A., & Maniam, S. (2016, November 9). Behind Trump's victory: Divisions by race, gender, education. Pew Research Center. https://www .pewresearch.org/short-reads/2016/11/09/behind-trumps-victory-divisions-by-race -gender-education/; **population data:** QuickFacts: California and North Dakota. (n.d.). US Census Bureau. Accessed January 10, 2024, from https://www.census.gov/quickfacts /fact/table/CA,ND/PST045222; **quote:** Lemann, N. (2022, October 24). The Democrats' midterm challenge. *The New Yorker.* https://www.newyorker.com/magazine/2022 /10/31/the-democrats-midterm-challenge.

5. **Statewide offices:** Leonhardt, D. (2023, June 13). How Democrats can win workers. *The New York Times.* https://www.nytimes.com/2023/06/13/briefing/democrats-elections -poll.html.

6. **Brexit—64 percent of manual workers and 43 percent of managers or professionals— and Le Pen vote shares:** Gidron, N., & Hall, P. A. (2017). The politics of social status: Economic and cultural roots of the populist right, p. S58. *The British Journal of Sociology*, 68(S1), S57–S84. https://doi.org/10.1111/1468–4446.12319.

7. **Reduces support:** Kurer, T. (2020). **The declining middle:** Occupational change, social status, and the populist right, p. 1798. *Comparative Political Studies*, 53(10–11), 1798– 1835. https://doi.org/10.1177/0010414020912283; **routine jobs:** Kurer, 2020, p. 1799; first quote: Kurer, 2020, p. 1819; **second quote:** Im, Z. J., Mayer, N., Paller, B., & Rovny, J. (2019). The "losers of automation": A reservoir of votes for the radical right?, p. 1798. *Research & Politics*, 6(1), 2053168018822395. https://doi.org/10.1177/2053168018822395.

8. **Quote:** Markovits, D. (2019). *The meritocracy trap: How America's foundational myth feeds inequality, dismantles the middle class, and devours the elite*, p. 69. Penguin Press; **81 percent of Trump voters:** Smith, S. (2016, October 20). 6 charts that show where Clinton and

Trump supporters differ. Pew Research Center. https://www.pewresearch.org/short-reads/2016/10/20/6-charts-that-show-where-clinton-and-trump-supporters-differ/.

9. **Both lifted and hurt:** Lakner, C., & Milanovic, B. (2016). Global income distribution: From the fall of the Berlin Wall to the Great Recession. *The World Bank Economic Review*, 30(2), 203–232. https://doi.org/10.1093/wber/lhv039.

10. **Quote:** Stricherz, M. (2007). *Why the Democrats are blue: How secular liberals hijacked the people's party*, p. 1. Encounter Books.

11. **36 percent of young and 11 percent of old Blacks support reducing police funding:** Cox, K., & Edwards, K. (2022). Black Americans have a clear vision for reducing racism but little hope it will happen. Pew Research Center. https://www.pewresearch.org/race-ethnicity/2022/08/30/black-americans-have-a-clear-vision-for-reducing-racism-but-little-hope-it-will-happen/.

12. **"Painful cuts":** Tankersley, J. (2023, February 8). President Biden is not backing off his big-government agenda. *The New York Times*. https://www.nytimes.com/2023/02/08/us/politics/biden-state-of-the-union-spending.html; **first quote:** Skocpol, T. (2000). *The missing middle: Working families and the future of American social policy*, p. 7. W. W. Norton; **second quote:** Kristof, N. (2024, July 20). Here's the hope if Biden withdraws. *The New York Times*. https://www.nytimes.com/2024/07/20/opinion/trump-biden-america.html; **Democrats tolerated:** Mishel, L., & Bivens, J. (2021). Identifying the policy levers generating wage suppression and wage inequality. Economic Policy Institute. https://www.epi.org/unequalpower/publications/wage-suppression-inequality/; **third quote:** S. Brown, personal communication, 2017, June 28; antitrust dropped: Lemann, 2022.

13. **Shifted away:** Kuziemko, I., Longuet-Marx, N., & Naidu, S. (2023). "Compensate the losers?" Economic policy and partisan realignment in the US (No. 31794). National Bureau of Economic Research. https://www.nber.org/papers/w31794; **quote:** Brooks, D. (2023, August 2). What if we're the bad guys here? *The New York Times*. https://www.nytimes.com/2023/08/02/opinion/trump-meritocracy-educated.html.

14. **"Scaffle" vote:** Leonhardt, D. (2023, May 25). Ron DeSantis and the "scaffle" vote. *The New York Times*. https://www.nytimes.com/2023/05/25/briefing/ron-desantis.html.

15. **Quote:** Cohen, P. (2020, October 24). Trump's biggest economic legacy isn't about the numbers. *The New York Times*. https://www.nytimes.com/2020/10/24/business/economy/trump-economy-manufacturing.html; **Trump entitlements:** Kapur, S. (2024, March 19). Donald Trump has been all over the map on Social Security and Medicare. NBC News. https://www.nbcnews.com/politics/donald-trump/donald-trump-map-social-security-medicare-rcna143475; **more than any other topic:** Ferguson et al., 2018, p. 32.

16. **Key group:** Oesch, D., & Rennwald, L. (2018). Electoral competition in Europe's new tripolar space: Class voting for the left, centre-right and radical right, pp. 787–788. *European Journal of Political Research*, 57(4), 783–807. https://doi.org/10.1111/1475-6765.12259; **workers identify with small business, US proportion twice that of Europe:** Hall, P. A., Evans, G., & Kim, S. I. (2023). *Political change and electoral coalitions in Western democracies*, p. 41. Cambridge University Press. https://doi.org/10.1017/9781009431378; **a third of business owners:** Annual business survey: Owner characteristics of respondent employer firms by sector, sex, ethnicity, race, and veteran status for the U.S., states, and metro areas: 2019. US Census Bureau. https://data.census.gov/cedsci/table?q=ab1900%2a&tid=ABSCBO2019.AB1900CSCBO&hidePreview=true&nkd=QDESC~O07.

17. **First, second, and third quotes:** Vanneman, R., & Cannon, L. W. (1987). *The American perception of class*, pp. 86–87. Temple University Press. https://doi.org/10.2307/j.ctv941wv0; **unusually close:** Hall et al., 2023, p. 41; **fourth quote:** Peck, R. (2019). *Fox populism: Branding conservatism as working class*, p. 123. Cambridge University Press. https://doi.org/10.1017/9781108634410; **sculpting support:** Lowenstein, A. M. (2024, February 16).

The stories corporations tell. *The American Prospect*. https://prospect.org/culture/books /2024–02–16-stories-corporations-tell-williams-waterhouse-review/; fifth quote: Ferguson et al., 2018, p. 19.

18. **19 percent anti-elites:** Ekins, E. (2017). The five types of Trump voters: Who they are and what they believe. Democracy Fund Voter Study Group, p. 4. https://www.voterstudygroup .org/publication/the-five-types-trump-voters; **83 percent system biased, 24 percent distribution fair, 64 percent warming happening, 67 percent warming serious, and plurality human activities:** Ekins, 2017, p. 17; **68 percent raise taxes wealthy:** Ekins, 2017, p. 11; 40 percent favorable Sanders: Ekins, 2017, p. 16; **59 percent women lose out:** Ekins, 2017, p. 12; **45 percent path to citizenship and most liberal same-sex marriage:** Ekins, 2017, p. 18; **warm feelings people of color:** Ekins 2017, p. 6.

19. **Top 20 percent cutoff:** Solum, A. (2022, July 20). Income thresholds to be a top earner in America's largest cities—2022 edition. SmartAsset. https://smartasset.com/data-studies /income-thresholds-to-be-a-top-earner-in-americas-largest-cities-2022; **fraction of the elite:** Bourdieu, 1984, p. 93; **top 1 percent and 10 percent cutoffs:** Gould, E., & Kandra, J. (2022, December 21). Inequality in annual earnings worsens in 2021. Economic Policy Institute. https://www.epi.org/publication/inequality-2021-ssa-data/; **deny privilege:** DiAngelo, R. (2018). *White fragility: Why it's so hard for white people to talk about racism*. Beacon Press.

20. **Truck driver wage:** Occupational outlook handbook: Heavy and tractor-trailer truck drivers. (n.d.). Bureau of Labor Statistics, US Department of Labor. Accessed January 18, 2024, from https://www.bls.gov/ooh/transportation-and-material-moving/heavy -and-tractor-trailer-truck-drivers.htm; **teller wage:** Occupational employment and wage statistics: Tellers. (n.d.). Bureau of Labor Statistics, US Department of Labor. Accessed January 18, 2024, from https://www.bls.gov/oes/current/oes433071.htm; **librarian wage:** Occupational outlook handbook: Librarians and library media specialists. (n.d.). Bureau of Labor Statistics, US Department of Labor. Accessed January 18, 2024, from https: //www.bls.gov/ooh/education-training-and-library/librarians.htm; **social worker wage:** Occupational outlook handbook: Social workers. (n.d.). Bureau of Labor Statistics, US Department of Labor. Accessed January 18, 2024, from https://www.bls.gov/ooh /community-and-social-service/social-workers.htm.

21. For a description of the methodology used to calculate these breakdowns from the US Census Bureau (2024). 2024 Annual Social and Economic Supplement, https://www .census.gov/data/datasets/2024/demo/cps/cps-asec-2024.html, see Williams, J. C., & Boushey, H. (2010). The three faces of work-family conflict: The poor, the professionals and the missing middle, p. 74. https://www.americanprogress.org/article/the-three-faces -of-work-family-conflict/ (data and methodological appendix).

22. **Typically self-describe:** Bettie, J. (2003). *Women without class: Girls, race, and identity*, pp. 81, 100. University of California Press; **clerical blue-collar:** Vanneman & Cannon, 1987, p. 78; **Missing Middle:** Skocpol, 2000; **police officers and bus drivers:** Vanneman & Cannon, 1987, p. 226; **whites more likely managerial:** Cose, E. (1993). *The rage of a privileged class*, p. 3. HarperCollins.

23. **62 percent of college grads and 46 percent of noncollege grads:** Cox, D., Lienesch, R., & Jones, R. P. (2017). Beyond economics: Fears of cultural displacement pushed the white working class to Trump, p. 9. PRRI / *The Atlantic*. https://www.prri.org/research/white -working-class-attitudes-economy-trade-immigration-election-donald-trump/.

Chapter 2: Isn't It Just the *White* Working Class?

1. **Quote:** Edsall, T. B. (2023, August 16). It's not your father's Democratic Party. But whose party is it? *The New York Times*. https://www.nytimes.com/2023/08/16/opinion /democrats-republicans-2024.html.

2. **65 percent of white noncollege, 42 percent of white college for Trump:** Igielnik, R.,

Keeter, S., & Hartig, H. (2021, June 30). Behind Biden's 2020 victory, p. 9. Pew Research Center. https://www.pewresearch.org/politics/2021/06/30/behind-bidens-2020-victory/; **startlingly higher:** Hartig, H., Daniller, A., Keeter, S., & Van Green, T. (2023, July 12). Republican gains in 2022 midterms driven mostly by turnout advantage, p. 20. Pew Research Center. https://www.pewresearch.org/politics/2023/07/12/republican-gains-in -2022-midterms-driven-mostly-by-turnout-advantage/.

3. **44 percent of the 2020 electorate:** Ghitza, Y., & Robinson, J. (2021, May 10). What happened in 2020? *Catalist.* https://catalist.us/wh-national/; **quote:** Cohn, N. (2023, September 6). Consistent signs of erosion in Black and Hispanic support for Biden. *The New York Times.* https://www.nytimes.com/2023/09/05/upshot/biden-trump-black-hispanic -voters.html; **compared to 2018:** Wolf, Z. B., & Merrill, C. (2023, January 10). Anatomy of a close election: How Americans voted in 2022 vs. 2018. CNN. https://www.cnn.com /interactive/2022/politics/exit-polls-2022-midterm-2018-shift/; **2024 data:** Wolf, Z. B., Merrill, C., & Mullery, W. (2024, November 6). Anatomy of three Trump elections: How Americans shifted in 2024 vs. 2020 and 2016. CNN. https://www.cnn.com/inter-active/2024/politics/2020-2016-exit-polls-2024-dg/.

4. **Quote:** Jones, J. M., & Saad, L. (2024, February 7). Democrats lose ground with Black and Hispanic adults. Gallup. https://news.gallup.com/poll/609776/democrats-lose -ground-black-hispanic-adults.aspx.

5. **2012 to 2020:** Cadava, G. (2024, August 21). Can Kamala Harris's campaign solve the Latino turnout problem? *The New Yorker.* https://www.newyorker.com/news/the-lede /can-kamala-harriss-campaign-solve-the-latino-turnout-problem; **Biden Latino support:** Cross-tabs: July 2024 Times/Siena poll of registered voters nationwide. (2024, July 3). *The New York Times.* https://www.nytimes.com/interactive/2024/07/03/us/elections /times-siena-poll-registered-voter-crosstabs.html; **2024 data:** Wolf et al., 2024; **Latino voting 2018 and 2020:** Igielnik, R., Keeter, S., & Hartig, H. (2021, June 30). Behind Biden's 2020 victory, p. 9. Pew Research Center. https://www.pewresearch.org/politics /2021/06/30/behind-bidens-2020-victory/.

6. **Shrank nearly 20 points:** Jones, J. M., & Saad, L. (2024, February 7). Democrats lose ground with Black and Hispanic adults. Gallup. https://news.gallup.com/poll/609776 /democrats-lose-ground-black-hispanic-adults.aspx; **quote:** Jain, L., & Lavelle, H. (2024, August 21). We dug into the 2024 polling crosstabs. What we found was stunning. *Politico.* https://www.politico.com/news/magazine/2024/08/21/kamala-harris-gains -polls-00175262; **2024 election:** Exit polls. (2024). CNN:https://www.cnn.com/elec tion/2024/exit-polls/national-results/general/president/0; **shifted 22 points:** McGill, B., & Day, C. (2022, November 14). How we voted in the 2022 midterm elections. *The Wall Street Journal.* https://www.wsj.com/articles/how-different-groups-voted-in-the-2022 -midterm-elections-11667955705; **10 points in 10 years:** Jones & Saad, 2024.

7. **Trump up 7 points:** How independents, Latino voters and Catholics shifted from 2016 and swung states for Biden and Trump. (2020, November 12). *The Washington Post.* https: //www.washingtonpost.com/graphics/2020/elections/exit-polls-changes-2016–2020/; **increased 8 points:** In tight presidential race, voters are broadly critical of both Biden and Trump, p. 4. (2024, April 24). Pew Research Center. https://www.pewresearch.org/politics /2024/04/24/in-tight-presidential-race-voters-are-broadly-critical-of-both-biden-and -trump/; **since 2020:** Igielnik et al., 2021, p. 9; **Trump Asian voting:** Exit polls. (2024). CNN; Exit polls. (2020). CNN. https://www.cnn.com/election/2020/exit-polls/president/ national-results; Exit polls (2016). CNN. https://www.cnn.com/election/2016/results/ exit-polls; **51 percent of Asian Americans:** Ruiz, N. G., Noe-Bustamante, L., & Shah, S. (2023, May 8). Diverse cultures and shared experiences shape Asian American identities. Pew Research Center. https://www.pewresearch.org/race-and-ethnicity/2023/05/08 /diverse-cultures-and-shared-experiences-shape-asian-american-identities/; **Black and Latino college:** Solman, P., & Koromvokis, L. (2021, October 26). Jobs requiring college

degrees disqualify most U.S. workers—especially workers of color. PBS News Hour. https://www.pbs.org/newshour/show/jobs-requiring-college-degrees-disqualify-most -u-s-workers-especially-workers-of-color; **more liberal:** Jones, J. M. (2010, February 3). Asian-Americans lean left politically. Gallup. https://news.gallup.com/poll/125579/asian -americans-lean-left-politically.aspx; **nearly 70 percent identify:** Ruiz et al., p. 43.

8. **Aspirational term:** Pérez, E. (2020, July 2). "People of color" are protesting. Here's what you need to know about this new identity. *The Washington Post.* https://www .washingtonpost.com/politics/2020/07/02/people-color-are-protesting-heres-what-you -need-know-about-this-new-identity/; **Indian and Bhutanese college:** Kochhar, R., & Cilluffo, A. (2018, July 12). Income inequality in the U.S. is rising most rapidly among Asians, p. 7. Pew Research Center. https://www.pewresearch.org/social-trends/2018/07 /12/income-inequality-in-the-u-s-is-rising-most-rapidly-among-asians/.

9. **First quote:** Grimmer, J., Marble, W., & Tanigawa-Lau, C. (2022). Measuring the contribution of voting blocs to election outcomes, p. 17. https://doi.org/10.31235/osf.io/c9fkg; **second quote:** Grimmer et al., 2022, p. 19; **third quote:** Grimmer et al., 2022, p. 23.

10. **Express dissatisfaction:** Green, J., & McElwee, S. (2019). The differential effects of economic conditions and racial attitudes in the election of Donald Trump. *Perspectives on Politics,* 17(2), 358–379. https://doi.org/10.1017/S1537592718003365; **low turnout:** McQuarrie, M. (2016, November 11). Trump and the revolt of the Rust Belt. LSE Blogs. https://blogs.lse.ac.uk/usappblog/2016/11/11/23174/; **high levels of nonvoting:** Kurer, T. (2020). The declining middle: Occupational change, social status, and the populist right, p. 1819. *Comparative Political Studies,* 53(10–11), 1798–1835. https://doi.org/10 .1177/0010414020912283; **unemployment and voting, see also:** Guiso, L., Herrera, H., Morelli, M., & Sonno, T. (2018). Populism: Demand and supply, p. 26. https://papers .ssrn.com/sol3/papers.cfm?abstract_id=2924731; **Black unemployment:** For the second consecutive month Black unemployment has increased. (2023, July 10). NPR. https: //www.npr.org/2023/07/10/1186712393/for-the-second-consecutive-monthly-black -unemployment-has-increased; **turnout advantage:** Hartig et al., 2023.

11. **Phillips:** Phillips, S. (2016). Brown is the new white. *The New Press;* **never been repeated:** Fabina, J. (2021, April 29). Despite pandemic challenges, 2020 election had largest increase in voting between presidential elections on record. US Census Bureau. https:// www.census.gov/library/stories/2021/04/record-high-turnout-in-2020-general-election .html; **cost Clinton the election:** McQuarrie, 2016.

12. **73 percent say being Black:** Cox, K., & Tamir, C. (2022, April 14). Race is central to identity for Black Americans and affects how they connect with each other, p. 20. Pew Research Center. https://www.pewresearch.org/race-and-ethnicity/2022/04/14/race -is-central-to-identity-for-black-americans-and-affects-how-they-connect-with-each -other/; **solidarity as their only reliable choice:** Cox, K. (2019, July 11). Most U.S. adults feel what happens to their own racial or ethnic group affects them personally. Pew Research Center. https://www.pewresearch.org/short-reads/2019/07/11/linked-fate -connectedness-americans/; **substantially more likely:** Americans' top policy priority for 2024: Strengthening the economy, p. 8. (2024, February 29). Pew Research Center. https: //www.pewresearch.org/politics/2024/02/29/americans-top-policy-priority-for-2024 -strengthening-the-economy/; **69 percent report discrimination:** Frasure, L., Wong, J., Vargas, E., & Barreto, M. (2016). Collaborative multiracial post-election survey. https:// doi.org/10.3886/ICPSR38040.v2; **the less they preferred:** Sidanius, J., & Pratto, F. (1999). *Social dominance: An intergroup theory of social hierarchy and oppression,* p. 238. Cambridge University Press. https://doi.org/10.1017/CBO9781139175043.

13. **Structural inequality:** Lamont, M. (2000). *The dignity of working men: Morality and the boundaries of race, class, and immigration,* pp. 3–6. Harvard University Press; **harder to be Latino:** Frasure et al., 2016; **weakest attachment:** Kaufmann, E. (2021, February 13).

How stable is the Democratic coalition. *The New York Times.* https://www.nytimes.com /2021/02/13/opinion/democrats-latino-hispanic-black-asian-american.html.

14. **Biggest gains:** 2020 post-mortem: part one: Portrait of a persuadable Latino, p. 4. (2021, April). Equis Research. https://downloads.ctfassets.net/ms6ec8hcu35u/5BR9iHBhsyQtq UU1gNgfaR/b0f4d0be5f55297c627a3f2373fb11b8/Equis_Post-Mortem_Part_One.pdf; **fueled by votes of men:** Igielnik et al., 2020, p. 8.

15. **Only about 25 percent:** Masuoka, N. (2006). Together they become one: Examining the predictors of panethnic group consciousness among Asian Americans and Latinos., p. 1002. *Social Science Quarterly,* 87(5), 993–1011. https://doi.org/10.1111/j .1540-6237.2006.00412.x; **only 22 percent of Latinos:** Memo to interested parties: Immigration and the 2022 elections. (2022, August 24). Hart Research Associates and BSP Research. https://static1.squarespace.com/static/5b60b2381aef1dbe876cd08f/t /63065b17c84f5751cdeafc94/1661360919967/ME-14335+Immigration+Battleground +Survey.pdf.

16. **Lower level:** Masuoka, 2006, p. 1008; **linked fate decrease:** Sanchez, G., Masuoka, N., & Adams, B. (2019). Revisiting the brown-utility heuristic: A comparison of Latino linked fate in 2006 and 2016. *Politics, Groups, and Identities,* 7(3), 673–683. https://doi.org/10 .1080/21565503.2019.1638803; **linked fate, see also:** Sanchez, G. R., & Masuoka, N. (2010). Brown-utility heuristic? The presence and contributing factors of Latino linked fate. *Hispanic Journal of Behavioral Sciences,* 32(4), 519–531. https://doi.org/10.1177 /0739986310383129; **quote:** Findell, E. (2020, November 8). Why Democrats lost so many South Texas Latinos—the economy. *The Wall Street Journal.* https://www.wsj.com /articles/how-democrats-lost-so-many-south-texas-latinosthe-economy-11604871650.

17. **Much smaller segment:** Hartig et al., 2023, p. 31; **gained 7 points:** Exit polls. (2020). CNN. Accessed May 21, 2024, from https://www.cnn.com/election/2020/exit-polls /president/national-results; Exit polls. (2016). CNN. Accessed May 21, 2024, from https: //www.cnn.com/election/2016/results/exit-polls.

18. **30–44 percent say:** Junn, J. & Masuoka, N. (2008). Asian-American identity: Shared racial status and political context, p. 733. *Perspectives on Politics,* 6(4), 729–740; **no group consciousness:** Masuoka, 2006, p. 1002; **major problem:** The rise of Asian Americans, p. 12. (2013, April 4). Pew Research Center. https://www.pewresearch.org/social-trends /2012/06/19/the-rise-of-asian-americans/#fn-41253–9.

19. **Quote:** Yang, J. (2021, September 2). Asian Americans are finally getting the heroes we deserve. *The New York Times.* https://www.nytimes.com/2021/09/02/opinion/asian -americans-superheroes-shang-chi.html.

20. **"Too sensitive about race":** Hawkins, S., Yudkin, D., Juan-Torres, M., & Dixon, T. (2018). Hidden tribes: A study of America's polarized landscape, p. 96. More in Common. https://hiddentribes.us/media/qfpekz4g/hidden_tribes_report.pdf; **36 percent of white-Asians quote:** Alba, R. (2016, January 11). The likely persistence of a white majority. *The American Prospect.* https://prospect.org/civil-rights/likely-persistence-white -majority/; **problems of the poor:** Pew Research Center, 2024, February 29; **get ahead quote:** The rise of Asian Americans, p. 82. (2013, April 4). Pew Research Center. https: //www.pewresearch.org/social-trends/2012/06/19/the-rise-of-asian-americans/.

21. **Quote:** Lee, J. (2021). Asian Americans, affirmative action & the rise in anti-Asian hate, p. 194. *Daedalus,* 150(2), 180–198. https://doi.org/10.1162/daed_a_01854.

22. **Quote:** Beltrán, C. (2021, January 15). To understand Trump's support, we must think in terms of multiracial whiteness. *The Washington Post.* https://www.washingtonpost.com /opinions/2021/01/15/understand-trumps-support-we-must-think-terms-multiracial -whiteness/; **Ostfeld study:** Ostfeld, M. C., & Yadon, N. D. (2021). ¿Mejorando la raza?: The political undertones of Latinos' skin color in the United States. *Social Forces,* 100(4), 1806–1832. https://doi.org/10.1093/sf/soab060; **supported Biden over Trump:** Haney

López, I. (2020, November 6). Trump exploited status anxiety in the Latino community. *The Washington Post.* https://www.washingtonpost.com/outlook/trump-exploited -status-anxiety-within-the-latino-community/2020/11/06/3164e77c-1f9f-11eb -b532-05c751cd5dc2_story.html.

23. **Haney López's findings:** Haney López, I. (2022). Project Juntos: Latinx race-class. Project Juntos. https://static1.squarespace.com/static/5ef377b623eaf41dd9df1311/t /5f6fd7e84ca040062e8dc0b9/1601165291980/Project+Juntos+Summary+Briefing +092620.pdf; **racial resentment strongly predicts:** 2020 post-mortem part two: The American Dream voter. (2021, December 14). Equis. https://assets.ctfassets.net /ms6ec8hcu35u/4E5a5nNoWi9JNFqeAylkmS/bf542d82f900dbfb62cc6e6d7253a24a /Post-Mortem_Part_Two_FINAL_Dec_14.pdf.

Chapter 3: Isn't It Bizarre When the Left Denies the Impact of Inequality on Politics?

1. **Quote:** Tesler, M. (2016, November 16). The education gap among whites this year wasn't about education. It was about race. *The Washington Post.* https://www.washingtonpost .com/news/monkey-cage/wp/2016/11/16/the-education-gap-among-whites-this-year -wasnt-about-education-it-was-about-race/.

2. **First quote:** Cohen, R. (2022, April 24). In Le Pen territory, as France votes, anger at a distant president. *The New York Times.* https://www.nytimes.com/2022/04/23/world /europe/france-election-runoff-le-pen-macron.html; **second quote:** Trump White House Archived. (2020, June 12). *President Trump will always fight for the forgotten men & women of America* [video]. *YouTube.* https://www.youtube.com/watch?v=U8pd5boPdLk; **feeling seen:** Lamont, M. (2023). *Seeing others: How recognition works—and how it can heal a divided world.* Atria/One Signal.

3. **First quote:** Lamont, M., Park, B. Y., & Ayala-Hurtado, E. (2017). Trump's electoral speeches and his appeal to the American white working class, p. S155. *The British Journal of Sociology, 68*(S1), S153–S180. https://doi.org/10.1111/1468-4446.12315; **second quote:** Lamont et al., 2017, p. S168; **18 percent of Democratic television ads:** Abbott, J. (2024). Understanding class dealignment, p. 128. *Catalyst, 7*(4). https://catalyst-journal .com/2024/03/understanding-class-dealignment.

4. **GOP cared more:** Yokley, E. (2023, September 25). Since Trump, voters have become more likely to see the GOP as caring about them. Morning Consult. https://pro .morningconsult.com/analysis/gop-working-class-survey; **helping the middle class:** CNN/SSRS Poll: November 1 to November 30, 2023. (2023, December 6). CNN/ SSRS. https://s3.documentcloud.org/documents/24193043/cnn-poll-bidens-job-approval -has-dropped-since-start-of-the-year-as-economic-concerns-remain-prevalent.pdf; **no influence on policy:** Gilens, M. (2012, July 1). Under the influence. *Boston Review.* https: //www.bostonreview.net/forum/lead-essay-under-influence-martin-gilens/.

5. **Eight times faster:** Frey, C. B., Berger, T., & Chen, C. (2018). Political machinery: Did robots swing the 2016 US presidential election?, p. 425. *Oxford Review of Economic Policy, 34*(3), 418–442. https://doi.org/10.1093/oxrep/gry007; **43 percent higher:** Mishel, L., Gould, E., & Bivens, J. (2015). Wage stagnation in nine charts, p. 10. Economic Policy Institute. https://files.epi.org/2013/wage-stagnation-in-nine-charts.pdf; **three-fourths of the decline:** Manyika, J., Mischke, J., Bughin, J., Woetzel, J., Krishnan, M., & Cudre, S. (2019, May 22). A new look at the declining labor share of income in the United States, p. 5. McKinsey Global Institute. https://www.mckinsey.com/featured-insights/employment -and-growth/a-new-look-at-the-declining-labor-share-of-income-in-the-united-states.

6. **Particularly marked:** Manyika et al., 2019, p. 5; **debt to GDP doubled:** Kumhof, M., Rancière, R., & Winant, P. (2015). Inequality, leverage, and crises, p. 1221. *American Economic Review, 105*(3), 1217–1245. https://doi.org/10.1257/aer.20110683; **most unequal:** Country comparisons—Gini index coefficient—distribution of family income.

(2019). The World Factbook, Central Intelligence Agency. Accessed January 31, 2024, from https://www.cia.gov/the-world-factbook/field/gini-index-coefficient-distribution -of-family-income/country-comparison/.

7. **Top 1 percent of earners:** Draut, T. (2016). *Strapped: Why Americans 20–30 something can't get ahead*, p. 21. Doubleday; **annual pay increases:** Mishel et al., 2015, p. 5; **CEO pay:** Leonhardt, D. (2023). *Ours was the shining future: The story of the American Dream*, pp. 75–76, 261. Random House.

8. **Economy polarized:** Autor, D. H., Katz, L. F., & Kearney, M. S. (2006). The polarization of the U.S. labor market, p. 189. *American Economic Review*, 96(2), 189–194. https://doi .org/10.1257/000282806777212620; **between 1982 and 2017:** Markovits, D. (2023, November 6). Bridging the diploma divide [PowerPoint slides]. Diploma Divide Working Group Conference, UC Law SF; **gig work:** Katz, L. F., & Krueger, A. B. (2016). The rise and nature of alternative work arrangements in the United States, 1995–2015. *ILR Review*, 72(2), 382–416. https://doi.org/10.1177/0019793918820008; **fissuring:** Mishel, L., & Bivens, J. (2021, May 13). Identifying the policy levers generating wage suppression and wage inequality, pp. 51–52. Economic Policy Institute. https://www.epi.org /unequalpower/publications/wage-suppression-inequality/.

9. **Increased by 83 percent:** Sosnik, D. (2023, April 17). The "diploma divide" is the new fault line in American politics. *The New York Times*. https://www.nytimes.com/2023/04 /17/opinion/education-american-politics.html; **college wage premium:** Mishel & Bivens, 2021, p. 11.

10. **Unemployment:** Case, A. & Deaton, A. (2020). *Deaths of despair and the future of capitalism*, p. 159. Princeton University Press; **deregulation of finance:** Palley, T. (2011). America's flawed paradigm: Macroeconomic causes of the financial crisis and Great Recession. *Empirica*, 38(1), 3–17. https://doi.org/10.1007/s10663-010-9142-3; **95th percentile recovers:** Pfeffer, F. T., Danziger, S., & Schoeni, R. F. (2013). Wealth disparities before and after the Great Recession. *The Annals of the American Academy of Political and Social Science*, 650(1), 98–123. https://doi.org/10.1177/0002716213497452; **lost about 85 percent:** Bartels, L. (2013, August 13). Power to (altruists concerned with) the poor? Good Authority. https://goodauthority.org/news/power-to-altruists-concerned-with-the-poor/; **own three-fourths:** Survey of Consumer Finances and Financial Accounts of the United States. (Updated September 2023). DFA: Distributional Financial Accounts. Federal Reserve. https://www.federalreserve.gov/releases/z1/dataviz/dfa/distribute/chart/.

11. **Cutbacks hurt:** Lacy, K. (2011, July 25). In Black middle class, the vulnerable and the comfortable. *The New York Times*. https://www.nytimes.com/roomfordebate/2011/07 /25/how-budget-cuts-will-change-the-black-middle-class/in-black-middle-class-the -vulnerable-and-the-comfortable; **quote:** Sherman, J. (2009). *Those who work, those who don't: Poverty, morality, and family in rural America*, p. 142. University of Minnesota Press.

12. **"Barely detectable":** Carbone, J., & Cahn, N. (2014). *Marriage markets: How inequality is remaking the American family*, p. 98. Oxford University Press; **middle-class incomes declined:** Chetty, R., Grusky, D., Hell, M., Hendren, N., Manduca, R., Narang, J. (2017). The fading American dream: Trends in absolute income mobility since 1940, p. 405. *Science*, 356(6336), 398–406. https://doi.org/10.1126/science.aal4617; **"great risk shift":** Hacker, J. S. (2008). *The great risk shift: The new economic insecurity and the decline of the American Dream*. Oxford University Press; **noncollege affected most:** Autor, D. H., Dorn, D., & Hanson, G. H. (2013). The China syndrome: Local labor market effects of import competition in the United States, p. 2144. *American Economic Review*, 103(6), 2121–2168. https://doi.org/10.1257/aer.103.6.2121; **quarter to half:** Autor, D. H., Dorn, D., & Hanson, G. H. (2013). The China syndrome: Local labor market effects of import competition in the United States, 2140. *American Economic Review*, 103(6), 2121–2168. 10.1257/aer.103.6.2121.

13. **Largest declines:** Chetty, R., Grusky, D., Hell, M., Hendren, N., Manduca, R., Narang, J. (2017). The fading American dream: Trends in absolute income mobility since 1940, p. 403. *Science*, 356(6336), 398–406. https://doi.org/10.1126/science.aal4617.

14. **90 percent mature economies, 90 percent Asia, low and middling incomes:** Lakner, C., & Milanovic, B. (2016). Global income distribution: From the fall of the Berlin Wall to the Great Recession. *The World Bank Economic Review*, 30(2), 203–232. https://doi.org /10.1093/wber/lhv039.

15. **Risen around 50 percent:** Bartscher, A. K., Kuhn, M., & Schularick, M. (2020). The college wealth divide: Education and inequality in America, 1956–2016, p. 23. *Federal Reserve Bank of St. Louis Review*, 102(1). https://papers.ssrn.com/sol3/papers.cfm?abstract _id=3587685; **earnings ratio:** Markovits, D. (2019). *The meritocracy trap: How America's foundational myth feeds inequality, dismantles the middle class and devours the elite*, p. 18. Penguin Press; **Gilded Age:** Rothman, L. (2018, February 5). How American inequality in the Gilded Age compares to today. *Time*. https://time.com/5122375/american -inequality-gilded-age/.

16. **Rise in despair deaths:** Stewart, M. (2018). The 9.9 percent is the new American aristocracy. *The Atlantic*. https://www.theatlantic.com/magazine/archive/2018/06/the-birth-of -a-new-american-aristocracy/559130/; **first quote:** Gerstle, G. (2022). *The rise and fall of the neoliberal order: America and the world in the free market era*, p. 233. Oxford University Press; **eight and a half years less:** Case, A., & Deaton, A. (2023, October 3). Without a college degree, life in America is staggeringly shorter. *The New York Times*. https://www .nytimes.com/2023/10/03/opinion/life-expectancy-college-degree.html; **rose nearly 40 percent:** Case, A., & Deaton, A. (2015). Rising morbidity and mortality among white non-Hispanic Americans in the 21st century, p. 15079. *Proceedings of the National Academy of Sciences*, 112(49), 15078–15083. https://doi.org/10.1073/pnas.1518393112; **second quote:** Sherman, 2009, p. 96; **opioid use, third quote:** Reeves, R. V. (2022). *Of boys and men: Why the modern male is struggling, why it matters, and what to do about it*, p. 62. Brookings Institution Press.

17. **"Nostalgic deprivation":** Gest, J., Reny, T., & Mayer, J. (2018). Roots of the radical right: Nostalgic deprivation in the United States and Britain. *Comparative Political Studies*, 51(13), 1694–1719. https://doi.org/10.1177/0010414017720705; **incomes doubled:** Markovits, 2019, p. 20; **increased support for Trump:** Gest et al., 2018, p. 1709.

18. **"Become a minor industry":** Arzheimer, K. (2009). Contextual factors and the extreme right vote in Western Europe, 1980–2002. *American Journal of Political Science*, 53(2), 259–275. https://www.jstor.org/stable/25548117; **two-thirds of the total effect:** Dippel, C., Gold, R., & Heblich, S. (2015). Globalization and its (dis-)content: Trade shocks and voting behavior (No. w21812). National Bureau of Economic Research. https://www .nber.org/papers/w21812; **tended to veer:** Autor, D., Dorn, D., Hanson, G., & Majlesi, K. (2020). Importing political polarization? The electoral consequences of rising trade exposure. *American Economic Review*, 110(10), 3139–3183. https://doi.org/10.1257/aer .20170011.

19. **At the expense:** Autor et al., 2020, p. 3139; **France:** Malgouyres, C. (2017). Trade shocks and far-right voting: Evidence from French presidential elections. Robert Schuman Centre for Advanced Studies Research Paper No. RSCAS, 21. https://papers.ssrn.com/sol3 /papers.cfm?abstract_id=2942173; **Germany:** Dippel. et al., 2015. **UK:** Colantone, I., & Stanig, P. (2018). Global competition and Brexit. American *Political Science Review*, 112(2), 201–218. https://doi.org/10.1017/S0003055417000685; **automation:** Frey et al., 2018; **automation decreases the wages:** Anneli, M., Colantone, I., & Stanig, P. (2021). Individual vulnerability to industrial robot adoption increases support for the radical right, p. 5. *Proceedings of the National Academy of Sciences*, 118(47), e2111611118. https:// www.pnas.org/doi/abs/10.1073/pnas.2111611118; **prefer a larger role for government:** Thewissen, S., & Rueda, D. (2019). Automation and the welfare state: Technological

change as a determinant of redistribution preferences. *Comparative Political Studies*, 52(2), 171–208. https://doi.org/10.1177/0010414017740600; **automation and redistribution, see also:** van Hoorn, A. (2022). Automatability of work and preferences for redistribution. *Oxford Bulletin of Economics and Statistics*, 84(1), 130–157. https://doi.org/10.1111/obes.12460.

20. **Quote:** Zonta, M., Edelman, S., & McArthur, C. (2016). The role of midwestern housing instability in the 2016 election. Center for American Progress. https://www.americanprogress.org/article/the-role-of-midwestern-housing-instability-in-the-2016-election/; **public health metrics:** Illness as indicator. (2016, November 19). *The Economist.* https://www.economist.com/united-states/2016/11/19/illness-as-indicator; **job growth, credit scores, social mobility, workforce participation:** Muravchik, S., & Shields, J. A. (2020). *Trump's Democrats*, p. 121. Brookings Institution Press; **life expectancy:** Bor, J. (2017). Diverging life expectancies and voting patterns in the 2016 US presidential election. *American Journal of Public Health*, 107(10), 1560–1562. https://doi.org/10.2105/ajph.2017.303945.

21. **Vote cluelessly:** Frank, T. (2004). *What's the matter with Kansas? How conservatives won the heart of America*. Metropolitan Books; **quote:** D. Mermin, personal communication, 2023, November.

22. **"Our Family Can Have a Future":** Boudette, N. E. (2023, November 9). "Our family can have a future": Ford workers on a new union contract. *The New York Times*. https://www.nytimes.com/2023/11/09/business/economy/ford-strike-wayne-michigan.html.

23. **Quotes:** Boudette, 2023.

24. **Quotes:** Boudette, 2023.

25. **Black intergenerational mobility:** Chetty, R., Hendren, N., Jones, M. R., & Porter, S. R. (2020). Race and economic opportunity in the United States: An intergenerational perspective. *The Quarterly Journal of Economics*, 135(2), 711–783. https://doi.org/10.1093/qje/qjz042; **fall out of the middle class:** Kochhar, R., & Sechopoulos, S. (2022, May 10). Black and Hispanic Americans, those with less education are more likely to fall out of the middle class each year. Pew Research Center. https://www.pewresearch.org/short-reads/2022/05/10/black-and-hispanic-americans-those-with-less-education-are-more-likely-to-fall-out-of-the-middle-class-each-year/; **mean wealth lost:** McKernan, S., Ratcliffe, C., Steuerle, C. E., & Zhang, S. (2014, April 21). Impact of the Great Recession and beyond: Disparities in wealth building by generation and race, p. 7. Urban Institute. https://www.urban.org/research/publication/impact-great-recession-and-beyond; **Black government jobs:** Cohen, P. (2015, May 24). Public-sector jobs vanish, hitting Blacks hard. *The New York Times*. https://www.nytimes.com/2015/05/25/business/public-sector-jobs-vanish-and-blacks-take-blow.html; **first quote:** Scott, R. E., Wilson, V., Kandra, J., & Perez, D. (2022). Botched policy responses to globalization have decimated manufacturing employment with often overlooked costs for Black, Brown, and other workers of color, pp. 2–3. Economic Policy Institute. https://www.epi.org/publication/botched-policy-responses-to-globalization/; **second quote:** Gould, E. D. (2021). Torn apart? The impact of manufacturing employment decline on Black and white Americans. *The Review of Economics and Statistics*, 103(4), 770–785, 711. https://doi.org/10.1162/rest_a_00918.

26. **Quotes:** Edin, K., Nelson, T., Cherlin, A., & Francis, R. (2019). The tenuous attachments of working-class men, p. 213. *Journal of Economic Perspectives*, 33(2), 221–228. 10.1257/jep.33.2.211; **Black despair deaths rising:** James, K., & Jordan, A. (2018). The opioid crisis in Black communities. *The Journal of Law, Medicine & Ethics*, 46(2), 404–421. https://doi.org/10.1177/1073110518782949; **Blacks more likely:** Lopez, G. A new insight into Donald Trump's rise. *The New York Times*. https://www.nytimes.com/2024/07/25/briefing/donald-trump-voters.html.

27. **First quote:** *Morning Joe*. (2024, February 26). "White rural rage" looks at the most likely group to abandon democratic norms [video]. MSNBC. https://www.msnbc.com

/morning-joe/watch/-white-rural-rage-looks-at-the-most-likely-group-to-abandon
-democratic-norms-204922949864; **second quote:** Etelson, E. (2023, August 24). If the
Left doesn't channel populist resentment, we know who will. *The Nation.* https://www
.thenation.com/article/culture/rich-men-richmond-liberals/.

Chapter 4: Why Are Rural and Rust Belts Red?

1. **Quote:** Bai, M. (2008, October 15). Working for the working-class vote. *The New York
   Times.* https://www.nytimes.com/2008/10/19/magazine/19obama-t.html.
2. **Rust Belt and Trump:** McQuarrie, M. (2016, November 11). Trump and the revolt of
   the Rust Belt. LSE Blogs. https://blogs.lse.ac.uk/usappblog/2016/11/11/23174/; **Rust
   Belt and Brexit:** Neal, S., Gawlewicz, A., Heley, J., & Jones, R. D. (2021, April 19).
   Don't forget the countryside: Rural communities and Brexit. LSE Blogs. https://blogs
   .lse.ac.uk/brexit/2021/04/19/dont-forget-the-countryside-the-social-impact-of-brexit
   -in-rural-communities-must-not-be-overlooked/; **Brexit, see also:** Faulconbridge, G.
   (2018, August 7). In England's forgotten "rust belt," voters show little sign of Brexit regret. Reuters. https://www.reuters.com/article/idUSKBN1KS0VM/; **Rust Belt, see also:**
   Westwood, A., & Austin, J. C. (2021, April 8). To counter extreme politics, revive global democracies' Rust Belts. Brookings. https://www.brookings.edu/articles/to-counter-extreme
   -politics-revive-global-democracies-rust-belts/; **quote:** Leonhardt, D., & Serkez, Y. (2020,
   May 13). What does opportunity look like where you live? *The New York Times.* https:
   //www.nytimes.com/interactive/2020/05/13/opinion/inequality-cities-life-expectancy
   .html; **stratified geographically:** Economic mobility of the states. (2012, April 2). Pew
   Charitable Trusts. https://www.pewtrusts.org/en/research-and-analysis/reports/0001/01
   /01/economic-mobility-of-the-states; **quote:** Leonhardt, D., & Serkez, Y. (2020, May 13).
   What does opportunity look like where you live? *The New York Times.* https://www.nytimes
   .com/interactive/2020/05/13/opinion/inequality-cities-life-expectancy.html; **Clinton and
   Trump counties:** Wilkinson, W. (2019, June). The density divide: Urbanization, polarization, and populist backlash, p. 9. Niskanen Center. https://niskanencenter.org/the-density
   -divide-urbanization-polarization-and-populist-backlash/.
3. **State legislatures:** Badger, E. (2019, May 21). How the rural-urban divide became
   America's political fault line. *The New York Times.* https://www.nytimes.com/2019/05/21
   /upshot/america-political-divide-urban-rural.html.
4. **Drives polarization:** Hyland, M., Mascherini, M., & Lamont, M. (2024, May 23). Europe's invisible provinces. *Foreign Affairs.* https://www.foreignaffairs.com/europe/europes
   -invisible-provinces.
5. **Furniture capital:** Furniture history. High Point Museum. Accessed March 20, 2024,
   from https://www.highpointnc.gov/841/Furniture-History.
6. **8 to 14 percent jump, 35 percent decrease:** Harris, K. (2020). Forty years of falling manufacturing employment. *Beyond the Numbers,* 9(16). https://www.bls.gov/opub/btn/volume
   -9/forty-years-of-falling-manufacturing-employment.htm; **rural hospitals:** Tkacik, M.
   (2023, May 23). Quackanomics. *The American Prospect.* https://prospect.org/health
   /2023-05-23-quackonomics-medical-properties-trust/.
7. **The New Economy:** Moretti, E. (2012). *The new geography of jobs.* HarperCollins; **Richard Florida:** Florida, R. (2002). *The rise of the creative class.* Basic Books; **quote:** Lochhead,
   T. (2024, March 23). The roots of rural rage [letter to the editor]. *The New York Times.*
   https://www.nytimes.com/2024/03/23/opinion/rural-rage.html.
8. **Quote:** Osnos, E. (2020, September 14). A political philosopher on why Democrats
   should think differently about merit. *The New Yorker.* https://www.newyorker.com/news
   /q-and-a/a-political-philosopher-on-why-democrats-should-think-differently-about
   -merit; **end of history:** Fukuyama, F. (1989). The end of history? *The National Interest,* 16,
   3–18. http://www.jstor.org/stable/24027184; **pinpoints its triumph:** Gerstle, G. (2022).
   The rise and fall of the neoliberal order: America and the world in the free market era. Oxford

University Press; **Clinton campaign:** McQuarrie, M. (2017). The revolt of the Rust Belt: Place and politics in the age of anger, p. S133. *The British Journal of Sociology*, 68(S1), S120–S152. https://doi.org/10.1111/1468-4446.12328.

9. **Exceeded the rate of loss:** Atkinson, R. D., Stewart, L. A., Andes, S. M., & Ezell, S. J. (2012). Worse than the Great Depression: What experts are missing about American manufacturing decline, p. 3. The Information Technology & Innovation Foundation. https://www.nist.gov/system/files/documents/2017/05/09/2012-american-manufacturing-decline.pdf; **growth and employment gains:** Muro, M., & Whiton, J. (2018, January 23). Geographic gaps are widening while U.S. economic growth increases. Brookings. https://www.brookings.edu/articles/uneven-growth/; **low or nil:** Wilkinson, 2019, p. 60; **quote:** Sherman, J. (2021). *Dividing Paradise: Rural inequality and the diminishing American Dream*, p. 169. University of California Press.

10. **Many in the Midwest fumed:** Lux, M. (2022, June 7). Winning back the factory towns that made Trumpism possible. American Family Voices. https://www.americanfamilyvoices.org/post/winning-back-the-factory-towns-that-made-trumpism-possible; **quote:** McQuarrie, 2017, p. S140; **China:** Stockman, F. (2020, October 16). Why they loved him. *The New York Times*. https://www.nytimes.com/2020/10/16/opinion/trump-working-class-economy.html.

11. **Shifted most sharply, factory towns:** Martin, R. J. (2021). Factory towns: A 10-state analysis of the Democratic presidential vote decline in working-class counties, 2012–2020. American Family Voices and 21st Century Democrats. https://e0f4aa21-1528-4579-b01b-5945b458d059.filesusr.com/ugd/d4d64f_5c5b228a260e4793ad6034c9dd535d36.pdf; **shifted hardest to the right:** Muro & Whiton, 2018.

12. **Graduation rates:** Educational attainment improved in rural America but educational gap with urban areas grew for bachelor's degrees and higher. US Department of Agriculture Economic Research Service. Accessed March 20, 2024, from https://www.ers.usda.gov/data-products/chart-gallery/gallery/chart-detail/?chartId=106147; **chicken-processing factories:** Striffler, S. (2005). *Chicken: The dangerous transformation of America's favorite food*. Yale University Press.

13. **Fell 50 percent to 15 percent, first quote:** Hogseth, B. (2020, December 1). Why Democrats keep losing rural counties like mine. *Politico*. https://www.politico.com/news/magazine/2020/12/01/democrats-rural-vote-wisconsin-441458; **second quote:** Lemann, N. (2022, October 24). The Democrats' midterm challenge. *The New Yorker*. https://www.newyorker.com/magazine/2022/10/31/the-democrats-midterm-challenge; **Robert Reich:** Reich, R. (2015). *Saving capitalism: For the many, not the few*. Knopf.

14. **First quote:** Walsh, K. C. (2011, June). Political understanding of economic crises: The shape of resentment toward public employees, p. 20. https://www.vanderbilt.edu/csdi/events/Walsh_Pol_Und_Eco_Crisis_112111.pdf; **dismissive of their concerns:** Cramer, K. J. (2016). *The politics of resentment: Rural consciousness in Wisconsin and the rise of Scott Walker*, p. 62. University of Chicago Press; **second quote:** Cramer, 2016, p. 146; **fair share:** Cramer, 2016, p. 105; **rural childcare:** Jessen-Howard, S., Malik, R., Workman, S., & Hamm, K. (2018, October 31). Understanding infant and toddler child care deserts, p. 10. Center for American Progress. https://www.americanprogress.org/article/understanding-infant-toddler-child-care-deserts/; **rural internet access:** Anderson, M. (2018, September 10). About a quarter of rural Americans say access to high-speed internet is a major problem. Pew Research Center. https://www.pewresearch.org/short-reads/2018/09/10/about-a-quarter-of-rural-americans-say-access-to-high-speed-internet-is-a-major-problem/.

15. **Opioid addiction:** Sparks, G., Montero, A., Kirzinger, A., Valdes, I., & Hamel, L. (2023, August 15). KFF tracking poll July 2023: Substance use crisis and accessing treatment. KFF. https://www.kff.org/other/poll-finding/kff-tracking-poll-july-2023-substance-use-crisis-and-accessing-treatment/; **Covid and hospital closures:** Saghafian, S., Song,

L. D., & Raja, A. S. (2022). Towards a more efficient healthcare system: Opportunities and challenges caused by hospital closures amid the COVID-19 pandemic. *Health Care Management Science*, 25, 187–190. https://doi.org/10.1007/s10729-022-09591-7; **rural hospital closures:** Holmes, G. M., Slifkin, R. T., Randolph, R. K., & Poley, S. (2006). The effect of rural hospital closures on community economic health. *Health Services Research*, 41(2), 467–485. https://doi.org/10.1111/j.1475–6773.2005.00497.x; **rural men out of work:** Male prime-age nonworkers: Evidence from the NLSY97. (2020, December). US Bureau of Labor Statistics. https://www.bls.gov/opub/mlr/2020/article/male-prime -age-nonworkers-evidence-from-the-nlsy97.htm; **first quote:** Hogseth, 2020; **widening urban-rural mortality gap:** Monnat, S. M. (2020). Trends in U.S. working-age non-Hispanic white mortality: Rural-urban and within-rural differences. *Population Research and Policy Review*, 39, 805–834. https://doi.org/10.1007/s11113-020-09607-6; **second quote:** Monnat, 2020, p. 813.

16. **Erosion of rural support:** Jacobs, N., & Munis, B. K. (2023). Place-based resentment in contemporary U.S. elections: The individual sources of America's urban-rural divide. *Political Research Quarterly*, 76(3), 1102–1118. https://doi.org/10.1177/10659129221124864; **Biden was in the 20s:** Martin, J. (2020, December 16). Senator Jon Tester on Democrats and rural voters: 'Our message is really, really flawed.' *The New York Times*. https://www .nytimes.com/2020/12/16/us/politics/jon-tester-democrats.html.

17. **Uneven recovery:** Davis, J. C., Cromartie, J., Farrigan, T., Genetin, B., Sanders, A., & Winikoff, J. B. (2023). Rural America at a glance: 2023 edition. US Department of Agriculture, Economic Research Service. https://doi.org/10.32747/2023.8134362.ers; **shipping everything:** McQuarrie, 2017, p. S135.

18. **Quote:** Stockman, 2020.

19. **First quote:** Tavernise, S. (2019, May 27). With his job gone, an autoworker wonders, "What am I as a man?" *The New York Times*. https://www.nytimes.com/2019/05/27/us /auto-worker-jobs-lost.html; **second and third quotes:** Martin, 2021.

20. **First and second quote:** McQuarrie, 2017, p. S138; **third quote:** McQuarrie, 2017, p. S146; **fourth quote:** McQuarrie, 2017, p. S144.

21. **Deep roots:** Nelsen, M. D., & Petsko, C. D. (2021). Race and white rural consciousness. *Perspectives on Politics*, 19(4), 1205–1218. https://doi.org/10.1017/S1537592721001948; **mentioned NAFTA:** Martin, 2021; **first quote:** Brown, L. (2019, June 9). The untapped power of rural voters. *The New York Times*. https://www.nytimes.com/2019/06/09/opinion /rural-voters-democrats.html; **farm subsidies:** Rappeport, A. (2020, October 12). Trump funnels record subsidies to farmers ahead of Election Day. *The New York Times*. https:// www.nytimes.com/2020/10/12/us/politics/trump-farmers-subsidies.html.

22. **First quote:** Stockman, 2020; trade wars: Autor, A., Beck, A., Dorn, D., & Hanson, G. H. (2024). Help for the heartland? The employment and electoral effects of the Trump tariffs in the United States (No. 32082). National Bureau of Economic Research. https: //www.nber.org/papers/w32082.

23. **First quote:** Cramer, 2016, p. 81; **second quote:** Cramer, 2016, p.158; **"takers":** Krugman, P. (2023, January 26). Can anything be done to assuage rural rage? *The New York Times*. https://www.nytimes.com/2023/01/26/opinion/rural-voters-economy.html; **third quote:** Krugman, 2023; **"mystery":** Krugman, P. (2024, February 26). The mystery of white rural rage. *The New York Times*. https://www.nytimes.com/2024/02/26/opinion/white-rural -voters.html; **progressive populist messaging:** Abbott, J., Fan, L., Guastella, D., Herz, G., Karp, M., Leach, J., Marvel, J., Rader, K., & Riz, F. (2021). Commonsense solidarity: How a working-class coalition can be built, and maintained, p. 29. *Jacobin*. https://jacobin .com/2021/11/common-sense-solidarity-working-class-voting-report.

24. **Rural people of color:** Martin, 2021; **first quote, attracted white workers:** McQuarrie, 2017, p. S144; **second quote:** Cullen, A. (2022, December 11). Want to know why

Democrats lose rural America? *The New York Times.* https://www.nytimes.com/2022/12
/11/opinion/democrats-iowa-caucus.html; **third quote, Clinton mass incarceration:**
McQuarrie, M. (2017). The revolt of the Rust Belt: Place and politics in the age of anger, p. S143. *The British Journal of Sociology,* 68(S1), S120–S152. https://doi.org/10.1111
/1468–4446.12328.

25. **Two-million-vote shift:** Martin, R. J. (2021). Factory towns: A 10-state analysis of the
Democratic presidential vote decline in working-class counties, 2012–2020. American Family Voices and 21st Century Democrats. https://e0f4aa21–1528–4579-b01b
-5945b458d059.filesusr.com/ugd/d4d64f_5c5b228a260e4793ad6034c9dd535d36.pdf;
47–48 percent of voters: Lux, M. (2022, June 7). Winning back the factory towns that
made Trumpism possible. American Family Voices. https://www.americanfamilyvoices
.org/post/winning-back-the-factory-towns-that-made-trumpism-possible.

26. **First quote:** Hogseth, 2020; **second and third quotes, gains in rural areas:** Brown, 2019;
pillars of communities: Lux, 2022.

27. **Quote:** Hogseth, 2020.

28. **Janitor's income:** Porter, E., & Gates, G. (2019, May 21). Why workers without college
degrees are fleeing big cities. *The New York Times.* https://www.nytimes.com/interactive
/2019/05/21/business/economy/migration-big-cities.html.

29. **"Levelling up":** Castle, S. (2021, October 2). Battered towns in England's north test
Johnson's plan to "level up." *The New York Times.* https://www.nytimes.com/2021/10/02
/world/europe/england-boris-johnson-development.html.

Chapter 5: Is the Solution to Move to the Center?

1. **Quote:** Glueck, K., & Mays, J. C. (2021, November 2). Eric Adams's win is a "watershed
moment" for Black leaders in New York. *The New York Times.* https://www.nytimes.com
/2021/07/13/nyregion/black-power-eric-adams-nyc.html; interview of Leah Daughtry
by Joan Williams, conducted June 29, 2024.

2. **First quote:** Democrats need to wake up and stop pandering to their extremes. (2022,
July 14). *The Economist.* https://www.economist.com/leaders/2022/07/14/the-democrats
-need-to-wake-up-and-stop-pandering-to-their-extremes; **commentators agree:** Zengerle, J. (2022, July 1). The vanishing moderate Democrat. *The New York Times.* https://www
.nytimes.com/2022/06/29/magazine/moderate-democrat.html; **second quote:** Abrams, S.,
& Groh-Wargo, L. (2021, February 11). Stacey Abrams and Lauren Groh-Wargo: How
to turn your red state blue. *The New York Times.* https://www.nytimes.com/2021/02/11
/opinion/stacey-abrams-georgia-election.html.

3. **"President par excellence":** Gerstle, G. (2022). *The rise and fall of the neoliberal order:
America and the world in the free market era,* p. 156. Oxford University Press; **Clinton and
China:** Associated Press. (2000, May 25). President Clinton's remarks on the passage of
the China trade bill. *The New York Times.* https://archive.nytimes.com/www.nytimes.com
/library/world/asia/052500clinton-trade-text.html; **Third Way free trade:** Our impact:
How Third Way spurred huge gains in free trade. (n.d.). Third Way. Accessed May 2,
2024, from https://www.thirdway.org/impact/how-third-way-spurred-huge-gains-in
-free-trade; **Third Way banking:** Liner, E., & Lapointe, P. (2016, May 5). A closer look at
market consolidation in banking. Third Way. https://www.thirdway.org/third-way-take/a
-closer-look-at-market-consolidation-in-banking.

4. **Move to the center:** Teixeira, R. (2022, December 15). Ten reasons why Democrats
should become more moderate. The Liberal Patriot. https://www.liberalpatriot.com/p
/ten-reasons-why-democrats-should; **Teixeira, see also:** Teixeira, R. (2023, June 1). Why
can't the Democrats be more moderate? The Liberal Patriot. https://www.liberalpatriot
.com/p/why-cant-the-democrats-be-more-moderate.

5. **Quote:** A long-term success strategy for Democrats, with Ruy Teixeira. Niskanen Center.

https://www.niskanencenter.org/a-long-term-success-strategy-for-democrats-with-ruy-teixeira/.

6. **Quote:** Kabaservice, G. (Host). (2023, May 30). A long-term success strategy for Democrats, with Ruy Teixeira (No. 47) [audio podcast episode]. In The vital center. The Niskanen Center. https://www.niskanencenter.org/a-long-term-success-strategy-for-democrats-with-ruy-teixeira/.

7. **Progressive activists:** Hawkins, S., Yudkin, D., Juan-Torres, M., & Dixon, T. (2018). Hidden tribes: A study of America's polarized landscape. More in Common. https://hiddentribes.us/media/qfpekz4g/hidden_tribes_report.pdf; **progressives, see also:** Beyond red vs. blue: The political typology. (2021, November). Pew Research Center. https://www.pewresearch.org/politics/2021/11/09/beyond-red-vs-blue-the-political-typology-2/; **8 percent of Americans:** Hawkins et al., 2018, p. 6; **demographic profile:** Hawkins et al., 2018, pp. 141–142; **quote:** Douthat, R. (2019, May 25). How liberalism loses. *The New York Times.* https://www.nytimes.com/2019/05/25/opinion/sunday/how-liberalism-loses.html.

8. **Ashamed to be American, luck and circumstance, more dangerous place (19 percent versus 38 percent), never pray (50 percent versus 19 percent):** Hawkins et al., 2018, p. 30.

9. **Hobby, proud of politics:** Hawkins et al., 2018, p. 30; **a lot in common, pressure to conform:** Hawkins et al., 2018, pp. 73–74.

10. **2.6 times more likely:** Hawkins et al., 2018, p. 59; **affirmative action:** Hawkins et al., 2018, p. 63; **gun owners:** Hawkins et al., 2018, p. 75; **rebuild institutions:** Pew Research Center, 2021, p. 7.

11. **Next most liberal:** Hawkins et al., 2018, p. 142; **identify as conservative, liberal:** Saad, L. (2022, January 17). U.S. political ideology steady; conservatives, moderates tie. Gallup. https://news.gallup.com/poll/388988/political-ideology-steady-conservatives-moderates-tie.aspx; **consistently progressive:** Haney López, I. (2019). Merge left: Fusing race and class, winning elections, and saving America, p. 78. *The New Press;* **"highly educated":** Commonsense solidarity: How a working-class coalition can be built, and maintained, 65. (2021, November 9). *Jacobin.* https://jacobin.com/2021/11/common-sense-solidarity-working-class-voting-report.

12. **Identify as liberal, conservative, moderate:** Saad, 2022.

13. **College versus noncollege:** Saad, 2022; **race and education breakdowns: 25 percentage points (66 percent versus 41 percent), 13 points (41 percent versus 28 percent), 11 points (43 percent versus 32 percent), 9 points (41 percent versus 32 percent):** Astrow, A. (2022, February 20). How does education level impact attitudes among voters of color? Third Way. https://www.thirdway.org/memo/how-does-education-level-impact-attitudes-among-voters-of-color.

14. **Democrats as liberal:** Saad, L. (2023, January 12). Democrats' identification as liberal now 54%, a new high. Gallup. https://news.gallup.com/poll/467888/democrats-identification-liberal-new-high.aspx; **mix of positions:** Haney López, 2019, p. 78; **persuasion, see also:** Haney López, 2019, p. 81.

15. ***The Hill* deep dive:** Williams, J. C. (2023, June 1). How Democrats can win noncollege voters without giving in to racism. *The Hill.* https://thehill.com/opinion/campaign/4029261-how-democrats-can-win-non-college-voters-without-giving-in-to-racism/.

16. **Avoid cultural issues:** Lux, M. (2022, June 6). Winning back the factory towns that made Trumpism possible. American Family Voices. https://www.americanfamilyvoices.org/post/winning-back-the-factory-towns-that-made-trumpism-possible; **first quote:** Gallagher, K. (2022, September 1). Meet Mary Peltola, the "pro-fish and pro-choice" Democrat who defeated Sarah Palin in Alaska's special House election. Business Insider. https://www.businessinsider.com/meet-mary-peltola-the-democrat-and-alaska-native-who-beat-sarah-palin-2022-9; **second quote:** C-SPAN. (2022, November 8).

John Fetterman victory speech [video]. *YouTube.* https://www.youtube.com/watch?v=iU _OyYRIMDg; **unions and jobs:** Firestone, D. (2023, March 9). A new voice for winning back lost Democratic voters. *The New York Times.* https://www.nytimes.com/2023/03/09 /opinion/marie-gluesenkamp-perez-democratic-voters.html; **apprenticeship programs:** Fertig, N. (2023, January 19). She fixes cars. Can she fix Congress' elitism problem? *Politico.* https://www.politico.com/news/magazine/2023/01/19/marie-gluenskamp-perez -democrats-middle-class-00078215; **Vasquez:** D'Ammassa, A. (2022, October 22). U.S. rep. Yvette Herrell, Gabe Vasquez present their cases to NM CD2 voters in TV debate. *Las Cruces Sun News.* https://www.lcsun-news.com/story/news/politics/elections/2022 /10/22/yvette-herrell-gabe-vasquez-present-cases-for-cd2-new-mexico-voters-in-tv -debate-nm-election-2022/69582156007/.

17. **Electric vehicle plants, Detroit plant:** Stryker, B. (2022, December 12). Gretchen Whitmer rejected false choices. All Democrats should. *The New York Times.* https://www .nytimes.com/2022/12/12/opinion/gretchen-whitmer-michigan-democrats.html; **economics of abortion:** Gardner, L. (2022, November 9). Whitmer beats back Dixon in Michigan governor's race. *Politico.* https://www.politico.com/news/2022/11/09/gretchen -whitmer-tudor-dixon-michigan-governor-race-results-2022–00064764; **talk traditions:** Parker, A. (2022, November 9). Whitmer vaults into national spotlight with double-digit reelection win. *The Washington Post.* https://www.washingtonpost.com/politics/2022/11 /09/gretchen-whitmer-michigan-governor-election/.

18. **Michigan Democrats:** Smith, M., & Londoño, E. (2023, March 9). Newly empowered Michigan Democrats move on labor, gay rights and guns. *The New York Times.* https:// www.nytimes.com/2023/03/09/us/michigan-democrats-right-to-work-lgbtq-guns.html.

19. **Day-to-day concerns:** Pennsylvania: Common touch key to Senate race. (2022, October 5). Monmouth University Poll. https://www.monmouth.edu/polling-institute/reports /monmouthpoll_pa_100522/; **quote:** Gabriel, T. (2022, October 8). Fetterman's blue-collar allure is tested as Pennsylvania race tightens. *The New York Times.* https://www .nytimes.com/2022/10/08/us/politics/fetterman-pennsylvania-senate-race.html; **championing clemency:** Hardison, E. (2020). Fetterman, Shapiro say they both believe in second chances. Pardons board votes tell two different stories. *Pennsylvania Capital-Star.* https: //penncapital-star.com/criminal-justice/fetterman-shapiro-say-they-both-believe-in -second-chances-pardons-board-votes-tell-two-different-stories/; **jogger incident, see:** Terruso, J., & Brennan, C. (2022, April 26). Everything to know about the 2013 John Fetterman jogger incident. *The Philadelphia Inquirer.* https://www.inquirer.com/politics /election/john-fetterman-black-jogger-2013-shotgun-20220425.html; **not perfect:** Wallace-Wells, B. (2024, July 1). John Fetterman's war. *The New Yorker.* https://www.newyorker .com/magazine/2024/07/01/john-fettermans-war.

20. **First quote:** Pennsylvania 8th congressional district debate [video]. (2022, October 20). CSPAN. https://www.c-span.org/video/?523538–1/pennsylvania-8th-congressional -district-debate; **second quote:** Bernal, R. (2022, September 14). Hispanic caucus endorses Latina in newly competitive Washington district. *The Hill.* https://thehill.com/latino /3642813-hispanic-caucus-endorses-latina-in-newly-competitive-washington-district/.

21. **Quote:** Fetterman, J. [@JohnFetterman]. (2022, August 15). "In PA, we call this a . . . veggie tray" [tweet]. Twitter. https://twitter.com/JohnFetterman/status/1559207673698127872; **mining:** Rolston, J. S. (2014). *Mining coal and undermining gender: Rhythms of work and family in the American west.* Rutgers University Press.

22. **First quote:** Schwartzman, P. (2022, April 18). A Democrat in gym shorts tries to rally blue votes in Trump country. *The Washington Post.* https://www.washingtonpost.com /lifestyle/2022/04/18/john-fetterman-pennsylvania-trump-country/; **second quote:** Fetterman, J. [@JohnFetterman]. (2022, August 23). "I had a stroke. I survived it. I'm truly so grateful to still be here today. I know politics can be nasty, but even then, I could *never*

imagine ridiculing someone for their health challenges" [tweet]. Twitter. https://twitter
.com/JohnFetterman/status/1562235945998553089; **third quote:** Marans, D. (2022,
October 4). How Rep. Matt Cartwright, a progressive Democrat, survives in Trump
country. Huff Post. https://www.huffpost.com/entry/matt-cartwright-defies-odds-trump
-country_n_6339b8f1e4b04cf8f363ca46/amp.

23. **First quote:** Stockburger, G. (2023, January 17). Read: Governor Josh Shapiro's inauguration speech. ABC27 WHTM. https://www.abc27.com/pennsylvania-governor-election
-2022/read-governor-josh-shapiros-inauguration-speech/; tradespeople: Fertig, 2023; **small
businesses:** French, D. (2023, February 12). Men need purpose more than "respect." *The New
York Times.* https://www.nytimes.com/2023/02/12/opinion/men-purpose-respect.html.

24. **First quote:** Release: Gabe Vasquez says New Mexico deserves better in first TV ad.
(2022, August 30). Gabe Vasquez for Congress. https://gabeforcongress.com/2022/08/30
/release-gabe-vasquez-says-new-mexico-deserves-better-in-first-tv-ad/; **second quote:**
D'Ammassa, 2022.

25. **First quote:** Perling, A. (2023, August 8). Driving change. *Reed Magazine.* https://www
.reed.edu/reed-magazine/articles/2023/marie-gluesenkamp-perez.html. https://www
.nytimes.com/2019/04/06/opinion/sunday/right-to-repair-elizabeth-warren-antitrust
.html; **"right to repair," see also:** NYT Editorial Board. (2019, April 6). It's your
iPhone. Why can't you fix it yourself? *The New York Times.* https://www.nytimes.com
/2019/04/06/opinion/sunday/right-to-repair-elizabeth-warren-antitrust.html; **Harris right to repair:** González-Ramírez, A. (2024, October 15). What to know about
Kamala Harris's policy proposals. *The Cut.* https://www.thecut.com/article/what-are
-kamala-harris-policies.html; **second quote:** Sokolove, M. (2022, November 15). How
Democrats can build a John Fetterman 2.0. *The New York Times.* https://www.nytimes
.com/2022/11/15/opinion/john-fetterman-democrats.html.

26. *Slate:* Sammon, A. (2023, August 10). With Democrats like Marie Gluesenkamp
Pérez, who needs Republicans? *Slate.* https://slate.com/news-and-politics/2023/08
/marie-gluesenkamp-perez-washington-congresswoman-sold-out-democrats.html;
defeated a MAGA Republican: Yglesias, M. (2023, August 15). Democrats need Marie Gluesenkamp Perez. Slow Boring. https://www.slowboring.com/p/democrats-need
-marie-gluesenkamp.

27. **Eric Adams:** Glueck & Mays, 2021; **quote:** Walley, C. J. (2013). *Exit zero: Family and
class in postindustrial Chicago,* p. 112. University of Chicago Press.

Part II: What's the Matter with Kansas?

1. **Quote:** Lamont, M. (2000). *The dignity of working men,* p. 2. Harvard University Press.

2. **Thomas Frank:** Frank, T. (2004). *What's the matter with Kansas? How conservatives
won the heart of America.* Metropolitan Books; **backed off this view:** Frank, T. (2016).
Listen, liberal: Or, what ever happened to the party of the people? Metropolitan Books;
quote: Leonhardt, D. (2021, November 4). What's the matter with Scarsdale? *The
New York Times.* https://www.nytimes.com/2021/11/04/briefing/democrats-election
-working-class-voters.html.

3. **Cramer:** Cramer, K. (2016). *The politics of resentment: Rural consciousness in Wisconsin and
the rise of Scott Walker,* p. 7. University of Chicago Press.

4. **First quote:** Bourdieu, P. (1984). *Distinction: A social critique on the judgment of taste* (R.
Nice, Trans.), pp. 170, 175, 372–396. Harvard University Press. (Original work published
1979); **second quote:** Bourdieu, P. (1990). *The logic of practice* (R. Nice, Trans.), p. 56.
Stanford University Press. (Original work published 1980); **third quote:** Bettie, J. (2003).
Women without class: Girls, race, and identity, p. 119. University of California Press; **alter-
nate routes:** Bettie, 2003, p. 112.

Chapter 6: Why Does the Culture Wars Formula Work So Well?

1. **Quote:** Peck, R. (2019). *Fox populism: Branding conservatism as working class*, p. 125. Cambridge University Press. https://doi.org/10.1017/9781108634410.

2. **Cultural voting:** van der Waal, J., Achterberg, P., & Houtman, D. (2007). Class is not dead—it has been buried alive: Class voting and cultural voting in postwar Western societies (1956–1990). *Politics & Society*, 35(3), 403–426. https://doi.org/10.1177/0032329207304314.

3. **Ronald Inglehart:** Inglehart, R. (1977). *The silent revolution: Changing values and political styles among Western publics*. Princeton University Press.

4. **Fundamental human motive:** Ridgeway, C. L. (2014). Why status matters for inequality. *American Sociological Review*, 79(1), 1–16. https://doi.org/10.1177/0003122413515997; **status is integral to identity:** Anderson, C., Hildreth, J. A. D., & Howland, L. (2015). Is the desire for status a fundamental human motive? A review of the empirical literature. *Psychological Bulletin*, 141(3), 574–601. https://doi.org/10.1037/a0038781; **quote:** Lamont, M. (2023). *Seeing others: How recognition works—and how it can heal a divided world*, p. 6. Atria/One Signal; **"dignity gap":** Andersson, M. A., & Hitlin, S. (2023). Measuring and explaining a college dignity divide in America. *Socius*, 9, 23780231231180381. https://doi.org/10.1177/23780231231180381.

5. **Quote:** Gidron, N., & Hall, P. A. (2017). The politics of social status: Economic and cultural roots of the populist right, p. S68. *The British Journal of Sociology*, 68(S1), S57–S84. https://doi.org/10.1111/1468-4446.12319.

6. **First and second quotes:** Lamont, M. (2000). *The dignity of working men: Morality and the boundaries of race, class, and immigration*, p. 19. Harvard University Press; **third quote:** Lamont, 2000, p. 20.

7. **Quote:** Lamont, 2000, p. 27.

8. **Quote:** Lareau, A. (2003). *Unequal childhoods: Class, race, and family life*, p. 238. University of California Press.

9. **Pride themselves:** Lamont, 2000, p. 20; **first quote:** Rodgers, D. (1978). *The work ethic in industrial America*, 1850–1920, p. 35. University of Chicago Press; **second quote:** Sherman, J. (2009). *Those who work, those who don't: Poverty, morality, and family in rural America*, p. 59. University of Minnesota Press; **third quote:** Rolston, J. S. (2014). *Mining coal and undermining gender: Rhythms of work and family in the American west*, p. 157. Rutgers University Press; **fourth quote:** Bageant, J. (2007). *Deer hunting with Jesus: Dispatches from America's class war*, pp. 69–70. Crown.

10. **Expressive independence:** Stephens, N. M., Markus, H. R., & Phillips, L. T. (2014). Social class culture cycles: How three gateway contexts shape selves and fuel inequality, p. 614. *Annual Review of Psychology*, 65, 611–634. https://doi.org/10.1146/annurev-psych-010213-115143; **quote:** Willis, P. (1977). *Learning to labor: How working class kids get working class jobs*, p. 177. Columbia University Press.

11. **Quote:** Cuban, M. (2020). Foreword, in J. C. Williams, *White working class: Overcoming class cluelessness in America*, p. xii. Harvard Business Review Press. (Original work published 2017); **trade creativity:** Duguid, M. M., & Goncalo, J. A. (2015). Squeezed in the middle: The middle status trade creativity for focus, 589. *Journal of Personality and Social Psychology*, 109(4), 589–603. https://doi.org/10.1037/a0039569.

12. **First quote:** Gest, J. (2016). *The new minority: White working class politics in an age of immigration and inequality*, p. 155. Oxford University Press; **second quote:** Goldmacher, S. (2022, November 10). The battle for blue-collar white voters raging in Biden's birthplace. *The New York Times*. https://www.nytimes.com/2022/10/30/us/politics/blue-collar-voters-pennsylvania.html; **third quote:** Gustafson, R. (2024, March 23). The roots of rural rage [letter to the editor]. *The New York Times*. https://www.nytimes.com/2024/03/23/opinion/rural-rage.html; **fourth quote:** Klein, E. (2011, March 8). Vilsack: "I took it as a slam on

rural America." *The Washington Post.* https://www.washingtonpost.com/blogs/wonkblog/post/vilsack-i-took-it-as-a-slam-on-rural-america/2011/03/08/ABF0l6O_blog.html.

13. **Hard-work worship:** Lamont, 2000, p. 28; **shifted away:** Hunt, M. O. (2007). African American, Hispanic, and White beliefs about Black/White inequality, 1977–2004. *American Sociological Review*, 72(3), 390–415. https://doi.org/10.1177/000312240707200304; **never missed a shift:** Obama, M. (2018). *Becoming*, p. 137. Crown; **first and second quotes:** Obama, 2018, p. 225; **stifle creativity and spontaneity:** Duguid & Goncalo, 2015.

14. **"Learning to labor":** Willis, 1977; **first quote:** Lubrano, A. (2004). *Limbo: Blue-collar roots, white-collar dreams*, p. 10. Wiley; **display less tolerance:** Stephens et al., 2014, p. 617; **second quote:** Terkel, S. (1974). *Working: People talk about what they do all day and how they feel about what they do*, p. 161. The New Press.

15. **Quote:** Prasad, M., Hoffman, S. G., & Bezila, K. (2016). Walking the line: The white working class and the economic consequences of morality, p. 281. *Politics & Society*, 44(2), 281–304. https://doi.org/10.1177/0032329216638062; **good moral standing:** Sherman, 2009, pp. 73–74.

16. **First and second quotes:** Obama, 2018, p. 137; **third and fourth quotes:** Obama, 2018, p. 33; **fifth quote:** Obama, 2018, p. 139; **Blacks' hard work:** Pougiales, R., & Fulton, J. (2019, December 30). A nuanced picture of what Black Americans want in 2020. Third Way. https://www.thirdway.org/memo/a-nuanced-picture-of-what-black-americans-want-in-2020; **Latinos' hard work:** Haney López, I. (2022). Project Juntos: Latinx race-class. Project Juntos. https://static1.squarespace.com/static/5ef377b623eaf41dd9df1311/t/5f6fd7e84ca040062e8dc0b9/1601165291980/Project+Juntos+Summary+Briefing+092620.pdf; **Latino college grads:** Krogstad, J. M., Passel, J. S., Moslimani, M., & Noe-Bustamante, L. (2023, September 22). Key facts about U.S. Latinos for national Hispanic heritage month. Pew Research Center. https://www.pewresearch.org/short-reads/2023/09/22/key-facts-about-us-latinos-for-national-hispanic-heritage-month/; **progressive activists:** Hawkins, S., Yudkin, D., Juan-Torres, M., & Dixon, T. (2018). Hidden tribes: A study of America's polarized landscape, p. 90. More in Common. https://hiddentribes.us/media/qfpekz4g/hidden_tribes_report.pdf.

17. **Food stamps:** Astrow, A. (2022, February 20). How does education level impact attitudes among voters of color? Third Way. https://www.thirdway.org/memo/how-does-education-level-impact-attitudes-among-voters-of-color.

18. **First quote:** Lamont, 2000, p. 26; **"keep it together":** Lamont, 2000, p. 23; **"religion of responsibility":** Lubrano, 2004, pp. 16–17; **second quote:** Tavernise, S. (2019, May 27). With his job gone, an autoworker wonders, "What am I as a man?" *The New York Times.* https://www.nytimes.com/2019/05/27/us/auto-worker-jobs-lost.html; **third quote:** Hochschild, A. (2016). *Strangers in their own land: Anger and mourning on the American right*, p. 218. The New Press.

19. **Class anger and redistribution:** Marchevsky, A., & Theoharis, J. (2000). Welfare reform, globalization, and the racialization of entitlement. *American Studies*, 41(2/3), 235–265. https://www.jstor.org/stable/40643238; **public employment:** Cramer, K. J. (2016). *The politics of resentment: Rural consciousness in Wisconsin and the rise of Scott Walker.* University of Chicago Press.

20. **Quotes:** Vance, J. D. (2016). *Hillbilly elegy: A memoir of a family and culture in crisis*, p. 174. HarperCollins.

21. **Honoring service members:** Hawkins, S., & Raghuram, T. (2020, December). American fabric: Identity and belonging, p. xliii. More in Common. https://www.moreincommon.com/media/s5jhgpx5/moreincommon_americanfabricreport.pdf; **quote:** French, D. (2023, February 12). Men need purpose more than "respect." *The New York Times.* https://www.nytimes.com/2023/02/12/opinion/men-purpose-respect.html; **military health care:** TRICARE Communications. (2023, November 7). Know your 2024 TRICARE health plan costs. TRICARE Newsroom/Department of Defense. https://newsroom.tricare.mil

/News/TRICARE-News/Article/3582211/know-your-2024-tricare-health-plan-costs; **subsidized college:** Military tuition assistance (n.d.). USAGov. Accessed January 12, 2024, from https://www.usa.gov/military-tuition-assistance; **military childcare:** Child care financial assistance for military families (n.d.). ChildCare.gov. Department of Health and Human Services. Accessed January 12, 2024, from https://childcare.gov/consumer -education/military-child-care-financial-assistance; **military retirement:** Military compensation: Retired pay. (n.d.). Department of Defense. Accessed January 12, 2024, from https://militarypay.defense.gov/Pay/Retirement/.

22. **Quote:** Vance, 2016, p. 164.
23. **Religion important in their lives:** Fetterolf, J., & Austin, S. (2023, April 20). Many people in U.S., other advanced economies say it's not necessary to believe in God to be moral. Pew Research Center. https://www.pewresearch.org/short-reads/2023/04/20 /many-people-in-u-s-other-advanced-economies-say-its-not-necessary-to-believe-in -god-to-be-moral/; **belief in God to be moral:** Fetterolf & Austin, 2023; **traditional morality:** Lamont, 2000, p. 21.
24. **Quote:** Vance, 2016, p. 94.
25. **First and second quotes:** Lamont, 2000, p. 40; **third quote:** Hochschild, 2016, p. 118.
26. **Quote:** Hochschild, 2016, p. 23.
27. **First quote:** Obama, 2018, p. 24; **second quote:** Obama, 2018, p. 236.
28. **Quote:** Lamont, 2000, p. 99.
29. **Quote:** Lamont, 2000, p. 108.
30. **First quote:** Lamont, 2000, p. 108; **second quote:** Lamont, 2000, p. 109; **high school girls:** Bettie, J. (2003). *Women without class: Girls, race, and identity*, p. 84. University of California Press.
31. **Quote:** Dews, C. L., & Law, C. L. (Eds.). (1995). *This fine place so far from home: Voices of academics from the working class*, p. 216. Temple University Press; **graduate in six years, lag behind:** Schaeffer, K. (2022, April 12). 10 facts about today's college graduates. Pew Research Center. https://www.pewresearch.org/short-reads/2022/04/12/10-facts-about -todays-college-graduates/; **college wealth premium:** Emmons, W. R., Kent, A. H., & Ricketts, L. R. (2019, February 7). Is college still worth it? It's complicated. Federal Reserve Bank of St. Louis. https://www.stlouisfed.org/on-the-economy/2019/february/is -college-still-worth-it-complicated.
32. **Quotes:** Glueck, K. (2023, February 22). Democratic report explores blue-collar struggles: "Our brand is pretty damaged." *The New York Times*. https://www.nytimes.com/2023 /02/22/us/politics/democrats-factory-towns-2024.html.
33. **Quote:** Edsall, T. B. (2021, December 8). Trump won't let America go. Can Democrats pry it away? *The New York Times*. https://www.nytimes.com/2021/12/08/opinion/trump -democrats-republicans.html.
34. **Language study:** Voelkel, J. G., & Willer, R. (2019). Resolving the progressive paradox: Conservative value framing of progressive economic policies increase candidate support. https://dx.doi.org/10.2139/ssrn.3385818.

Chapter 7: Isn't It Ironic that Red "Family Values" States Have Weaker Families than Blue States?

1. **Quote:** Gest, J. (2016). *The new minority: White working class politics in an age of immigration and inequality*, p. 159. Oxford University Press.
2. **Pornography:** Broderick, R. (2014, April 11). Who watches more porn: Republicans or Democrats? BuzzFeed News. https://www.buzzfeednews.com/article/ryanhatesthis /who-watches-more-porn-republicans-or-democrats; **"red families, blue families":** Cahn, N., & Carbone, J. (2010). *Red families v. blue families: Legal polarization and the creation of culture*. Oxford University Press; **teen pregnancy rates:** Cahn & Carbone, 2010, p. 2; **high divorce rates:** Glass, J., & Levchak, P. (2014). Red states, blue

states, and divorce: Understanding the impact of conservative Protestantism on regional variation in divorce rates. *American Journal of Sociology*, 119(4), 1002–1046. https://doi.org/10.1086/674703; Penman-Aguilar, A., Carter, M., Snead, M. C., & Kourtis, A. P. (2013). Socioeconomic disadvantage as a social determinant of teen childbearing in the U.S. Public Health Reports, 128(2_suppl1), 5–22. https://doi.org/10.1177%2F00333549131282S102.

3. **Poor families:** Penman-Aguilar et al., 2013; **college grad divorce rates:** Mounk, Y. (2023, October 4). Nothing defines America's social divide like a college education. *The Atlantic.* https://www.theatlantic.com/ideas/archive/2023/10/education-inequality-economic -opportunities-college/675536/; **divorce and nonmarital childbearing:** McLanahan, S. (2004). Diverging destinies: How children are faring under the second demographic transition, pp. 612–613. *Demography*, 41(4), 607–627. https://doi.org/10.1353/dem.2004 .0033; **births outside marriage:** Wildsmith, E., Manlove, J., & Cook, E. (2018, August 8). Dramatic increase in the proportion of births outside of marriage in the United States from 1990 to 2016. Child Trends. https://www.childtrends.org/publications /dramatic-increase-in-percentage-of-births-outside-marriage-among-whites-hispanics -and-women-with-higher-education-levels.

4. **Downward mobility, quote:** Newman, K. S. (1999). *Falling from grace: Downward mobility in the age of affluence*, p. 135. University of California Press; **40 percent of the decline, wives earn more:** Reeves, R. V. (2022). *Of boys and men: Why the modern male is struggling, why it matters, and what to do about it*, p. 37. Rowman & Littlefield; **fight about money:** Meyer, D., & Sledge, R. (2022). The relationship between conflict topics and romantic relationship dynamics. *Journal of Family Issues*, 43(2), 306–323. https://doi.org/10.1177 /0192513X21993856; **Black marriage rates, when work disappears:** Wilson, W. J. (1996). *When work disappears: The world of the new urban poor.* Knopf; **white marriage rates:** Murray, C. (2012). *Coming apart: The state of white America, 1960–2010.* Random House; **81 percent believe:** Reeves, 2022, p. 36.

5. **Working mothers:** Sherman, J. (2009). *Those who work, those who don't: Poverty, morality, and family in rural America*, pp. 59–60. University of Minnesota Press.

6. **Black noncollege more conservative:** Pougiales, R., & Fulton, J. (2019, December 30). A nuanced picture of what Black Americans want in 2020. Third Way. https://www .thirdway.org/memo/a-nuanced-picture-of-what-black-americans-want-in-2020.

7. **First and second quotes:** Sherman, 2009, p. 78; **third quote:** Lamont, M. (2000). *The dignity of working men: Morality and the boundaries of race, class, and immigration*, p. 9. Harvard University Press.

8. **More dedicated to family life:** Sherman, 2009, p. 107; **Thomas Fell:** Tom Rice Buick, 167 L.R.R.M. 1343 (2001).

9. **Physicians' wives, first quote:** Shows, C., & Gerstel, N. (2009). Fathering, class, and gender: A comparison of physicians and emergency medical technicians, pp. 173–174. *Gender & Society*, 23(2), 161–187. https://doi.org/10.1177/0891243209333872; **second quote:** Shows & Gerstel, 2009, p. 175; **swapped shifts:** Shows & Gerstel, 2009, p. 176; **take time out of the labor market:** Reeves, 2022, p. 66.

10. **First quote:** Lamont, 2000, p. 30; **second quote:** Sherman, 2009, pp. 125–126; **third quote:** Sherman, 2009, p. 105.

11. **First quote:** Kefalas, M. (2003). *Working-class heroes: Protecting home, community, and nation in a Chicago neighborhood*, p. 66. University of California Press; **second quote:** Fiske, S. T. (2011). *Envy up, scorn down: How status divides us*, p. 76. Russell Sage Foundation; **social ties:** Myers, D. G. (2000). The funds, friends, and faith of happy people. *American Psychologist*, 55(1), 56–67. https://doi.org/10.1037/0003-066X.55.1.56; **third quote:** Myers, 2000, p. 59.

12. **Quote:** Sherman, 2009, p. 120; **care for nonbiological children:** Sherman, 2009, p. 113.

13. **First quote:** Sherman, 2009, p. 127; **second, third, fourth, and fifth quotes:** Kefalas,

2003, p. 5; **sixth quote:** Bettie, J. (2003). *Women without class: Girls, race, and identity,* p. 128. University of California Press.

14. **First quote:** Kefalas, 2003, p. 103; **Covid and housing prices:** Median sales price for new houses sold in the United States. (2023, December 22). US Census Bureau and US Department of Housing and Urban Development. Accessed January 23, 2024, from FRED (Federal Reserve Bank of St. Louis) at https://fred.stlouisfed.org/series/MSPNHSUS; **second quote:** Sherman, J., [unpublished] research interview conducted in December 2014; **third quote:** Kefalas, 2003, p. 31.

15. **First and second quotes:** Kefalas, 2003, pp. 12–13; **symbolic boundary, "white trash":** Kefalas, 2003, p. 11; **"loving and orderly home":** Obama, M. (2018). *Becoming,* p. 60. Crown; **third quote:** Obama, 2018, p. 46.

16. **First quote:** Sherman, 2009, p. 112; **second quote:** Sherman, 2009, p. 110; **third and fourth quotes:** Sherman, 2009, p. 134.

17. **Quote, so little to lose, middle-class vigilance:** Duguid, M. M., & Goncalo, J. A. (2015). Squeezed in the middle: The middle status trade creativity for focus, pp. 589–590. *Journal of Personality and Social Psychology,* 109(4), 589–603. https://doi.org/10.1037/a0039569; Ridgeway, C. L., & Fisk, S. R. (2012). Class rules, status dynamics, and "gateway" interactions, p. 130. In S. T. Fiske & H. R. Markus (Eds.), *Facing social class: How societal rank influences interaction,* pp. 131–151. Russell Sage Foundation.

18. **Quote:** Lamont, 2000, p. 43; **1985 abortion ethnography:** Luker, K. (1985). *Abortion and the politics of motherhood.* University of California Press; **1998 abortion ethnography:** Ginsburg, F. D. (1998). *Contested lives: The abortion debate in an American community.* University of California Press; **33 points more likely:** Majority of public disapproves of Supreme Court's decision to overturn Roe v. Wade. (2022, July 6). Pew Research Center. https://www.pewresearch.org/politics/2022/07/06/majority-of-public-disapproves-of -supreme-courts-decision-to-overturn-roe-v-wade/; **noncollege voters of every race:** Astrow, A. (2022, February 20). How does education level impact attitudes among voters of color? Third Way. https://www.thirdway.org/memo/how-does-education-level-impact -attitudes-among-voters-of-color; **abortion and careers untrue:** Finer, L. B., Frohwirth, L. F., Dauphinee, L. A., Singh, S., & Moore, A. M. (2005). Reasons U.S. women have abortions: Quantitative and qualitative perspectives. *Perspectives on Sexual and Reproductive Health,* 37(3), 110–118. https://doi.org/10.1111/j.1931–2393.2005.tb00045.x.

19. **45 percent of high school or less and 25 percent of postgrads gay marriage:** Borelli, G. (2022, November 15). About six-in-ten Americans say legalization of same-sex marriage is good for society. Pew Research Center. https://www.pewresearch.org/short-reads/2022 /11/15/about-six-in-ten-americans-say-legalization-of-same-sex-marriage-is-good-for -society/.

Chapter 8: Can't People See Through Trump's Truculent Retro Masculinity?

1. **Quote:** Tavernise, S. (2019, May 27). With his job gone, an autoworker wonders, 'what am I as a man?' *The New York Times.* https://www.nytimes.com/2019/05/27/us/auto-worker -jobs-lost.html.

2. **Gender gap:** Norrander, B. (1999). The evolution of the gender gap. *The Public Opinion Quarterly,* 63(4), 566–576. https://doi.org/10.1086/297871; **2024 gender gap:** Exit polls. (2024). CNN. https://www.cnn.com/election/2024/exit-polls/national-results/general /president/0; **quote:** Keil, A. (2020). "We need to rediscover our manliness . . .": The language of gender authenticity in German right-wing populism. *Journal of Language and Politics,* 19(1), 107–124. https://doi.org/10.1075/jlp.19091.kei.

3. **Trump's white noncollege support:** Igielnik et al., 2021, p. 9; **Latino voting in the 2022 midterms:** Hartig, H., Daniller, A., Keeter, S., & Van Green, T. (2023, July 12). Republican gains in 2022 midterms driven mostly by turnout advantage, p. 20. Pew Research Center. https://www.pewresearch.org/politics/2023/07/12/republican-gains-in

-2022-midterms-driven-mostly-by-turnout-advantage/; **2024 election:** Clement, S., Guskin, E., Keating, D., & Ledur, J. (2024, November 8). What the 2024 election tells us about Trump's voters. *The Washington Post.* https://www.washingtonpost.com/poli tics/2024/11/08/trump-voter-demographic-shifts-election/; see also: Robertson, C., & Tesler, M. (2024, December 11). How sexism cost both Biden and Harris votes among Black men. Good Authority. https://goodauthority.org/news/sexism-black-men-voters -2024-election-cost-both-biden-and-harris/.

4. **Northern and Southern men experiment:** Cohen, D., Nisbett, R. E., Bowdle, B. F., & Schwarz, N. (1996). Insult, aggression, and the southern culture of honor: An "experimental ethnography." *Journal of Personality and Social Psychology,* 70(5), 945–960. https://doi.org/10.1037/0022–3514.70.5.945; **"dragon energy":** Muravchik, S., & Shields, J. A. (2020). *Trump's Democrats,* p. 37. Brookings Institution Press; **"the don":** Muravchik & Shields, 2020, p. 69; **public performance:** Bostdorff, D. M. (2023). Donald Trump, Access Hollywood, and the rhetorical performance of aggrieved white masculinity, p. 220. *Western Journal of Communication,* 87(2), 215–238. https://doi.org/10 .1080/10570314.2022.2118549.

5. **Bad-but-bold:** Glick, P., Lameiras, M., Fiske, S. T., Eckes, T., Masser, B., Volpato, C., Manganelli, A. M., Pek, J. C. X., Huang, L.-l., Sakalli-Uğurlu, N., Castro, Y. R., D'Avila Pereira, M. L., Willemsen, T. M., Brunner, A., Six-Materna, I., & Wells, R. (2004). Bad but bold: Ambivalent attitudes toward men predict gender inequality in 16 nations. *Journal of Personality and Social Psychology,* 86(5), 713–728. https://doi.org/10.1037/0022–3514 .86.5.713; **taking on political correctness:** Dignam, P., Schrock, D., Erichsen, K., & Dowd-Arrow, B. (2021). Valorizing Trump's masculine self: Constructing political allegiance during the 2016 presidential election. *Men and Masculinities,* 24(3), 367–392. https://doi.org/10.1177 /1097184X19873692; **first quote:** Graham, R., & Homans, C. (2024, January 10). Trump is connecting with a different type of evangelical voter. *The New York Times.* https://www .nytimes.com/2024/01/08/us/politics/donald-trump-evangelicals-iowa.html; **Fox News emotional connection:** Peck, R. (2019). *Fox populism: Branding conservatism as working class.* Cambridge University Press. https://doi.org/10.1017/9781108634410; **second quote:** Peck, R. (2023). Comparing populist media: From Fox News to The Young Turks, from cable to YouTube, from right to left. *Television & New Media,* 24(6), 599–615. https:// doi.org/10.1177/15274764221114349.

6. **First quote:** Dignam et al., 2021, p. 368; **second quote:** Peck, 2019, p. 11; **young men trust Trump:** Barker, G., Hayes, C., Heilman, B., & Reichert, M. (2023). The state of American men: From crisis and confusion to hope, p. 34. Equimundo. https://www .equimundo.org/resources/state-of-american-men/.

7. **Quote:** Otis, J. (2022, August 13). Brazil's firearm ownership booms, and gun laws loosen, under President Bolsonaro. NPR. https://www.npr.org/2022/08/13/1116989125/brazil -firearm-ownership-booms-gun-laws-loosen-bolsonaro.

8. **First quote:** Dutta, S., & Abbas, T. (2024). Protecting the people: populism and masculine security in India and Hungary, p. 2. *Journal of Political Ideologies,* 1–23. https://doi.org/10 .1080/13569317.2024.2337181; **second quote:** Edsall, T. B. (2021, September 22). "It's become increasingly hard for them to feel good about themselves." *The New York Times.* https://www.nytimes.com/2021/09/22/opinion/economy-education-women-men.html.

9. **Hostile sexism second only to orientation:** Glick, P. (2019). Gender, sexism, and the election: Did sexism help Trump more than it hurt Clinton? *Politics, Groups, and Identities,* 7(3), 713–723. https://doi.org/10.1080/21565503.2019.1633931; **hostile sexism Latinos:** 2020 post-mortem part two: The American Dream voter. (2021, December 14). Equis. https://assets.ctfassets.net/ms6ec8hcu35u/4E5a5nNoWi9JNFqeAylkmS/b f542d82f900dbfb62cc6e6d7253a24a/Post-Mortem_Part_Two_FINAL_Dec_14.pdf; **hegemonic masculinity:** Schermerhorn, N. E., Vescio, T. K., & Lewis, K. A. (2023).

Hegemonic masculinity predicts support for U.S. political figures accused of sexual assault. *Social Psychological and Personality Science*, 14(5), 475–486. https://doi.org/10.1177/19485506221077861; **hostile sexism Trump voting:** Bock, J., Byrd-Craven, J., & Burkley, M. (2017). The role of sexism in voting in the 2016 presidential election. *Personality and Individual Differences*, 119, 189–193. https://doi.org/10.1016/j.paid.2017.07.026; **quote:** Miller, C. C., & Gupta, A. H. (2020, November 3). What makes a man manly? Trump and Biden offer competing answers. *The New York Times*. https://www.nytimes.com/2020/10/30/upshot/trump-biden-masculinity-fatherhood.html.

10. **Quote:** Brooks, D. (2022, September 29). The crisis of men and boys. *The New York Times*. https://www.nytimes.com/2022/09/29/opinion/crisis-men-masculinity.html; **male despair deaths:** Emba, C. (2023, July 10). Men are lost. Here's a map out of the wilderness. *The Washington Post*. https://www.washingtonpost.com/opinions/2023/07/10/christine-emba-masculinity-new-model/; **four key components of manhood:** Townsend, N. (2002). *Package deal: Marriage, work and fatherhood in men's lives.* Temple University Press; **expressing masculinity when threatened:** Fowler, S. L., & Geers, A. L. (2017). Does trait masculinity relate to expressing toughness? The effects of masculinity threat and self-affirmation in college men. *Psychology of Men & Masculinity*, 18(2), 176–186. https://doi.org/10.1037/men0000053.

11. **First quote:** Gidron, N., & Hall, P. A. (2017). The politics of social status: Economic and cultural roots of the populist right, p. S66. *The British Journal of Sociology*, 68(S1), S57–S84. https://doi.org/10.1111/1468-4446.12319; **second quote:** Bourdieu, P. (1984). *Distinction: A social critique on the judgment of taste* (R. Nice, Trans.), p. 384. Harvard University Press. (Original work published 1979); **hypermasculine ethos:** Embrick, D. G., Walther, C. S., & Wickens, C. M. (2007). Working class masculinity: Keeping gay men and lesbians out of the workplace. *Sex Roles*, 56, 757–766. https://doi.org/10.1007/s11199-007-9234-0; **"hidden injuries of class":** Sennett, R., & Cobb, J. (1972). *The hidden injuries of class.* Knopf; **"men should be men":** Bracic, A., Israel-Trummel, M., & Shortle, A. F. (2019). Is sexism for white people? Gender stereotypes, race, and the 2016 presidential election. *Political Behavior*, 41(2), 281–307. https://doi.org/10.1007/s11109-018-9446-8.

12. **Unemployed husbands:** Willer, R., Rogalin, C. L., Conlon, B., Wojnowicz, M. T. (2013). Overdoing gender: A test of the masculine overcompensation thesis. *American Journal of Sociology*, 118(4), 980–1022. https://doi.org/10.1086/668417; **husbands earning less:** MacMillan, R., & Gartner, R. (1999). When she brings home the bacon: Labor-force participation and the risk of spousal violence against women. *Journal of Marriage and the Family*, 61(4), 947–958. https://doi.org/10.2307/354015; McCloskey, L. A. (1996). Socioeconomic and coercive power within the family. *Gender & Society*, 10(4), 449–463. https://www.jstor.org/stable/189681; **men do less housework:** Brines, J. (1994). Economic dependency, gender, and the division of labor at home. *American Journal of Sociology*, 100(3), 652–688. https://www.jstor.org/stable/2782401; **sexual harassment:** Maass, A., Cadinu, M., Guarnieri, G., & Grasselli, A. (2003). Sexual harassment under social identity threat: The computer harassment paradigm. *Journal of Personality and Social Psychology*, 85(5), 853–870. https://doi.org/10.1037/0022-3514.85.5.853; **identities threatened:** Willer et al., 2013.

13. **Feel more praised:** Barker et al., 2023, p. 36; **manhood is earned:** Vandello, J. A., Bosson, J. K., Cohen, D., Burnaford, R. M., & Weaver, J. R. (2008). Precarious manhood. *Journal of Personality and Social Psychology*, 95(6), 1325–1339. https://doi.org/10.1037/a0012453; **statuses of men and women in the US and Europe:** Gidron & Hall, 2017, p. S75; **quote:** Gidron & Hall, 2017, p. S57; **Susan Faludi:** Faludi, S. (1999). *Stiffed: The roots of modern male rage.* HarperCollins; **signaled precarious masculinity:** DiMuccio, S. H., & Knowles, E. D. (2021). Precarious manhood predicts support for aggressive policies and

politicians. *Personality and Social Psychology Bulletin*, 47(7), 1169–1187. https://doi.org/10 .1177/0146167220963577.

14. **First quote:** Lamont, M. (2000). *The dignity of working men: Morality and the boundaries of race, class, and immigration*, p. 34. Harvard University Press; **second quote:** Sherman, J. (2009). *Those who work, those who don't: Poverty, morality, and family in rural America*, p. 152. University of Minnesota Press; **"privilege men's employment," "division of labor":** Yavorsky, J. E., Keister, L. A., Qian, Y., & Thébaud, S. (2023). Separate spheres: The gender division of labor in the financial elite, p. 625. *Social Forces*, 102(2), 609–632. https://doi .org/10.1093/sf/soad061.

15. **Obama's mother:** Obama, M. (2018). *Becoming*, p. 45. Crown; **59 percent grew up with homemaker moms, quote:** Sherman, 2009, p. 60.

16. **Three-fourths of Americans:** Parker, K., & Stepler, R. (2017, September 20). Americans see men as the financial providers, even as women's contributions grow. Pew Research Center. https://www.pewresearch.org/short-reads/2017/09/20/americans-see-men -as-the-financial-providers-even-as-womens-contributions-grow/; **"one parent" stays home:** Smith, M. (2023, May 9). Women are now out-earning or making the same as their husbands in nearly half of marriages. CNBC. https://www.cnbc.com/2023/04 /20/more-women-are-out-earning-their-husbands-in-the-us.html; **quotes:** Legerski, E. M., & Cornwall, M. (2010). Working-class job loss, gender, and the negotiation of household labor, p. 464. *Gender & Society*, 24(4), 447–474. https://doi.org/10.1177 /0891243210374600; **elite women earn less:** Carbone, J., & Cahn, N. (2014). *Marriage markets: How inequality is remaking the American family*, p. 66. Oxford University Press.

17. **Women and blue-collar jobs:** Liu, Y., Trueblood, A. B., Yohannes, T., Brooks, R. D., Harris, W., West, G. H., & Memarian, B. (2023, May). Women in construction: Employment, business owner, and injury trends, p. 2. The Center for Construction and Research Training, Centers for Disease Control and Prevention. https://stacks.cdc.gov/view/cdc/128163.

18. **Providing:** Lamont, 2000, p. 21; **quote:** Lamont, M., Park, B. Y., & Ayala-Hurtado, E. (2017, November 8). What Trump's campaign speeches show about his lasting appeal to the white working class. *Harvard Business Review*. https://hbr.org/2017/11/what-trumps -campaign-speeches-show-about-his-lasting-appeal-to-the-white-working-class.

19. **Quotes:** Rubin, L. B. (1994). *Families on the fault line: America's working class speaks about the family, the economy, race, and ethnicity*, pp. 94, 96–97. HarperCollins; **divorce rate:** Shulman, B. (2003). *The betrayal of work: How low-wage jobs fail 30 million Americans*, p. 37. The New Press.

20. **Hobbies, first and second quotes:** Sherman, 2009, pp. 66–67; **deer meat:** Sherman, 2009, p. 96; **men on disability, third quote:** Sherman, 2009, pp. 69–70; **fourth quote:** Smialek, J. (2021, February 4). Toll worker job losses highlight long-term fallout of pandemic. *The New York Times*. https://www.nytimes.com/2021/02/04/business/economy/toll-workers -layoffs-coronavirus.html.

21. **Quote:** Sherman, 2009, p. 69.

22. **Being a protector:** Lamont, 2000, p. 21; **victim of violent crime:** Economist/YouGov Poll. (2021, September). YouGov. https://d3nkl3psvxxpe9.cloudfront.net/documents /econTabReport_RNOZtwi.pdf.

23. **Quotes:** Lamont, 2000, pp. 32–33.

24. **Quote:** Grose, J. (2023, February 15). Are men the overlooked reason for the fertility decline? *The New York Times*. https://www.nytimes.com/2023/02/15/opinion/fertility -decline.html; **prefer women earning less:** Greitemeyer, T. (2007). What do men and women want in a partner? Are educated partners always more desirable? *Journal of Experimental Social Psychology*, 43(2), 180–194. https://doi.org/10.1016/j.jesp.2006.02.006.

25. **Quote:** Martin, R. (2016, November 13). Feeling left behind, white working-class voters turned out for Trump. NPR. https://www.npr.org/2016/11/13/501904167/feeling-left

-behind-white-working-class-voters-turned-out-for-trump; **more marital tension:** Carbone & Cahn, 2014, p. 100.

26. **Falling earnings tied to falling marriage rates:** Reeves, R. V. (2022). *Of boys and men: Why the modern male is struggling, why it matters, and what to do about it*, p. 65. Brookings Institution Press; **Black marriage rates, women not marrying:** Wilson, W. J. (1996). *When work disappears: The world of the new urban poor*, pp. 94–96. Knopf; **living with parents not wives:** Brooks, 2022; **childless men:** Grose, 2023.

27. **Cost of pre-K:** Clark, C. (2023, August 29). Is preschool free? Here's what you need to know. Tinybeans. https://tinybeans.com/is-preschool-free-united-states/.

28. **Real wage growth:** Weinstein, A. L. (2017). Working women in the city and urban wage growth in the United States, p. 604. *Journal of Regional Science*, 57(4), 591–610. https://doi.org/10.1111/jors.12336.

Chapter 9: Doesn't the Diploma Divide Just Reflect "Grievance Politics"?

1. **Quote:** Bierman, N., Mascaro, L. (2016, February 16). Donald Trump supporter in South Carolina: "We're voting with our middle finger." *Los Angeles Times*. https://www.latimes.com/local/lanow/la-na-trump-south-carolina-20160216-story.html.

2. **Rage in the face of injustice:** Friedrich, J. (2024). The bellwether of oppression: Anger, critique, and resistance. https://www.cambridge.org/core/journals/hypatia/article/bellwether-of-oppression-anger-critique-and-resistance/DF30CB83597D6CC098AE5CF930BC2ECB; **discounted as "grievance":** Farrell, J. A. (2020, April 16). Breaking the grip of white grievance. *The New Republic*. https://newrepublic.com/article/157173/2020-election-referendum-trumpism-white-grievance-politics.

3. **Assertive not angry:** Livingston, R. W., Rosette, A. S., & Washington, E. F. (2012). Can an agentic Black woman get ahead? The impact of race and interpersonal dominance on perceptions of female leaders. *Psychological Science*, 23(4), 354–358. https://doi.org/10.1177/0956797611428079.

4. **Submissive and deferential:** Berdahl, J. L., & Min, J. A. (2012). Prescriptive stereotypes and workplace consequences for East Asians in North America, p. 141. *Cultural Diversity and Ethnic Minority Psychology*, 18(2), 141–152. https://doi.org/10.1037/a0027692.

5. **First quote:** Fiske, S. T. (2011). *Envy up, scorn down: How status divides us*, p. 13. Russell Sage Foundation; **second quote:** Fiske, 2011, p. 15; **third quote:** Fiske, 2011, pp. 17–18; **read facial expressions:** Galinsky, A. D., Magee, J. C., Inesi, M. E., & Gruenfeld, D. H. (2006). Power and perspectives not taken. *Psychological Science*, 17(12), 1068–1074. https://doi.org/10.1111/j.1467-9280.2006.01824.x; **fourth quote:** Fiske, 2011, p. 21; **fifth quote:** Fiske, 2011, p. 24.

6. **Status by race:** Fiske, 2011, p. 49; **race, class, status, and competence, see also:** Fiske, S. T., Cuddy, A. J. C., Glick, P., & Xu, J. (2002). A model of (often mixed) stereotype content: Competence and warmth respectively follow from perceived status and competition. *Journal of Personality and Social Psychology*, 82(6), 878–902. https://doi.org/10.1037/0022-3514.82.6.878.

7. **Letters:** Kavesh, R., Milsap, R., & Schwartz, D. S. (2024, September 14). How Democrats treat Trumpites [letters to the editor]. *The New York Times*. https://www.nytimes.com/2024/09/14/opinion/democrats-donald-trump-voters.html; **Trump supporters stupid:** [@Riverrat423]. (2023, October 14). Do you ever feel your opinion of someone instantly decline when they talk about how they support Donald Trump? [online forum post] Reddit. https://www.reddit.com/r/TooAfraidToAsk/comments/1777h24/do_you_ever_feel_your_opinion_of_someone/; **Trump supporters racist:** [@Overall-Put-1165]. (2024, January 18). CMV: The MAGA crowd is a cult full of hate [online forum post]. Reddit. https://www.reddit.com/r/changemyview/comments/199unuw/cmv_the_maga_crowd_is_a_cult_full_of_hate/; **T-shirt:** Racist crazy fraud moron stupid Trump anti

Trump t-shirt. (n.d.). Amazon. Accessed June 27, 2024, from https://www.amazon.com /Racist-Crazy-Stupid-Trump-T-Shirt/dp/B07F29RGNF.

8. **Quote:** Wray, M. (2006). *Not quite white: White trash and the boundaries of whiteness*, p. 39. Duke University Press; **"deplorables":** Chozick, A. (2016, September 10). Hillary Clinton calls many Trump backers "deplorables," and G.O.P. pounces. *The New York Times.* https://www.nytimes.com/2016/09/11/us/politics/hillary-clinton-basket-of-deplorables .html; **guns and religion:** Smith, B. (2008, April 11). Obama on small-town Pa.: Clinging to religion, guns, xenophobia. *Politico.* https://www.politico.com/blogs/ben-smith /2008/04/obama-on-small-town-pa-clinging-to-religion-guns-xenophobia-007737; **Reece Peck:** Peck, R. (2019). *Fox populism: Branding conservatism as working class.* Cambridge University Press. https://doi.org/10.1017/9781108634410; **Anthony Nadler:** Nadler, A. M., & Bauer, J. (2020). *News on the right: Studying conservative news cultures.* Oxford University Press.

9. **First and second quote:** Ehrenreich, B. (2015, December 1). Barbara Ehrenreich: Dead, white, and blue. *Guernica.* https://www.guernicamag.com/barbara-ehrenreich-dead-white -and-blue/; **third quote:** Fiske, 2011, p. 151 (quoting Margaret Canovan).

10. **Quote:** MacGillis, A., & ProPublica. (2016, September). The original underclass. *The Atlantic.* https://www.theatlantic.com/magazine/archive/2016/09/the-original-underclass /492731/; **"deep story":** Hochschild, 2016.

11. **Quote:** Hochschild, 2016, pp. 136–137.

12. **Black-white wealth gap:** Gerstle, G. (2022). *The rise and fall of the neoliberal order: America and the world in the free market era*, pp. 234–235. Oxford University Press.

13. **Parents and grandparents:** Cherlin, A. J. (2016, February 22). Why are white death rates rising? *The New York Times.* https://www.nytimes.com/2016/02/22/opinion/why-are -white-death-rates-rising.html; **first quote:** Edin, K., Nelson, T., Cherlin, A., & Francis, R. (2019). The tenuous attachments of working-class men, p. 223. *Journal of Economic Perspectives*, 33(2), 211–228. https://doi.org/10.1257/jep.33.2.211; **household incomes:** Monnat, S. M., & Brown, D. L. (2017). More than a rural revolt: Landscapes of despair and the 2016 presidential election, p. 229. *Journal of Rural Studies*, 55, 227–236. https://doi.org/10.1016/j.jrurstud.2017.08.010; **second quote:** Boudette, N. E. (2023, November 9). "Our family can have a future": Ford workers on a new union contract. *The New York Times.* https://www.nytimes.com/2023/11/09/business/economy/ford-strike -wayne-michigan.html.

14. **Distress doubled:** Blanchflower, D. G., & Oswald, A. J. (2020). Trends in extreme distress in the United States, 1993–2019, p. 1538. *American Journal of Public Health*, 110(10), 1538–1544. https://doi.org/10.2105/AJPH.2020.305811; **physical pain:** Blanchflower, D. G., & Oswald, A. J. (2019). Unhappiness and pain in modern America: A review essay, and further evidence, on Carol Graham's Happiness for All?, pp. 390–391. *Journal of Economic Literature*, 57(2), 385–402. https://doi.org/10.1257/jel.20171492; **opioid deaths and employment loss:** McGranahan, D. A., & Parker, T. S. (2021). The opioid epidemic: A geography in two phases, p. 27. US Department of Agriculture Economic Research Service. https://www.ers.usda.gov/webdocs/publications/100833/err-287.pdf; **noncollege overdose deaths:** Powell, D. (2023). Educational attainment and US drug overdose deaths, p. 1. *JAMA Health Forum*, 4(10), e233274. https://doi.org/10.1001%2Fjamahealthforum .2023.3274.

15. **Happiness gap:** Blanchflower & Oswald, 2019, p. 385; **income satisfaction gap:** Blanchflower & Oswald, 2019, pp. 395, 397; **definition of success:** Lamont, M. (2000). *The dignity of working men: Morality and the boundaries of race, class, and immigration*, p. 28. Harvard University Press; **suicide rates:** Curtin, S. C., Brown, K. A., & Jordan, M. E. (2022). Suicide rates for the three leading methods by race and ethnicity: United States, 2000–2020. NCHS Data Brief, 450. https://www.cdc.gov/nchs/products/databriefs /db450.htm.

16. **First quote:** Prasad, M., Hoffman, S. G., & Bezila, K. (2016). Walking the line: The white working class and the economic consequences of morality, p. 294. *Politics & Society*, 44(2), 281–304. https://doi.org/10.1177/0032329216638062; **second and third quotes:** Tavernise, S. (2019, May 27). With his job gone, an autoworker wonders, "what am I as a man?" *The New York Times.* https://www.nytimes.com/2019/05/27/us/auto-worker-jobs -lost.html; **fourth quote:** McDermott, M. (2006). *Working-class white: The making and unmaking of race relations*, p. 149. University of California Press.

17. **Drug, alcohol, and suicide deaths:** Case, A., & Deaton, A. (2022). The great divide: Education, despair and death, p. 2. *Annual Review of Economics*, 14, 1–21. https://doi.org /10.1146/annurev-economics-051520–015607; **post-recession increase:** Case & Deaton, 2022, p. 16; **first quote:** Mounk, Y. (2023, October 4). Nothing defines America's social divide like a college education. *The Atlantic.* https://www.theatlantic.com/ideas/archive /2023/10/education-inequality-economic-opportunities-college/675536/; **second quote:** Monnat & Brown, 2017, p. 229.

18. **Disruptive behavior and suspensions:** Bertrand, M., & Pan, J. (2013). The trouble with boys: Social influences and the gender gap in disruptive behavior, pp. 60–61. *American Economic Journal: Applied Economics*, 5(1), 32–64. https://www.jstor.org/stable/43189418; **single motherhood:** Carbone, J., & Cahn, N. (2014). *Marriage markets: How inequality is remaking the American family*, p. 17. Oxford University Press; **quote:** Autor, D., & Wasserman, M. (2013). Wayward sons: The emerging gender gap in labor markets and education, p. 50. Third Way. https://www.thirdway.org/report/wayward-sons-the-emerging-gender -gap-in-labor-markets-and-education.

19. **Quote:** Bettie, J. (2003). *Women without class: Girls, race, and identity*, p. 168. University of California Press.

20. **Distress rose steadily:** Blanchflower & Oswald, 2020, p. 1540; **happiness:** Trends: General happiness (General Social Survey). (n.d.). National Opinion Research Center (NORC). Accessed January 24, 2024, from https://gssdataexplorer.norc.org/trends ?category=Gender%20%26%20Marriage&measure=happy; **optimism:** Graham, C., & Pinto, S. (2019). Unequal hopes and lives in the USA: Optimism, race, place, and premature mortality. *Journal of Population Economics*, 32(2), 665–733. https://doi.org/10.1007 /s00148-018-0687-y.

21. **Trump performed better:** Monnat & Brown, 2017, P. 805–808; **nonwhite noncollege despair deaths:** Case & Deaton, 2022, p. 2.

22. **"Grip of white grievance":** Farrell, 2020.

Chapter 10: How Can I Respect People Who Deny Facts and Science?

1. **Quote:** Hands Across the Hills. (2021, April 7). *Guns, coal, vaccines, and abortion: East KY meets western MA* [video]. *YouTube.* https://www.youtube.com/watch?v=dVe-O9–6gko.

2. **Anti-intellectualism:** Hofstadter, R. (1966). *Anti-intellectualism in American life.* Vintage; **character flaw:** Hofstadter, R. (1964, November). The paranoid style in American politics. *Harper's Magazine.* https://harpers.org/archive/1964/11/the-paranoid-style-in -american-politics/; **first quote:** Sandel, M. (2020). *The tyranny of merit: What's become of the common good?*, p. 73. Farrar, Straus, and Giroux; **second quote:** Vanneman, R., & Cannon, L. W. (1987). *The American perception of class*, p. 79. Temple University Press. https:// doi.org/10.2307/j.ctv941wv0; **common sense of ordinary people:** Cross-tabs: July 2023 Times/Siena poll of the 2024 race and national issues. (2023, August 1). *The New York Times.* https://www.nytimes.com/interactive/2023/07/31/us/elections/times-siena-poll -republican-primary-crosstabs.html.

3. **First quote:** Sample, T. (2006). *Blue collar resistance and the politics of Jesus: Doing ministry with working class whites*, p. 61. Abingdon Press; **second quote:** Vanneman & Cannon, 1987, p. 65.

4. **First quote:** Calarco, J. M. (2018). *Negotiating opportunities: How the middle class secures*

advantages in school, p. 3. Oxford University Press; **second quote:** Carr, P. J., & Kefalas, M. J. (2009). *Hollowing out the middle: The rural brain drain and what it means for America*, p. 163. Beacon Press; **elicit help:** Calarco, 2018, p. 3. **third quote:** Bettie, J. (2003). *Women without class: Girls, race, and identity*, p. 108. University of California Press; **predict school performance:** Calarco, 2018, p. 3.

5. **"Agency capture":** Gerstle, G. (2022). *The rise and fall of the neoliberal order: America and the world in the free market era*, p. 159. Oxford University Press; **second quote:** Cramer, K. J. (2016). *The politics of resentment: Rural consciousness and the rise of Scott Walker*, p. 129. University of Chicago Press.

6. **Quote:** Hochschild, A. R. (2016). *Strangers in their own land: Anger and mourning on the American right*, p. 43. The New Press.

7. **Less likely to consistently wear masks:** Cassino, D., & Besen-Cassino, Y. (2020). Of masks and men? Gender, sex, and protective measures during COVID-19. *Politics & Gender*, 16(4), 1052–1062. https://doi.org/10.1017/S1743923X20000616; **1.5 times less likely:** Haischer, M. H., Beilfuss, R., Hart, M. R., Opielinski, L., Wrucke, D., Zirgaitis, G., Uhrich, T. D., & Hunter, S. K. (2020). Who is wearing a mask? Gender-, age-, and location-related differences during the COVID-19 pandemic. *PloS one*, 15(10), e0240785. https://doi.org/10.1371/journal.pone.0240785; **first quote:** North, A. (2020, May 12). What Trump's refusal to wear a mask says about masculinity in America. Vox. Retrieved July 15, 2022, from https://www.vox.com/2020/5/12/21252476/masks-for-coronavirus -trump-pence-honeywell-covid-19; **same pattern with vaccines:** Cassino & Besen-Cassino, 2020, p. 1056; **"show no weakness":** Berdahl, J. L., Copper, M., Glick, P., Livingston, R. W., & Williams, J. C. (2018, September 13). Work as a masculinity contest, p. 433. *Journal of Social Issues*, 74 (3), 422–448. https://doi.org/10.1111/josi.12289; **second quote:** Glick, P. (2020, April 30). Masks and emasculation: Why some men refuse to take safety precautions. *Scientific American* Blog Network. https://blogs.scientificamerican .com/observations/masks-and-emasculation-why-some-men-refuse-to-take-safety -precautions/; **third quote:** Victor, D. (2021, January 20). Coronavirus safety runs into a stubborn barrier: Masculinity. *The New York Times*. https://www.nytimes.com/2020/10 /10/us/politics/trump-biden-masks-masculinity.html.

8. **Feel talked down to:** Lunz Trujillo, K. (2022). Rural identity as a contributing factor to anti-intellectualism in the U.S. *Political Behavior*, 44, 1509–1532. https://doi.org/10 .1007/s11109-022-09770-w; **share their values:** Evans, J. H., & Hargittai, E. (2020). Who doesn't trust Fauci? The public's belief in the expertise and shared values of scientists in the COVID-19 pandemic. *Socius*, 6, 2378023120947337. https://doi.org/10.1177 /2378023120947337.

9. **Shared false information:** Littrell, S., Klofstad, C., Diekman, A., Funchion, J., Murthi, M., Premaratne, K., Seelig, M., Verdear, D., Wuchty, S., & Uscinski, J. E. (2023, August 25). Who knowingly shares false political information online? *Harvard Kennedy Schools Misinformation Review*. https://misinforeview.hks.harvard.edu/article/who-knowingly -shares-false-political-information-online/; **quote:** Littrell et al., 2023, p. 4; **14 percent of respondents:** Littrell et al., 2023, p. 5.

10. **First quote:** Jetten, J., Peters, K., & Casara, B. G. S. (2022). Economic inequality and conspiracy theories, p. 1. *Current Opinion in Psychology*, 47, 101358. https://doi.org/10.1016/j .copsyc.2022.101358; **populist anti-elitism:** Christner, C. (2022). Populist attitudes and conspiracy beliefs: Exploring the relation between the latent structures of populist attitudes and conspiracy beliefs. *Journal of Social and Political Psychology*, 10(1), 72–85. https:// doi.org/10.5964/jspp.7969; **conspiracy index:** Cordonier, L., Cafiero, F., & Bronner, G. (2021). Why are conspiracy theories more successful in some countries than in others? An exploratory study on internet uses from 22 Western and non-Western countries. *Social Science Information*, 60(3), 436–456. https://doi.org/10.1177/05390184211018961.

11. **Institutions:** van Prooijen, J. W., Spadaro, G., & Wang, H. (2022). Suspicion of insti-

tutions: How distrust and conspiracy theories deteriorate social relationships. *Current Opinion in Psychology,* 43, 65–69. https://doi.org/10.1016/j.copsyc.2021.06.013; **support for democracy:** Papaioannou, K., Pantazi, M., & van Prooijen, J. W. (2023). Is democracy under threat? Why belief in conspiracy theories predicts autocratic attitudes. *European Journal of Social Psychology,* 53(5), 846–856. https://doi.org/10.1002/ejsp.2939; **authoritarian values:** Hogg, M. A. (2021). Uncertain self in a changing world: A foundation for radicalisation, populism, and autocratic leadership. *European Review of Social Psychology,* 32(2), 235–268. https://doi.org/10.1080/10463283.2020.1827628; **strong leader:** Sprong, S., Jetten, J., Wang, Z., Peters, K., Mols, F., Verkuyten, M., Bastian, B., Ariyanto, A., Autin, F., Ayub, N., Badea, C., Besta, T., Butera, F., Costa-Lopes, R., Cui, L., Fantini, C., Finchilescu, G., Gaertner, L., Gollwitzer, M., . . . & Wohl, M. J. A. (2019): "Our country needs a strong leader right now": Economic inequality enhances the wish for a strong leader. *Psychological Science,* 30(11), 1625–1637. https://doi.org/10.1177/0956797619875472.

12. **First quote:** Klein, E. (Host). (2022, February 25). Are we measuring our lives in all the wrong ways? [Audio Podcast Episode]. In *The Ezra Klein Show. The New York Times.* https://www.nytimes.com/2022/02/25/podcasts/transcript-ezra-klein-interviews-c-thi-nguyen.html; **second quote:** Jetten et al., 2022, p. 2; **third quote:** Jetten et al., 2022, p. 3; **fourth quote:** van Prooijen, J. M. (2022). Psychological benefits of believing conspiracy theories, p. 1. *Current Opinion in Psychology,* 47, 101352. https://doi.org/10.1016/j.copsyc.2022.101352.

13. **Powerlessness and lack of status:** Douglas, K. M., Uscinski, J. E., Sutton, R. M., Cichocka, A., Nefes, T., Ang, C. S., & Deravi, F. (2019). Understanding conspiracy theories. *Political Psychology,* 40(S1), 3–35. https://doi.org/10.1111/pops.12568; **first quote:** van Prooijen, J. W. (2016). Why education predicts decreased belief in conspiracy theories, p. 50. *Applied Cognitive Psychology,* 31(1), 50–58. https://doi.org/10.1002/acp.3301; **second quote:** Markovits, D. (2019). *The meritocracy trap: How America's foundational myth feeds inequality, dismantles the middle class and devours the elite,* pp. xvi–xvii. Penguin Press; **third quote:** Cramer, 2016, p. 81.

14. **Reassuring structure:** Nguyen, C. T. (2020). *Games: Agency as art.* Oxford University Press; **points and control:** Klein, E. (Host). (2022, February 25). Are we measuring our lives in all the wrong ways? [audio podcast episode]. In The Ezra Klein Show. *The New York Times.* https://www.nytimes.com/2022/02/25/podcasts/transcript-ezra-klein-interviews-c-thi-nguyen.html.

15. **Quote:** French, D. (2023, July 6). The rage and joy of MAGA America. *The New York Times.* https://www.nytimes.com/2023/07/06/opinion/maga-america-trump.html.

16. **Quote:** Egger, A. (2020, June 11). For Trump superfans, huge rallies can't resume soon enough. The Dispatch. https://thedispatch.com/article/for-trump-superfans-huge-rallies/; **Trump is "fun":** French, 2023.

17. **Quote:** van Prooijen, 2022, p. 3.

18. **Quote:** Oliver, J. E., & Wood, T. J. (2014). Conspiracy theories and the paranoid style(s) of mass opinion, p. 952. *American Journal of Political Science,* 58(4), 952–966. https://doi.org/10.1111/ajps.12084.

19. **Trust in institutions:** Saad, L. (2023, July 6). Historically low faith in U.S. institutions continues. Gallup. https://news.gallup.com/poll/508169/historically-low-faith-institutions-continues.aspx.

20. **Quote:** Smallpage, S. M., Enders, A. M., & Uscinski, J. E. (2017). The partisan contours of conspiracy theory beliefs, p. 1. *Research & Politics,* 4(4), 1–7. https://doi.org/10.1177/2053168017746554; **Stop the Steal:** Agiesta, J., & Edwards-Levy, A. (2023, August 3). CNN poll: Percentage of Republicans who think Biden's 2020 win was illegitimate ticks back up near 70%. CNN. https://www.cnn.com/2023/08/03/politics/cnn-poll-republicans-think-2020-election-illegitimate/index.html; **"seriously but not literally":**

Zito, S. (2016, September 23). Taking Trump seriously, not literally. *The Atlantic*. https://www.theatlantic.com/politics/archive/2016/09/trump-makes-his-case-in-pittsburgh/501335/; **Sanders rigged economy:** Sanders, B. [@BernieSanders]. (2019, January 9). "This is what a rigged economy is all about. We must work to transform American society by making our political and economic systems work for all of us, not just the 1 percent" [tweet]. Twitter. https://twitter.com/BernieSanders/status/1083079711259951104; **anti-elites agreed:** Ekins, E. (2017, June). The five types of Trump voters: Who they are and what they believe. Democracy Fund Voter Study Group. https://www.voterstudygroup.org/publication/the-five-types-trump-voters.

21. **Quote:** Mason, L. (2018). *Uncivil agreement: How politics became our identity*, p. 4. University of Chicago Press.

22. **Tribe more powerful than facts:** Mason, 2018, p. 4; **quote:** MacGillis, A. (2016, November 10). Revenge of the forgotten class. ProPublica. https://www.propublica.org/article/revenge-of-the-forgotten-class.

Part III: What's the Matter with Cambridge?

1. **Quote:** Ridgeway, C. L., & Fisk, S. R. (2012). Class rules, status dynamics, and "gateway" interactions, p. 139. In S. T. Fiske & H. R. Markus (Eds.), *Facing social class: How societal rank influences interaction*, pp. 131–151. Russell Sage Foundation.

2. **First quote:** Skeggs, B. (2005). The re-branding of class: Propertising culture, p. 64. In F. Devine, M. Savage, R. Crompton, & J. Scott (Eds.), *Rethinking class: Cultures, identities, and lifestyles*, pp. 46–68. Palgrave Macmillan; **second quote:** Gray, B., & Kish-Gephart, J. J. (2013). Encountering social class differences at work: How "class work" perpetuates inequality, p. 680. *Academy of Management Review*, 38(4), 670–699. https://doi.org/10.5465/amr.2012.0143; **third quote:** Gray & Kish-Gephart, 2013, p. 679; **"I only have," "not that rich":** Stuber, J. M. (2010). Class dismissed? The social-class worldviews of privileged college students, p. 134. In A. Howard & R. A. Gaztambide-Fernandez, *Educating elites: Class privilege and educational advantage*, pp. 131–152. Rowman & Littlefield.

3. **"Double consciousness":** Du Bois, W. E. B. (2008). *The souls of Black folk* (B. H. Edwards, Ed.). Oxford University Press. (Original work published 1903).

Chapter 11: Smart People Get Ahead; Isn't That Just the Reality?

1. **Challenger School:** Challenger School: Mission and philosophy. (n.d.). Challenger School. Accessed July 2, 2024, from https://www.challengerschool.com/philosophy.

2. **Anxiety and depression:** Luthar, S. S., & Latendresse, S. J. (2005). Children of the affluent: Challenges to well-being. *Current Directions in Psychological Science*, 14(1), 49–53. https://doi.org/10.1111/j.0963-7214.2005.00333.x; **major depressive episode:** Peterson, C. (2006). *A primer in positive psychology*, p. 84. Oxford University Press.

3. **Villain:** The history of the word "villain." (n.d.). Merriam-Webster Dictionary. Accessed January 24, 2024, from https://www.merriam-webster.com/wordplay/the-villain-in-the-history-of-the-word-villain-isnt-the-villain; **mean:** Mean. (n.d.). Online Etymology Dictionary. Accessed January 24, 2024, from https://www.etymonline.com/word/mean; **poor:** Poor. (n.d.). Online Etymology Dictionary. Accessed January 24, 2024, from https://www.etymonline.com/search?q=poor; **class act:** Class act. (n.d.). Merriam-Webster Dictionary. Accessed January 24, 2024, from https://www.merriam-webster.com/dictionary/class%20act#dictionary-entry-1.

4. **Meritocracy as derision:** Young, M. (1958). *The rise of the meritocracy*. Thames and Hudson.

5. **Obama and smartness:** Sandel, M. (2020). *The tyranny of merit: What's become of the common good?*, p. 107. Farrar, Straus, and Giroux; **"bending the cost curve":** Sandel, 2020, p. 106; **"incentivizing" development:** Sandel, 2020, p. 107.

6. **First quote:** Sandel, 2020, p. 86; **second quote:** Sandel, 2020, p. 87; **third quote:** Suskind, R. (2012). *Confidence men: Wall Street, Washington and the education of a president*, p. 197.

Harper Perennial; **fourth quote:** Frank, T. (2017). *Listen, liberal: Or, what ever happened to the party of the people?*, pp. 34–35. Metropolitan Books; **co-opting the share:** Sandel, 2020, p. 88; **fifth quote:** Roush, T. (2024, August 21). Here's Barack Obama's speech at the DNC in full. *Forbes.* https://www.forbes.com/sites/tylerroush/2024/08/21/heres-barack -obamas-speech-at-the-dnc-in-full/.

7. **Blame less educated more:** Kuppens, T., Spears, R., Manstead, A. S. R., Spruyt, B., & Easterbrook, M. J. (2018). Educationism and the irony of meritocracy: Negative attitudes of higher educated people towards the less educated. *Journal of Experimental Social Psychology*, 76(1), 429–447. https://doi.org/10.1016/j.jesp.2017.11.001; **quote:** Sandel, M. J. (2020, September 2). Disdain for the less educated is the last acceptable prejudice. *The New York Times.* https://www.nytimes.com/2020/09/02/opinion/education-prejudice.html.

8. **Quotes:** Weishan, M. (2016, August 2). "A second bill of rights" [video]. The Franklin Delano Roosevelt Foundation. https://fdrfoundation.org/a-second-bill-of-rights-video/.

9. **Graduation rate 2010:** Mini digest of education statistics, 2010: Educational outcomes. (2011, March). National Center for Education Statistics (NCES), US Department of Education. https://nces.ed.gov/pubs2011/2011016/outcomes.asp?type=8; **enrollment falling 2022:** Total undergraduate fall enrollment in degree-granting postsecondary institutions, by attendance status, sex of student, and control and level of institution: Selected years, 1970 through 2031. (n.d.). National Center for Education Statistics (NCES), US Department of Education. Accessed July 2, 2024, from https://nces.ed.gov/programs /digest/d23/tables/dt23_303.70.asp; **quote:** Lemann, N. (2022, October 24). The Democrats' midterm challenge. *The New Yorker.* https://www.newyorker.com/magazine/2022 /10/31/the-democrats-midterm-challenge.

10. **Blue-collar German earnings:** Ahsan Finance. (2023, April 10). *Why plumbers earn more than engineers in Germany* [video]. *YouTube.* https://www.youtube.com/watch?v=5p1GW _np3So&t=182s.

11. **Construction delays:** Hall, K. G. (2016, September 2). Electricians, roofers and plumbers have their pick of jobs, and demand is expected to grow. *Los Angeles Times.* https://www .latimes.com/business/la-fi-skilled-workers-jobs-20160902-snap-story.html; **confidence in higher education:** Brenan, M. (2023, July 11). Americans' confidence in higher education down sharply. Gallup. https://news.gallup.com/poll/508352/americans-confidence -higher-education-down-sharply.aspx.

12. **Top 20 percent and Ivy Leagues:** Chetty, R., Friedman, J. N., Saez, E., Turner, N., & Yagan, D. (2020). Income segregation and intergenerational mobility across colleges in the United States, p. 1584. *The Quarterly Journal of Economics*, 135(3), 1567–1633. https:// doi.org/10.1093/qje/qjaa005; **more from 1 percent:** Aisch, G., Buchanan, L., Cox, A., & Quealy, K. (2017, January 18). Some colleges have more students from the top 1 percent than the bottom 60. Find yours. *The New York Times.* https://www.nytimes.com/interactive /2017/01/18/upshot/some-colleges-have-more-students-from-the-top-1-percent-than -the-bottom-60.html; **three times more likely:** Pruitt, L. R. (2015). The false choice between race and class and other affirmative myths, p. 1038. *Buffalo Law Review*, 63, 981; **twice the earnings advantage:** Corak, M. (2006). Do poor children become poor adults? Lessons from a cross-country comparison of generational earnings mobility, p. 145. In J. Creedy and G. Kalb (Eds.). *Dynamics of inequality and poverty*, pp. 143–188. Emerald Publishing Group Limited. https://doi.org/10.1016/S1049–2585(06)13006–9.

13. **Quote:** Sandel, 2020, p. 164; **suspect grade point averages:** Leonhardt, D. (2024, January 7). The misguided war on the SAT. *The New York Times.* https://www.nytimes.com/2024 /01/07/briefing/the-misguided-war-on-the-sat.html; **organized activities:** Lareau, A. (2003). *Unequal childhoods: Class, race, and family life*, pp. 264, 282. University of California Press; **college graduate earnings:** Schmitt, J., & Boushey, H. (2010, December). The college conundrum: Why the benefits of a college education may not be so clear, especially to men, pp. 3, 8, 9. Center for American Progress. https://www.americanprogress.org/article

/the-college-conundrum/; **college admission rates:** Wallace, J. B. (2023). *Never enough: When achievement culture becomes toxic—and what we can do about it*, p. 41. Penguin Publishing Group.

14. **Quote:** Lareau, 2003, p. 43; **"concerted cultivation":** Lareau, 2003, p. 2.

15. **Work hours increased:** Williams, J. C. (2013, February 11). The daddy dilemma: Why men face a "flexibility stigma" at work. *The Washington Post*. https://www.washingtonpost.com /national/on-leadership/the-daddy-dilemma-why-men-face-a-flexibility-stigma-at-work /2013/02/11/58350f4e-7462-11e2-aa12-e6cf1d31106b_story.html; **college-educated men work hours:** Jacobs, J. A. (2004). *The time divide: Work, family, and gender inequality*. Harvard University Press; **college-educated women work hours:** Williams, J. C., & Boushey, H. (2010, January 25). The three faces of work-family conflict: The poor, the professionals, and the missing middle. The Center for American Progress. https://www.americanprogress .org/article/the-three-faces-of-work-family-conflict/; **1960s law schedule:** Fontaine, V. (n.d.). The billable hours crunch. SeltzerFontaine. Accessed May 8, 2024, from https://www .seltzerfontaine.com/the-billable-hours-crunch/; **path to partnership:** Olson, E. G. (2012, May 15). Dewey's decline and the rise of high-risk Big Law. *Fortune*. https://fortune.com /2012/05/15/deweys-decline-and-the-rise-of-high-risk-big-law/; **"profits per partner":** ALM Staff. (2024, April 16). The 2024 Am Law 100: Ranked by profits per equity partner. *The American Lawyer*. https://www.law.com/americanlawyer/2024/04/16/the-2024-am-law -100-ranked-by-profits-per-equity-partner/.

16. **First and second quotes:** Rolston, J. S. (2014). *Mining coal and undermining gender: Rhythms of work and family in the American West*, p. 164. Rutgers University Press; **third quote:** Lamont, M. (2000). *The dignity of working men: Morality and the boundaries of race, class, and immigration*, pp. 115–116. Harvard University Press.

17. **First quote:** Sherman, J. (2009). *Those who work, those who don't: Poverty, morality, and family in rural America*, p. 135. University of Minnesota Press; **second quote:** Lythcott-Haims, J. (2015). *How to raise an adult: Break free of the overparenting trap and prepare your kid for success*, p. 7. Henry Holt and Co.

18. **"Intensive mothering":** Hays, S. (1996). *The cultural contradictions of motherhood*. Yale University Press; **sibling relations:** Lareau, 2003, pp. 45, 55–57, 76–77; **determine for the whole family:** Lareau, 2003, p. 42.

19. **"More of a priority":** Lareau, 2003, p. 58.

20. **First quote:** Wallace, 2003, p. 30; **fear of falling:** Ehrenreich, B. (1989). *Fear of falling: The inner life of the middle class*. Pantheon Books; **millennial wealth:** Kurz, C., Li, G., & Vine, D. J. (2018). Are millennials different? Finance and Economics Discussion Series 2018–080. Washington: Board of Governors of the Federal Reserve System, https://doi.org/10 .17016/FEDS.2018.080; **second quote:** Wallace, 2023, p. 30; **third quote:** Wallace, 2023, p. 50; **loved more when successful:** Wallace, 2023, p. 55; **trophy child:** Wallace, 2023, p. 59; **fourth quote:** Wallace, 2023, p. 112; **Palo Alto suicides, fifth quote:** Markovits, D. (2019). *The meritocracy trap: How America's foundational myth feeds inequality, dismantles the middle class, and devours the elite*, p. 42. Penguin Press.

21. **"Good kids":** Bettie, J. (2003). *Women without class: Girls, race, and identity*, p. 134. University of California Press; **first quote:** Lareau, 2003, p. 250; **second, third, and fourth quotes:** Lareau, 2003, pp. 250, 45, 79, 80; **fifth quote:** Lareau, 2003, p. 81; **sixth quote:** Glass, I. (Host). (2008, March 7). Return to childhood: People who try to revisit their childhoods—what they find and what they do not find [audio podcast episode]. *In This American Life*. https://www.thisamericanlife.org/351/return-to-childhood; **seventh and eighth quotes:** Lareau, 2003, p. 251.

Chapter 12: It's a Battle Between Sophisticated Global Citizens and Parochial Ethno-Nationalists, Right?

1. **Quote:** Coman, J. (2020, September 6). Michael Sandel: The populist backlash has been

a revolt against the tyranny of merit. *The Guardian*. https://www.theguardian.com/books
/2020/sep/06/michael-sandel-the-populist-backlash-has-been-a-revolt-against-the
-tyranny-of-merit.

2. **Dutch elections:** Corder, M., & Casert, R. (2023, November 23). In a shock for Europe, anti-Islam populist Geert Wilders records a massive win in Dutch elections. Associated Press. https://apnews.com/article/netherlands-election-candidates-prime-minister-f31f 57a856f006ff0f2fc4984acaca6b.

3. **Achievers, Stayers, and Boomerangs:** Carr, P. J., & Kefalas, M. J. (2010). *Hollowing out the middle: The rural brain drain and what it means for America*. Beacon Press; **those who leave and those who stay:** Ferrante, E. (2014). *Those who leave and those who stay* (A. Goldstein, Trans.). Europa Editions. (Original work published 2013); **quotes:** Carr & Kefalas, 2009, pp. 39–40.

4. **Quotes:** Carr & Kefalas, 2009, pp. 65, 69, 152, 73.

5. **Quotes:** Carr & Kefalas, 2009, pp. 129, 128.

6. **Quote:** Carr & Kefalas, 2009, p. 129.

7. **First quote:** Carr & Kefalas, 2009, p. 81; **extroverts and moving:** Jokela, M. (2009). Personality predicts migration within and between U.S. states. *Journal of Research in Personality*, 43(1), 79–83. https://doi.org/10.1016/j.jrp.2008.09.005; **second quote:** Wilkinson, W. (2019, June). The density divide: Urbanization, polarization, and populist backlash, p. 41. Niskanen Center. https://niskanencenter.org/the-density-divide-urbanization-polarization -and-populist-backlash/.

8. **Quote:** Brooks, D. (2021, September). How the bobos broke America. *The Atlantic*. https://www.theatlantic.com/magazine/archive/2021/09/blame-the-bobos-creative -class/619492/; **the bobos:** Brooks, D. (2001). *Bobos in paradise: The new upper class and how they got there*. Simon & Schuster; **"Insubordi(nation)":** Haidt, J. (2012). *The righteous mind: Why good people are divided by politics and religion*, p. 169. Knopf Doubleday Publishing Group.

9. **Ferrante:** Ferrante, 2014; **car study:** Stephens, N. M., Markus, H. R., & Townsend, S. S. M. (2007). Choice as an act of meaning: The case of social class. *Journal of Personality and Social Psychology*, 93(5), 814–830. https://doi.org/10.1037/0022–3514.93.5.814; **quotes:** Rolston, J. S. (2014). *Mining coal and undermining gender: Rhythms of work and family in the American West*, pp. 164, 166. Rutgers University Press.

10. **Rural communality:** Enke, B. (2020). Moral values and voting. *Journal of Political Economy*, 128(10), 3679–3729. https://doi.org/10.1086/708857; **89% of respondents:** Haney López, I. (2019). *Merge left: Fusing race and class, winning elections, and saving America*, p. 175. The New Press; **Tommy and Liza:** Sherman, J. (2009). *Those who work, those who don't: Poverty, morality, and family in rural America*, pp. 76, 78. University of Minnesota Press.

11. **Live in or near hometown:** Cox, D., Lienesch, R., & Jones, R. P. (2017). Beyond economics: Fears of cultural displacement pushed the white working class to Trump, p. 7. PRRI / *The Atlantic*. https://www.prri.org/research/white-working-class-attitudes-economy -trade-immigration-election-donald-trump/; **first quote:** Muravchik, S., & Shields, J. A. (2020). *Trump's Democrats*, p. 97. Brookings Institution Press; **second quote:** Muravchik & Shields, 2020, p. 96; **third and fourth quotes:** Muravchik & Shields, 2020, p. 100; **fifth quote:** Muravchik & Shields, 2020, p. 101; **"remained stubbornly protectionist":** Huntington, S. (2004). *Who are we? The challenges to America's national identity*, p. 329. Simon & Schuster.

12. **US is the best country:** In a politically polarized era, sharp divides in both partisan coalitions, p. 30. (2019, December 17). Pew Research Center. https://www.pewresearch .org/politics/2019/12/17/in-a-politically-polarized-era-sharp-divides-in-both-partisan -coalitions/; **being American important to identity:** Hawkins, S., & Raghuram, T. (2020, December). American fabric: Identity and belonging, p. xvi. More in Common. https:// www.moreincommon.com/media/s5jhgpx5/moreincommon_americanfabricreport.pdf.

13. **Displaying the flag:** Hawkins & Raghuram, 2020, p. xliv.
14. **First quote:** Lamont, M. (2000). *The dignity of working men: Morality and the boundaries of race, class, and immigration*, p. 36. Harvard University Press; **second quote:** Klein, E. (2011, March 8). Vilsack: "I took it as a slam on rural America." *The Washington Post*. https://www.washingtonpost.com/blogs/wonkblog/post/vilsack-i-took-it-as-a-slam-on-rural-america/2011/03/08/ABF0l6O_blog.html; **"America is a better country":** Hawkins, S., Yudkin, D., Juan-Torres, M., & Dixon, T. (2018). Hidden tribes: A study of America's polarized landscape, p. 119. More in Common. https://hiddentribes.us/media/qfpekz4g/hidden_tribes_report.pdf.
15. **First quote:** Bourdieu, P. (1984). *Distinction: A social critique on the judgment of taste* (R. Nice, Trans.), p. 197. Harvard University Press. (Original work published 1979); **second quote:** DeVault, M. L. (1991). *Family discourse and everyday practice: Gender and class at the dinner table*, pp. 5–6. Syracuse Scholar (1979–1991), 11(1). https://surface.syr.edu/suscholar/vol11/iss1/2; **third quote:** Lamont, 2000, p. 11; **fourth quote:** Lareau, A. (2003). *Unequal childhoods: Class, race, and family life*, 57. University of California Press.
16. **Childcare:** Williams, J. C., & Boushey, H. (2010, January 25). The three faces of work-family conflict: The poor, the professionals, and the Missing Middle. Center for American Progress. https://www.americanprogress.org/article/the-three-faces-of-work-family-conflict/.
17. **Janitor income:** Porter, E., & Gates, G. (2019, May 21). Why workers without college degrees are fleeing big cities. *The New York Times*. https://www.nytimes.com/interactive/2019/05/21/business/economy/migration-big-cities.html; **noncollege leaving big cities see also:** Autor, D. (2020, July 8). The faltering escalator of urban opportunity, p. 111. Securing Our Economic Future, 108–136. https://www.economicstrategygroup.org/wp-content/uploads/2020/12/Autor_Urban-Opportunity.pdf.
18. **Road to Somewhere:** Goodhart, D. (2017). *The road to somewhere: The populist revolt and the future of politics*. Hurst; **Klein's algorithm:** Klein, E. (Host). (2024, January 9). How to discover your own taste [audio podcast episode]. In The Ezra Klein Show. *The New York Times*. https://www.nytimes.com/2024/01/09/opinion/ezra-klein-podcast-kyle-chayka.html.

Chapter 13: Aren't the College-Educated Just More Enlightened?

1. **Feeling rules:** Hochschild, A. R. (1979). Emotion work, feeling rules, and social structure. *American Journal of Sociology*, 85(3), 551–575. https://doi.org/10.1086/227049.
2. **Limbaugh:** Hochschild, A. R. (2016). *Strangers in their own land: Anger and mourning on the American right*, p. 22. The New Press.
3. **Quote:** Haskell, T. L. (1985). Capitalism and the origins of the humanitarian sensibility, part 1, pp. 354–355. *The American Historical Review*, 90(2), 339–361. https://doi.org/10.2307/1852669.
4. **First quote:** Haskell, 1985, p. 355; **second quote:** Haskell, 1985, p. 361.
5. **Hunger and violence:** FAO, IFAD, UNICEF, WFP, and WHO. (2023). The state of food security and nutrition in the world 2023. Urbanization, agrifood systems transformation and healthy diets across the rural–urban continuum. Food and Agriculture Organization of the United Nations. https://doi.org/10.4060/cc3017en.
6. **Quote:** Goodnough, A. (2016, November 12). Michigan voters say Trump could see their problems "right off the bat." *The New York Times*. https://www.nytimes.com/2016/11/13/us/politics/michigan-voters-donald-trump.html.
7. **Quote:** Greenberg, S., & Zdunkewicz, N. (2017, March 10). *Macomb County in the Age of Trump: Report from focus groups with Independent & Democratic Trump voters in Macomb County*. Democracy Corps. https://democracycorps.com/wp-content/uploads/2017/03/Dcor_Macomb_FG-Memo_3.10.2017_FINAL.pdf.

8. **US foreign policy and immigration:** Gordon, R. (2019, August 16). The current migrant crisis was created by US foreign policy, not Trump. *The Nation.* https://www.thenation.com /article/archive/central-america-migrant-crisis-foreign-policy-trump/; **migrants world-wide:** International Migration 2020 Highlights. (2020). United Nations Department of Economic and Social Affairs, Population Division. https://www.un.org/development /desa/pd/sites/www.un.org.development.desa.pd/files/undesa_pd_2020_international_ migration_highlights.pdf.

9. **Tech entrepreneurs:** Broockman, D. E., Ferenstein, G., & Malhotra, N. (2019). Predispositions and the political behavior of American economic elites: Evidence from technology entrepreneurs. *American Journal of Political Science,* 63(1), 212–233. https://doi.org/10 .1111/ajps.12408; **contractors and freelancers:** State of tech employment: For enterprise employers and contractors. (2022). Motion Recruitment. https://motionrecruitment.com /it-salary/state-of-tech-employment-enterprise-contracting.

10. **Cold feelings:** Hawkins, S., Yudkin, D., Juan-Torres, M., & Dixon, T. (2018). Hidden tribes: A study of America's polarized landscape, p. 103. More in Common. https://hiddentribes .us/media/qfpekz4g/hidden_tribes_report.pdf; **quote:** Chozick, A. (2016, September 10). Hillary Clinton calls many Trump backers "deplorables," and G.O.P. pounces. *The New York Times.* https://www.nytimes.com/2016/09/11/us/politics/hillary-clinton-basket-of -deplorables.html.

11. **"Poor, illiterate, and strung out":** Midler, B. [@BetteMidler]. (2021, December 20). "What #JoeManchin, who represents a smaller population than Brooklyn, has done to the rest of America, who wants to move forward, not backward, like his state, is horrible. He sold us out. He wants us all to be just like his state, West Virginia. Poor, illiterate and strung out" [tweet]. Twitter. https://twitter.com/BetteMidler/status/1472955243935711236; **persistent poverty:** Klein, E. (2011, March 8). Vilsack: "I took it as a slam on rural America." *The Washington Post.* https://www.washingtonpost.com/blogs/wonkblog /post/vilsack-i-took-it-as-a-slam-on-rural-america/2011/03/08/ABF0l6O_blog.html; **opioid use:** Keyes, K. M., Cerdá, M., Brady, J. E., Havens, J. R., & Galea, S. (2014). Understanding the rural-urban differences in nonmedical prescription opioid use and abuse in the United States. *American Journal of Public Health,* 104(2), e52–e59. https://doi.org /10.2105%2FAJPH.2013.301709; **later apologized:** Midler, B. [@BetteMidler]. (2021, December 20). "I apologize to the good people of WVA for my last outburst. I'm just seeing red; #JoeManchin and his whole family are a criminal enterprise. Is he really the best WV has to offer its own citizens? Surely there's someone there who has the state's interests at heart, not his own!" [tweet]. Twitter. https://twitter.com/BetteMidler/status /1472964848875188226; **comments:** Potts, M. (2019, October 4). In the land of self-defeat [Comments section]. *The New York Times.* https://www.nytimes.com/2019/10/04 /opinion/sunday/trump-arkansas.html; **SundaeDivine:** Sundae_Gurl [@SundaeDivine]. (2023, October 15). "Rural America, you didn't get left behind—you chose not to keep up. Your resentment toward politicians you don't like or people who look different from you is nothing but scapegoating. Turn off Fox News and join the rest of us in electing people who'll make your life better" [tweet]. Twitter. https://twitter.com/SundaeDivine/status /1713655199892402599.

12. **"Backlash" thesis:** Norris, P., & Inglehart, R. (2019). *Cultural backlash: Trump, Brexit, and authoritarian populism.* Cambridge University Press; **like a tide:** Klein, E. (Host). (2022, November 1). A powerful theory of why the far right is thriving across the globe [audio podcast episode]. In *The Ezra Klein Show. The New York Times.* https://www.nytimes .com/2022/11/01/opinion/ezra-klein-podcast-pippa-norris.html; **roundly criticized:** Schäfer, A. (2022). Cultural backlash? How (not) to explain the rise of authoritarian populism, p. 1977. *British Journal of Political Science,* 52(4), 1977–1993. https://doi.org /10.1017/S0007123421000363; Johnston, R. (2019, June 5). Book review: Cultural

backlash: Trump, Brexit and authoritarian populism by Pippa Norris and Ronald Inglehart. LSE Blogs. https://blogs.lse.ac.uk/lsereviewofbooks/2019/06/05/book-review -cultural-backlash-trump-brexit-and-authoritarian-populism-by-pippa-norris-and -ronald-inglehart/.

13. **First quote:** Klein, 2022; **coded as "authoritarian":** Norris & Inglehart, 2019, pp. 103–105; **second quote:** Norris & Inglehart, 2019, p. 3.

14. **Quote:** Obschonka, M., Stuetzer, M., Rentfrow, P. J., Lee, N., Potter, J., & Gosling, S. (2018). Fear, populism, and the geopolitical landscape: The "sleeper effect" of neurotic personality traits on voting behavior in the 2016 Brexit and Trump elections, p. 285. *Social Psychology and Personality Science*, 9(3), 285–298. https://doi.org/10.1177 /1948550618755874.

15. **Theodor Adorno:** Adorno, T. W., Frenkel-Brunswik, E., Levinson, D., & Sanford, N. (1950). *The authoritarian personality*. Harper.

16. **Influential:** Feinberg, M., Wehling, E., Chung, J. M., Saslow, L. R., & Melvær Paulin, I. (2020). Measuring moral politics: How strict and nurturant family values explain individual differences in conservatism, liberalism, and the political middle, p. 779. *Journal of Personality and Social Psychology*, 118(4), 777–804. https://doi.org/10.1037/pspp0000255; **quotes:** Lakoff, G. (1996). *Moral politics: What conservatives know that liberals don't*, p. 34. University of Chicago Press.

17. **Chooses sides:** Lakoff, 1996, pp. 339–340; **nurturing parent:** Lakoff, 1996, pp. 33–35; **working-class mom:** Sherman, J. (2009). *Those who work, those who don't: Poverty, morality, and family in rural America*, p. 133. University of Minnesota Press.

18. **Long been ignored:** Leonhardt, D. (2023, May 25). Ron DeSantis and the "scaffle" vote. *The New York Times*. https://www.nytimes.com/2023/05/25/briefing/ron-desantis.html; **first quote:** Klein, 2022; **second quote:** Potts, 2019; **third quote:** Norris & Inglehart, 2019, p. 87; **fourth quote:** Podhorzer, M. (2023, July 25). Confirmation bias is a hell of a drug. Weekend Reading. https://www.weekendreading.net/p/confirmation-bias-is -a-hell-of-a.

Chapter 14: Aren't Elites Just Less Racist?

1. **Quote:** Bettie, J. (2003). *Women without class: Girls, race, and identity*, p. 173. University of California Press.

2. **Implicit bias scores:** Mooney, C. (2014, December 1). The science of why cops shoot young Black men. *Mother Jones*. https://www.motherjones.com/politics/2014/12/science -of-racism-prejudice/; **racism not binary:** Leonhardt, D. (2023). *Ours was the shining future: The story of the American Dream*, p. 199. Random House.

3. **Paul Willis:** Willis, P. E. (1977). *Learning to labour: How working class kids get working class jobs*. Columbia University Press; **racist logic:** Lamont, M. (2000). *The dignity of working men: Morality and the boundaries of race, class, and immigration*, p. 59. Harvard University Press; **quote:** Lamont, 2000, p. 61.

4. **First quote:** Lamont, 2000, p. 63; **overt prejudice:** Flemmen, M., & Savage, M. (2017). The politics of nationalism and white racism in the UK. *The British Journal of Sociology*, 68(S1), S233–S264. https://doi.org/10.1111/1468–4446.12311; **second quote:** 100 days into the Trump era, working-class 'searchers' who voted for him are having doubts, open to appeals. (2017, April 26). Working America. https://workingamerica.org/news/post /research/100days/.

5. **Quote:** Working America, 2017.

6. **First quote:** Williams, J. C., Phillips, K. W., & Hall, E. V. (2014). Double jeopardy? Gender bias against women in science, p. 12. The Center for WorkLife Law. https://worklifelaw .org/publications/Double-Jeopardy-Report_v6_full_web-sm.pdf; **never get tenure:** Williams et al., 2014, p. 16; **second quote:** Williams, J. C., Korn, R. M., & Ghani, A. (2022,

April). Pinning down the jellyfish: The workplace experiences of women of color in tech, p. 22. The Center for WorkLife Law. https://worklifelaw.org/wp-content/uploads/2022 /04/Pinning-Down-the-Jellyfish-The-Workplace-Experiences-of-Women-of-Color-in -Tech.pdf.

7. **Quote:** Williams et al., 2022, p. 25.

8. **First quote:** Williams et al., 2022, p. 24; **second quote:** Williams et al., 2014, p. 47.

9. **High status and competence:** Fiske, S. T., Cuddy, A. J. C., Glick, P., & Xu, J. (2002). A model of (often mixed) stereotype content: Competence and warmth respectively follow from perceived status and competition. *Journal of Personality and Social Psychology*, 82(6), 878–902. https://doi.org/10.1037/0022–3514.82.6.878; **one-third of white men and half to three-quarters of people of color:** Williams, J. C. (2021). Bias interrupted: Creating inclusion for real and for good, p. 37. Harvard Business Review Press; **over three-quarters of Black women:** Williams, 2021, p. 38; **first quote:** Williams, 2021, p. 8; **second quote:** Williams, 2021, p. 39; **dismissed as luck:** Williams, J. C., Korn, R. M., & Maas, R. (2021). The elephant in the (well-designed) room: An investigation into bias in the architecture profession, p. 38. Center for WorkLife Law. https://biasinterrupters.org /wp-content/uploads/2024/03/AIA_An_Investigation_Into_Bias_Study.pdf; **third quote:** Williams et al., 2014, p. 8.

10. **Jamal-and-Greg study:** Bertrand, M., & Mullainathan, S. (2004). Are Emily and Greg more employable than Lakisha and Jamal? A field experiment on labor market discrimination. *American Economic Review*, 94(4), 991–1013. 10.1257/0002828042002561; **memos with mistakes:** Reeves, A. N. (2014). Written in Black & White: Exploring confirmation bias in racialized perceptions of writing skills. Nextions. https://nextions.com/wp-content /uploads/2022/06/2014–04–01–14-Written-in-Black-and-White-Yellow-Paper-Series -ANR-Differences-Based-on-Race-Implicit-Bias-Bias-Breakers-Effective-Recruiting -and-Hiring-.pdf; **quote:** Williams et al., 2014, p. 12.

11. **Women of color in tech:** Williams et al., 2022, p. 17.

12. **About the same warmth:** Ekins, E. (2017). The five types of Trump voters: Who they are and what they believe. Democracy Fund Voter Study Group. https://www.voterstudygroup .org/publication/the-five-types-trump-voters.

13. **First quote:** Carney, R. K., & Enos, R. D. (2017, October). Conservatism and fairness in contemporary politics: Unpacking the psychological underpinnings of modern racism. In NYU CESS Experiments Conference; **second quote:** Kinder, D. R., & Sears, D. O. (1981). Prejudice and politics: Symbolic racism versus racial threats to the good life, p. 416. *Journal of Personality and Social Psychology*, 40(3), 414–431. https://doi.org/10.1037 /0022–3514.40.3.414; **noncollege higher racial resentment:** Smith, C. W., Kreitzer, R. J., & Suo, F. (2020). The dynamics of racial resentment across the 50 US states. *Perspectives on Politics*, 18(2), 527–538. https://doi.org/10.1017/S1537592719002688.

14. **Four items:** Kinder, D. R., & Sanders, L. M. (1996). *Divided by color: Racial politics and democratic ideals.* University of Chicago Press.

15. **Structural or individual reasons:** Kam, C. D., & Burge, C. D. (2018). Uncovering reactions to the racial resentment scale across the racial divide. *The Journal of Politics*, 80(1), 314–320. https://doi.org/10.1086/693907; **quotes:** Kristof, N. (2024, January 20). Bill Beard was a good man. Then he committed a terrible crime. *The New York Times.* https://www .nytimes.com/2024/01/20/opinion/trauma-pain-assault.html.

16. **First quote:** Hochschild, J. L. (1995). *Facing up to the American Dream: Race, class, and the soul of the nation*, p. 164. Princeton University Press; **second quote:** Kristof, N. (2021, February 13). Can Biden save Americans like my old pal Mike? *The New York Times.* https://www.nytimes.com/2021/02/13/opinion/sunday/working-class-dignity.html; **get ahead if they work hard:** Pougiales, R., & Fulton, J. (2019, December 30). A nuanced picture of what Black Americans want in 2020. Third Way. https://www.thirdway.org

/memo/a-nuanced-picture-of-what-black-americans-want-in-2020; **Latinos hard work, luck, and circumstance:** Haney López, I. (2022). Project Juntos: Latinx race-class. Project Juntos. https://static1.squarespace.com/static/5ef377b623eaf41dd9df1311 /t/5f6fd7e84ca040062e8dc0b9/1601165291980/Project+Juntos+Summary+Briefing +092620.pdf; **similar proportions found dog whistle convincing:** Haney López, I. (2019). *Merge left: Fusing race and class, winning elections, and saving America*, p. 90. The New Press.

17. **Authoritative seen as angry:** Livingston, R. W., & Pearce, N. A. (2009). The teddy-bear effect: Does having a baby face benefit black chief executive officers? *Psychological Science*, 20(10), 1229–1236. https://doi.org/10.1111/j.1467–9280.2009.02431.x; **prescriptive stereotypes and intersectionality, see also:** Hudson, S. K. T., & Ghani, A. (2024). Sexual orientation and race intersectionally reduce the perceived gendered nature of normative stereotypes in the United States. *Psychology of Women Quarterly*, 48(1), 56–79. https:// doi.org/10.1177/03616843231187851; **perceived stereotypes and intersectionality, see also:** Ghavami, N., & Peplau, L. A. (2013). An intersectional analysis of gender and eth-nic stereotypes: Testing three hypotheses. *Psychology of Women Quarterly*, 37(1), 113–127. https://doi.org/10.1177/0361684312464203; **first quote:** Williams et al., 2022, p. 32; **second quote:** Williams et al., 2022, p. 30.

18. **More integrated environments:** Dawson, M. C. (1995). *Behind the mule: Race and class in African-American politics*. Princeton University Press; **Latino education and linked fate:** Masuoka, N. (2006). Together they become one: Examining the predictors of panethnic group consciousness among Asian Americans and Latinos, p. 1009. *Social Science Quarterly*, 87(5), 993–1011. https://doi.org/10.1111/j.1540–6237.2006.00412.x; **quote:** Hochschild, J. L. (1995). *Facing up to the American Dream: Race, class, and the soul of the nation*, p. 73. Princeton University Press; **working class more likely to identify with their group:** Harris, F. C., & McKenzie, B. D. (2015). Unreconciled strivings and warring ideals: The complexities of competing African-American political identities. *Politics, Groups, and Identities*, 3(2), 239–254. https://doi.org/10.1080/21565503.2015.1024260; **most important problem:** Hochschild, 1995, p. 213; **discrimination negatively affected ability to succeed:** Anderson, M. (2019, May 2). For black Americans, experiences of racial discrimination vary by education level, gender. Pew Research Center. https://www .pewresearch.org/short-reads/2019/05/02/for-black-americans-experiences-of-racial -discrimination-vary-by-education-level-gender/.

19. **Black class-linked linked-fate patterns:** Cose, E. (1993). *The rage of a privileged class*, p. 7. HarperCollins; **Latino education and linked fate:** Masuoka, 2006, p. 1009; **quotes:** Findell, E. (2020, November 8). Why Democrats lost so many South Texas Latinos. *The Wall Street Journal*. https://www.wsj.com/articles/how-democrats-lost-so-many-south -texas-latinosthe-economy-11604871650.

20. **Mute button:** Wasserman, J. (2017, October 16). Visiting author talks about the de-cline of the white working class. *The Review*. https://udreview.com/visiting-author-talks -decline-white-working-class/.

21. **Lower levels of belonging:** Equality Action Center. (2024). Unpublished research; **new first-generation professionals:** Profile of undergraduate students: Attendance, distance and remedial education, degree program and field of study, demographics, financial aid, financial literacy, employment, and military status: 2015–16. (2019, January). National Center for Education Statistics. https://nces.ed.gov/pubs2019/2019467.pdf.

22. **Data points:** Williams, J. C., Ray, R. L., Korn, R. M., Ghani, A., & Ali Khan, R. (2024). Traditional bias training doesn't work—Bias Interrupters do. The Conference Board. https://www.conference-board.org/publications/traditional-bias-training-does-not -work-bias-interrupters-do; Korn, R. M., Ghani, A., & Williams, J. C. (2024, July 15). How to equitably assign high-profile work. *Harvard Business Review*. https://hbr.org /2024/07/how-to-equitably-assign-high-profile-work.

Part IV: The Path Past Far-Right Populism
1. **Quote:** Evans, R. H. (2021). *Wholehearted faith*, pp. 89–90. HarperCollins.
2. **1971:** Vanneman, R., & Cannon, L. W. (1987). *The American perception of class*, p. 43. Temple University Press. https://doi.org/10.2307/j.ctv941wv0; **staff writers study:** Wai, J., & Perina, K. (2018). Expertise in journalism: Factors shaping a cognitive and culturally elite profession. *Journal of Expertise*, 1(1), 57–78. https://www.journalofexpertise.org /articles/volume1_issue1/JoE_2018_1_1_Wai_Perina.pdf.

Chapter 15: Of Covid and Playground Design: How Class Blindness Distorts Public Policy
1. **Quote:** Leonhardt, D. (2021, September 7). One in 5,000. *The New York Times*. https:// www.nytimes.com/2021/09/07/briefing/risk-breakthrough-infections-delta.html.
2. **More at risk, quote:** Schiffman, R. (2019, May 10). Making playgrounds a little more dangerous. *The New York Times*. https://www.nytimes.com/2019/05/10/well/family /adventure-playgrounds-junk-playgrounds.html; **British playgrounds:** Talarowski, M., Cohen, D. A., Williamson, S., & Han, B. (2019). Innovative playgrounds: Use, physical activity, and implications for health. *Public Health*, 174, 102–109. https://doi.org/10.1016 /j.puhe.2019.06.002.
3. **First quote:** Brussoni, M., Olsen, L. L., Pike, I., & Sleet, D. A. (2012). Risky play and children's safety: Balancing priorities for optimal child development, p. 3134. *International Journal of Environmental Research and Public Health*, 9(9) 3134–3148. https://doi .org/10.3390/ijerph9093134; **play and mental health:** Gray, P. (2011). The decline of play and the rise of psychopathology in children and adolescents. *American Journal of Play*, 3(4), 443–463. https://files.eric.ed.gov/fulltext/EJ985541.pdf; **anxiety, see also:** Twenge, J. M. (2000). The age of anxiety? The birth cohort change in anxiety and neuroticism, 1952–1993. *Journal of Personality and Social Psychology*, 79(6), 1007–1021. https:// doi.org/10.1037/0022–3514.79.6.1007; **second quote:** Brussoni et al., 2012, p. 3138.
4. **First quote:** Lythcott-Haims, J. (2015). *How to raise an adult*, p. 7. Henry Holt and Co; **second and third quotes:** Brooks, K. (2020, August 14). Parents are frightened, and not just about contagion. *The New York Times*. https://www.nytimes.com/2020/08/14/opinion /coronavirus-parenting-education.html; **fourth and fifth quotes:** Brooks, K. (2018). *Small animals: Parenthood in the age of fear*, pp. 19–20. Flatiron Books; **sixth quote:** Fass, P. S. (2016). *The end of American childhood: A history of parenting from life on the frontier to the managed child*, p. 221. Princeton University Press.
5. **News more pessimistic:** Sacerdote, B., Sehgal, R., & Cook, M. (2020). Why is all COVID-19 news bad news?, para. 17. (No. w28110). National Bureau of Economic Research. https://www.nber.org/papers/w28110; **six-to-one ratio:** Sacerdote et al., 2020, para. 22; **by a factor of 5.5:** Sacerdote et al., 2020, abstr.; **1.5 standard deviations:** Sacerdote et al., 2020, para. 17; **quote:** Sacerdote et al., 2020, para. 5.
6. **Bleaker US coverage:** Leonhardt, D. (2021, April 22). Bad news bias. *The New York Times*. https://www.nytimes.com/2021/03/24/briefing/boulder-shooting-george-segal -astrazeneca.html; **quote:** Sacerdote et al., 2020, para. 6; **91 percent of US and 54 percent of foreign media were negative:** Sacerdote et al., 2020, abstr.; **reopening schools:** Sacerdote et al., 2020, para. 2.
7. **First quote:** Sacerdote et al., 2020, para. 1; **second quote:** Sacerdote et al., 2020, paras. 16, 19; **"stay safe during the holidays":** Blum, D. (2022, December 15). How to make holiday plans as Covid cases climb. *The New York Times*. https://www.nytimes.com/2022 /10/15/well/covid-holiday-plans.html; **third quote:** Gandhi, M. (2023). *Endemic: A post-pandemic playbook*, p. 86. Mayo Clinic Press.
8. **DeSantis:** Sullivan, K. (2020, July 10). Florida Gov. DeSantis says schools can be open if Walmart and Home Depot are open. CNN. https://cnn.com/2020/07/10/politics/florida -desantis-walmart-home-depot-schools-reopen/index.html; **Youngkin:** Goldstein,

D. (2021, November 14). In Virginia, frustration with schooling during the pandemic played a part in Youngkin's win. *The New York Times*. https://www.nytimes.com/2021/11/14/us/elections/in-virginia-frustration-with-schooling-during-the-pandemic-played-a-part-in-youngkins-win.html; **quotes:** Marshall, M., & Tran, L. (2021, May). 2020 post-election analysis, slide 27. Third Way. https://www.thirdway.org/report/2020-post-election-analysis.

9. **British expert:** Landler, M., & Castle, S. (2021, October 29). Britons, unfazed by high Covid rates, weigh their "price of freedom." *The New York Times*. https://www.nytimes.com/2021/08/28/world/europe/coronavirus-britain-uk.html; **quotes:** Leonhardt, 2021, September 7.

10. **Risks of Covid poll:** Rothwell, J., & Desai, S. (2020, December 22). How misinformation is distorting COVID policies and behaviors. Brookings. https://www.brookings.edu/articles/how-misinformation-is-distorting-covid-policies-and-behaviors/; **downplayed the benefits:** Lewis, T. (2021, March 11). How the U.S. pandemic response went wrong—and what went right—during a year of COVID. *Scientific American*. https://www.scientificamerican.com/article/how-the-u-s-pandemic-response-went-wrong-and-what-went-right-during-a-year-of-covid/; **quotes:** Leonhardt, D. (2022, March 18). Covid and the "very liberal." *The New York Times*. https://www.nytimes.com/2022/03/18/briefing/covid-risks-poll-americans.html.

11. **Quotes:** Leonhardt, 2022.

12. **Known very early:** Gandhi, 2023, p. 101; **infection fatality rates:** Smith, C., Odd, D., Harwood, R., Ward, J., Linney, M., Clark, M., Hargreaves, D., Ladhani, S. N., Draper, E., Davis, P. J., Kenny, S. E., Whittaker, E., Lyut, K., Viner, R., & Fraser, L. K. (2022). Deaths in children and young people in England after SARS-CoV-2 infection during the first pandemic year. *Nature Medicine*, 28(1), 185–192. https://doi.org/10.1038/s41591-021-01578-1; **sick for six days:** Molteni, E., Sudre, C. H., Canas, L. S., Bhopal, S. S., Hughes, R. C., Antonelli, M., Murray, B., Kläser, K., Kerfoot, E., Chen, L., Deng, J., Hu, C., Selvachandran, S., Read, K., Pujol, J. C., Hammers, A., Spector, T. D., Ourselin, S., Steves, C. J., . . . & Duncan, E. L. (2021). Illness duration and symptom profile in symptomatic UK school-aged children tested for SARS-CoV-2. *The Lancet Child & Adolescent Health*, 5(10), 708–718. https://doi.org/10.1016/s2352-4642(21)00198-x; **long Covid rare:** Farhadian, S., & Doron, S. (2022, February 14). Controlled studies ease worries of widespread long COVID in kids. STAT. https://www.statnews.com/2022/02/14/controlled-studies-ease-worries-widespread-long-covid-kids/; **school transmission uncommon:** Biggs, A. T., & Littlejohn, L. F. (2021). Revisiting the initial COVID-19 pandemic projections. *The Lancet Microbe*, 2(3), e91–e92. https://doi.org/10.1016/S2666-5247(21)00029-X; **quote:** Gandhi, 2023, p. 109; **children not the primary driver:** Ladhani, S. N., & sKIDs Investigation Team. (2021). Children and COVID-19 in schools. *Science*, 374(6568), 680–682. https://doi.org/10.1126/science.abj2042; **adult staff:** Gold, J. A., Gettings, J. R., Kimball, A., Franklin, R., Rivera, G., Morris, E., Scott, C., Marcet, P. L., Hast, M., Swanson, M., McCloud, J., Mehari, L., Thomas, E. S., Kirking, H. L., Tate, J. E., Memark, J., Drenzek, C., Vallabhaneni, S., & Georgia K–12 School COVID-19 Investigation Team. (2021). Clusters of SARS-CoV-2 infection among elementary school educators and students in one school district—Georgia, December 2020–January 2021. *Morbidity and Mortality Weekly Report*, 70(8), 289–292. http://dx.doi.org/10.15585/mmwr.mm7008e4; **37 percent lower in schools:** Falk, A., Benda, A., Falk, P., Steffen, S., Wallace, Z., & Høeg, T. B. (2021). COVID-19 cases and transmission in 17 K–12 schools—Wood County, Wisconsin, August 31–November 29, 2020. *Morbidity and Mortality Weekly Report*, 70(4), 136–140. http://dx.doi.org/10.15585/mmwr.mm7004e3; **teachers vaccinated:** Nearly 80 percent of teachers, school staff, and childcare workers receive at least one shot of COVID-19 vaccine. (2021, April 6). Centers for Disease Control and Prevention. https://archive.cdc.gov/www_cdc_gov/media/releases/2021/s0406

-teachers-staff-vaccine.html; **nine pieces:** Gandhi, 2023, p. 196; **longer closures in blue states:** Burbio's K-12 school opening tracker. (2022). Burbio. https://about.burbio.com/school-opening-tracker; **San Francisco closures:** Stone, J. R. (2021, August 15). "I'm going back to school!": San Francisco Unified students react as full in-person learning starts. ABC7 News. https://abc7news.com/sf-schools-reopen-back-to-school-sfusd-open-in-person-learning/10954172/; **Jennifer Nuzzo:** Nuzzo, J. (2010, March 10). We don't need to close schools to fight the coronavirus. *The New York Times.* https://www.nytimes.com/2020/03/10/opinion/coronavirus-school-closing.html; **US experts:** Jenkins, R. (2020, March 13). Op-ed: LAUSD just closed schools. Ebola taught us why that may be extreme. *Los Angeles Times.* https://www.latimes.com/opinion/story/2020–03–13/op-ed-lausd-just-closed-schools-ebola-taught-us-why-that-may-be-extreme; **UK experts:** Van Lancker, W., & Parolin, Z. (2020). COVID-19, school closures, and child poverty: A social crisis in the making. *The Lancet Public Health*, 5(5), E243–E244. https://doi.org/10.1016/S2468–2667(20)30084–0; **Italian experts:** Fantini, M. P., Reno, C., Bisernie, G. B., Savoia, E., & Lanari, M. (2020). COVID-19 and the re-opening of schools: A policy maker's dilemma. *Italian Journal of Pediatrics*, 46(79), 1–3. https://doi.org/10.1186/s13052-020-00844–1; **Hong Kong experts:** Lee, J. (2020). Mental health effects of school closures during COVID-19. *The Lancet Child & Adolescent Health*, 4(6), 421. https://doi.org/10.1016/S2352–4642(20)30109–7; **weight gain:** Rundle, A. G., Park, Y., Herbstman, J., Kinsey, E. W., & Wang, Y. C. (2020). COVID-19–related school closings and risk of weight gain among children. *Obesity*, 28(6), 1008–1009. https://doi.org/10.1002/oby.22813; **weight gain, see also:** Increase seen in pediatric BMI during pandemic, study finds. (2022, October 7). American Academy of Pediatrics. https://www.aap.org/en/news-room/news-releases/conference-news-releases/increase-seen-in-pediatric-bmi-during-pandemic-study-finds/; **health screenings and vaccines:** Gandhi, 2023, p. 115; **suicide:** Yard, E., Radhakrishnan, L., Ballesteros, M. F., Sheppard, M., Gates, A., Stein, Z., Harnett, K., Kite-Powell, A., Rodgers, L., Adjemian, J., Ehlman, D. C., Holland, K., Idaikkadar, N., Ivey-Stephenson, A., Martinez, P., Law, R., & Stone, D. M. (2021). Emergency department visits for suspected suicide attempts among persons aged 12–25 years before and during the COVID-19 pandemic—United States, January 2019–May 2021. *Morbidity and Mortality Weekly Report*, 70(24), 888–894. http://dx.doi.org/10.15585/mmwr.mm7024e1; **child abuse:** Baron, E. J., Goldstein, E. G., & Wallace, C. T. (2020). Suffering in silence: How COVID-19 school closures inhibit the reporting of child maltreatment. *Journal of Public Economics*, 190, 104258. https://doi.org/10.1016/j.jpubeco.2020.104258; **all came to pass:** Mervosh, S., Miller, C. C., & Paris, F. (2024, March 19). What the data says about pandemic school closures, four years later. *The New York Times.* https://www.nytimes.com/2024/03/18/upshot/pandemic-school-closures-data.html.

13. **Lost more jobs, pay during shutdowns:** Bennet, J. (2021, April 15). Fewer jobs have been lost in the EU than in the U.S. during the COVID-19 downturn. Pew Research Center. https://www.pewresearch.org/short-reads/2021/04/15/fewer-jobs-have-been-lost-in-the-eu-than-in-the-u-s-during-the-covid-19-downturn/; **third largest job loss gap:** Rothwell, J. (2021, May 3). How social class affects Covid-related layoffs worldwide. *The New York Times.* https://www.nytimes.com/2021/05/03/upshot/covid-layoffs-worldwide.html.

14. **Would not accept:** R. H. Langhoff, personal communication, October 18, 2021.

15. **Denmark reopening schools:** Kingsley, P. (2020, April 17). In Denmark, the rarest of sights: Classrooms full of students. *The New York Times.* https://www.nytimes.com/2020/04/17/world/europe/denmark-schools-coronavirus.html; **quote:** Firth, E. (2020, May 29). How Denmark got its children back to school so soon after lockdown. The Local. https://www.thelocal.com/20200528/how-denmark-got-its-children-back-to-school.

16. **CDC school reopenings:** Leidman, E., Duca, L. M., Omura, J. D., Proia, K., Stephens, J. W., & Sauber-Schatz, E. K. (2021). COVID-19 trends among persons aged 0–24 years—United States, March 1–December 12, 2020. *Morbidity and Mortality Weekly Report*,

70(3), 88–94. https://doi.org/10.15585%2Fmmwr.mm7003e1; **Norwegian reopenings:** Stebbings, S., Rotevatn, T. A., Larsen, V. B., Surén, P., Elstrøm, P., Greve-Isdahl, M., Johansen, T. B., & Astrup, E. (2022). Experience with open schools and preschools in periods of high community transmission of COVID-19 in Norway during the academic year of 2020/2021. *BMC Public Health*, 22, 1454; **Australian and Korean reopenings:** Viner, R. M., Mytton, O. T., Bonell, C., Melendez-Torres, G. J., Ward, J., Hudson, L., Waddington, C., Thomas, J., Russell, S., van der Klis, F., Koirala, A., Ladhani, S., Panovska-Griffiths, J., Davies, N. G., Booy, R., & Eggo, R. M. (2020). Susceptibility to SARS-CoV-2 infection among children and adolescents compared with adults: A systematic review and meta-analysis. *JAMA Pediatrics*, 175(2), 143–156. https://doi.org/10.1001/jamapediatrics.2020.4573; **Italian reopenings:** Larosa, E., Djuric, O., Cassinadri, M., Cilloni, S., Bisaccia, E., Vicentini, M., Venturelli, F., Rossi, P. G., Pezzotti, P., Bedeschi, E., & the Reggio Emilia Covid-19 Working Group. (2020). Secondary transmission of COVID-19 in preschool and school settings in northern Italy after their reopening in September 2020: a population-based study. *Eurosurveillance*, 25(49), 2001911. https://doi.org/10.2807/1560–7917.es.2020.25.49.2001911; **first quote:** Firth, 2020; **disruptive strategies:** Gandhi, 2023, p. 120; **second quote:** R. H. Langhoff, personal communication, October 18, 2021.

17. **Vaccination rates:** Holder, J. (2023, March 13). Tracking coronavirus vaccinations around the world. *The New York Times*. https://nytimes.com/interactive/2021/world/covid-vaccinations-tracker.html; Langhoff, 2021.

18. **Chilean vaccination rate:** Holder, 2023; quote: Londoño, E., Politi, D., & Milhorance, F. (2021, September 29). Covid ravaged South America. Then came a sharp drop in infections. *The New York Times*. https://www.nytimes.com/2021/09/05/world/americas/covid-south-america-reprieve-vaccines.html; **65 percent of Americans, 80 percent in developing countries, second only to Russia:** Solís Arce, J. S., Warren, S. S., Meriggi, N. F., Scacco, A., McMurry, N., Voors, M., Syunyaev, G., Malik, A. A., Aboutajdine, S., Adeojo, O., Anigo, D., Armand, A., Asad, S., Atyera, M., Augsburg, B., Awasthi, M., Ayesiga, G. E., Bancalari, A., Nyqvist, M. B., . . . & Omer, S. B. (2021). COVID-19 vaccine acceptance and hesitancy in low-and middle-income countries. *Nature Medicine*, 27(8), 1385–1394. https://doi.org/10.1038/s41591-021-01454-y.

19. **Higher mortality rate:** Mortality analyses. Johns Hopkins Coronavirus Resource Center. Accessed August 3, 2022, from https://coronavirus.jhu.edu/data/mortality; **50 percent and 13 percent shut:** Global monitoring of school closures caused by COVID-19. UNESCO Institute of Statistics. Accessed July 17, 2022, from https://covid19.uis.unesco.org/global-monitoring-school-closures-covid19/country-dashboard/; **red and blue counties:** Kates, J., Tolbert, J., & Rouw, A. (2022, January 19). The red/blue divide in COVID-19 vaccination rates continues: An update. KFF. https://www.kff.org/policy-watch/the-red-blue-divide-in-covid-19-vaccination-rates-continues-an-update/; **trust in public health:** Pollard, M. S., & Davis, L. M. (2022). Decline in trust in the Centers for Disease Control and Prevention during the COVID-19 pandemic. *Rand Health Quarterly*, 9(3). https://www.ncbi.nlm.nih.gov/pmc/articles/PMC9242572/; **trust in government, schools, and media:** Saad, L. (2023, July 6). Historically low faith in U.S. institutions continues. Gallup. https://news.gallup.com/poll/508169/historically-low-faith-institutions-continues.aspx; **African Americans and less educated:** Suhay, E., Soni, A., Persico, C., & Marcotte, D. E. (2022). Americans' trust in government and health behaviors during the COVID-19 pandemic. *RSF: The Russell Sage Foundation Journal of the Social Sciences*, 8(8), 221–244. https://doi.org/10.7758/RSF.2022.8.8.10; **trust in Netherlands increased:** Groeniger, J. O., Noordzij, K., Van Der Waal, J., & De Koster, W. (2021). Dutch COVID-19 lockdown measures increased trust in government and trust in science: A difference-in-differences analysis. *Social Science & Medicine*, 275, 113819. https://doi.org/10.1016/j.socscimed.2021.113819.

20. **CDC suggestions:** Centers for Disease Control and Prevention. (2007, February). Interim pre-pandemic planning guidance: Community strategy for pandemic influenza mitigation in the United States: Early, targeted, layered use of nonpharmaceutical interventions. https://stacks.cdc.gov/view/cdc/11425; **WHO suggestions:** World Health Organization. (2019). Non-pharmaceutical public health measures for mitigating the risk and impact of epidemic and pandemic influenza. https://www.who.int/publications/i/item/non-pharmaceutical-public-health-measuresfor-mitigating-the-risk-and-impact-of-epidemic-and-pandemic-influenza; **public school exodus:** Dee, T. S. (2023, February 9). Where the kids went: Nonpublic schooling and demographic change during the pandemic exodus from public schools. Urban Institute. https://www.urban.org/research/publication/where-kids-went-nonpublic-schooling-and-demographic-change-during-pandemic; **chronic absenteeism:** Gandhi, 2023, p. 119; **declines in scores:** Reading and mathematics scores decline during COVID-19 pandemic. (2022). National Center for Education Statistics. https://www.nationsreportcard.gov/highlights/ltt/2022/.
21. **Remote learning inequities:** Hoofman, J., & Secord, E. (2021). The effect of COVID-19 on education. *Pediatric Clinics of North America*, 68(5), 1071–1079. https://doi.org/10.1016/j.pcl.2021.05.009; **high-poverty schools and remote learning:** Goldhaber, D., Kane, T. J., McEachin, A., Morton, E., Patterson, T., & Staiger, D. O. (2022). The consequences of remote and hybrid instruction during the pandemic. Harvard University Center for Education Policy Research. https://cepr.harvard.edu/files/cepr/files/5-4.pdf?m=1651690491; **46 percent of low-income parents:** Schaeffer, K. (2021, October 1). What we know about online learning and the homework gap amid the pandemic. Pew Research Center. https://www.pewresearch.org/short-reads/2021/10/01/what-we-know-about-online-learning-and-the-homework-gap-amid-the-pandemic/; **quote:** Agostinelli, F., Doepke, M., Sorrenti, G., & Zilibotti, F. (2022). When the great equalizer shuts down: Schools, peers, and parents in pandemic times, p. 1. *Journal of Public Economics*, 206, 104574. https://doi.org/10.1016/j.jpubeco.2021.104574; **poor not catching up:** Fahle, E. M., Kane, T. J., Patterson, T., Reardon, S. F., Staiger, D. O., & Stuart, E. A. (2023). School district and community factors associated with learning loss during the COVID-19 pandemic. Center for Education Policy Research at Harvard University. https://cepr.harvard.edu/sites/hwpi.harvard.edu/files/cepr/files/explaining_covid_losses_5.23.pdf.
22. **Quote:** Dagsputa, S. (2022). School in the time of Covid, p. 140. *Monash Bioethics Review*, 40(1), 120–144. https://doi.org/10.1007/s40592-022-00161-9.

Chapter 16: Nothing Is as Dangerous as a Man Without a Future (Even If You Offer Universal Basic Income)

1. **Quote:** Stockman, F. (2021). *American made: What happens to people when work disappears*, pp. 9–10. Random House.
2. **Quote:** Sherman, J. (2009). *Those who work, those who don't: Poverty, morality and family in rural America*, 146, University of Minnesota Press; **promised good jobs 2016:** Lamont, M., Park, B. Y., & Ayala-Hurtado, E. (2017). Trump's electoral speeches and his appeal to the American white working class. *The British Journal of Sociology*, 68(S1), S153–S180. https://doi.org/10.1111/1468-4446.12315; **promised good jobs 2020:** Klar, R. (2020, September 8). Trump touts job gains in new ad. The Hill. https://thehill.com/homenews/campaign/515433-trump-touts-job-gains-in-new-ad/.
3. **Weaker support for redistribution:** Oser, J., & Hooghe, M. (2018). Give me your tired, your poor? Support for social citizenship rights in the United States and Europe. *Sociological Perspectives*, 61(1), 14–38. https://doi.org/10.1177/0731121417697305; **stronger support predistribution:** McCall, L. (2013). *The undeserving rich: American beliefs about inequality, opportunity and redistribution.* Cambridge University Press. https://doi.org/10.1017/CBO9781139225687; **quote:** Kuziemko, I., Marx, N. L., & Naidu, S. (2023).

"Compensate the losers?" Economic policy and partisan realignment in the US (No. w31794), p. 3. National Bureau of Economic Research. https://www.nber.org/papers /w31794; **half of the loss:** Kuziemko et al., 2023, p. 30.

4. **Quote:** Abou-Chadi, T., & Hix, S. (2021). Brahmin Left versus Merchant Right? Education, class, multiparty competition, and redistribution in Western Europe, p. 88. *The British Journal of Sociology*, 72(1), 79–92. https://doi.org/10.1111/1468–4446.12834; **middle income ($47,900–$143,600) provide more assistance:** Americans' views of government's role: Persistent divisions and areas of agreement, p. 18. (2024, June 24). Pew Research Center. https://www.pewresearch.org/politics/2024/06/24/americans-views -of-governments-role-persistent-divisions-and-areas-of-agreement/; **middle income ($40,100–$120,400) oppose UBI:** Gilberstadt, H. (2020, August 19). More Americans oppose than favor the government providing a universal basic income for all adult citizens. Pew Research Center. https://www.pewresearch.org/short-reads/2020/08/19/more -americans-oppose-than-favor-the-government-providing-a-universal-basic-income -for-all-adult-citizens/; **70 percent tax rate:** Poll: A majority of Americans supporting raising the top tax rate to 70 percent. (2019, January 15). The Hill. https://thehill.com /hilltv/what-americas-thinking/425422-a-majority-of-americans-support-raising-the -top-tax-rate-to-70/.

5. **Tech executives:** Broockman, D. E., Ferenstein, G., & Malhotra, N. (2018). Predispositions and the political behavior of American economic elites: Evidence from technology entrepreneurs. *American Journal of Political Science*, 63(1), 212–233. https://doi.org/10 .1111/ajps.12408; **"fissured workers":** NYT Editorial Board. (2019, May 29). Google should google the definition of "employee." *The New York Times*. https://www.nytimes.com /2019/05/29/opinion/google-contract-labor.html; **quote:** Sperling, G. B. (2020, April 24). Martin Luther King Jr. predicted this moment. *The New York Times*. https://www .nytimes.com/2020/04/24/opinion/sunday/essential-workers-wages-covid.html; **"wage inequality":** Katz, L. F., & Krueger, A. B. (2019). The rise and nature of alternative work arrangements in the United States, 1995–2015. *ILR Review*, 72(2), 382–416. https://doi .org/10.1177/0019793918820008; **janitor subcontracting:** Dorn, D., Schmieder, J. F., & Spletzer, J. R. (2018). Domestic outsourcing in the United States. *US Department of Labor Technical Report*, 14. https://www.dol.gov/sites/dolgov/files/OASP/legacy/files/Domestic -Outsourcing-in-the-United-States.pdf; **janitor health insurance:** Hinkley, S., Bernhardt, A., & Thomason, S. (2016). Race to the bottom: How low-road subcontracting affects working conditions in California's property services industry. UC Berkeley Labor Center. https://escholarship.org/content/qt9bk1r6pq/qt9bk1r6pq.pdf; **security guards:** Dube, A., & Kaplan, E. (2010). Does outsourcing reduce wages in the low-wage service occupations? Evidence from janitors and guards. *ILR Review*, 63(2), 287–306. https://doi .org/10.1177/001979391006300206.

6. **"Kitchen table" issues:** Lux, M. (2022, June 7). Winning back the factory towns that made Trumpism possible. American Family Voices. https://www.americanfamilyvoices .org/post/winning-back-the-factory-towns-that-made-trumpism-possible; **kitchen table issues, see also:** Abbott, J., Fan, L., Guastella, D., Herz, G., Karp, M., Leach, J., Marvel, J., Rader, K., & Riz, F. (2021). Commonsense solidarity: How a working-class coalition can be built, and maintained. *Jacobin*. https://jacobinmag.com/2021/11/common-sense -solidarity-working-class-voting-report; **dismissing inflation:** Krugman, P. (2023, September 19). Inflation is down, disinflation denial is soaring. *The New York Times*. https:// nytimes.com/2023/09/19/opinion/core-inflation-rate-data.html; **dismissing inflation, see also:** Krugman, P. (2024, February 22). Bidenomics is still working very well. *The New York Times*. https://www.nytimes.com/2024/02/22/opinion/biden-economy.html; **inflation college and noncollege grads:** Halpin, J. (2022, October 25). "One-third of a nation." The Liberal Patriot. https://www.liberalpatriot.com/p/one-third-of-a-nation;

car loans and credit cards: Cramer, K. J., & Cohen, J. D. (2024, February 21). Many Americans believe the economy is rigged. *The New York Times*. https://www.nytimes.com /2024/02/21/opinion/economy-research-greed-profit.html.

7. **Quote:** Vance, J. D. (2016). *Hillbilly elegy: A memoir of a family and culture in crisis*, p. 148. HarperCollins.

8. **Pass a drug test:** Vance, 2016, p. 130; **first and second quotes:** Vance, 2016, p. 91; **third quote:** Howell, J. T. (1973). *Hard living on Clay Street: Portraits of blue collar families*, p. 355. Waveland Press.

9. **First quote:** Pruitt, L. R. (2019). What Hillbilly Elegy reveals about race in twenty-first-century America, p. 116. In A. Harkins & M. McCarroll (Eds.), *Appalachian reckoning: A region responds to Hillbilly Elegy*, pp. 105–133. West Virginia University Press; **second quote:** Sherman, J. (2009). *Those who work, those who don't: Poverty, morality, and family in rural America*, p. 57. University of Minnesota Press; **American Families Plan:** National tracking poll #2104156. (2021, May). Morning Consult. https://assets.morningconsult .com/wp-uploads/2021/05/05062006/2104156_crosstabs_POLITICO_RVs_v1_SH .pdf; **child tax credit permanent:** Americans support a generous child benefit tied to work. (2021, September). American Compass. https://americancompass.org/child -tax-credit-expansion-survey/; **third quote:** Brown, P. T. (2021, September 14). Why working-class parents don't buy what D.C. is selling. *The New York Times*. https://www .nytimes.com/2021/09/14/opinion/child-tax-credit-biden.html.

10. **First quote:** Fiske, S. T. (2011). *Envy up, scorn down: How status divides us*, p. 67. Russell Sage Foundation; **second and third quotes:** Obama, M. (2018). *Becoming*, p. 342. Crown; **dislike for irresponsibility:** Lamont, 2000, p. 28; **Black support for redistribution:** Lindh, A., & McCall, L. (2023). Bringing the market in: An expanded framework for understanding popular responses to economic inequality. *Socio-Economic Review*, 21(2), 1035–1055. https://doi.org/10.1093/ser/mwac018.

11. **Americans blame the poor:** Lamont, 2000, p. 234.

12. **Quote:** Peck, R. (2019). *Fox populism: Branding conservatism as working class*, p. 162. Cambridge University Press; **whites feelings toward welfare:** Soss, J., & Schram, S. F. (2006). Welfare reform as a failed political strategy: Evidence and explanations for the stability of public opinion. *Focus*, 24(3), 17–23. https://irp.wisc.edu/publications/focus /pdfs/foc243c.pdf; **work ethic:** Weissmann, J. (2016, June 1). The failure of welfare reform. *Slate*. https://slate.com/news-and-politics/2016/06/how-welfare-reform-failed .html; *Dog Whistle Politics*: Haney López, I. (2013). *Dog whistle politics: How coded racial appeals have wrecked the middle class*. Oxford University Press.

13. **Latinos hard work:** López, M. H., Gonzalez-Barrera, A., & Krogstad, J. M. (2018, September 11). Latinos are more likely to believe in the American dream, but most say it's hard to achieve. Pew Research Center. https://www.pewresearch.org/short-reads/2018 /09/11/latinos-are-more-likely-to-believe-in-the-american-dream-but-most-say-it-is -hard-to-achieve/; **hard-work worship:** Sandel, M. J. (2020). *The tyranny of merit: What's become of the common good?*, p. 74. Farrar, Straus, and Giroux.

14. **First quote:** Halpern-Meekin, S., Edin, K., Tach, L., & Sykes, J. (2015). *It's not like I'm poor: How working families make ends meet in a post-welfare world*, p. 107. University of California Press; **second quote:** Halpern-Meekin et al., 2015, p. 115; **inequality and redistribution:** Kelly, N. J., & Enns, P. K. (2010). Inequality and the dynamics of public opinion: The self-reinforcing link between economic inequality and mass preferences. *American Journal of Political Science*, 54(4), 855–870. https://www.jstor.org/stable/20788774; **government should do more to solve problems:** Americans see broad responsibilities for government; little change since 2019, p. 16. (2021, May 17). Pew Research Center. https: //www.pewresearch.org/politics/2021/05/17/americans-see-broad-responsibilities-for -government-little-change-since-2019/.

15. **Work requirements:** Astrow, A. (2022, February 20). How does education level impact attitudes among voters of color? Third Way. https://www.thirdway.org/memo/how-does -education-level-impact-attitudes-among-voters-of-color.

16. **Quotes:** Sherman, 2009, p. 78; **First and second quotes:** Boucher, D., & Spangler, T. (2020, September 11). Trump makes wild claims about revitalizing auto industry at Michigan rally. *Detroit Free Press.* https://www.freep.com/story/news/politcs/elections /2020/09/10/trump-michigan-rally-auto-claims/5768672002/; **manufactoring losses in Michigan:** US Bureau of Labor Statistics. All employees: Manufactoring in Michigan. Federal Reserve Bank of St.Louis. Accessed May 9, 2024, from https://fred.stlouisfeed .org/series/MIMFG; **manufacturing losses nationwide:** Employment, hours, and earnings from the current employment statistics survey: Manufacturing. US Bureau of Labor Statistics. Accessed May 9, 2024, from https://datat.bls.gov/timeseries/CES3000000001; **third quote:** 2020 post-mortem part two: The American Dream voter. (2021, December 14). Equis. https://assests.ctfassets.net/ms6ec8hcu35u/4E5a5nNoWi9JNFqeAylkmS /bf542d82f900dbfb62cc6e6d7253a24/Post-Mortem_Part_Two_FINAL_Dec_14.pdf.

17. **Quotes:** Sherman, 2009, p. 78; **First and second quotes:** Boucher & Spangler, 2020; **manufacturing losses in Michigan:** US Bureau of Labor Statistics. All employees: Manufacturing in Michigan. Federal Reserve Bank of St. Louis. Accessed May 9, 2024, from https://fred.stlouisfeed.org/series/MIMFG; **manufacturing losses nationwide:** Employment, hours, and earnings from the current employment statistics survey: Manufacturing. US Bureau of Labor Statistics. Accessed May 9, 2024, from https://datat.bls .gov/timeseries/CES3000000001; **third quote:** 2020 post-mortem part two: The American Dream voter. (2021, December 14). Equis. https://assets.ctfassets.net/ms6ec8hcu35u /4E5a5nNoWi9JNFqeAylkmS/bf542d82f900dbfb62cc6e6d7253a24a/Post-Mortem _Part_Two_FINAL_Dec_14.pdf.

18. **Apprenticeships:** Economic trust gap survey toplines—June 2021. (2021, July 1). Third Way. https://www.thirdway.org/polling/economic-trust-gap-survey-toplines-june-2021; **debt relief priority:** Samuels, A. (2023, March 3). Americans like Biden's student debt forgiveness plan. The Supreme Court . . . not so much. FiveThirtyEight. https://fivethirtyeight .com/features/samuels-student-debt-forgiveness-0303/.

19. **Expanded child tax credit:** *The Economist* / YouGov Poll. (2021, July). YouGov. https: //d3nkl3psvxxpe9.cloudfront.net/documents/econTabReport_OIWJU67.pdf; **permanent child tax credit:** Americans support a generous child benefit tied to work. (2021, September). American Compass. https://americancompass.org/child-tax-credit-expansion -survey/; **helping working parents:** Third Way, 2021.

20. **First quote:** Sperling, 2020; **second quote:** Stockman, 2021, p. 11.

21. **Technical job applications, quotes:** Yang, M. (2023, January 5). America needs carpenters and plumbers. Gen Z doesn't seem interested. NPR. https://www.npr.org/2023/01 /05/1142817339/america-needs-carpenters-and-plumbers-try-telling-that-to-gen-z.

22. **"Four million jobs per year":** Hersh, A. S. (2021, September 16). "Build back better" agenda will ensure strong, stable recovery in coming years. Economic Policy Institute. https://www.epi.org/publication/iija-budget-reconciliation-jobs/; **IRA investments in noncollege counties:** Nostrand, E. V., & Feiveson, L. (2023, August 16). The Inflation Reduction Act and U.S. business investment. US Department of the Treasury. https:// home.treasury.gov/news/featured-stories/the-inflation-reduction-act-and-us-business -investment; **Biden and antitrust:** Sisco, J. (2024, January 2). Biden administration readies a big swing at big businesses in 2024. *Politico.* https://www.politico.com/news/2023 /12/30/heres-how-biden-may-cement-his-antitrust-legacy-in-2024–00132756.

23. **Quote:** Gest, J. (2016). *The new minority: White working class politics in an age of immigration and inequality*, p. 158. Oxford University Press.

24. **Get ahead by working hard:** Newport, F. (2018, March 7). Majority in U.S. satisfied with opportunity to get ahead. Gallup. https://news.gallup.com/poll/228914/majority

-satisfied-opportunity-ahead.aspx; **Republicans income divide:** In a politically polarized era, sharp divides in both partisan coalitions, p. 44. Pew Research Center. https://www .pewresearch.org/politics/2019/12/17/in-a-politically-polarized-era-sharp-divides-in -both-partisan-coalitions/; **support for unions:** Labor unions. (n.d.). Gallup. Accessed June 13, 2024, from https://news.gallup.com/poll/12751/Labor-Unions.aspx.

25. **Income differences:** McCall, 2013, pp. 5, 102, 155, 161.

26. **UBI benefits the poor:** West, S., Baker, A. C., Samra, S., & Coltrera, E. (2021). Preliminary analysis: SEED's first year. Stockton Economic Empowerment Demonstration. https://static1 .squarespace.com/static/6039d612b17d055cac14070f/t/603ef1194c474b329f33c329 /1614737690661/SEED_Preliminary+Analysis-SEEDs+First+Year_Final+Report _Individual+Pages+-2.pdf; **quote:** 100 days into the Trump era, working-class "searchers" who voted for him are having doubts, open to appeals. (2017, April). Working America. https://www.workingamerica.org/sites/default/files/documents/2017–04/100%20Days%20 FPFG%20Report%20100AFINAL.pdf.

27. **Means testing, European welfare support:** Alesina, A., Sacerdote, B., & Glaeser, E. (2001). Why doesn't the United States have a European-style welfare state? *Brookings Papers on Economic Activity*, 2, 187–277. https://www.brookings.edu/articles/why-doesnt -the-united-states-have-a-european-style-welfare-state/; **quote:** Rieder, J. (1985). *Canarsie: The Jews and Italians of Brooklyn against liberalism*, p. 106. Harvard University Press; **Kansas family Medicaid:** Cramer & Cohen, 2024.

28. **Middle-income government support:** Gilberstadt, 2020; **make child tax credit permanent:** American Compass, 2021; **child poverty doubled:** Parrot, S. (2023, September 12). Record rise in poverty highlights importance of Child Tax Credit; health coverage marks a high point before pandemic safeguards ended. Center on Budget and Policy Priorities. https://www.cbpp.org/press/statements/record-rise-in-poverty-highlights-importance -of-child-tax-credit-health-coverage.

29. **Pointed this out:** Skocpol, T. (1991). Targeting within universalism: Politically viable policies to combat poverty in the United States. In C. Jencks & P. E. Peterson, Eds., The urban underclass, pp. 411–436. The Brookings Institution; **Tim Walz:** Toussaint, K. (2024, August 6). How Tim Walz made school meals free for all students. *Fast Company*. https: //www.fastcompany.com/91168428/how-tim-walz-made-school-meals-free-for-all -minnesota-students.

30. **"Social housing":** Mari, F. (2023, May 26). Imagine a renters' utopia. It might look like Vienna. *The New York Times*. https://www.nytimes.com/2023/05/23/magazine/vienna -social-housing.html.

31. **92 percent preferred:** Norton, M. I., & Ariely, D. (2011). Building a better America— One wealth quintile at a time. *Perspectives on Psychological Science*, 6(1), 9–12. https://doi .org/10.1177/1745691610393524.

32. **First quote:** Halpern-Meekin, S., Edin, K., Tach, L., & Sykes, J. (2015). *It's not like I'm poor: How working families make ends meet in a post-welfare world*, p. 103. University of California Press; **second quote:** Williams, J. C. (2017). *White working class: Overcoming class cluelessness in America*, p. 19. Harvard Business Review Press.

33. **Earned Income Tax Credit:** Earned Income Tax Credit: Halpern-Meekin et al., 2015, pp. 100–105.

34. *Washington Post* **middle class:** Fowers, A., Guskin, E., & Clement, S. (2024, February 15). How Americans define a middle-class lifestyle—and why they can't reach it. *The Washington Post*. https://www.washingtonpost.com/business/2024/02/15/middle-class-financial -security/; **quotes:** Cramer & Cohen, 2024.

35. **College wage premium:** Mishel, L., & Bivens, J. (2021, May 13). Identifying the policy levers generating wage suppression and wage inequality. Economic Policy Institute. https:// www.epi.org/unequalpower/publications/wage-suppression-inequality/; **does not predictably enhance wealth:** Bartscher, A. K., Kuhn, M., & Schularick, M. (2020). The

college wealth divide: Education and inequality in America, 1956–2016. https://papers
.ssrn.com/sol3/papers.cfm?abstract_id=3587685; **average debt doubled:** Schmitt, J., &
Boushey, H. (2010, December 3). The college conundrum: Why the benefits of a college
education may not be so clear, especially to men, p. 5. Center for American Progress.
https://www.americanprogress.org/article/the-college-conundrum/; **student loan debt,
see also:** Yellen, J. L. (2016). Perspectives on inequality and opportunity from the survey
of consumer finances, p. 54. *RSF: The Russell Sage Foundation Journal of the Social Sciences*, 2(2), 44–59. https://doi.org/10.7758/RSF.2016.2.2.02; **student debt at graduation:**
Draut, T. (2006). *Strapped: Why America's 20- and 30-somethings can't get ahead*, p. 7. Doubleday; **college graduate earnings:** Draut, 2006, p. 11.

36. **Male graduate earnings gap:** Schmitt & Boushey, 2010, p. 8; **earn less than high school
grad:** Schmitt & Boushey, 2010, p. 3; **quote:** Kurz, C., Li, G., & Vine, D. J. (2018, November). Are millennials different?, abstr. Board of Governors of the Federal Reserve
System Finance and Economics Discussion Series. https://doi.org/10.17016/FEDS
.2018.080; **own a home, student debt:** Hobbes, M. (2017, December 14). Why millennials are facing the scariest financial future of any generation since the Great Depression.
HuffPost. https://highline.huffingtonpost.com/articles/en/poor-millennials/.

37. **Youth unemployment:** Unemployment, youth total (% of total labor force ages 15–24).
The World Bank. Accessed March 20, 2024, from https://data.worldbank.org/indicator
/SL.UEM.NEET.ZS?end=2022&start=1976&view=chart.

38. **Quote:** Waters, C. (2023, February 22). Wall Street has purchased hundreds of thousands of single-family homes since the Great Recession. Here's what that means for rental
prices. CNBC. https://www.cnbc.com/2023/02/21/how-wall-street-bought-single-family
-homes-and-put-them-up-for-rent.html; **Harris wasted no time:** Maruf, R., Wallace, A.,
Delouya, S., & Lopez, L. (2024, August 16). Harris has a plan to fix one of America's
biggest economic problems. Here's what it means for you. CNN. https://www.cnn.com
/2024/08/16/business/harris-housing-plan/index.html; **youth pessimism, children better
off than parents:** Miller, C. C., & Parlapiano, A. (2021, November 23). Where are young
people most optimistic? In poorer nations. *The New York Times*. https://www.nytimes.com
/2021/11/17/upshot/global-survey-optimism.html.

39. **"It sucks to be 33":** Barbaro, M. [Host]. (2024, March 14). It sucks to be 33 [audio podcast episode]. In *The Daily*. *The New York Times*. https://www.nytimes.com/2024/03/14
/podcasts/the-daily/millennial-economy.html; traditional accoutrements of adulthood:
Draut, 2006, p. 6.

40. **Rents in major cities:** Draut, 2006, p. 13; **housing second to inflation:** Smialek, J., Tankersley, J., & Dougherty, C. (2023, December 15). American Dream deferred: Why housing
prices may pose a problem for Biden. *The New York Times*. https://www.nytimes.com/2023
/12/15/us/politics/housing-prices-biden.html; **rents climbed 22 percent:** Consumer price
index for all urban consumers: Rent of primary residence in U.S. city average. (n.d.). US
Bureau of Labor Statistics. Accessed February 21, 2024, from https://fred.stlouisfed.org
/series/CUUR0000SEHA; **home prices rose 46 percent:** S&P CoreLogic Case-Shiller
20-city composite home price index. (n.d.). US Bureau of Labor Statistics. Accessed
February 21, 2024, from https://fred.stlouisfed.org/series/SPCS20RSA; **TikTok video:**
Calvillo, B. [@bjcalvillo]. (2024, January 24). Buying a house 30 years ago vs today [video].
TikTok. https://www.tiktok.com/@bjcalvillo/video/7327834209597574446.

Chapter 17: Understand Why Demography Wasn't Destiny

1. **Quote:** Blow, C. M. (2024, March 13). Some Black voters are souring on Democrats. It
may be part of a natural drift. *The New York Times*. https://www.nytimes.com/2024/03/13
/opinion/black-democrats-trump-biden.html.

2. **Liberal or very liberal:** Saad, L. (2023, January 12). Democrats' identification as liberal now 54%, a new high. Gallup. https://news.gallup.com/poll/467888/democrats

-identification-liberal-new-high.aspx; **abortion, gay marriage, and pathway to citizenship:** Cross-tabs: July 2023 Times/Siena poll of the 2024 race and national issues. (2023, August 1). *The New York Times.* https://www.nytimes.com/interactive/2023/08/01/us/elections/times-siena-poll-registered-voters-crosstabs.html; **graduation rates:** Solman, P., & Koromvokis, L. (2021, October 26). Jobs requiring college degrees disqualify most U.S. workers—especially workers of color. PBS News Hour. https://www.pbs.org/newshour/show/jobs-requiring-college-degrees-disqualify-most-u-s-workers-especially-workers-of-color.

3. **Two-thirds of Latinos, first quote:** Haney López, I. (2022). Project Juntos: Latinx race-class. Project Juntos. https://static1.squarespace.com/static/5ef377b623eaf41dd9df1311/t/5f6fd7e84ca040062e8dc0b9/1601165291980/Project+Juntos+Summary+Briefing+092620.pdf; **second quote:** Haney López, I. (2019). *Merge left: Fusing race and class, winning elections, and saving America,* p. 111. The New Press; **third quote:** Haney López, 2019, p. 111.

4. **Asian Americans:** Budiman, A., Passel, J. S., & Im, C. (2024, January 10). Key facts about Asian American eligible voters in 2024. Pew Research Center. https://www.pewresearch.org/short-reads/2024/01/10/key-facts-about-asian-american-eligible-voters-in-2024/.

5. **Black liberals:** Gilberstadt, H., & Daniller, A. (2020, January 17). Liberals make up the largest share of Democratic voters, but their growth has slowed in recent years. Pew Research Center. https://www.pewresearch.org/short-reads/2020/01/17/liberals-make-up-largest-share-of-democratic-voters/; **under forty-five shifted:** McGill, B., & Day, C. (2022, November 14). How we voted in the 2022 midterm elections. *The Wall Street Journal.* https://www.wsj.com/articles/how-different-groups-voted-in-the-2022-midterm-elections-11667955705.

6. **Trailing economic issues:** Americans' top policy priority for 2024: Strengthening the economy, p. 8. (2024, February 29). Pew Research Center. https://www.pewresearch.org/politics/2024/02/29/americans-top-policy-priority-for-2024-strengthening-the-economy/; **Black-white pay gap:** Leonhardt, D. (2023). *Ours was the shining future: The story of the American Dream,* p. 114. Random House.

7. **Treated fairly, changes in policing:** Brown, M. C., II., & Lloyd, C. (2023, September 18). Black Americans less confident, satisfied with local police. Gallup. https://news.gallup.com/poll/511064/black-americans-less-confident-satisfied-local-police.aspx; **criminal justice reform:** Public's top priority for 2022: Strengthening the nation's economy, p. 11. (2022, February 16). Pew Research Center. https://www.pewresearch.org/politics/2022/02/16/publics-top-priority-for-2022-strengthening-the-nations-economy/; **71 percent of white liberals and 53 percent of Blacks defund the police:** Cox, D. A. (2022, February 22). Crime, policing and the racial divide on the left. Survey Center on American Life. https://www.americansurveycenter.org/crime-policing-and-the-racial-divide-on-the-left/; **half of Blacks agreed:** Harper Pope, L. (2023, December 19). Black Democrats are moderate. Slow Boring. https://www.slowboring.com/p/black-democrats-are-moderate.

8. **Border patrols, border security:** Harper Pope, 2023.

9. **Climate change:** Harper Pope, 2023.

10. **Helping the poor:** Pew Research Center, 2024, p. 8; **managing the economy:** Economic trust gap survey toplines—June 2021. (2021, July 1). Third Way. https://www.thirdway.org/polling/economic-trust-gap-survey-toplines-june-2021.

11. **Get ahead if they work hard:** Pougiales, R., & Fulton, J. (2019, December 30). A nuanced picture of what Black Americans want in 2020. Third Way. https://www.thirdway.org/memo/a-nuanced-picture-of-what-black-americans-want-in-2020; **redistribution suspicion and racism:** Quadagno, J. S. (1994). *The color of welfare: How racism undermined the war on poverty.* Oxford University Press; **redistribution and racism, see also:** Lee, W., & Roemer, J. E. (2006). Racism and redistribution in the United States: A solution to the

problem of American exceptionalism. *Journal of Public Economics*, 90(6–7), 1027–1052. https://doi.org/10.1016/j.jpubeco.2005.08.008; quotes: Haney López, 2019, pp. 90–91; **vigorously monitor:** Hochschild, J. L. (1995). *Facing up to the American Dream: Race, class, and the soul of the nation*, p. 124. Princeton University Press.

12. **Jobs and prosperity:** Haney López, 2019, p. 90; **Black Republicans:** Fields, C. D. (2016). *Black elephants in the room: The unexpected politics of African American Republicans*, pp. 120, 136. University of California Press; **recent polling:** Abbott, J., DeVeaux, F., Fan, L., Guadron, C., Guastella, D., Herz, G., Karp, M., Marvel, J., Rader, K., Riz, F., & Rabbani, I. (2023). Trump's kryptonite: How progressives can win back the working class, p. 32. *Jacobin.* https://jacobin.com/2023/06/trumps-kryptonite-progressive -working-class-voting-report.

13. **Men shift right, first quote:** Dent, D. J. (2022, December 4). Why are more Black men voting Republican? *Rolling Stone.* https://www.rollingstone.com/politics/politics-features /black-men-voting-republican-obama-trump-romney-1234641210/; **being providers:** Lamont, M. (2000). *The dignity of working men: Morality and the boundaries of race, class, and immigration*, p. 21. Harvard University Press; **second quote:** Dent, 2022.

14. **Quote:** McGrady, C. (2020, November 20). Some famous rappers backed Trump's campaign. Did it matter? *The Washington Post.* https://www.washingtonpost.com/lifestyle /rappers-trump-maga-ice-cube-lil-wayne-lil-pump/2020/11/19/f4aec62e-2316-11eb -8599-406466ad1b8e_story.html.

15. **First and second quotes:** Barker, G., Hayes, C., Heilman, B., & Reichert, M. (2023). The state of American men: From crisis and confusion to hope, p. 36. Equimundo. https:// www.equimundo.org/resources/state-of-american-men/; **third quote:** Dent, 2022.

16. **Quote:** Harris, F. C., & Rivera-Burgos, V. (2021). The continuing dilemma of race and class in the study of American political behavior, p. 187. *Annual Review of Political Science*, 24, 175–191. https://doi.org/10.1146/annurev-polisci-050317-071219; **polling:** Pougiales & Fulton, 2019.

17. **More pro-life:** Political and religious activation and polarization in the wake of the *Roe v. Wade* overturn. (2022, July 7). PRRI. https://www.prri.org/research/political-and-religious -activation-and-polarization-in-the-wake-of-the-roe-overturn/; **believing is necessary:** Pougiales & Fulton, 2019; **religious sects:** Masci, D., Mohamed, B., & Smith, G. A. (2018, April 23). Black Americans are more likely than overall public to be Christian, Protestant. Pew Research Center. https://www.pewresearch.org/short-reads/2018/04/23/black -americans-are-more-likely-than-overall-public-to-be-christian-protestant/; **attend services regularly:** Frasure, L., Wong, J., Vargas, E., & Barreto, M. (2016). Collaborative multiracial post-election survey. https://cmpsurvey.org/2016-survey/; **homosexual sex:** General Social Survey. (2018). National Opinion Research Center (NORC). https://gss .norc.org/.

18. **Effect on voting behavior:** Kidd, Q., Diggs, H., Farooq, M., & Murray, M. (2007). Black voters, Black candidates and social issues: Does party identification matter? *Social Science Quarterly*, 88(1), 165–176. https://doi.org/10.1111/j.1540-6237.2007.00452.x.

19. **First quote:** Taladrid, S. (2020, October 26). How pro-Trump disinformation is swaying a new generation of Cuban-American voters. *The New Yorker.* https://www.newyorker .com/news/us-journal/how-pro-trump-disinformation-is-swaying-a-new-generation-of -cuban-american-voters; **Trump 2020:** Exit polls: Florida. (2020). CNN. https://www.cnn .com/election/2020/exit-polls/president/florida; **Trump 2016:** Exit polls: Florida. (2016). CNN. https://www.cnn.com/election/2016/results/exit-polls/florida/president; **second, third, and fourth quotes:** Paz, C. (2020, October 29). What liberals don't understand about pro-Trump Latinos. *The Atlantic.* https://www.theatlantic.com/politics/archive/2020 /10/trump-latinos-biden-2020/616901/.

20. **Trump Latinos 2020:** Ghitza, Y., & Robinson, J. (2021). What happened in 2020. Catalist. https://catalist.us/wh-national/.

21. **First quote, identify as white:** Herrera, J. (2021, October). Why Democrats are losing Texas Latinos. *Texas Monthly.* https://www.texasmonthly.com/news-politics/democrats -losing-texas-latinos-trump/; **paths to the middle class:** Medina, J. (2022, March 1). How immigration politics drives some Hispanic voters to the G.O.P. in Texas. *The New York Times.* https://www.nytimes.com/2022/02/28/us/politics/border-grievance-politics .html; **second quote:** Findell, E. (2020, November 8). Why Democrats lost so many South Texas Latinos. *The Wall Street Journal.* https://www.wsj.com/articles/how-democrats-lost -so-many-south-texas-latinosthe-economy-11604871650; **third quote:** Goodman, J. D., Sandoval, E., & Gebeloff, R. (2023, November 13). What it means to be a Texan is changing in surprising ways. *The New York Times.* https://www.nytimes.com/2023/11/13 /us/texas-identity-population-politics-future.html; **fourth quote:** Memo to interested parties: New Hispanic realignment survey shows broad dissatisfaction with Democrats, GOP poised to make big gains in November. (2022, August 11). Texas Latino Conservatives. https://echeloninsights.com/wp-content/uploads/TLC-Hispanic-Realignment -Memo-August-2022.pdf.

22. **Trump Hispanics 2020:** Ghitza & Robinson, 2021; **New York Hispanics:** Thomas, M. (2021, August 16). Queens is more diverse than ever and more Republican than 20 years ago. Vulgar Marxism. https://vulgarmarxism.substack.com/p/queens-is-more-diverse -than-ever?fbclid=IwAR03gZTPjmd_ZHWQMuU1qs0Mb5D-Vvoc9xUaSZOyYDW 6NBN7xg6oLuFoXNw.

23. **Quote:** Medina, J. (2021, October 8). A vexing question for Democrats: What drives Latino men to Republicans? *The New York Times.* https://www.nytimes.com/2021/03/05 /us/politics/latino-voters-democrats.html; **hard work:** Haney López et al., 2018; **reward hard work, tax big business and the rich:** Economic trust gap survey toplines—June 2021. (2021, July 1). Third Way. https://www.thirdway.org/polling/economic-trust-gap-survey -toplines-june-2021; **American dream:** Echelon Insights. (2020, October). Opening doors to opportunity: Generation Z and millennials speak. Walton Family Foundation. https://8ce82b94a8c4fdc3ea6d-b1d233e3bc3cb10858bea65ff05e18f2.ssl.cf2.rackcdn.com /b1/02/ddcbc1d6434d91e8494f0070fa96/echelon-insights-walton-family-foundation -generation-z-millennials-and-opportunity-report-october-2020–10–6–20.pdf.

24. **Abortion and crime:** Sanchez, G. R. (2022, November 3). Will Democratic focus on abortion policy help reverse decrease in Democratic vote share among Latinas over time? Brookings. https://www.brookings.edu/articles/will-democratic-focus-on-abortion -policy-help-reverse-decrease-in-democratic-vote-share-among-latinas-over-time/; **first quote:** Medina, 2021; **second quote:** Medina, J. (2024, February 11). Latino, working class and proud. *The New York Times.* https://www.nytimes.com/2024/02/11/us/politics /democrats-latinos-biden-trump.html.

25. **Economic issues:** Tausanovitch, C., & Vavreck, L. (2021). Democracy Fund + UCLA Nationscape data set. Democracy Fund Voter Study Group. https://www.voterstudygroup .org/data/nationscape; **first quote:** Herrera, 2021; **over 70 percent:** Tausanovitch & Vavreck, 2021; **second quote:** Brownstein, R. (2022, July 21). Are Latinos really realigning towards Republicans? *The Atlantic.* https://www.theatlantic.com/politics/archive/2022/07 /working-class-latino-voters-political-alignment/670593/; **third quote:** C. Odio, personal communication, August 8, 2021; **Democrats do better:** Third Way, 2021.

26. **Trump the businessman, quote:** 2020 post-mortem part one: Portrait of a persuadable Latino. (2021, April). Equis Research. https://downloads.ctfassets.net/ms6ec8hcu35u /5BR9iHBhsyQtqUU1gNgfaR/b0f4d0be5f55297c627a3f2373fb11b8/Equis_Post -Mortem_Part_One.pdf; pandemic hurt small business: Findell, 2020; hard work: Haney López, 2022.

27. **Latinos redistribution:** Barreto, M. (2023, November 6). Latino voters and the diploma divide: The importance of generation [PowerPoint slides]. Diploma Divide Working Group Conference, UC Law SF.

28. **Quote:** Midterm persuasion messaging for Latino voters. (2022, August 17). Equis. https: //www.weareequis.us/en-US/labs/labs-our-work/midterm-persuasion-messaging-for -latino-voters; **gun control:** Equis key states series: Gun safety memo. (2022, September 6). Equis. https://weareequis.us/en-US/institute/insitute-our-work/equis-key-states-series -gun-safety-memo; *Roe v. Wade:* Equis key states series: Abortion memo. (2022, September 6). Equis. https://assets.ctfassets.net/ms6ec8hcu35u/1nvzEQPJa6TmkurJkyS48f/51 600c5f85113777f2e0dc1931508899/-ABORTION-_Equis_Key_States_Series_Memo _09062022.pdf; **Mayra Flores:** Svitek, P., & Choi, M. (2022, November 4). Republican confidence grows as they eye South Texas congressional sweep. *Texas Tribune.* https://www .texastribune.org/2022/11/04/south-texas-republicans-congressional-districts/; **believe in God to be moral:** In a politically polarized era, sharp divides in both partisan coalitions, p. 74. (2019, December 17). Pew Research Center. https://www.pewresearch.org/politics /2019/12/17/in-a-politically-polarized-era-sharp-divides-in-both-partisan-coalitions/.

29. **Attend church, abortion by generation:** Franco, M. E., & Contreras, R. (2022, June 28). Latinos split on abortion by generation. Axios. https://www.axios.com/2022/06/28 /abortion-views-latinos-supreme-court-roe-poll; abortion by race: PRRI, 2022.

30. **Path to citizenship:** Gonzalez-Barrera, A., Krogstad, J. M., & Noe-Bustamante, L. (2020, February 11). Path to legal status for the unauthorized is top immigration policy goal for Hispanics in the U.S. Pew Research Center. https://www.pewresearch .org/short-reads/2020/02/11/path-to-legal-status-for-the-unauthorized-is-top -immigration-policy-goal-for-hispanics-in-u-s/; **"Remain in Mexico":** Contreras, R. (2022, June 30). Exclusive poll: Majority of Latinos support Trump-era COVID border policy. Axios. https://www.axios.com/2022/06/30/title-42-latino-support-border -immigration; **first and second quotes:** Medina, 2022; **third quote, Trump will help address:** Paz, 2020.

31. **Leading to more crime:** Noe-Bustamante, L. (2024, March 4). Latinos' views on the migrant situation at the U.S.-Mexico border, p. 5. Pew Research Center. https://www .pewresearch.org/race-and-ethnicity/2024/03/04/latinos-views-on-the-migrant -situation-at-the-us-mexico-border/.

32. **Assimilation into whiteness:** Fiske, S. T. (2011). *Envy up, scorn down: How status divides us,* p. 124. Russell Sage Foundation; quote: Findell, 2020.

Chapter 18: Understand the Flaws in the Conventional Wisdom That MAGA Is About Racism and Status Anxiety, Not Economics

1. **Quote:** Mutz, D. (2018). Status threat, not economic hardship, explains the 2016 presidential vote. Proceedings of the National Academy of Sciences (PNAS), 115(19), E4330-E4339. https://doi.org/10.1073/pnas.1718155115.

2. **PRRI/***Atlantic:* Cox, D., Lienesch, R., & Jones, R. P. (2017). Beyond economics: Fears of cultural displacement pushed the white working class to Trump. *PRRI / The Atlantic.* https://www.prri.org/research/white-working-class-attitudes-economy-trade-immigration -election-donald-trump; **Diana Mutz:** Mutz, 2018.

3. *Washington Post* **op-ed:** Carnes, N., & Lupu, N. (2017, June 5). It's time to bust the myth: Most Trump voters were not working class. *The Washington Post.* https://www .washingtonpost.com/news/monkey-cage/wp/2017/06/05/its-time-to-bust-the-myth -most-trump-voters-were-not-working-class/; **Trump attracted middle status:** Kurer, T. (2020). The declining middle: Occupational change, social status, and the populist right. Comparative Political Studies, 53(10–11), 1798–1835. https://doi.org/10.1177 /0010414020912283.

4. **60-point increase:** Schaffner, B. F., Macwilliams, M., & Nteta, T. (2018). Understanding white polarization in the 2016 vote for president: The sobering role of racism and sexism, p. 25. *Political Science Quarterly,* 133(1), 9–34. https://doi.org/10.1002/polq.12737.

5. **Bacon's Rebellion:** Africans in America: Bacon's Rebellion. (n.d.). PBS/KQED. Accessed

May 1, 2024, from https://www.pbs.org/wgbh/aia/part1/1p274.html; **quote:** Adams, J. Q. (2017). *John Quincy Adams: Diaries 1821–1848* (D. Waldstreicher, Ed.), 537–545. Library of America. https://www.loa.org/books/548-diaries-1821–1848/.

6. **Dog whistle politics:** Haney López, I. (2013). Dog whistle politics: How coded racial appeals have reinvented racism and wrecked the middle class. Oxford University Press.

7. **Low correlations:** Marble, W. (2023, September). What explains educational polarization among white voters?, p. 32. https://williammarble.co/docs/EducPolarization.pdf; **same weight on race:** Marble, 2023, p. 34; **quote:** Ferguson, T., Page, B., Rothschild, J., Chang, A., & Chen, J. (2018). The economic and social roots of populist rebellion: Support for Donald Trump in 2016. Institute for New Economic Thinking Working Paper Series, (83). https://papers.ssrn.com/sol3/papers.cfm?abstract_id=3306267; **measure 1: resentment:** Hooghe, M., & Dassonneville, R. (2018). Explaining the Trump vote: The effect of racist resentment and anti-immigrant sentiments. PS: Political Science and Politics, 51(3), 528–534. https://doi.org/10.1017/S1049096518000367; **measure 2: animus:** Mason, L., Wronski, J., & Kane, J. V. (2021). Activating animus: The uniquely social roots of Trump support. American Political Science Review, 115(4), 1508–1516. https://doi.org/10.1017/S0003055421000563; **measure 3: white identity politics:** Jardina, A. (2019). White identity politics. Cambridge University Press. https://doi.org/10.1017/9781108645157; **measure 4: anti-anti-racism:** Feldman, S., & Huddy, L. (2005). Racial resentment and white opposition to race-conscious programs: Principles or prejudice? *American Journal of Political Science*, 49(1), 168–183. https://doi.org/10.1111/j.0092–5853.2005.00117.x.

8. **Quote:** Lamont, M., Park, B. Y., & Ayala-Hurtado, E. (2017). Trump's electoral speeches and his appeal to the American white working class, p. S157. *The British Journal of Sociology*, 68(S1), S153–S180. https://doi.org/10.1111/1468–4446.12315; **Trump's tweets:** Miller, Z. (2020, June 28). Trump tweets video with "white power" chant, then deletes it. Associated Press. https://apnews.com/article/donald-trump-race-and-ethnicity-tim-scott-fl-state-wire-ap-top-news-7eea48b80f14474b7057967a9654c4f0; **refusal to distance himself:** McCammon, S. (2020, September 30). From debate stage, Trump declines to denounce white supremacy. NPR. https://www.npr.org/2020/09/30/918483794/from-debate-stage-trump-declines-to-denounce-white-supremacy.

9. **American preservationists:** Ekins, E. (2017). The five types of Trump voters: Who they are and what they believe. Democracy Fund Voter Study Group. https://www.voterstudygroup.org/publication/the-five-types-trump-voters#share-content.

10. **Blacks lost more jobs:** Scott, R. E., Wilson, V., Kandra, J., & Perez, D. (2022, January 31). Botched policy responses to globalization have decimated manufacturing employment with often overlooked costs for Black, brown, and other workers of color. Economic Policy Institute. https://www.epi.org/publication/botched-policy-responses-to-globalization/; **Black unemployment:** Labor force characteristics by race and ethnicity, 2022. (2023, November). US Bureau of Labor Statistics. https://www.bls.gov/opub/reports/race-and-ethnicity/2022/home.htm; **Black underemployment:** Nunn, R., Parsons, J., & Shambaugh, J. (2019, August 1). Race and underemployment in the US labor market. Brookings. https://www.brookings.edu/articles/race-and-underemployment-in-the-u-s-labor-market/.

11. **Quote:** Sides, J., Tesler, M., & Vavreck, L. (2017). The 2016 U.S. election: How Trump lost and won, p. 40. *Journal of Democracy*, 28(2), 34–44. https://doi.org/10.1353/jod.2017.0022.

12. **First and second quotes:** Tesler, M., & Sides, J. (2016, March 3). How political science helps explain the rise of Trump: The role of white identity and grievances. *The Washington Post*. https://www.washingtonpost.com/news/monkey-cage/wp/2016/03/03/how-political-science-helps-explain-the-rise-of-trump-the-role-of-white-identity-and-grievances/; **racial animus:** Mason et al., 2021; **discount class:** Schaffner et al., 2018.

13. **Obama-era backlash:** Tesler, M. (2016). *Post-racial or most-racial? Race and politics in the Obama era.* University of Chicago Press; **grew at each step:** Edsall, T. B. (2023, March 22). The unsettling truth about Trump's first great victory. *The New York Times.* https: //www.nytimes.com/2023/03/22/opinion/trump-racial-resentment-2016–2020.html; **most and least resentful:** Grimmer, J., Marble, W., & Tanigawa-Lau, C. (2022). Measuring the contribution of voting blocs to election outcomes. https://doi.org/10.31235 /osf.io/c9fkg.

14. **First quote:** Grimmer et al., 2022, p. 28; **second quote:** Grimmer et al., 2022, p. 34; **third quote:** Edsall, 2023.

15. **Anti-elites:** Ekins, 2017.

16. **Diana Mutz:** Mutz, 2018; **quote:** Cox et al., 2017, sec. I; **predicts support for populists:** Kurer, 2020, p. 1804; **populism, see also:** Mughan, A., & Lacy, D. (2002). Economic performance, job insecurity and electoral choice. *British Journal of Political Science,* 32(3), 513–533. https://doi.org/10.1017/S0007123402000212.

17. **Quote:** Cox et al., 2017, sec. VI.

18. **Three times as likely, 14 percent of noncollege:** Cox et al., 2017, sec. III; **American dream, best days behind:** Cox et al., 2017, sec. VI.

19. **Quote:** Mutz, 2018, p. E4330; **China shock:** Autor, D. H., Dorn, D., & Hanson, G. H. (2016). The China shock: Learning from labor-market adjustment to large changes in trade. *Annual Review of Economics,* 8, 205–240. https://doi.org/10.1146/annurev -economics-080315–015041.

20. **Globalization:** Mutz, 2018, p. E4332.

21. **Quote:** Mutz, 2018, p. E4332.

22. **Quotes:** Cox et al., 2017, sec. VIII.

23. **First quote:** Cox et al., 2017, sec. XI; **second and third quotes, experience discrimination, immigrant citizenship:** Cox et al., 2017, sec. VIII; **linked with fears of foreign influence:** Cox et al., 2017, sec. I.

24. **Deportations and discrimination against whites:** Cox et al., 2017, sec. XI.

25. **Higher in anxiety:** Duguid, M. M., & Goncalo, J. A. (2015). Squeezed in the middle: The middle status trade creativity for focus, p. 589. *Journal of Personality and Social Psychology,* 109(4), 589–603. https://psycnet.apa.org/doi/10.1037/a0039569; **others don't worry:** Duguid & Goncalo, 2015, p. 590; **"fear of falling":** Ehrenreich, B. (1989). *Fear of falling: The inner life of the middle class.* Pantheon Books; **quote:** Fiske, S. (2011). *Envy up, scorn down: How status divides us,* p. 153. Russell Sage Foundation.

26. **Quote:** Gest, J. (2016). *The new minority: White working class politics in an age of immigration and inequality,* p. 164. Oxford University Press; see also: Lakner, C., & Milanovic, B. (2016). Global income distribution: From the fall of the Berlin Wall to the Great Recession. *The World Bank Economic Review,* 30(2), 203–232. https://doi.org/10.1093/wber /lhv039.

Chapter 19: Talking Across Class Lines

1. **Quote:** Vargas, C. (2020, August 18). Who gives a shit if the majority of Hispanics don't know or use Latinx. Latino Rebels. https://www.latinorebels.com/2020/08/18 /latinxopinion/.

2. **Found Latinx offensive:** Torregrosa, L. L. (2021, December 14). Many Latinos say "Latinx" offends or bothers them. Here's why. NBC News. https://www.nbcnews.com/think /opinion/many-latinos-say-latinx-offends-or-bothers-them-here-s-ncna1285916; **3 percent use it:** Noe-Bustamante, L., Mora, L., & López, M. H. (2020). About one-in-four U.S. Hispanics have heard of Latinx, but just 3% use it. Pew Research Center. https://www .pewresearch.org/hispanic/2020/08/11/about-one-in-four-u-s-hispanics-have-heard-of -latinx-but-just-3-use-it/; **79 percent lack degrees:** Solman, P., & Koromvokis, L. (2021, October 26). Jobs requiring college degrees disqualify most U.S. workers—especially

workers of color. PBS News Hour. https://www.pbs.org/newshour/show/jobs-requiring
-college-degrees-disqualify-most-u-s-workers-especially-workers-of-color; **political correctness:** Hawkins, S., Yudkin, D., Juan-Torres, M., & Dixon, T. (2018). *Hidden tribes:
A study of America's polarized landscape*, p. 130. https://hiddentribes.us/media/qfpekz4g
/hidden_tribes_report.pdf; **quote:** Bazelon, E. (2021, June 14). Speaking truth to both the
right and left. *The New York Times*. https://www.nytimes.com/2021/06/14/books/review
/george-packer-last-best-hope-jonathan-rauch-the-constitution-of-knowledge.html;
focus on virtue: Hochschild, J. (1996). *Facing up to the American Dream: Race, class, and
the soul of the nation*, p. 24. Princeton University Press.

3. **34 percent of liberals and 14 percent of conservatives fail to tailor arguments:** Feinberg, M., & Willer, R. (2015). From gulf to bridge: When do moral arguments facilitate
political influence. *Personality and Social Psychology Bulletin*, 41(12), 1665–1681. https:
//doi.org/10.1177/0146167215607842; **"woke":** Fox News. (2022, August 17). *DeSantis: Florida is where "woke" goes to die* [video]. *YouTube*. https://www.youtube.com/watch
?v=gexHjhwIC0Q; **first quote:** Nadler, A. (2022). Political identity and the therapeutic
work of US conservative media, p. 2621. *International Journal of Communication*, 16, p. 13.
https://ijoc.org/index.php/ijoc/article/view/18366/3778; **second quote:** Nadler, 2022, p.
2622; **third quote:** Nadler, 2022, p. 2625; **fourth and fifth quotes, anti-lockdown protestors:** Nadler, 2022, p. 2626; **sixth quote:** Nadler, 2022, p. 2628.

4. **Negative stereotypes:** Cramer, K. J. (2016). *The politics of resentment: Rural consciousness
and the rise of Scott Walker*, p. 66. University of Chicago Press; **first quote:** Nadler, A. (2020,
October 2). The great anti-left show. *Los Angeles Review of Books*. https://lareviewofbooks
.org/article/the-great-anti-left-show/; **second quote:** Krugman, P. (2024, January 29).
MAGA is based on fear, not grounded in reality. *The New York Times*. https://www
.nytimes.com/2024/01/29/opinion/trump-maga-fear.html.

5. **Quote:** MSNBC. (2024, February 26). *"White Rural Rage" looks at the most likely group
to abandon democratic norms* [video]. *YouTube*. https://www.youtube.com/watch?v
=rcsxO6rbhlI.

6. **Quote:** Kleeb, J. [@janekleeb]. (2024, March 2). "I am not sure I could HATE a book
more than this (which is saying a lot because its [sic] up there with Hillbilly Elegy) . . .
please don't write books about us like we are zoo animals to be observed from a tower
above. Racism exists everywhere, it is not only in rual [sic] towns. What a perfect way
to alienate MORE voters by calling them every stereotype in the book. How long have
these guys lived in a rural town? Or did they study us with their polls and focus groups?
Do not read this trash. Books like this set us BACK even more with voters. This would
be like a bunch of rural folks writing a book about every stereotype of the cities. That
too would be wrong. Some rural authors to read their books, blogs or listen to podcasts
instead: @mhildreth; @MrRural; @chloemaxmin; Sarah Smarsh; @TedGenoways + @
MaryAnneAndrei; @WillieNelson; @FarmAid podcast" [tweet]. Twitter. https://twitter
.com/janekleeb/status/1763929359885185133; **inner city gun violence:** del Pozo, B.,
Knorre, A., Mello, M. J., & Chalfin, A. (2022). Comparing risks of firearm-related death
and injury among young adult males in selected US cities with wartime service in Iraq
and Afghanistan. *JAMA Network Open*, 5(12), e2248132–e2248132. https://doi.org/10
.1001%2Fjamanetworkopen.2022.48132.

7. **Maddow and O'Reilly:** Peck, R. (2019). *Fox populism: Branding conservatism as working-
class*, p. 11. Cambridge University Press. https://doi.org/10.1017/9781108634410; **first
quote:** Peck, 2019, p. 11; **second quote:** Peck, 2019, p. 113.

8. **Quote:** Poniewozik, J. (2023, June 20). This land is his land. *The New York Times*. https:
//www.nytimes.com/2022/11/10/arts/television/yellowstone-taylor-sheridan.html.

9. **First quote:** Otterbein, H. (2021, April 16). The Democrats' giant dilemma. *Politico*.
https://www.politico.com/news/magazine/2021/04/16/john-fetterman-profile-2022
-senate-politics-pennsylvania-481259; **second quote:** Chamlee, V. (2021, February

21). At home with Pennsylvania's headline-making second couple as they prepare their next big campaign. *People*. https://people.com/politics/at-home-with-john-gisele -fetterman/; **tattoos:** Fetterman, J. (2022, September 25). Tucker Carlson wants to talk about my tattoos. So let's talk about them. NBC News. https://www.nbcnews.com/think /opinion/fox-news-tucker-carlson-attack-john-fetterman-tattoos-ignorant-rcna48573; **third quote:** Slisco, A. (2022, September 26). Dr. Oz denounces John Fetterman's clothing for undermining "authority." *Newsweek*. https://www.newsweek.com/dr-oz-denounces -john-fettermans-clothing-undermining-authority-1746460; **not a progressive:** Kapur, S. (2023, December 15). "I'm not a progressive": Fetterman breaks with the left, showing a maverick side. NBC News. https://www.nbcnews.com/politics/congress/-not-progressive -fetterman-breaks-left-israel-immigration-rcna129747.

10. **Fetterman ad:** John Fetterman. (2022, September 22). *Make more sh*t in America* [video]. *YouTube*. https://www.youtube.com/watch?v=Z7WQn2NBTe0; **right to repair:** Gault, M. (2023, May 24). Minnesota passes right to repair. Vice. https://www.vice.com /en/article/minnesota-passes-right-to-repair/; **marijuana:** Sokolove, M. (2022, November 15). How Democrats can build a John Fetterman 2.0. *The New York Times*. https:// www.nytimes.com/2022/11/15/opinion/john-fetterman-democrats.html; **first quote:** Roush, T. (2024, August 21). Here's Barack Obama's speech at the DNC in full. *Forbes*. https://www.forbes.com/sites/tylerroush/2024/08/21/heres-barack-obamas-speech -at-the-dnc-in-full/; **second quote:** Epstein, R. J., Green, E. L., & Glueck, K. (2024, August 6). Walz, throwing punches at Republicans, makes his big entrance with Harris. *The New York Times*. https://www.nytimes.com/2024/08/06/us/politics/harris-tim -walz-rally.html; **third quote:** Amiri, F. (2024, August 6). Tim Walz became beloved by young voters with a message that the GOP is 'weird.' Associated Press. https://apnews .com/article/kamala-walz-vp-weird-trump-gen-z-f9d718890c3ca907f42dba59340753 82; **fourth quote:** Karnowski, S. (2023, April 19). Minnesota Gov. Walz draws sharp contrasts with red states. Associated Press. https://apnews.com/article/minnesota-walz -republicans-red-states-ed890f65fd18a85a3cad2a482e624a65; **fifth quote:** Bidgood, J. (2024, August 6). Introducing Coach Walz: Five takeaways from Philadelphia. *The New York Times*. https://www.nytimes.com/2024/08/06/us/politics/harris-walz-rally-speech -takeaways.html; **sixth quote:** Democratic vice presidential nominee Tim Walz campaigns in Omaha, Nebraska [video]. (2024, August 17). C-SPAN. https://www.c-span .org/video/?537741–1/democratic-vice-presidential-nominee-tim-walz-campaigns -omaha-nebraska; **runza:** Genoways, T. (2024, August 21). Vance thinks he knows rural America. Walz begs to differ. *The New York Times*. https://www.nytimes.com/2024/08 /21/opinion/walz-vance-rural-midwest.html.

11. **Fixing cars:** Hogg, D. [@davidhogg111]. (2024, August 5). Another Tim Walz gem [tweet]. Twitter. https://x.com/davidhogg111/status/1820523166277795858; **snowbanks:** Bartolotta, D., & Howard, H. (2024, August 6). Tim Walz, Kamala Harris' running mate once helped WWL anchor get her vehicle out of Minnesota ditch. 4WWL. https:// www.wwltv.com/article/news/local/orleans/tim-walz-once-helped-wwl-anchor-get-her -vehicle-out-of-minnesota-ditch/289-c3348b5c-706b-4ad9–8b06-a82c4b77c329; **farm work:** Hess, A. J. (2024, August 6). Tim Walz's first job was working on a farm. *Fast Company*. https://www.fastcompany.com/91168539/tim-walzs-first-job-was-working-on-a -farm; **enacting reverence:** Walz, T. [@Tim_Walz]. (2024, August 6). My dad served in the army during the Korean War. With his encouragement, at 17, I joined the Army National Guard for 24 years. Service gave me the strength of a shared commitment to something greater than ourselves. And just as it did for my dad and millions of others, the GI Bill gave me a shot at a college education [tweet]. Twitter. https://x.com/Tim_Walz /status/1820956562875433010?lang=en; **best shot:** Peterson, K., & Ferek, K. S. (2024, August 7). 'Top Gun Democrat' Tim Walz cultivated centrist record in Washington. *The*

Wall Street Journal. https://www.wsj.com/politics/elections/tim-walz-governing-record -vice-president-87ea3660.

12. **Quote:** Peck, 2019, p. 11.

13. **First quote:** Gambino, L. (2019, May 11). "I have a plan for that": Elizabeth Warren leads the Democratic "ideas primary." *The Guardian.* https://www.theguardian.com/us-news /2019/may/11/i-have-a-plan-for-that-elizabeth-warren-democratic-policy-primary; **second quote:** Abrams, S., & Groh-Wargo, L. (2021, February 11). Stacey Abrams and Lauren Groh-Wargo: How to turn your red state blue. *The New York Times.* https://www .nytimes.com/2021/02/11/opinion/stacey-abrams-georgia-election.html.

14. **"Ordinary" and "authentic":** Peck, 2019, p. 97; **first quote:** Peck, 2019, p. 104; **slang and sports references, second quote:** Peck, 2019, p. 107.

15. **Quote:** Lamont, M. (2000). *The dignity of working men: Morality and the boundaries of race, class, and immigration,* p. 147. Harvard University Press; **"irony-free" zone:** Reitman, J. (2009, May 14). John Fetterman: The mayor of hell. *Rolling Stone.* https://www .rollingstone.com/culture/culture-features/john-fetterman-pennsylvania-mayor-hell -allegheny-county-100493/.

16. **Distinction:** Bourdieu, P. (1984). *Distinction: A social critique on the judgment of taste* (R. Nice, Trans.). Harvard University Press. (Original work published 1979).

17. **Close work bonds:** Rolston, J. S. (2014). *Mining coal and undermining gender: Rhythms of work and family in the American West,* p. 171. Rutgers University Press; **quote:** Delano, J. (2022, July 15). John Fetterman uses Snooki to tweak Dr. Oz on his New Jersey residency. CBS News. https://www.cbsnews.com/pittsburgh/news/john-fetterman-uses -snooki-to-tweak-dr-oz-on-his-new-jersey-residency/; **second quote:** Fetterman, J. [@JohnFetterman]. (2024, February 23). "To any same-sex couples in Tennessee, it would be my pleasure to travel to your beautiful state and officiate your wedding. DM me" [tweet]. Twitter. https://twitter.com/JohnFetterman/status/1761037859182563490.

18. **Appeal with facts versus emotions:** Shapiro, J., & Newby, A. (2015, October 29). Republicans are from the heart; Democrats are from the head. Brookings. https://www .brookings.edu/articles/republicans-are-from-the-heart-democrats-are-from-the-head/; **quote:** Marshall, M., & Tran, L. (2021, May). 2020 post-election analysis. Third Way. https://www.thirdway.org/report/2020-post-election-analysis; **more consistent policy views:** Marble, W. (2023, September). What explains educational polarization among white voters?, p. 21. https://williammarble.co/docs/EducPolarization.pdf.

19. **Kusnet:** Kusnet, D. (1992) *Speaking American: How the Democrats can win in the Nineties.* Thunder's Mouth Press.

20. **First quote:** Lamont, M., Park, B. Y., & Ayala-Hurtado, E. (2017). Trump's electoral speeches and his appeal to the American white working class, p. S164. *The British Journal of Sociology,* 68(S1), S153–S180. https://doi.org/10.1111/1468–4446.12315; **second quote:** Oltermann, P. (2021, September 8). Olaf Scholz: "Merit in society must not be limited to top-earners." *The Guardian.* https://www.theguardian.com/world/2021/sep/08 /olaf-scholz-merit-society-not-be-limited-top-earners-germany-election; **third quote:** *The Guardian* view on Europe's centre-left: New grounds for optimism. (2021, September 24). *The Guardian.* https://www.theguardian.com/commentisfree/2021/sep/24/the -guardian-view-on-europes-centre-left-new-grounds-for-optimism.

21. **First quote:** Zengerle, J. (2014, April 29). How Barack Obama sold out the kale crowd. *The New Republic.* https://newrepublic.com/article/117504/obama-failed-foodies; **Iowa college graduates:** Burke, S. C. (2023, April 7). Educational attainment in Iowa: 1940– 2021. Iowa State University Extension Indicators Program. https://indicators.extension .iastate.edu/Indicators/Census/educational%20attainment%20decennial%20ACS%20 1940–2021.pdf; **second quote:** McCormick, J. (2018, June 10). Obama talks arugula— again—in Iowa. *Chicago Tribune.* https://www.chicagotribune.com/2007/10/05/obama

-talks-arugula-again-in-iowa/; **Dean and Dukakis:** Dowd, M. (2008, April 16). Egg-heads and cheese balls. *The New York Times*. https://www.nytimes.com/2008/04/16/opinion/16dowd.html; **signal sophistication:** Bourdieu, 1984, pp. 79, 194.

22. **Windsurfing:** Zernike, K. (2004, September 5). Who among us does not love windsurfing? *The New York Times*. https://www.nytimes.com/2004/09/05/weekinreview/who-among-us-does-not-love-windsurfing.html; **bowling score:** Van Natta, D., Jr. (2008, April 6). They got game. It just may be the wrong game. *The New York Times*. https://www.nytimes.com/2008/04/06/weekinreview/06vannatta.html.

23. **First quote:** Can Democrats succeed in rural America?: Executive summary, p. 4. (2022, November). Rural Urban Bridge Initiative. https://ruralurbanbridge.org/our-work/distilling-best-practices; **second quote:** Rural Urban Bridge Initiative, 2022, pp. 7–8; **"pivot" plays poorly:** Rural Urban Bridge Initiative, 2022, p. 7; **third quote:** Rural Urban Bridge Initiative, 2022, p. 8.

24. **Quote:** Abbott, J., Fan, L., Guastella, D., Herz, G., Karp, M., Leach, J., Marvel, J., Rader, K., & Riz, F. (2021). Commonsense solidarity: How a working-class coalition can be built, and maintained, p. 11. *Jacobin*. https://jacobinmag.com/2021/11/common-sense-solidarity-working-class-voting-report.

25. **Polled better key demographics, won 63 percent support:** Abbott et al., 2021, p. 12; **also responded positively:** Abbott et al., 2021, pp. 12, 17.

26. **Quote:** Abbott et al., 2021, p. 11.

27. **Notably higher:** Abbott et al., 2021, p. 34.

28. **Low-education whites:** Abbott et al., 2021, p. 12; **liked by upper-middle class:** Abbott et al., 2021, p. 32; **quote:** Yourish, K., Buchanan, L., & Cai, W. (2022, April 30). How 'Tucker Carlson Tonight' fuels extremism and fear. *The New York Times*. https://www.nytimes.com/interactive/2022/04/30/us/tucker-carlson-tonight.html.

29. **Structural disadvantage:** Schaeffer, K., & Edwards, K. (2022, November 15). Black Americans differ from other U.S. adults over whether individual or structural racism is a bigger problem. Pew Research Center. https://www.pewresearch.org/short-reads/2022/11/15/black-americans-differ-from-other-u-s-adults-over-whether-individual-or-structural-racism-is-a-bigger-problem/.

30. **Quote:** Lemann, N. (2022, October 24). The Democrats' midterm challenge. *The New Yorker*. https://www.newyorker.com/magazine/2022/10/31/the-democrats-midterm-challenge.

31. **First quote:** Khanna, R. (2022). *Progressive capitalism: How to make tech work for all of us*, p. 8. Simon & Schuster; **second quote:** Khanna, 2022, p. 17; **third quote:** Khanna, 2022, p. 7.

Chapter 20: Redirect Anti-Elitist Anger

1. **Quote:** Kusnet, D. [@DavidKusnet]. (2024, March 7). "There are two populist messages: 1. Left populism: They're robbing you blind. 2. Right populism: They think they're better than you. Progressives should stick with #1 and not fall into #2" [tweet]. Twitter. https://twitter.com/DavidKusnet/status/1765732635114938449.

2. **Quotes:** Yourish, K., Buchanan, L., & Cai, W. (2022, April 30). How "Tucker Carlson Tonight" fuels extremism and fear. *The New York Times*. https://www.nytimes.com/interactive/2022/04/30/us/tucker-carlson-tonight.html.

3. **Critiqued elites:** Abbott, J. (2024). Understanding class dealignment, p. 113. *Catalyst*, 7(4). https://catalyst-journal.com/2024/03/understanding-class-dealignment; **quote:** Bhargava, D., Shams, S., & Hanbury, H. (2024). The death of deliverism: Why policy alone is not enough. *New Labor Forum*, 33(1), 6–16. https://doi.org/10.1177/10957960231221761.

4. **Quotes:** Baker, P. (2024, August 21). 'I am the only person stupid enough to speak after Michelle Obama.' *The New York Times*. https://www.nytimes.com/2024/08/21/us/politics/obamas-convention.html.

5. **Anti-elitism see also:** Sokolove, 2022; **quotes:** C-SPAN, 2024; **Harris anti-elitism:**

Full transcript of Kamala Harris's Democratic convention speech. (2024, August 23). *The New York Times.* https://www.nytimes.com/2024/08/23/us/politics/kamala-harris -speech-transcript.html.

6. **First quote:** Abbott, J., DeVeaux, F., Fan, L., Guadron, C., Guastella, D., Herz, G., Karp, M., Marvel, J., Rader, K., Riz, F., & Rabbani, I. (2023). Trump's kryptonite: How progressives can win back the working class, p. 6. *Jacobin.* https://jacobin.com/2023/06/trumps -kryptonite-progressive-working-class-voting-report; **2021 study:** Abbott, J., Fan, L., Guastella, D., Herz, G., Karp, M., Leach, J., Marvel, J., Rader, K., & Riz, F. (2021). Commonsense solidarity: How a working-class coalition can be built, and maintained. *Jacobin.* https://jacobinmag.com/2021/11/common-sense-solidarity-working-class-voting-report; **second quote:** Abbott et al., 2023, p. 14.

7. **Invoked political elites:** Oliver, J. E., & Rahn, W. M. (2016). Rise of the "Trumpenvolk": Populism in the 2016 election. *The Annals of the Academy of Political and Social Science,* 667(1), 189–206. https://doi.org/10.1177/0002716216662639; **quotes:** Noordzij, K., de Koster, W., & van der Waal, J. (2021). "They don't know what it's like to be at the bottom": Exploring the role of perceived cultural distance in less-educated citizens' discontent with politicians, p. 566. *The British Journal of Sociology,* 72(3), 566–579. https://doi .org/10.1111/1468–4446.12800.

8. **Dissatisfied with corporations:** Big business. (n.d.). Gallup. https://news.gallup.com /poll/5248/big-business.aspx; **Harris anti-elitism:** Nehamas, N., & Duehren, A. (2024, November 9). Harris had a Wall Street-approved economic pitch. It fell flat. *The New York Times.* https://www.nytimes.com/2024/11/09/us/politics/harris-trump-economy .html.

9. **20 percent more likely:** In a politically polarized era, sharp divides in both partisan coalitions, p. 37. (2019, December). Pew Research Center. https://www.pewresearch.org /politics/2019/12/17/in-a-politically-polarized-era-sharp-divides-in-both-partisan -coalitions/; **hard work no guarantee:** Pew Research Center, 2019, p. 44; **even more supportive:** Abbott, 2024, p. 105.

10. **Working America:** 100 days into the Trump era, working-class "searchers" who voted for him are having doubts, open to appeals. (2017, April 26). Working America. https: //workingamerica.org/news/post/research/100days/; **quotes, a third of swing voters:** 100 days into the Trump era, working-class 'searchers' who voted for him are having doubts, open to appeals. (2017, April 26). Working America. https://workingamerica.org/news /post/research/100days/.

11. **Preferred by 7.2 points:** Abbott et al., 2023, p. 32; **performed significantly better:** Abbott, J., DeVeaux, F., Guastella, D., Loewer, M., & Rabbani, I. (2024). Where are all the left populists? Progressives, populists, and the working class among 2022 Democratic candidates, p. 31. *Jacobin.* https://jacobin.com/2024/03/left-populists-working-class -voters; **increased support for Trump:** Gest, J., Reny, T., & Mayer, J. (2018). Roots of the radical right: Nostalgic deprivation in the United States and Britain, p. 1709. *Comparative Political Studies,* 51(13), 1694–1719. https://doi.org/10.1177/0010414017720705.

12. **Is particularly strong:** Abbott et al., 2021, p. 30; **53 percent of the time:** Abbott et al., 2021, p. 37.

13. **Sense of being deprived:** Gest et al., 2018, p. 1709; **Trump voters trust him:** Working America, 2017; **second quote:** McQuarrie, M. (2017). The revolt of the Rust Belt: Place and politics in the age of anger, p. S146. *The British Journal of Sociology,* 68(S1), S120–S152. https://doi.org/10.1111/1468–4446.12328.

14. **Higher rates than whites:** Igielnik, R., Keeter, S., & Hartig, H. (2021, June 30). Behind Biden's 2020 victory. Pew Research Center. https://www.pewresearch.org/politics/2021 /06/30/behind-bidens-2020-victory/.

15. **Quote:** Kuttner, R. (2017, August 16). Steve Bannon, unrepentant. *The American*

Prospect. https://prospect.org/power/steve-bannon-unrepentant/; **George Wallace:** Peck, R. (2019). *Fox populism: Branding conservatism as working class*, p. 113. Cambridge University Press. https://doi.org/10.1017/9781108634410; favors people of color: Peck, 2019, p. 130; **Jesse Helms ad:** SnakesOnABlog. (2006, October 16). *Jesse Helms "Hands" ad* [video]. *YouTube.* https://www.youtube.com/watch?v=KIyewCdXMzk.

16. **Conventional wisdom:** Haney López, I. (2019). *Merge left: Fusing race and class, winning elections, and saving America*, p. 9. The New Press; **first quote:** Haney López, 2019, p. 102; **second quote:** Sandel, M. (2020). *The tyranny of merit: What's become of the common good?*, p. 18. Farrar, Straus, and Giroux; **third quote:** Haney López, 2019, p. 102.

17. **Quote:** Haney López, 2019, p. 5.

18. **Quote:** Haney López, 2019, p. 184.

19. **"Living hell," quote:** Rutz, D. (2023, August 17). Oliver Anthony says he's turned down $8 million offers since going viral: "Nothing special about me." Fox News. https://www .foxnews.com/media/oliver-anthony-turned-down-8-milliondollar-offers-since-going -viral-nothing-special-about-me.

20. **Racist dog whistle:** Levitz, E. (2023, August 17). Oliver Anthony and the incoherence of right-wing populism. *New York* magazine. https://nymag.com/intelligencer/2023/08 /oliver-anthony-and-the-incoherence-of-right-wing-populism.html; **YouTube commentary:** No Life Shaq. (2023, August 17). *FOR THE PEOPLE! | Oliver Anthony— Rich Men North Of Richmond (REACTION!!!)* [video]. *YouTube.* https://www.youtube .com/watch?v=lflNGWchZ3o; **commentary, see also:** Half and Jai. (2023, August 15). *WTF!!! OLIVER ANTHONY—RICH MEN NORTH OF RICHMOND* [video]. *YouTube.* https://www.youtube.com/watch?v=e9BpqjToKBQ; **hit number one:** Oliver Anthony Music chart history: Hot 100. (n.d.). *Billboard.* Accessed May 13, 2024, from https://www.billboard.com/artist/oliver-anthony-music/chart-history/hsi/.

21. **Defended the poor:** Oliver Anthony Music. (2024, March 31). "Doggonit" [song]. On *Hymnal of a Troubled Man's Mind.* Self-released; **first quote:** Oliver Anthony Music. (2023, August 25). *It's a pleasure to meet you—part 2* [video]. *YouTube.* https://www .youtube.com/watch?v=cv9uMXiY29s; **second quote:** Tabb, K. (2023, August 18). Virginia songwriter Oliver Anthony to play free Saturday show in eastern N.C. *The Virginian Pilot.* https://www.pilotonline.com/2023/08/18/virginia-songwriter-oliver -anthony-to-play-free-outer-banks-show-saturday/; **third quote:** Oliver Anthony Music, 2023.

22. **First quote:** Pandolfo, C. (2023, August 26). Democratic Sen. Chris Murphy rebukes left for mocking "Rich Men North of Richmond" singer Oliver Anthony. Fox News. https: //www.foxnews.com/politics/dem-sen-chris-murphy-rebukes-left-mocking-rich-men -north-richmond-singer-oliver-anthony; **second quote:** @solent802. (2023, August 26). Rich Men North of Richmond singer condemns Republicans after song used in debate. *The Guardian.* https://www.theguardian.com/us-news/2023/aug/25/rich-men-north-of -richmond-oliver-anthony-republicans.

23. **Quote:** Haney López, 2019, p. 13.

24. **"Economic justice":** Voelkel, J. G., Mernyk, J. S., & Willer, R. (2023). Moral reframing increases support for economically progressive candidates. *PNAS Nexus*, 2(6), pgad154. https://doi.org/10.1093/pnasnexus/pgad154.

25. **Quote:** Haney López, 2019, p. 49.

26. **First quote:** UAW president Shawn Fain speaks at 2024 DNC. (2024, August 20). Rev. https://www.rev.com/blog/transcripts/uaw-president-shawn-fain-speaks-at-2024-dnc; **second quote:** Habeshian, S. (2024, September 10). Harris skewers Trump's history of racism. Axios. https://www.axios.com/2024/09/11/harris-trump-racism-debate.

27. **Polled better than, first quote:** Haney López, 2019, p. 13; **second quote:** Haney López, 2019, p. 49.

28. **First quote:** Haney López, 2019, p. 49; **second and third quotes:** Haney López, 2019, p. 11; **fourth quote:** Haney López, 2019, p. 17; **more enthusiastic:** Haney López, 2019, p. 186.
29. **First quote:** Haney López, 2019, p. 51; **second quote:** Haney López, 2019, p. 175.
30. **Simultaneously call out:** English, M., & Kalla, J. (2021, April 23). Racial equality frames and public policy support: Survey experimental evidence. https://doi.org/10.31219/osf.io/tdkf3.
31. **"Like likes like":** Brewer, M. B. (1996). In-group favoritism: The subtle side of intergroup discrimination. In D. M. Messick & A. E. Tenbrunsel (Eds.), *Codes of conduct: Behavioral research into business ethics*, pp. 160–170. Russell Sage Foundation; **lowers racial resentment:** Frymer, P., & Grumbach, J. M. (2020). Labor unions and white racial politics. *American Journal of Political Science*, 65(1), 225–240. https://doi.org/10.1111/ajps.12537; **quote:** Fiske, S. T. (2011). *Envy up, scorn down: How status divides us*, p. 118. Russell Sage Foundation; **increased understanding:** Dietze, P., McCall, L., Craig, M. A., Richeson, J. A. (2022). Rising income inequality in the multidimensional perception of unequal economic opportunity. Unpublished.
32. **Quote:** Transcript of Dr. Martin Luther King speaking at The New School, February 6, 1964. (n.d.). Amherst College Library Archives. Accessed May 13, 2024, from https://www.amherst.edu/library/archives/holdings/mlk/transcript.

Chapter 21: Therapy's Expensive, but Praying Is Free

1. **Self-reported happiness:** Gruber, J. H., & Mullainathan, S. (2005). Do cigarette taxes make smokers happier? *The BE Journal of Economic Analysis and Policy*, 5(1), 000010151515153806371412. https://doi.org/10.1515/1538–0637.1412.
2. **84 percent of white evangelicals:** Burge, R. (2021, August 29) A more secular America is not just a problem for Republicans. *The New York Times*. https://www.nytimes.com/2021/08/25/opinion/republicans-democrats-america-religion.html; **quote:** Haney López, I. (2019). *Merge left: Fusing race and class, winning election and saving America*, p. 83. The New Press; **better predictor:** Podhorzer, M. (2023, July 25). Confirmation bias is a hell of a drug. Weekend Reading. https://www.weekendreading.net/p/confirmation-bias-is-a-hell-of-a; **"strong taproot":** Haney López, 2019, p. 84; **voted for Trump five to one:** Haney López, 2019, p. 83; **associated with churches:** Jones, R. P. (2016). *The end of white Christian America*, pp. 56, 106. Simon & Schuster; **second quote:** Spruill, M. (2017). *Divided we stand: The battle over women's rights and family values that polarized American politics*, p. 304. Bloomsbury Publishing.
3. **Cold feelings:** Hawkins, S., Yudkin, D., Juan-Torres, M., & Dixon, T. (2018). *Hidden tribes: A study of America's polarized landscape*, p. 105. More in Common. https://hiddentribes.us/media/qfpekz4g/hidden_tribes_report.pdf; **evangelicals gay marriage:** Romney Garrett, S. (2022, November 10). Perspective: Love thy neighbor, America. *Deseret News*. https://www.deseret.com/magazine/2022/11/10/23404376/class-system-religious-community-economic-mobility/; **began identifying as evangelicals:** Smith, G. A. (2021, September 15). More white Americans adopted than shed evangelical label during Trump presidency, especially his supporters. Pew Research Center. https://www.pewresearch.org/short-reads/2021/09/15/more-white-americans-adopted-than-shed-evangelical-label-during-trump-presidency-especially-his-supporters/; **"master identity":** Graham, R., & Homans, C. (2024, January 10). Trump is connecting with a different type of evangelical voter. *The New York Times*. https://www.nytimes.com/2024/01/08/us/politics/donald-trump-evangelicals-iowa.html.
4. **Religion and racism:** Gjelten, T. (2020, July 1). White supremacist ideas have historical roots in U.S. Christianity. NPR. https://www.npr.org/2020/07/01/883115867/white-supremacist-ideas-have-historical-roots-in-u-s-christianity; **Second Great Awakening:** McKivigan, J. R. (1984). *The war against proslavery religion: Abolitionism and the*

Northern churches, 1830–1865, pp. 13–184. Cornell University Press; **abolitionism, see also:** Harrold, S. (2019). *American abolitionism: Its direct impact from colonial times to Reconstruction*, p. 15. University of Virginia Press.

5. **Largest group:** DeRose, J. (2024, January 24). Religious "nones" are now the largest single group in the U.S. NPR. https://www.npr.org/2024/01/24/1226371734/religious -nones-are-now-the-largest-single-group-in-the-u-s; **somewhat important, 15 percent go to services:** Burge, R., & Michel, A. A. (2023, June 13). Who are the nones?: An in-depth interview with Ryan Burge. Lewis Center for Church Leadership. https://www .churchleadership.com/leading-ideas/who-are-the-nones-an-in-depth-interview-with -ryan-burge/; Smith, G. A., Tevington, P., Nortey, J., Rotolo, M., Kallo, A., & Alper, B. A. (2024, January 24). Religious "nones" in America: Who they are and what they believe, p. 57. Pew Research Center. https://www.pewresearch.org/religion/2024/01/24/religious -nones-in-america-who-they-are-and-what-they-believe/.

6. **More education equals less:** In America, does more education equal less religion? (2017, April 26). Pew Research Center. https://www.pewresearch.org/religion/2017/04/26/in -america-does-more-education-equal-less-religion/; **say they are religious:** Alper, B. A., Rotolo, M., Tevington, P., Nortey, J., & Kallo, A. (2023, December 7). Spirituality among Americans, p. 71. Pew Research Center. https://www.pewresearch.org/religion/2023/12 /07/spirituality-among-americans/; **important in their lives:** Pew Research Center, 2017, p. 7; **"absolute certainty":** Pew Research Center, 2017, p. 4; **neither spiritual nor religious:** Alper et al., 2023, p. 71.

7. **Unstable scheduling:** Williams, J. C., Lambert, S. J., Kesavan, S., Ospina, L. A., Rapoport, E. D., Jarpe, M., Bellisle, D., Pendem, P., McCorkell, L., & Adler-Milstein, S. (2018). Stable scheduling increases productivity and sales: The stable scheduling study. The Center for WorkLife Law. https://worklifelaw.org/publications/Stable-Scheduling-Study-Report.pdf.

8. **Quote:** Burge and Michel, 2023; **new atheists:** Cragun, R. T. (2014). Who are the "new atheists"? In L. G. Beaman & S. Tomlins (Eds.), *Atheist identities—spaces and social contexts*, pp. 195–211. Springer. https://doi.org/10.1007/978-3-319-09602-5_12; **"spiritual but not religious":** Alper et al., 2023, p. 71; **"heavy stigma":** Sakurai, J. (1999, June 6). Japanese pay high price to rest in peace. *Los Angeles Times.* https://www.latimes.com /archives/la-xpm-1999-jun-06-mn-44669-story.html.

9. **College degrees, less than $50,000, quote:** Burge, R. (2023). The religious landscape is undergoing massive change. It could decide the 2024 election. *Politico.* https://www .politico.com/news/magazine/2023/05/14/democrats-religion-census-secular-00095858.

10. **Vance:** Vance, J. D. (2016). *Hillbilly elegy: A memoir of a family and culture in crisis*, p. 92. HarperCollins; **reduces risk-taking behaviors:** Dionne, E. J., Jr. (2023, September 10). We need a truce in our wars over religion. Here's a glimmer of hope. *The Washington Post.* https://www.washingtonpost.com/opinions/2023/09/10/religion-politics-loneliness -community/.

11. **Jobs and safety net:** Romney Garrett, 2022; **predict economic mobility:** Chetty, R., Jackson, M. O., Kuchler, T., Stroebel, J., Hendren, N., Fluegge, R. B., Gong, S., Gonzalez, F., Grondin, A., Jacob, M., Johnston, D., Koenen, M., Laguna-Muggenburg, E., Mudekereza, F., Rutter, T., Thor, N., Townsend, W., Zhang, R., Bailey, M., . . . & Wernerfelt, N. (2022). Social capital I: Measurement and associations with economic mobility. *Nature*, 608(7921), 108–121. https://doi.org/10.1038/s41586-022-04996-4; **social integration:** Bradley, C. S., Hill, T. D., Burdette, A. M., Mossakowski, K. N., & Johnson, R. J. (2020). Religious attendance and social support: Integration or selection? *Review of Religious Research*, 62(1), 83–99. https://doi.org/10.1007/s13644-019-00392-z; **social support:** Krause, N. (2006). Church-based social support and change in health over time. *Review of Religious Research*, 48(2), 125–140. https://www.jstor.org/stable/20058128; **donate money:** Shepherd, A. M., Schnitker, S. A., & Greenway, T. S. (2019). Religious service attendance, moral foundations, God concept, and in-group giving: Testing moderated

mediation. *Review of Religious Research*, 61(4), 301–322. https://doi.org/10.1007/s13644 -019-00384-z.

12. **Cost of therapy:** Lauretta, A., & Hall, A. (2024, March 1). How much does therapy cost in 2024? *Forbes.* https://www.forbes.com/health/mind/how-much-does-therapy -cost/; **better mental health:** Ellison, C. G., & Fan, D. (2008). Daily spiritual experiences and psychological well-being among US adults. *Social Indicators Research*, 88(2), 247–271. https://doi.org/10.1007/s11205-007-9187-2; **twice as likely:** Myers, D. G., & Diener, E. (1995). Who is happy? *Psychological Science*, 6(1), 10–19. https://doi.org /10.1111/j.1467–9280.1995.tb00298.x; **offset depression:** Krause, 2006; **stronger God-mediated control:** Krause, N. (2010). God-mediated control and change in self-rated health. The *International Journal for the Psychology of Religion*, 20(4), 267–287. https://doi .org/10.1080/10508619.2010.507695; **three-fourths of U.S. adults:** Stark, R., & Bader, C. D. (2008). *What Americans really believe: New findings from the Baylor surveys of religion.* Baylor University Press; **God has protected them:** When Americans say they believe in God, what do they mean? (2018, April 25). Pew Research Center. https://www .pewresearch.org/religion/2018/04/25/when-americans-say-they-believe-in-god-what -do-they-mean/; **quote:** Hochschild, A. R. (2016). *Strangers in their own land: Anger and mourning on the American right*, p. 172. The New Press.

13. **Optimism and health:** Peterson, C. (2006). *A primer in positive psychology*, pp. 123–124. Oxford University Press; **optimism predicts:** Peterson, 2006, pp. 120, 124; **promotes positive mood:** Peterson, 2006, pp. 109, 114; **quote:** Peterson, 2006, p. 128.

14. **Gratitude predicts happiness:** Peterson, 2006, p. 33; **three good things:** Peterson, 2006, p. 39; **reported higher gratitude:** Lambert, N. M., Fincham, F. D., Braithwaite, S. R., Graham, S. M., & Beach, S. R. H. (2009). Can prayer increase gratitude? *Psychology of religion and spirituality*, 1(3), 139–149. https://doi.org/10.1037/a0016731; **associated with higher levels:** Whittington, B. L., & Scher, S. J. (2010). Prayer and subjective well-being: An examination of six different types of prayer. The *International Journal for the Psychology of Religion*, 20(1), 59–68. https://doi.org/10.1080/10508610903146316; **grit:** Duckworth, A. (2016). *Grit: The power of passion and perseverance.* Simon & Schuster; **externalizing and internalizing disorders:** Kendler, K. S., Liu, X., Gardner, C. O., McCullough, M. E., Larson, D., & Prescott, C. A. (2003). Dimensions of religiosity and their relationship to lifetime psychiatric and substance abuse disorders. *The American Journal of Psychiatry*, 160(3), 496–503. https://doi.org/10.1176/appi.ajp.160.3.496.

15. **Frightened and bummed out:** Ano, G. G., & Vasconcelles, E. B. (2005). Religious coping and psychological adjustment to stress: A meta-analysis. *Journal of Clinical Psychology*, 61(4), 461–480. https://doi.org/10.1002/jclp.20049; **sin and punishment:** Bruce, M. A., Bowie, J. V., Barge, H., Beech, B. M., LaVeist, T. A., Howard, D. L., & Thorpe, R. J., Jr. (2020). Religious coping and quality of life among Black and white men with prostate cancer, p. 5. *Cancer Control*, 27(3), 1073274820936288. https://doi.org/10.1177/1073274820936288.

16. **"Epidemic of loneliness":** Seitz, A. (2023, May 2). Loneliness poses risks as deadly as smoking: Surgeon general. Associated Press. https://apnews.com/article/surgeon-general -loneliness-334450f7bb5a77e88d8085b178340e19; **quote, more likely than nonmembers:** Dionne, 2023; **strong association:** Solan, M. (2017, October 5). The secret to happiness? Here's some advice from the longest-running study on happiness. *Harvard Health.* https: //www.health.harvard.edu/blog/the-secret-to-happiness-heres-some-advice-from-the -longest-running-study-on-happiness-2017100512543; **less distress, greater life satisfaction:** Ellison, C. G., Boardman, J. D., Williams, D. R., & Jackson, J. S. (2001). Religious involvement, stress and mental health: Findings from the 1995 Detroit Area Study. *Social Forces*, 80(1), 215–249. https://doi.org/10.1353/sof.2001.0063; **less depression:** Baetz, M., Bowen, R., Jones, G., & Koru-Sengul, T. (2006). How spiritual values and worship attendance relate to psychiatric disorders in the Canadian population. *The Canadian Journal of Psychiatry*, 51(10), 654–661. https://doi.org/10.1177/070674370605101005; **greater**

happiness: Ellison, C. G., Burdette, A. M., & Hill, T. D. (2009). Blessed assurance: Religion, anxiety, and tranquility among US adults. *Social Science Research*, 38(3), 656–667. https://doi.org/10.1016/j.ssresearch.2009.02.002; **greater self-esteem:** Krause, N., & Ellison, C. G. (2007). Parental religious socialization practices and self-esteem in late life. *Review of Religious Research*, 49(2), 109–127. https://www.jstor.org/stable/20447484; **emotional and practical support:** Ellison, C. G., Shepherd, B. C., Krause, N. M., & Chaves, M. A. (2009). Size, conflict, and opportunities for interaction: Congregational effects on members' anticipated support and negative interaction. *Journal for the Scientific Study of Religion*, 48(1), 1–15. https://www.jstor.org/stable/20486977; **aid and counseling:** Chaves, M., & Tsitsos, W. (2001). Congregations and social services: What they do, how they do it, and with whom. *Nonprofit and Voluntary Sector Quarterly*, 30(4), 660–683. https://doi.org/10.1177/0899764001304003; **anticipated support:** Krause, 2006; **may be more important than:** Ellison, C. G., & Henderson, A. K. (2011). Religion and mental health: Through the lens of the stress process. In A. Blasi (Ed.), Toward a sociological theory of religion and health (pp. 11–44). Brill. https://doi.org/10.1163/ej.9789004205970.i-277.7; **replaced functions of unions:** Newman, L., & Skocpol, T. (2023). *Rust Belt union blues: Why working-class voters are turning away from the Democratic Party*. Columbia University Press.

17. **Quote:** Bruce, M. A., Martins, D., Duru, K., Beech, B. M., Sims, M., Harawa, N., Vargas, R., Kermah, D., Nicholas, S. B., Brown, A., Norris, K. C. (2017). Church attendance, allostatic load and mortality in middle aged adults, p. 8. *PLoS ONE, 12*(5), e0177618. https://doi.org/10.1371/journal.pone.0177618.

18. **Quote:** Bai, M. (2008, October 15). Working for the working-class vote. *The New York Times*. https://www.nytimes.com/2008/10/19/magazine/19obama-t.html.

19. **Quote:** Hale, L., Drummond, S., & Martin, R. (2023, June 1). Actor Jeff Hiller feels fortunate to play a character who is both queer and religious. NPR. https://www.npr.org/2023/06/01/1179524276/actor-jeff-hiller-feels-fortunate-to-play-a-character-who-is-both-queer-and-reli.

20. **Quote:** Hale et al., 2023.

21. **Quote:** Siebert, T. (2020, September 16). Cradle to the grave—Birth, marriage and death in Japan. InsideJapan Tours. https://www.insidejapantours.com/blog/2020/09/16/cradle-to-the-grave-birth-marriage-and-death-in-japan/.

Chapter 22: Understand How We Won the Gay Marriage Battle: Rinse and Repeat

1. **Quote:** Sherman, J. (2009). *Those who work, those who don't: Poverty, morality, and family in rural America*, p. 137. University of Minnesota Press.

2. **Gay marriage polling:** LGBTQ+ rights: Gallup historical trends. (n.d.). Gallup. Accessed April 4, 2024, from https://news.gallup.com/poll/1651/gay-lesbian-rights.aspx; **quote:** AmRev360: Well-behaved women seldom make history with Laurel Thatcher Ulrich. (2022, March). Museum of the American Revolution. https://www.amrevmuseum.org/amrev360-well-behaved-women-seldom-make-history-with-laurel-thatcher-ulrich.

3. **First quote:** Hunter, N. D. (2017). Varieties of constitutional experience: Democracy and the marriage equality campaign, p. 1684. *UCLA Law Review*, 64, 1662; **alternatives to marriage, see also:** Ashley, C. P. (2015). Gay liberation: How a once radical movement got mainstreamed and settled down, 28. *New Labor Forum*, 24(3), 28–32. https://doi.org/10.1177/1095796015597453.

4. **Windsor case:** *United States v. Windsor*, 570 U.S. 744 (2013).

5. **First quote:** Adams, M., Bonauto, M., Broaddus, T., Carey, R., Coles, M., Kilbourn, S., Minter, S., Robinson, A., Thorpe, R., & Wolfson, E. (2005, June 21). Winning marriage: What we need to do. Accessed May 14, 2024, from https://s3-us-west-2.amazonaws.com/ftm-assets/ftm/archive/files/images/Final_Marriage_Concept_Paper-revised_(1).pdf; **sec-**

ond quote: Hunter, 2017, p. 1692; **third quote:** Messaging, messengers and public support. (n.d.). Freedom to Marry. Accessed May 14, 2024, from https://perma.cc/AS5E-V7AD.

6. **Quote:** Hunter, 2017, p. 1716.

7. **Join marriage:** Hunter, 2017, p. 1663.

8. **Individualizing and binding foundations:** Graham, J., Nosek, B. A., Haidt, J., Iyer, R., Koleva, S., & Ditto, P. H. (2011). Mapping the moral domain, p. 369. *Journal of Personality and Social Psychology*, 101(2), 366–385. https://doi.org/10.1037/a0021847; **liberal versus conservative morality, see also:** Voelkel, J. G., Redekopp, C., & Willer, R. (2022). Changing Americans' attitudes about immigration: Using moral framing to bolster factual arguments. *The ANNALS of the American Academy of Political and Social Science*, 700(1), 73–85. https://doi.org/10.1177/00027162221083877.

9. **Quote:** Haidt, J. (2012). *The righteous mind: Why good people are divided by politics and religion*, p. 191. Knopf Doubleday Publishing Group.

10. **Quote:** Fiske, S. T. (2011). *Envy up, scorn down: How status divides us*, p. 71. Russell Sage Foundation.

11. **Quote:** Frimer, J. A. (2020). Do liberals and conservatives use different moral languages? Two replications and six extensions of Graham, Haidt, and Nosek's (2009) moral text analysis, p. 1. *Journal of Research in Personality*, 84, 103906. https://doi.org/10.1016/j.jrp.2019.103906.

12. **Quote:** Hunter, 2017, p. 1691.

13. **2003 and 2013 polling:** Growing support for gay marriage: Changed minds and changing demographics, p. 12. (2013, March 20). Pew Research Center. https://www.pewresearch.org/politics/2013/03/20/growing-support-for-gay-marriage-changed-minds-and-changing-demographics/; **2023 polling:** McCarthy, J. (2023, June 5). U.S. same-sex marriage support holds at 71% high. Gallup. https://news.gallup.com/poll/506636/sex-marriage-support-holds-high.aspx.

14. **Validators, first quote, "journey stories":** Hunter, 2017, p. 1710; **focus on identification:** Hunter, 2017, p. 1712; **second quote:** Hunter, 2017, p. 1711; **third quote:** Hunter, 2017, p. 1724.

15. **Quotes:** Willer, R., & Feinberg, M. (2015, November 13). The key to political persuasion. *The New York Times*. https://www.nytimes.com/2015/11/15/opinion/sunday/the-key-to-political-persuasion.html; **reframed arguments more effective:** Feinberg, M., & Willer, R. (2015). From gulf to bridge: When do moral arguments facilitate political influence? *Personality and Social Psychology Bulletin*, 41(12), 1665–1681. https://doi.org/10.1177/0146167215607842.

16. **Binding rather than individualistic:** Voelkel, J. G., Mernyk, J. S., & Willer, R. (2023). Moral reframing increases support for economically progressive candidates. *PNAS Nexus*, 2(6), pgad154. https://doi.org/10.1093/pnasnexus/pgad154.

17. S. Marshall, personal communication, 2024, Sept. 16.

18. **Quote:** Nagourney, A., & Peters, J. W. (2023, April 17). How a campaign against transgender rights mobilized conservatives. *The New York Times*. https://www.nytimes.com/2023/04/16/us/politics/transgender-conservative-campaign.html.

19. **Bathroom bans:** Levin, S. (2021, March 23). How trans children became "a political football" for the Republican Party. *The Guardian*. https://www.theguardian.com/us-news/2021/mar/23/anti-trans-bills-us-transgender-youth-sports; **quote:** Nagourney & Peters, 2023.

20. **Quote:** Leonhardt, D. (2022, May 18). Unfussy and plain-spoken. *The New York Times*. https://www.nytimes.com/2022/05/18/briefing/john-fetterman-pennsylvania-primary.html.

21. **Support antidiscrimination legislation:** Americans' support for key LGBTQ rights continues to tick upward: Findings from the 2021 American Values Atlas. (2022, March 14).

PRRI. https://www.prri.org/research/americans-support-for-key-lgbtq-rights-continues -to-tick-upward/; **trans job discrimination:** Granberg, M., Andersson, P. A., & Ahmed, A. (2020). Hiring discrimination against transgender people: Evidence from a field experiment. *Labour Economics*, 65, 101860. https://doi.org/10.1016/j.labeco.2020.101860.

22. **Hate crimes:** FBI releases 2022 Crime in the Nation statistics. (2023, October 16). Federal Bureau of Investigation. https://www.fbi.gov/news/press-releases/fbi-releases-2022 -crime-in-the-nation-statistics.

23. **First quote:** Hersh, E. (2020). *Politics is for power: How to move beyond political hobbyism, take action, and make real change*, p. 3. Scribner; **belong to zero organizations, community issue, second quote:** Hersh, 2020, p. 136.

24. **Spent actually volunteering:** Hersh, 2020, p. 186; **first quote:** Hersh, 2020, p. 5; **60 percent more likely to identify, second quote:** Hersh, 2020, p. 6.

25. **Predicts feelings of moral conviction:** Hersh, 2020, p. 125.

Chapter 23: Deploy Alternative Masculinities to Build Support for Vaccinations, Sane Gun Policies, and More

1. **Quote:** Featherstone, L. (2021, December 4). Josh Hawley and the Republican obsession with manliness. *The New York Times*. https://www.nytimes.com/2021/12/04/opinion/josh -hawley-republican-manliness.html.

2. **Thirty times lower:** Fernández, E., & Moynihan, Q. (2020, April 23). Portugal shares a border with Spain but its death toll is 30 times lower. Here's how the country curbed the spread of the coronavirus. Business Insider. https://www.businessinsider.com/portuguese -covid-19-died-infected-outbreak-pandemic-crisis-2020-4.

3. **Vaccinated in nine months:** Hatton, B. (2021, September 23). Rear admiral becomes household name in Portugal as head of Covid vaccine drive. *Irish Examiner*. https://www .irishexaminer.com/world/arid-40704371.html.

4. **Vaccination, mask-wearing:** Economist/YouGov Poll. (2021, September). YouGov. https://d3nkl3psvxxpe9.cloudfront.net/documents/econTabReport_RNOZtwi.pdf.

5. **Higher death rate:** Bennett, G., & Cuevas, K. (2022, February 2). Why the COVID death rate in the U.S. is so much higher than other wealthy nations. PBS. https://www.pbs.org /newshour/show/why-the-covid-death-rate-in-the-u-s-is-so-much-higher-than-other -wealthy-nations; **kids falling behind:** Tai, D. B. G., Shah, A., Doubeni, C. A., Sia, I. G., & Wieland, M. L. (2021). The disproportionate impact of COVID-19 on racial and ethnic minorities in the United States. *Clinical Infectious Diseases*, 72(4), 703–706. https: //doi.org/10.1093/cid/ciaa815; **most trusted institution:** French, D. (2023, February 12). Men need purpose more than "respect." *The New York Times*. https://www.nytimes.com /2023/02/12/opinion/men-purpose-respect.html.

6. **Masculine swagger:** Smith, J. (2017, January 18). Blind spots of liberal righteousness. Society for Cultural Anthropology. https://culanth.org/fieldsights/blind-spots-of-liberal -righteousness; **Musk cheats workers:** Mitchell, R. (2022, November 14). Is the world's richest person the world's worst boss? What it's like working for Elon Musk. *Los Angeles Times*. https://www.latimes.com/business/story/2022-11-14/elon-musk-toxic-boss -timeline; **Trump cheats workers:** Reilly, S. (2018, April 25). USA TODAY exclusive: Hundreds allege Donald Trump doesn't pay his bills. *USA Today*. https://www.usatoday .com/story/news/politics/elections/2016/06/09/donald-trump-unpaid-bills-republican -president-laswuits/85297274/; **enact a protest masculinity:** Willis, P. E. (1977). *Learning to labour: How working class kids get working class jobs*. Saxon House.

7. **First and second quotes:** Roush, T. (2024, August 21). Here's Barack Obama's speech at the DNC in full. *Forbes*. https://www.forbes.com/sites/tylerroush/2024/08/21/heres-barack -obamas-speech-at-the-dnc-in-full/; **third quote:** *Time* Staff. (2024, August 21). A full transcript of Michelle Obama's speech at the 2024 Democratic National Convention. *Time*. https://time.com/7013289/michelle-obama-2024-dnc-speech-full-transcript/.

8. **Suitable humility:** WFAA. (2024, August 6). *Tim Walz full speech from rally in Pennsylvania* [video]. *YouTube.* https://www.youtube.com/watch?v=ZOdPrKao1YA; **march on stage:** Bidgood, J. (2024, August 22). Wednesday Night Lights: To vouch for Coach Walz, his old players step up. *The New York Times.* https://www.nytimes.com/2024/08/22/us/politics/football-players-walz-dnc.html.

9. **First quote:** Reitman, J. (2009, May 14). John Fetterman: The mayor of hell. *Rolling Stone.* https://www.rollingstone.com/culture/culture-features/john-fetterman-pennsylvania-mayor-hell-allegheny-county-100493/; **free store:** Hall, R. (2022, September 12). Braddock, the town that made John Fetterman, speaks on his run for Senate: "Our town got a battery jolt." *The Independent.* https://www.independent.co.uk/news/world/americas/us-politics/john-fetterman-braddock-senate-trump-b2165538.html; **second quote:** Muravchik, S., & Shields, J. A. (2020). *Trump's Democrats*, p. 71. Brookings Institution Press; **higher levels of support:** Ranehill, E., & Weber, R. A. (2022). Gender preference gaps and voting for redistribution. *Experimental Economics*, 25, 845–875. https://doi.org/10.1007/s10683-021-09741-8.

10. **First quote:** Donahue, B. (2022, June 20). How 2022 became the year of over-the-top masculinity in politics. *The Washington Post.* https://www.washingtonpost.com/magazine/2022/06/20/he-man-politics/; **masculinity polling:** Many Americans grapple with attitudes around masculinity. (2023, July 14). Ipsos. https://www.ipsos.com/en-us/politico-magazine-ipsos-poll-masculinity; **second quote:** Emba, C. (2023, July 10). Men are lost. Here's a map out of the wilderness. *The Washington Post.* https://www.washingtonpost.com/opinions/2023/07/10/christine-emba-masculinity-new-model/.

11. **Guns and masculinity:** Cassino, D., & Besen-Cassino, Y. (2020). Sometimes (but not this time), a gun is just a gun: Masculinity threat and guns in the United States, 1999–2018. *Sociological Forum*, 35(1), 5–23. https://doi.org/10.1111/socf.12565; **guns and masculinity see also:** Carlson, J. (2015). Mourning Mayberry: Guns, masculinity, and socioeconomic decline. *Gender & Society*, 29(3), 386–409. https://doi.org/10.1177/0891243214554799; Connell, R. W., & Messerschmidt, J. W. (2005). Hegemonic masculinity: Rethinking the concept. *Gender & Society*, 19(6), 829–859. https://doi.org/10.1177/0891243205278639; Stroud, A. (2012). Good guys with guns: Hegemonic masculinity and concealed handguns. *Gender & Society*, 26(2), 216–238. https://doi.org/10.1177/0891243211434612; **significantly more interest:** Borgogna, N. C., McDermott, R. C., & Brasil, K. M. (2022). The precarious masculinity of firearm ownership. *Psychology of Men & Masculinities*, 23(2), 173–182. https://doi.org/10.1037/men0000386; **quote:** Cassino & Besen-Cassino, 2020, p. 12; **concealed carry permits:** Astrow, A. (2022, February 20). How does education level impact attitudes among voters of color? Third Way. https://www.thirdway.org/memo/how-does-education-level-impact-attitudes-among-voters-of-color.

12. **First quote:** Cassino & Besen-Cassino, 2020, p. 18; **second quote:** Cassino & Besen-Cassino, 2020, p. 19; **"be a man among men":** McIntire, M., Thrush, G., & Lipton, E. (2022, June 22). Gun sellers' message to Americans: Man up. *The New York Times.* https://www.nytimes.com/2022/06/18/us/firearm-gun-sales.html.

13. **Quote:** Cassino & Besen-Cassino, 2020, p. 6; **2023 Pew survey:** Schaeffer, K. (2023, September 13). Key facts about Americans and guns. Pew Research Center. https://www.pewresearch.org/short-reads/2023/09/13/key-facts-about-americans-and-guns/; **stressed the need:** Stroud, A. (2012). Good guys with guns: Hegemonic masculinity and concealed handguns. *Gender & Society*, 26(2), 216–238. https://doi.org/10.1177/0891243211434612; **assuming the protector role:** Carlson, J. (2015). Mourning Mayberry: Guns, masculinity, and socioeconomic decline. *Gender & Society*, 29(3), 386–409. https://doi.org/10.1177/0891243214554799.

14. **Moral and emotional empowerment:** Mencken, F. C., & Froese, P. (2019). Gun culture in action, p. 2. *Social Problems*, 66(1), 3–27. https://doi.org/10.1093/socpro/spx040;

Imagined as men of color: Carlson, J. (2015). Mourning Mayberry: Guns, masculinity, and socioeconomic decline. *Gender & Society*, 29(3), 386–409. https://doi.org/10.1177 /0891243214554799; **people of color, see also:** Collins, P. H. (2004). *Black sexual politics: African Americans, gender and the new racism.* Routledge; **crime rates:** Thompson, A., & Tapp, S. N. (2022, September). Criminal victimization, 2021. Bureau of Justice Statistics. https://bjs.ojp.gov/content/pub/pdf/cv21.pdf.

15. **First quote:** Cramer, K. J. (2016). *The politics of resentment: Rural consciousness in Wisconsin and the rise of Scott Walker*, p. 67. University of Chicago Press; **second quote:** Bai, M. (2008, October 15). Working for the working-class vote. *The New York Times.* https: //www.nytimes.com/2008/10/19/magazine/19obama-t.html.

16. **First quote:** Cramer, 2016, p. 181; **second quote:** Bai, 2008; **Maureen Dowd:** Dowd, M. (2010, December 7). Pass the caribou stew. *The New York Times.* https://www.nytimes .com/2010/12/08/opinion/08dowd.html.

17. **Hidden injuries of class:** Sennett, R., & Cobb, J. (1972). *The hidden injuries of class.* Knopf.

18. **Quote:** Rabin, R. C. (2023, October 6). Gun deaths rising sharply among children, study finds. *The New York Times.* https://www.nytimes.com/2023/10/05/health/gun-deaths -children.html.

Chapter 24: Talk About Solutions—Not the Causes—of "Extreme Weather"

1. **Quote:** Rérolle, R. (2018, November 25). "Yellow Vests": "The elites talk about the end of the world, when we talk about the end of the month." *Le Monde.* https://www.lemonde.fr /politique/article/2018/11/24/gilets-jaunes-les-elites-parlent-de-fin-du-monde-quand -nous-on-parle-de-fin-du-mois_5387968_823448.html.

2. **Wind farm:** Humes, E. (2013, March 1). Anywhere it blows: Wind is no longer the energy source of the future. It's ready today. Sierra. https://www.sierraclub.org/sierra /2013–2-march-april/feature/anywhere-it-blows.

3. **US culture war:** Hornsey, M. J., Harris, E. A., & Fielding, K. S. (2018). Relationships among conspiratorial beliefs, conservatism and climate scepticism across nations. *Nature Climate Change*, 8(7), 614–620. https://doi.org/10.1038/s41558-018-0157–2; **country comparisons:** Flynn, C., & Yamasumi, E. (2021, January 26). The people's climate vote. United Nations Development Programme. https://www.undp.org/publications/peoples -climate-vote.

4. **Ignored political realities:** Gilligan, J. M., & Vandenbergh, M. P. (2014). Accounting for political feasibility in climate instrument choice. *Virginia Environmental Law Journal*, 32(1), 1–26. https://www.jstor.org/stable/24789329.

5. **Quote:** Mildenberger, M., Lachapelle, E., Harrison, K., & Stadelmann-Steffen, I. (2022). Limited impacts of carbon tax rebate programmes on public support for carbon pricing, p. 141. *Nature Climate Change*, 12(2), 141–147. https://doi.org/10.1038/s41558-021 -01268–3.

6. **Colossal drop:** McCall, L. (2013). *The undeserving rich: American beliefs about inequality, opportunity, and redistribution*, p. 201. Cambridge University Press.

7. **Climate changes as a culture-wars issue:** Worland, J. (2017, July 27). Climate change used to be a bipartisan issue. Here's what changed. *Time.* https://time.com/4874888 /climate-change-politics-history/.

8. **First quote:** Lemola, J. (2019, April 14). The Finns Party campaigned against climate action. It came in 2nd. *The New York Times.* https://www.nytimes.com/2019/04/14/world /europe/finland-election-climate.html; **Yellow Vests protestors:** Nossiter, A. (2018, December 5). How France's 'Yellow Vests' differ from populist movements elsewhere. *The New York Times.* https://www.nytimes.com/2018/12/05/world/europe/yellow-vests-france.html; **second quote:** Zhou, L. (2024, March 12). The dangerous resurgence of Germany's far right, explained. Vox. https://www.vox.com/world-politics/2024/3/12/24080074/germany -afd-far-right.

9. **Prioritize the economy, job loss:** Abbott, J., Fan, L., Guastella, D., Herz, G., Karp, M., Leach, J., Marvel, J., Rader, K., & Riz, F. (2021). Commonsense solidarity: How a working-class coalition can be built, and maintained, p. 53. *Jacobin.* https://jacobinmag .com/2021/11/common-sense-solidarity-working-class-voting-report; **laid off refinery worker:** Ngo, M. (2023, July 12). The energy transition is underway. Fossil fuel workers could be left behind. *The New York Times.* https://www.nytimes.com/2023/07/12/us /politics/coal-gas-workers-transition.html.

10. **Latinos southern Texas:** Ferman, M. (2020, November 13). Donald Trump made inroads in South Texas this year. These voters explain why. *Texas Tribune.* https://www .texastribune.org/2020/11/13/south-texas-voters-donald-trump/.

11. **Quote:** Roberts, D. (2017, September 20). Hillary Clinton's "coal gaffe" is a microcosm of her twisted treatment by the media. Vox. https://www.vox.com/energy-and-environment /2017/9/15/16306158/hillary-clinton-hall-of-mirrors.

12. **Ranked fourteenth:** Pew Research Center. (2022). Public's top priority for 2022: Strengthening the nation's economy. https://www.pewresearch.org/politics/2022/02/16/publics -top-priority-for-2022-strengthening-the-nations-economy/; **top concern:** Biden & the issues facing the nation: NPR / PBS NewsHour / Marist National Poll. (2023, March 29). Marist Poll. https://maristpoll.marist.edu/polls/biden-the-issues-facing-the-nation/; **7–10 points more:** Hanley, K., & Adcox, G. (2023, August 24). Voters broadly reject key climate components of the conservative "Project 2025." Data for Progress. https://www .filesforprogress.org/datasets/2023/8/dfp_climate_power_p2025_tabs.pdf.

13. **Saul Griffith:** Griffith, S., Calisch, S., & Fraser, L. (2020). The rewiring America handbook: A guide to winning the climate fight. Rewiring America. https://www.rewiringamerica .org/policy/rewiring-america-handbook; **Jesse Jenkins:** Larson, E., Greig, C., Jenkins, J., Mayfield, E., Pascale, A., Zhang, C., Drossman, J., Williams, R., Pacala, S., Socolow, R., Baik, E., Birdsey, R., Duke, R., Jones, R., Haley, B., Leslie, E., Paustian, K., & Swan, A. (2021). *Net-zero America: Potential pathways, infrastructure and impacts.* Princeton University. https://www.dropbox.com/s/ptp92f65lgds5n2/Princeton%20NZA%20 FINAL%20REPORT%20%2829Oct2021%29.pdf?dl=0; **twenty-five million jobs:** Griffith et al., 2020; more modest figure: Princeton University C-Pree. (2022, September 15). Jesse Jenkins: *The Inflation Reduction Act and the path to a net zero America* [video]. YouTube. https://www.youtube.com/watch?v=_4DeCE-QC0A; **single-largest investment:** Inflation Reduction Act of 2022. (2023, September 22). Loans Program Office, US Department of Energy. Accessed April 11, 2024, from https://www.energy.gov/lpo/inflation -reduction-act-2022; **quote:** Jenkins, J. D. [@JesseJenkins]. "#InflationReductionAct in one tweet: Billion-dollar corporations and people who have been cheating on their taxes paying for us all to get cheaper, cleaner, energy and manufacture clean energy technologies in America. Watch my Princeton seminar for more: https://www.youtube .com/watch?v=_4DeCE-QC0A" [tweet]. Twitter. https://x.com/JesseJenkins/status /1570495144696369154.

14. **Areas left behind:** Klein, E. (Host). (2022, September 20). The single best guide to decarbonization I've heard [audio podcast episode]. In The Ezra Klein Show. *The New York Times.* https://www.nytimes.com/2022/09/20/podcasts/transcript-ezra-klein-interviews -jesse-jenkins.html; **wind turbine technician:** Fastest growing occupations. (2023). US Bureau of Labor Statistics. https://www.bls.gov/ooh/fastest-growing.htm; **dependent on fossil fuels:** Van Nostrand, E., & Ashenfarb, M. (2023, November 29). The Inflation Reduction Act: A place-based analysis. US Department of the Treasury. https://home .treasury.gov/news/featured-stories/the-inflation-reduction-act-a-place-based-analysis; **quote:** Abrams, S., & Groh-Wargo, L. (2021, February 11). Stacey Abrams and Lauren Groh-Wargo: How to turn your red state blue. *The New York Times.* Retrieved June 2, 2022, from https://www.nytimes.com/2021/02/11/opinion/stacey-abrams-georgia -election.html.

15. **Quote:** Hochschild, A. R. (2016). *Strangers in their own land: Anger and mourning on the American right*, p. 176. The New Press.

16. **Quotes:** Hochschild, 2016, pp. 72, 77.

17. **Nine hundred thousand workers:** Ngo, 2023; **protect workers' interests:** Griffith et al., 2020; **protect workers, see also:** Klein, 2022.

18. **Comparable wages:** Ngo, 2023; **quote:** Scheiber, N. (2021, December 8). The Achilles' heel of Biden's climate plan? Coal miners. *The New York Times*. https://www.nytimes.com /2021/12/08/business/economy/coal-miners-unions-climate.html.

19. **Comparable wages:** Ngo, 2023; **quote:** Scheiber, N. (2021, December 8). The Achilles' heel of Biden's climate plan? Coal miners. *The New York Times*. https://www.nytimes.com /2021/12/08/business/economy/coal-miners-unions-climate.html.

20. **70 percent of Americans:** Hayhoe, K. (2019, October 31). I'm a climate scientist who believes in God. Hear me out. *The New York Times*. https://www.nytimes.com/2019/10 /31/opinion/sunday/climate-change-evangelical-christian.html; **quote:** Renkl, M. (2022, July 25). How to talk about 'extreme weather' with your angry uncle. *The New York Times*. https://nytimes.com/2022/07/25/opinion/climate-change-conservatives.html.

21. **Quote:** Renkl, 2022.

22. **Conservatives' support increased:** Feinberg, M., & Willer, R. (2013). The moral roots of environmental attitudes. *Psychological Science*, 24(1), 56–62. https://doi.org/10.1177 /0956797612449177.

23. **Coastal areas:** Kaufman, L. (2022, April 26). 81% of flood insurance policyholders will see rate increases, report says. *Bloomberg*. https://www.bloomberg.com/news/articles /2022–04–26/flood-insurance-policyholders-set-to-see-rate-increases-report?leadSource =uverify%20wall; **fire-prone areas:** Finney, M., & Koury, R. (2019, October 25). Thousands of homeowners in fire zones are losing their insurance. ABC7 News. https://abc7news .com/homeowners-insurance-fire-for-wildfire-area-dropped-from/5647865/.

24. **Watered down:** Baldwin, S. (2022, September 7). Inflation Reduction Act benefits: Electric vehicle tax incentives for consumers and U.S. automakers. *Forbes*. https://www.forbes .com/sites/energyinnovation/2022/09/07/inflation-reduction-act-benefits-electric-vehicle -tax-incentives-for-consumers-and-us-automakers/?sh=463bb5d5117e.

25. **Indiana:** Miniard, D., & Attari, S. Z. (2021). Turning a coal state to a green state: Identifying themes of support and opposition to decarbonize the energy system in the United States. *Energy Research & Social Science*, 82. https://doi.org/10.1016/j.erss.2021.102292; **younger Republicans:** Funk, C., & Kennedy, B. (2022, April 22). For earth day 2020, how Americans see climate change and the environment in 7 charts. Pew Research Center. https://www.pewresearch.org/fact-tank/2020/04/21/how-americans-see-climate-change -and-the-environment-in-7-charts/; **people greatly overestimate:** Roberts, D. (2016, October 28). America isn't using nearly as much renewable energy as Americans think. Vox. https://www.vox.com/energy-and-environment/2016/10/28/13427822/americans -overestimate-renewable-energy; **proposes a model:** Ochoa, C., Cook, K., & Weil, H. (2022). Deals in the heartland: Renewable energy projects, local resistance, and how law can help. *Minnesota Law Review*, 107. https://ssrn.com/abstract=4061042.

26. **Concern over air pollution:** Miniard & Attari, 2021; **lower rates:** Ambient (outdoor) air pollution. (2022, December 19). World Health Organization. https://www.who.int /news-room/fact-sheets/detail/ambient-(outdoor)-air-quality-and-health; **quote:** Pod Save America. (2023, March 30). *DONALD TRUMP INDICTED BY MANHATTAN GRAND JURY, would become first president charged with a crime* [video]. *YouTube*. https: //www.youtube.com/watch?v=Rvh1SD7WFHQ.

27. **Pay their bills:** Saad, L. (2022, May 16). Americans' financial worries tick up in past year. Gallup. https://news.gallup.com/poll/392432/americans-financial-worries-tick-past-year .aspx; **heat pumps and home upgrades:** Klein, 2022; **40 percent of the reduction:** Ca-

ballero, M. D., Vandenbergh, M. P., Gilligan, J. M., & Currier, E. O. (2024). Incentivizing household action: Exploring the behavioral wedge in the 2021 Infrastructure Investment and Jobs Act and the 2022 Inflation Reduction Act. *Energy Policy*, 186, 113992. https://doi .org/10.1016/j.enpol.2024.113992; **$1,900 a year:** Griffith et al., 2020.

28. **Thoroughly demonized:** Tyson, A., & Kennedy, B. (2021, July 12). Two-thirds of Americans think government should do more on climate. Pew Research Center. https://www .pewresearch.org/science/2020/06/23/two-thirds-of-americans-think-government -should-do-more-on-climate/.

29. **"Extreme weather":** Hayhoe, 2022.

30. **Montana farmer:** LeVaux, A. (2017, December 13). Climate change threatens Montana's barley farmers—and possibly your beer. Food & Environment Reporting Network. https: //thefern.org/2017/12/climate-change-threatens-montanas-barley-farmers-possibly -beer/.

Chapter 25: Reframe the Immigration Debate to Tap Working-Class Values

1. **Quote:** Seib, G. F. (2024, January 18). What Republicans used to believe. *The Wall Street Journal*. https://www.wsj.com/politics/policy/what-republicans-used-to-believe -71a77c22.

2. **Quote:** Spierings, N., & Zaslove, A. (2015). Gendering the vote for populist radical-right parties, p. 150. *Patterns of Prejudice*, 49(1–2), 135–162. https://doi.org/10.1080 /0031322X.2015.1024404; **without mobilizing grievances:** Ivarsflaten, E. (2008). What unites right-wing populists in Western Europe?: Re-examining grievance mobilization models in seven successful cases. *Comparative Political Studies*, 41(1), 3–23. https://doi .org/10.1177/0010414006294168; **strong determinant:** Hooghe, M., & Dassonneville, R. (2018). Explaining the trump vote: The effect of racist resentment and anti-immigrant sentiments. *PS: Political Science and Politics*, 51(3), 528–534. https://doi.org/10.1017 /S1049096518000367; **closer to their views, 39% college and 24% non-college grads:** CNN/SSRS Poll: November 1 to November 30, 2023. (2023, December 6). CNN/ SSRS. https://s3.documentcloud.org/documents/24193043/cnn-poll-bidens-job-appro val-has-dropped-since-start-of-the-year-as-economic-concerns-remain-prevalent.pdf; **burden: 42% of rural and 16% of city folk; share values: 50% of rural and 39% of city folk:** Sacchetti, M., & Guskin, E. (2017, June 17). In rural America, fewer immigrants and less tolerance. *The Washington Post*. https://www.washingtonpost.com/local/in-rural -america-fewer-immigrants-and-less-tolerance/2017/06/16/7b448454–4d1d-11e7 bc1bfddbd8359dee_story.html.

3. **Over one hundred interviews, quote:** Glass, I. (Host). (2017, December 15). Our town—part two (No. 633) [audio podcast episode]. In *This American Life*. https://www .thisamericanlife.org/633/our-town-part-two.

4. **Quote:** Pod Save America. (2023, March 30). *DONALD TRUMP INDICTED BY MANHATTAN GRAND JURY, would become first president charged with a crime* [Video]. *YouTube*. https://www.youtube.com/watch?v=Rvh1SD7WFHQ.

5. **Intertwined with racism:** Hutchings, V. L., & Wong, C. (2014). Racism, group position, and attitudes about immigration among Blacks and Whites. *Du Bois Review: Social Science Research on Race*, 11(2), 419–442. https://doi.org/10.1017/S1742058X14000198; **more from Norway:** Kirby, J. (2018, January 11). Trump wants fewer immigrants from "shithole countries" and more from places like Norway. Vox. https://www.vox.com/2018/1/11 /16880750/trump-immigrants-shithole-countries-norway; **quote:** Lamont, M. (2000). *The dignity of working men: Morality and the boundaries of race, class, and immigration*, p. 89. Harvard University Press; **"basically good, honest people":** Lapinski, J. S., Peltola, P., Shaw, G., & Yang, A. (1997). Trends: Immigrants and immigration, p. 367. *The Public Opinion Quarterly*, 61(2), 356–383. https://www.jstor.org/stable/2749556; **more likely to**

endorse: Filindra, A., & Pearson-Merkowitz, S. (2013). Together in good times and bad? How economic triggers condition the effect of intergroup threat. *Social Science Quarterly*, 94(5), 1328–1345. https://doi.org/10.1111/ssqu.12028.

6. **Very likely to oppose:** Hutchings & Wong, 2014.

7. **Immigration and GDP:** Boubtane, E., Coulibaly, D., & Rault, C. (2013). Immigration, growth and unemployment: Panel VAR evidence from OECD countries. *Labour*, 27(4), 399–420. https://doi.org/10.1111/labr.12017; **GDP, see also:** The budget and economic outlook: 2024 to 2034, p. 43. (2024, February 1). Congressional Budget Office (CBO). https://www.cbo.gov/system/files/2024–02/59710-Outlook-2024.pdf; **boost by $7 trillion:** CBO, 2024; **$100 billion annually:** Baxandall, P., Capote, A., & Dyssegaard, D. (2024, February 7). Economic projections for asylum seekers and new immigrants: Massachusetts. Massachusetts Budget & Policy Center. https://massbudget.org/2024/02/07 /economic-projections-immigrants/.

8. **Wages fell in regions, nursing less likely:** Leonhardt, D. (2023). *Ours was the shining future: The story of the American Dream*, p. 316. Random House; **quote:** Caiumi, A., & Peri, G. (2024). *Immigration's effect on US wages and employment* redux, abstr. (No. w32389). National Bureau of Economic Research. https://www.nber.org/papers/w32389; **small negative impacts:** Shierholz, H. (2010, February 4). *Immigration and wages: Methodological advancements confirm modest gains for native workers*. Economic Policy Institute. https://www.epi.org/publication/bp255/; boosted tax revenues: CBO, 2024; **predicted increases:** Baxandall et al., 2024; **tame inflation:** Jerome Powell: Full 2024 *60 Minutes* interview transcript. (2024, February 4). CBS News. https://www.cbsnews.com/news/full -transcript-fed-chair-jerome-powell-60-minutes-interview-economy/.

9. **Quote:** García, M. (2024, February 17). Are immigrants a burden or a benefit? *The Boston Globe*. https://www.bostonglobe.com/2024/02/17/opinion/immigrants-burden -or-benefit/.

10. **Quote:** García, 2024.

11. **Quote:** Glass, I. (Host). (2017, December 8). Our town—part one (No. 632) [audio podcast episode]. In *This American Life*. https://www.thisamericanlife.org/632/our-town -part-one.

12. **Quote:** Mohan, G. (2017, May 25). To keep crops from rotting in the field, farmers say they need Trump to let in more temporary workers. *Los Angeles Times*. https://www .latimes.com/projects/la-fi-farm-labor-guestworkers/.

13. **Belief that immigrants take jobs:** Hutchings & Wong, 2014; **40 percent of immigrants:** Lay, J. C. (2012). *A midwestern mosaic: Immigration and political socialization of rural America*, p. 15. Temple University Press.

14. **Quote:** Glass, 2017, December 8.

15. **Quote:** Glass, 2017, December 8.

16. **80–95 percent unionized:** Glass, 2017, December 8; **relationship is complex:** Ness, I. (2005). *Immigrants, unions, and the new U.S. labor market*. Temple University Press; **Justice for Janitors:** Wikipedia, Justice for Janitors, https://en.wikipedia.org/wiki/Justice _for_Janitors#:~:text=The%20Los%20Angeles%20Justice%20for,the%20buildings%20 where%20they%20worked.

17. **Quote:** Glass, 2017, December 8.

18. **Quote:** Carr, P. J., & Kefalas, M. (2009). *Hollowing out the middle: The rural brain drain and what it means for America*, pp. 152–153. Beacon Press.

19. **Quote:** Lay, 2012, p. 13.

20. **About $1,200 less, half of 1974 pay:** Glass, 2017, December 8; **5 percent of the increase:** Card, D. (2009). Immigration and inequality (NBER Working Paper No. 14683). National Bureau of Economic Research. https://www.nber.org/papers/w14683.

21. **Burden on the country:** DelReal, J. A., & Clement, S. (2017, June 17). Rural divide. *The*

Washington Post. https://www.washingtonpost.com/graphics/2017/national/rural-america/; **quote:** Glass, 2017, December 8.

22. **Quote:** Glass, 2017, December 8; **first vote:** Roll call vote 109th Congress—2nd session: Vote number 157. (2006, May 25). United States Senate. https://www.senate.gov /legislative/LIS/roll_call_votes/vote1092/vote_109_2_00157.htm; **second vote:** Roll call vote 113th Congress—1st session: Vote number 168. (2013, June 27). United States Senate. https://www.senate.gov/legislative/LIS/roll_call_votes/vote1131/vote_113_1_00168 .htm.

23. **Trusted Republicans more:** Memo to interested parties: Immigration and the 2022 elections. (2022, August 24). Hart Research Associates. https://static1.squarespace.com /static/5b60b2381aef1dbe876cd08f/t/63065b17c84f5751cdeafc94/1661360919967/ME -14335+Immigration+Battleground+Survey.pdf.

24. **Lack of timely farm labor:** Mohan, 2017; **supported a path to citizenship:** Hart Research Associates, 2022.

25. **10,000 workers, nurses and health aides:** Maag, C., & Vilchis, R. (2023, July 14). As politicians cry "crisis," some migrants are finding their way. *The New York Times.* https://www .nytimes.com/2023/07/13/nyregion/migrants-nyc-politics.html; **shortfall of 460,000 workers:** Portes, J., & Springford, J. (2023). The impact of the post-Brexit migration system on the UK labour market. *Contemporary Social Science,* 18(2), 132–149. https://doi .org/10.1080/21582041.2023.2192516; **foreign-born doctors:** Mathema, S. (2019, July 29). Immigrant doctors can help lower physician shortages in rural America. Center for American Progress. https://www.americanprogress.org/article/immigrant-doctors-can -help-lower-physician-shortages-rural-america/; **57 percent of battleground voters, 67 percent of battleground voters:** Hart Research Associates, 2022; **start businesses:** Rampell, C. (2024, April 23). You don't want immigrants? Then tell grandma she can never retire. *The Washington Post.* https://www.washingtonpost.com/opinions/2024/04/23 /immigration-jobs-economy/; **quote:** Lemann, N. (2022, October 24). The Democrats' midterm challenge. *The New Yorker.* https://www.newyorker.com/magazine/2022/10/31 /the-democrats-midterm-challenge.

26. **Replacement rate:** Peri, G. (2020, March). Immigrant swan song. *International Monetary Fund Finance and Development Magazine.* https://www.imf.org/en/Publications /fandd/issues/2020/03/can-immigration-solve-the-demographic-dilemma-peri; **era of labor scarcity:** America's demography is looking European. (2021, January 2). *The Economist.* https://www.economist.com/united-states/2021/01/02/americas-demography-is -looking-european.

27. **"America is a better country":** Nowrasteh, A., & Forrester, A. (2019). Immigrants recognize American greatness: Immigrants and their descendants are patriotic and trust America's governing institutions. Cato Institute Immigration Research and Policy Brief, 10. https://papers.ssrn.com/sol3/papers.cfm?abstract_id=3382348; **choose to live in the US:** Hawkins, S., & Raghuram, T. (2020, December). American fabric: Identity and belonging, p. 15. More in Common. https://www.moreincommon.com/media/s5jhgpx5 /moreincommon_americanfabricreport.pdf; **less likely to be college grads:** Mora, L. (2022, October 7). Hispanic enrollment reaches new high at four-year colleges in the U.S., but affordability remains an obstacle. Pew Research Center. https://www.pewresearch.org /short-reads/2022/10/07/hispanic-enrollment-reaches-new-high-at-four-year-colleges -in-the-u-s-but-affordability-remains-an-obstacle/.

28. **"Very serious concern":** Hart Research Associates, 2022; **strongest motivator:** Midterm persuasion messaging for Latino voters. (2022, August 17). Equis. https://www .weareequis.us/en-US/labs/labs-our-work/midterm-persuasion-messaging-for-latino -voters.

29. **Respect for hard work:** Haney López, I. (2022). Project Juntos: Latinx race-class.

Project Juntos. https://static1.squarespace.com/static/5ef377b623eaf41dd9df1311/t/5f6fd7e84ca040062e8dc0b9/1601165291980/Project+Juntos+Summary+Briefing+092620.pdf.

30. **Quote:** Hart Research Associates, 2022.

31. **Quote:** Carr & Kefalas, 2009, p. 151.

32. **Planning quinceañeras:** Glass, 2017, December 8; **lumps refugees with immigrants:** Lamont, M., Park, B. Y., & Ayala-Hurtado, E. (2017). Trump's electoral speeches and his appeal to the American white working class, p. 157. *The British Journal of Sociology,* 68(S1), S153–S180. https://doi.org/10.1111/1468–4446.12315; **refused to support:** Galston, W. A. (2024, February 8). The collapse of bipartisan immigration reform: A guide for the perplexed. Brookings. https://www.brookings.edu/articles/the-collapse-of-bipartisan-immigration-reform-a-guide-for-the-perplexed/.

33. **60 percent of swing voters:** Hart Research Associates, 2022.

34. **Easy to exploit:** Chassamboulli, A., & Peri, G. (2015). The labor market effects of reducing the number of illegal migrants. *Review of Economic Dynamics,* 18(4), 792–821. https://doi.org/10.1016/j.red.2015.07.005; **regularize workers' status:** Borjas, G. J., & Edo, A. (2023, July). Monopsony, efficiency, and the regularization of undocumented immigrants (No. 31457). National Bureau of Economic Research. https://www.nber.org/papers/w31457; **executives indicted:** Jackson, R. L. (2001, December 20). Tyson Foods is indicted in immigrant smuggling. *Los Angeles Times.* https://www.latimes.com/archives/la-xpm-2001-dec-20-mn-16761-story.html.

35. **Quotes:** Lamont, 2000, pp. 90–91.

36. **First quote:** Lay, 2012, p. 18; **second quote:** Lay, 2012, p. 140; **third quote:** Chetty, R., Hendren, N., Jones, M. R., & Porter, S. R. (2020). Race and economic opportunity in the United States: An intergenerational perspective, p. 736. *The Quarterly Journal of Economics,* 135(2), 711–783. https://doi.org/10.1093/qje/qjz042; **reach the 50th percentile, fastest assimilation:** Smith, N. (2022). Interview: Leah Boustan, economist. Noahpinion. https://www.noahpinion.blog/p/interview-leah-boustan-economist. **Jose/Jesus:** Roberts, S. (2009, May 28). Study reveals changes among second-generation Hispanics. *The New York Times.* https://www.nytimes.com/2009/05/29/us/29hispanic.html.

37. **Proud to be an American:** Nowrasteh & Forrester, 2019, p. 4; **speak English:** National Academies of Sciences, Engineering, and Medicine. (2015). *The integration of immigrants into American society,* p. 309. The National Academies Press. https://doi.org/10.17226/21746.

38. **Place loyal and community-minded:** Muravchik, S., & Shields, J. A. (2020). *Trump's Democrats,* pp. 96–104. Brookings Institution Press; **well-kept home:** Carr & Kefalas, 2009, p. 81; **"outsiders," piled into houses:** Glass, 2017, December 15.

39. **Quote:** Glass, 2017, December 15.

40. **16 percent of college and 41 percent of noncollege grads:** Goodhart, D. (2017). *The road to somewhere: The populist revolt and the future of politics,* p. 42. Hurst.

41. **Stories of violence:** Quiroz, L. (2022, September 24). Is the American dream worth the risk? These migrants hope so. NPR. https://www.npr.org/2022/09/24/1123867466/migrants-marthas-vineyard-migration-border-us-american-dream; **chaotic border towns:** Garsd, J. (2024, January 27). A California community sees a dip in immigration. Where have all the people gone? NPR. https://www.npr.org/2024/01/27/1226570548/border-migrants-mexico-jacumba-california-desert-immigration; **family separations:** Quiroz, L., Martin, R., & Whelan, C. (2021, June 22). Separated at the border, a father reunites with his son. But struggles remain. NPR. https://www.npr.org/2021/06/15/1006477931/how-families-separated-at-the-border-by-trump-policies-are-coping.

42. **Quotes:** *Morning Joe.* (2024, February 26). "White rural rage" looks at the most likely group to abandon democratic norms [video]. MSNBC. https://www.msnbc.com/morning

-joe/watch/-white-rural-rage-looks-at-the-most-likely-group-to-abandon-democratic
-norms-204922949864.

Conclusion

1. **Quote:** Cuban, M. (2020). Foreword, pp. xiii–xiv. In J. C. Williams, *White working class: Overcoming class cluelessness in America*. Harvard Business Review Press. (Original work published 2017).
2. **Quotes:** CNN live event/special: Memorial service for Senator Edward M. Kennedy [transcript]. (2009, August 28). CNN. https://transcripts.cnn.com/show/se/date/2009–08–28/segment/01.
3. **Quotes:** Leonhardt, D. (2023). *Ours was the shining future: The story of the American Dream*, p. 209. Random House.
4. **First quote:** Hochschild, A. R. (2016). *Strangers in their own land: Anger and mourning on the American right*, p. 131. The New Press; **second and third quotes:** Bettie, J. (2002). *Women without class: Girls, race, and identity*, p. 161. University of California Press; **"multiracial whiteness":** Beltrán, C. (2021, January 15). To understand Trump's support, we must think in terms of multiracial whiteness. *The Washington Post*. https://www.washingtonpost.com/opinions/2021/01/15/understand-trumps-support-we-must-think-terms-multiracial-whiteness/.
5. **Obama fared better:** Leonhardt, 2023). *Ours was the shining future: The story of the American Dream*, p. 386. Random House; **quotes:** Bai, M. (2008, October 15). Working for the working-class vote. *The New York Times*. https://www.nytimes.com/2008/10/19/magazine/19obama-t.html; **rural activists' recommendations:** Can Democrats succeed in rural America? (2022, November). Rural Urban Bridge Initiative. https://ruralurbanbridge.org/our-work/distilling-best-practices.
6. **Quote:** Bai, 2008.
7. **Defending coal, Second Amendment:** Bai, 2008.
8. **Quote:** Klein, E. (2024, November 7). Where does this leave Democrats? *The New York Times*. https://www.nytimes.com/2024/11/07/opinion/ezra-klein-podcast-election.html.

Index

About the Author

Olena Jacenko

Joan C. Williams, described as having "something approaching rock-star status" in her field by *The New York Times Magazine*, is an award-winning scholar of social inequality. She is the author of *White Working Class* and has written about class dynamics in *The New York Times*, *The Washington Post*, *The Atlantic*, *The New Republic*, and other publications. She is the Distinguished Professor of Law and Founding Director of the Equality Action Center at University of California College of the Law, San Francisco.